Yamaha XJ900S Diversion
Service and Repair Manual

by Matthew Coombs

Models covered
XJ900S. 892cc. 1994 to 2000

(3739-240)

ABCDE
FGHIJ
KLMNO
PQRST

© Haynes Publishing 2000

A book in the **Haynes Service and Repair Manual Series**

All rights reserved. No part of this book may be reproduced or transmitted in any form or by any means, electronic or mechanical, including photocopying, recording or by any information storage or retrieval system, without permission in writing from the copyright holder.

ISBN **1 85960 739 X**

British Library Cataloguing in Publication Data
A catalogue record for this book is available from the British Library.

Library of Congress Catalog Card Number 00 131364

Printed by **J H Haynes & Co Ltd, Sparkford, Nr Yeovil, Somerset BA22 7JJ, England**

Haynes Publishing
Sparkford, Nr Yeovil, Somerset BA22 7JJ, England

Haynes North America, Inc
861 Lawrence Drive, Newbury Park, California 91320, USA

Editions Haynes S.A.
Tour Aurore – IBC, 18 Place des Reflets,
92975 Paris La Defense 2, Cedex, France

Haynes Publishing Nordiska AB
Box 1504, 751 45 UPPSALA, Sweden

Contents

LIVING WITH YOUR YAMAHA XJ

Introduction

Yamaha – Musical instruments to motorcycles	Page	0•4
Acknowledgements	Page	0•9
About this manual	Page	0•9
Safety first!	Page	0•10
Identification numbers	Page	0•11
Buying spare parts	Page	0•11

Daily (pre-ride checks)

Engine/transmission oil level check	Page	0•12
Brake fluid level checks	Page	0•13
Suspension, steering and final drive checks	Page	0•14
Tyre checks	Page	0•15
Legal and safety checks	Page	0•15

MAINTENANCE

Routine maintenance and servicing

Specifications	Page	1•2
Recommended lubricants and fluids	Page	1•2
Maintenance schedule	Page	1•3
Component locations	Page	1•4
Maintenance procedures	Page	1•6

Contents

REPAIRS AND OVERHAUL

Engine, transmission and associated systems

Engine, clutch and transmission	Page	**2•1**
Fuel and exhaust systems	Page	**3•1**
Ignition system	Page	**4•1**

Chassis components

Frame	Page	**5•1**
Suspension	Page	**5•1**
Final drive	Page	**5•1**
Brakes	Page	**6•1**
Wheels	Page	**6•1**
Tyres	Page	**6•1**
Fairing and bodywork	Page	**7•1**

Electrical system
Page **8•1**

Wiring diagrams
Page **8•22**

REFERENCE

Dimensions and Weights	Page	**REF•1**
Tools and Workshop Tips	Page	**REF•2**
Conversion factors	Page	**REF•20**
Motorcycle Chemicals and Lubricants	Page	**REF•21**
MOT Test Checks	Page	**REF•22**
Storage	Page	**REF•27**
Fault Finding	Page	**REF•30**
Fault Finding Equipment	Page	**REF•39**
Technical Terms Explained	Page	**REF•43**

Index
Page **REF•47**

0•4 Introduction

Yamaha
Musical instruments to motorcycles

**The FS1E -
first bike of many sixteen year olds in the UK**

The Yamaha Motor Company

The Yamaha name can be traced back to 1889, when Torakusu Yamaha founded the Yamaha Organ Manufacturing Company. Such was the success of the company, that in 1897 it became Nippon Gakki Limited and manufactured a wide range of reed organs and pianos.

During World War II, Nippon Gakki's manufacturing base was utilised by the Japanese authorities to produce propellers and fuel tanks for their aviation industry. The end of the war brought about a huge public demand for low cost transport and many firms decided to utilise their obsolete aircraft tooling for the production of motorcycles. Nippon Gakki's first motorcycle went on sale in February 1955 and was named the 125 YA-1 Red Dragonfly. This machine was a copy of the German DKW RT125 motorcycle, featuring a single cylinder two-stroke engine with a four-speed gearbox. Due to the outstanding success of this model the motorcycle operation was separated from Nippon Gakki in July 1955 and the Yamaha Motor Company was formed.

The YA-1 also received acclaim by winning two of Japan's biggest road races, the Mount Fuji Climbing race and the Asama Volcano race. The high level of public demand for the YA-1 led to the development of a whole series of two-stroke singles and twins.

Having made a large impact on their home market, Yamahas were exported to the USA in 1958 and to the UK in 1962. In the UK the signing of an Anglo-Japanese trade

Introduction

agreement during 1962 enabled the sale of Japanese lightweight motorcycles and scooters in Britain. At that time, competition between the many motorcycle producers in Japan had reduced numbers significantly and by the end of the sixties, only the big-four which are familiar with today remained.

Yamaha Europe was founded in 1968 and based in Holland. Although originally set up to market marine products, the Dutch base is now the official European Headquarters and distribution centre. Yamaha motorcycles are built at factories in Holland, Denmark, Norway, Italy, France, Spain and Portugal. Yamahas are imported into the UK by Yamaha Motor UK Ltd, formerly Mitsui Machinery Sales (UK) Ltd. Mitsui and Co. were originally a trading house, handling the shipping, distribution and marketing of Japanese products into western countries. Ultimately Mitsui Machinery Sales was formed to handle Yamaha motorcycles and outboard motors.

Based on the technology derived from its motorcycle operation, Yamaha have produced many other products, such as automobile and lightweight aircraft engines, marine engines and boats, generators, pumps, ATVs, snowmobiles, golf cars, industrial robots, lawnmowers, swimming pools and archery equipment.

Two-strokes first

Part of Yamaha's success was a whole string of innovations in the two-stroke world. Autolube engine lubrication, torque induction, multi-ported engines, reed valves and power valves kept their two-strokes at the forefront of technology. Many advances were achieved with the use of racing as a development laboratory. They went to the USA in the late 1950s with an air-cooled 250cc twin but didn't hit the GPs until the early 1960s when Fumio Ito scored a hat-trick of sixth places in the Isle of Man TT, the Dutch TT and the Belgian GP. This experiment gave rise to the idea of the over-the-counter racer, an idea that became reality in the TD1, the first in an unmatched series of two-stroke racers that were the standard issue for privateers at national and international level for years and helped Yamaha develop their road engines. While privateers raced the twins, Yamaha built the outrageously complicated vee-four 250 for Phil Read and followed it with a vee-four 125 that Bill Ivy lapped the Isle of Man on at over 100mph! When the FIM regulations were changed to limit the smaller GP classes to two cylinders, these exotic bikes died but set the scene for an unparalleled dynasty of mass-produced racers based on the same technology as the road bikes.

In the 1960s and 70s the two-stroke engined YAS3 125, YDS1 to YDS7 250 and YR5 350 formed the core of Yamaha's range. By the mid-70s they had been superseded by the RD (Race-Developed) 125, 250, and 350 range of two-stroke twins, featuring improved 7-port engines with reed valve induction. Braking was improved by the use of an hydraulic brake on the front wheel of DX models, instead of the drum arrangement used previously, and cast alloy wheels were available as an option on later RD models. The RD350 was replaced by the RD400 in 1976.

Running parallel with the RD twins was a range of single-cylinder two-strokes. Used in a variety of chassis types, the engine was used in the popular 50 cc FS1-E moped, the V50 to 90 step-thrus, RS100 and 125, YB100 and the DT trail range.

The TD racers got water-cooling in 1973 to become the TZs, the most successful and numerous over-the-counter racers ever built. That same year, Jarno Saarinen became the first rider to win a 500cc GP on a four-cylinder two-stroke on the new in-line four which was effectively a pair of TZs side-by-side. TZs won everywhere – including the Daytona 200 and 500 races when overbored to 351cc. A 700cc TZ also appeared, one year later taken out to 750cc. Steve Baker won the first Formula 750 world title – one of the precursors of Superbike – on one in 1977. The following year Kenny Roberts won Yamaha's first world 500 title and would be succeeded by Wayne Rainey and Eddie Lawson before Mick Doohan and the NSR500 took over.

The air-cooled single and twin cylinder RD road bikes were eventually replaced by the LC series in 1980, featuring liquid-cooled engines, radical new styling, spiral pattern cast wheels and cantilever rear suspension (Yamaha's Monoshock). Of all the LC models, the RD350LC, or RD350R as it was later known, has made the most impact in the market. Later models had YPVS (Yamaha Power Valve System) engines, another first for Yamaha – this was essentially a valve located in the exhaust ports which was electronically operated to alter port timing to achieve maximum power output. The RD500LC was the largest two-stroke made by Yamaha and differed from the other LCs by the use of its vee-four cylinder engine.

With the exception of the RD350R, now manufactured in Brazil, the LC range has been discontinued. Two-stroke engined models have given way to environmental pressure, and thus with a few exceptions, such as the TZR125 and TZR250, are used only in scooters and small capacity bikes.

The distinctive paintwork and trim of the RD models

Introduction

The Four-strokes

Yamaha concentrated solely on two-stroke models until 1970 when the XS1 was produced, their first four-stroke motorcycle. It was perhaps Yamaha's success with two-strokes that postponed an earlier move into the four-stroke motorcycle market, although their work with Toyota during the 1960s had given them a sound base in four-stroke technology.

The XS1 had a 650 cc twin-cylinder SOHC engine and was later to become known as the XS650, appearing also in the popular SE custom form. Yamaha introduced a three cylinder 750 cc engine in 1976, fitted in a sport-tourer frame and called the XS750, TX750 in the USA . The XS750 established itself well in the sport tourer class and remained in production with very few changes until uprated to 850 cc in 1980.

Other four-strokes followed in 1976, with the introduction of the XS250/360/400 series twins. The XS range was strengthened in 1978 by the four-cylinder XS1100.

The 1980s saw a new family of four-strokes, the XJ550, 650, 750 and 900 Fours. Improvements over the XS range amounted to a slimmer DOHC engine unit due to the relocation of the alternator behind the cylinders, electronic ignition and uprated braking and suspension systems. Models were available mainly in standard trim, although custom-styled Maxims were produced especially for the US market. The

The XS650 led the way for Yamaha's four-stroke range

Yamaha's XS750 was produced from 1976 to 1982 and then uprated to 850 cc

Introduction 0•7

XJ650T was the first model from Yamaha to have a turbo-charged engine. Although these early XJ models have now been discontinued, their roots live on in the XJ600S and XJ900S Diversion (Seca II) models.

The FZR prefix encompasses the pure sports Yamaha models. With the exception of the 16-valve FZR400 and FZR600 models, the FZ/FZR750 and FZR1000 used 20-valve engines, two exhaust valves and three inlet valves per cylinder. This concept was called Genesis and gave improved gas flow to the combustion chambers. Other features of the new engine were the use of down-draught carburetors and the engine's inclined angle in the frame, plus the change to liquid-cooling. Lightweight Deltabox design aluminium frames and uprated suspension improved the bikes's handling. The Genesis engine lives on in the YZF750 and 1000 models.

The Genesis concept was the basis of Yamaha's foray into four-stroke racing, first with a bike known simply as 'The Genesis', an FZ750 motor in a TT Formula 1 bike with which the factory attempted to steal the Honda RVF750's thunder at important events like the Suzuka 8 Hours and the Bol d'Or although they never fielded it for a whole World Championship season. That had to wait for the advent of the World Superbike Championship, although there was no full works team until 1995, instead it was left to individual importers to support teams. It was the Australian Dealer Team Yamaha which scored the factory's first World Superbike win in the series debut year of 1988. The rider? Mick Doohan. Slightly, embarrassingly, it was the steel framed FZ750 rather than the FZR homologation special that won races. The OW01 was a race winner, mainly in the hands of Fabrizio Pirovano, the factory's most successful Superbike racer with ten victories, but national success in the UK, Japan, and in the Daytona 200 has not been translated into World Championships for any of Yamaha's 750s.

The vee-twin engine has been the mainstay of the XV Virago range. Since 1981 XVs have been produced in 535, 700, 750, 920, 1000 and 1100 engine sizes, all using the same basic air-cooled sohc vee-twin engine. Other uses of vee engines have been in the XZ550 of the early 1980s, the XVZ12 Venture and the mighty VMX-12 V-Max.

A new family of four-strokes was released in 1980 with the introduction of the XJ range

The XV535 Virago vee-twin

0•8 Introduction

1995 XJ900S Diversion

Yamaha has always been a sporting-orientated company whose motto could be 'Racing Improves the Breed', so it's no surprise that the latest generation of lightweight sportsters are at the cutting edge of performance on and off the track. The R6 won more races than any other machine in the inaugural year of the World Supersports Championship, the R7 won a race in its debut year in World Superbike in the hands of the mercurial Noriyuki Haga, and the mighty 1000cc R1 ended Honda's domination of the Isle of Man F1 TT when David Jefferies won three races in a week in 1999.

In Grand Prix racing, the factory took several years to get over the shock of Wayne Rainey's crippling accident. and first 500cc win since the American's enforced retirement didn't come until 1998 when Simon Crafar won at Donington Park. For 1999, Yamaha refocussed their ambitions and signed Italian superstar Max Biaggi plus Spanish trier Carlos Checa for the works team, while dashing young Frenchman Regis Laconi and tough little Aussie Gary McCoy rode for the WCM satellite team. Both teams got a win in the '99 season and with a new TZ250 being developed for 2000 it looks as if Yamaha's spirit of competition will go on unabated into the new Millenium.

The XJ900S Diversion – function not fashion

The bigger Diversion can trace its ancestry to two of Yamaha's long lived models. The motor and, to some extent, chassis are firmly based on the old XJ900F that appeared eleven years before the S-model Diversion in 1983 and stayed around long enough to overlap with the Diversion in the company's range. The two bikes' motors share a bore and stroke of 68.5 x 60.5 mm, but the later model of course benefits from a deal of fine-tuning and some weight loss, plus the Diversion styling from the XJ600S model. Nevertheless, it is instantly recognisable as the original power plant despite everything from camshafts to gearbox being redesigned. The block is slanted forward à la Genesis to give the inlet tracts a straight path from the big airbox to the downdraft carbs – modern thinking there. The shaft final drive system is lifted direct from the old XJ, though.

Chassis-wise the main difference is the change from twin rear shocks to the Monocross cantilever system – more advanced but not Yamaha's latest rising-rate linkage rear suspension system for reasons that will become apparent. Neither were the front forks the latest thing – they had no facilities for adjustment on the early models.

The model the Diversion was destined to replace in Yamaha's range was the FJ1100/1200, one of the best all-rounders to come out of Japan in the 1980s. Originally, it had sporting pretensions but they were soon dismissed in favour of its astonishing all-round people- and luggage-carrying abilities. Thus the Diversion had to come with long-distance ability: a decent-sized tank; comfortable seat; screen as standard equipment; luggage not a problem.

There was another major design requirement: price. The old FJ was good but pricey and the new Diversion, like its 600 cc sibling, had to come in at a much lower price. The smaller Diversion arrived a couple of years before the bigger bike and was also based around a revamped version of an old XJ motor, but was labelled as an all-rounder that would stay in the range basically unchanged for a substantial period of time. The XJ900S had to do the same but at a much reduced price tag compared to the FJ.

When it first appeared in the UK range at the end of 1994 it was priced at £6199. That was £500 more than the old XJ but a whopping £2350 cheaper than the ABS-equipped version of the FJ1200 – a lot of money even today and a stunning 27.5% lower than the bigger bike. Objective achieved.

There is another aspect to price and that is

1999 XJ900S Diversion

Introduction

running costs. Launch publicity for the Diversion majored on the low running costs, and the one advantage the newer bike had in that respect over the FJ is shaft drive. Add in low maintenance requirements for the air-cooled motor and Yamaha got that right, too.

On the road, the big Diversion felt very much like what it was: an uprated and modified XJ900F. And like its ancestor it attracted a stolid, no-nonsense type of rider – who, in the main, specified the optional hard luggage when ordering. To help them keep their purchases, Yamaha built in storage for a U-lock under the seat. A small detail but a significant one. This was one of the first times that a Japanese factory acknowledged that theft prevention was an issue for owners.

The way the Diversion was built down to a price was twofold. Obviously, using the parts from previous models was a good start (clocks and controls came off the FJ1200) in the economy stakes but the pre-planned longevity of the model was equally significant – as was the status of the Diversion as a 'world bike'. The Diversion was in planning when the Japanese factories were used to building bikes for three different markets: Europe, the USA, and the Japanese home market. The economic imperative of the booming Japanese economy demanded that the manufacturers build bikes that could be sold in at least two, and preferably all three, markets – the so-called 'world bike'. Add in the long model life over which fixed costs could be amortised and you have a strategy for much-reduced price tags, and it worked.

Happily, the strategy also produced a good working motorcycle. Not a fashionable, flavour of the month motorcycle, but a solid do-anything bike that fulfilled its design objectives. And you can't ask more of any design than that.

Acknowledgements

Our thanks are due to Taylors Motorcycles of Crewkerne who supplied the machines featured in the illustrations throughout this manual. We would also like to thank Mitsui Machinery Sales (UK) Ltd for permission to reproduce certain illustrations used in this manual and for supplying some of the cover photographs, also NGK Spark Plugs (UK) Ltd for supplying the colour spark plug condition photos, the Avon Rubber Company for supplying information on tyre fitting, and Draper Tools Ltd for supplying some of the workshop tools.

About this manual

The aim of this manual is to help you get the best value from your motorcycle. It can do so in several ways. It can help you decide what work must be done, even if you choose to have it done by a dealer; it provides information and procedures for routine maintenance and servicing; and it offers diagnostic and repair procedures to follow when trouble occurs.

The XJ's forward sloping cylinders allow the use of downdraught carbs

We hope you use the manual to tackle the work yourself. For many simpler jobs, doing it yourself may be quicker than arranging an appointment to get the motorcycle into a dealer and making the trips to leave it and pick it up. More importantly, a lot of money can be saved by avoiding the expense the shop must pass on to you to cover its labour and overhead costs. An added benefit is the sense of satisfaction and accomplishment that you feel after doing the job yourself.

References to the left or right side of the motorcycle assume you are sitting on the seat, facing forward.

We take great pride in the accuracy of information given in this manual, but motorcycle manufacturers make alterations and design changes during the production run of a particular motorcycle of which they do not inform us. No liability can be accepted by the authors or publishers for loss, damage or injury caused by any errors in, or omissions from, the information given.

0•10 Safety first!

Professional mechanics are trained in safe working procedures. However enthusiastic you may be about getting on with the job at hand, take the time to ensure that your safety is not put at risk. A moment's lack of attention can result in an accident, as can failure to observe simple precautions.

There will always be new ways of having accidents, and the following is not a comprehensive list of all dangers; it is intended rather to make you aware of the risks and to encourage a safe approach to all work you carry out on your bike.

Asbestos

● Certain friction, insulating, sealing and other products - such as brake pads, clutch linings, gaskets, etc. - contain asbestos. Extreme care must be taken to avoid inhalation of dust from such products since it is hazardous to health. If in doubt, assume that they do contain asbestos.

Fire

● Remember at all times that petrol is highly flammable. Never smoke or have any kind of naked flame around, when working on the vehicle. But the risk does not end there - a spark caused by an electrical short-circuit, by two metal surfaces contacting each other, by careless use of tools, or even by static electricity built up in your body under certain conditions, can ignite petrol vapour, which in a confined space is highly explosive. Never use petrol as a cleaning solvent. Use an approved safety solvent.

● Always disconnect the battery earth terminal before working on any part of the fuel or electrical system, and never risk spilling fuel on to a hot engine or exhaust.

● It is recommended that a fire extinguisher of a type suitable for fuel and electrical fires is kept handy in the garage or workplace at all times. Never try to extinguish a fuel or electrical fire with water.

Fumes

● Certain fumes are highly toxic and can quickly cause unconsciousness and even death if inhaled to any extent. Petrol vapour comes into this category, as do the vapours from certain solvents such as trichloro-ethylene. Any draining or pouring of such volatile fluids should be done in a well ventilated area.

● When using cleaning fluids and solvents, read the instructions carefully. Never use materials from unmarked containers - they may give off poisonous vapours.

● Never run the engine of a motor vehicle in an enclosed space such as a garage. Exhaust fumes contain carbon monoxide which is extremely poisonous; if you need to run the engine, always do so in the open air or at least have the rear of the vehicle outside the workplace.

The battery

● Never cause a spark, or allow a naked light near the vehicle's battery. It will normally be giving off a certain amount of hydrogen gas, which is highly explosive.

● Always disconnect the battery ground (earth) terminal before working on the fuel or electrical systems (except where noted).

● If possible, loosen the filler plugs or cover when charging the battery from an external source. Do not charge at an excessive rate or the battery may burst.

● Take care when topping up, cleaning or carrying the battery. The acid electrolyte, evenwhen diluted, is very corrosive and should not be allowed to contact the eyes or skin. Always wear rubber gloves and goggles or a face shield. If you ever need to prepare electrolyte yourself, always add the acid slowly to the water; never add the water to the acid.

Electricity

● When using an electric power tool, inspection light etc., always ensure that the appliance is correctly connected to its plug and that, where necessary, it is properly grounded (earthed). Do not use such appliances in damp conditions and, again, beware of creating a spark or applying excessive heat in the vicinity of fuel or fuel vapour. Also ensure that the appliances meet national safety standards.

● A severe electric shock can result from touching certain parts of the electrical system, such as the spark plug wires (HT leads), when the engine is running or being cranked, particularly if components are damp or the insulation is defective. Where an electronic ignition system is used, the secondary (HT) voltage is much higher and could prove fatal.

Remember...

✗ **Don't** start the engine without first ascertaining that the transmission is in neutral.

✗ **Don't** suddenly remove the pressure cap from a hot cooling system - cover it with a cloth and release the pressure gradually first, or you may get scalded by escaping coolant.

✗ **Don't** attempt to drain oil until you are sure it has cooled sufficiently to avoid scalding you.

✗ **Don't** grasp any part of the engine or exhaust system without first ascertaining that it is cool enough not to burn you.

✗ **Don't** allow brake fluid or antifreeze to contact the machine's paintwork or plastic components.

✗ **Don't** siphon toxic liquids such as fuel, hydraulic fluid or antifreeze by mouth, or allow them to remain on your skin.

✗ **Don't** inhale dust - it may be injurious to health (see Asbestos heading).

✗ **Don't** allow any spilled oil or grease to remain on the floor - wipe it up right away, before someone slips on it.

✗ **Don't** use ill-fitting spanners or other tools which may slip and cause injury.

✗ **Don't** lift a heavy component which may be beyond your capability - get assistance.

✗ **Don't** rush to finish a job or take unverified short cuts.

✗ **Don't** allow children or animals in or around an unattended vehicle.

✗ **Don't** inflate a tyre above the recommended pressure. Apart from overstressing the carcass, in extreme cases the tyre may blow off forcibly.

✔ **Do** ensure that the machine is supported securely at all times. This is especially important when the machine is blocked up to aid wheel or fork removal.

✔ **Do** take care when attempting to loosen a stubborn nut or bolt. It is generally better to pull on a spanner, rather than push, so that if you slip, you fall away from the machine rather than onto it.

✔ **Do** wear eye protection when using power tools such as drill, sander, bench grinder etc.

✔ **Do** use a barrier cream on your hands prior to undertaking dirty jobs - it will protect your skin from infection as well as making the dirt easier to remove afterwards; but make sure your hands aren't left slippery. Note that long-term contact with used engine oil can be a health hazard.

✔ **Do** keep loose clothing (cuffs, ties etc. and long hair) well out of the way of moving mechanical parts.

✔ **Do** remove rings, wristwatch etc., before working on the vehicle - especially the electrical system.

✔ **Do** keep your work area tidy - it is only too easy to fall over articles left lying around.

✔ **Do** exercise caution when compressing springs for removal or installation. Ensure that the tension is applied and released in a controlled manner, using suitable tools which preclude the possibility of the spring escaping violently.

✔ **Do** ensure that any lifting tackle used has a safe working load rating adequate for the job.

✔ **Do** get someone to check periodically that all is well, when working alone on the vehicle.

✔ **Do** carry out work in a logical sequence and check that everything is correctly assembled and tightened afterwards.

✔ **Do** remember that your vehicle's safety affects that of yourself and others. If in doubt on any point, get professional advice.

● If in spite of following these precautions, you are unfortunate enough to injure yourself, seek medical attention as soon as possible.

Identification numbers 0•11

Frame and engine numbers

The frame serial number is stamped into the right-hand side of the steering head. The engine number is stamped into the top of the crankcase on the right-hand side of the engine. The model code label is on the top of the right-hand sub-frame spar under the seat. These numbers should be recorded and kept in a safe place so they can be furnished to law enforcement officials in the event of a theft. There is also a carburettor identification number on each carburettor body.

The frame serial number, engine serial number, carburettor identification number and model code should be recorded and kept in a handy place (such as with your driver's licence) so they are always available when purchasing or ordering parts for your machine.

The procedures in this manual identify the bikes by production year (i.e. 1998 model) which is not necessarily the same as the year of first registration. Refer to the table below to establish the production year from the model code or engine/frame number. Note that the model codes given apply to UK market models.

Model	Prod Yr	Code	Engine/frame No.
XJ900S	1994/95	4KM1	4KM-000101-on
XJ900S	1996	4KM3	4KM-025101-on
XJ900S	1997	4KM5	Not available
XJ900S	1998/99	4KM7	Not available
XJ900S	2000	4KM9	Not available

The model code label (arrowed) is on the sub-frame under the seat

The frame number is stamped on the right-hand side of the steering head

The engine number is stamped into the top of the crankcase

Buying spare parts

Once you have found all the identification numbers, record them for reference when buying parts. Since the manufacturers change specifications, parts and vendors (i.e. companies that manufacture the various components on the machine), providing the ID numbers is the only way to be reasonably sure that you are buying the correct parts.

Whenever possible, take the worn part to the dealer so direct comparison with the new component can be made. Along the trail from the manufacturer to the parts shelf, there are numerous places where the part can end up with the wrong number or be listed incorrectly.

The two places to purchase new parts for your motorcycle – the accessory store and the franchised dealer – differ in the type of parts they carry. While dealers can obtain virtually every part for your motorcycle, the accessory dealer is usually limited to normal high-wear items such as shock absorbers, tune-up parts, various engine gaskets, cables, chains, brake parts, etc. An accessory outlet will rarely have major suspension components, cylinders, transmission gears, or cases.

Used parts can be obtained for roughly half the price of new ones, but you can't always be sure of what you're getting. Once again, take your worn part to the breaker's yard for direct comparison.

Whether buying new, used or rebuilt parts, the best course is to deal directly with someone who specialises in parts for your particular make.

0•12 Daily (pre-ride) checks

1 Engine/transmission oil level check

Note: *The daily (pre-ride) checks outlined in the owner's manual covers those items which should be inspected on a daily basis.*

Before you start:

✔ Support the motorcycle on its centrestand, making sure it is on level ground.
✔ Start the engine and let it idle for several minutes to allow it to reach normal operating temperature.
Caution: Do not run the engine in an enclosed space such as a garage or workshop.
✔ Leave the motorcycle undisturbed for a few minutes to allow the oil level to stabilise.

Bike care:

● If you have to add oil frequently, you should check whether you have any oil leaks. If there is no sign of oil leakage from the joints and gaskets the engine could be burning oil (see *Fault Finding*).

The correct oil

● Modern, high-revving engines place great demands on their oil. It is very important that the correct oil for your bike is used.

● Always top up with a good quality oil of the specified type and viscosity and do not overfill the engine.

Caution: Do not use chemical additives or oils with a grade of CD or higher, or use oils labelled 'ENERGY CONSERVING II'. Such additives or oils could cause clutch slip.

Oil type	API grade SE, SF or SG
Oil viscosity	SAE 10W40 or 20W40*

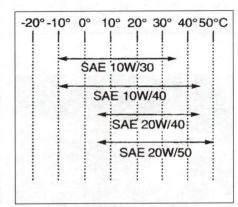

Oil viscosity table; select the oil best suited to your conditions

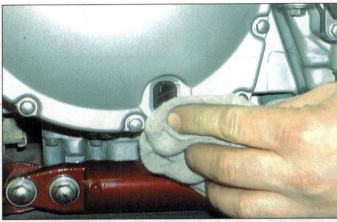

1 Wipe the oil level inspection window, located on the right-hand side of the engine, so that it is clean.

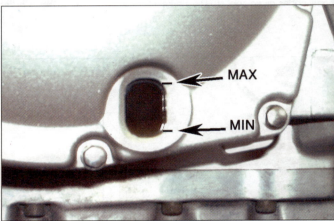

2 With the motorcycle vertical, the oil level should lie between the maximum and minimum levels on the window (arrowed).

3 If the level is below the minimum line, remove the filler cap from the top of the clutch cover.

4 Top the engine up with the recommended grade and type of oil, to bring the level up to the maximum level on the window.

Daily (pre-ride) checks   0•13

2 Brake fluid level checks

> ⚠ **Warning:** Brake hydraulic fluid can harm your eyes and damage painted surfaces, so use extreme caution when handling and pouring it and cover surrounding surfaces with rag. Do not use fluid that has been standing open for some time, as it absorbs moisture from the air which can cause a dangerous loss of braking effectiveness.

Before you start:

✔ Support the motorcycle in an upright position, using an auxiliary stand if required. Turn the handlebars until the top of the front master cylinder is as level as possible. The rear master cylinder reservoir is located behind the right-hand side panel.
✔ Make sure you have the correct hydraulic fluid. DOT 4 is recommended.
✔ Wrap a rag around the reservoir being worked on to ensure that any spillage does not come into contact with painted surfaces.

Bike care:

● The fluid in the front and rear brake master cylinder reservoirs will drop slightly as the brake pads wear down.
● If any fluid reservoir requires repeated topping-up this is an indication of an hydraulic leak somewhere in the system, which should be investigated immediately.
● Check for signs of fluid leakage from the hydraulic hoses and components – if found, rectify immediately.
● Check the operation of both brakes before taking the machine on the road; if there is evidence of air in the system (spongy feel to lever or pedal), it must be bled as described in Chapter 6.

FRONT BRAKE FLUID LEVEL

1 The front brake fluid level is visible through the reservoir body – it must be above the LOWER level line.

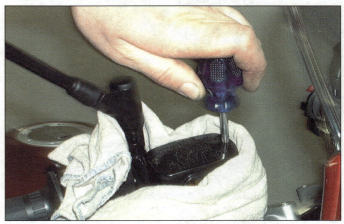

2 If the level is below the LOWER level line, remove the reservoir cover screws and lift off the cover, then remove the diaphragm.

3 Top up with new clean DOT 4 hydraulic fluid, until the level is above the LOWER level line. Take care to avoid spills (see **Warning** above).

4 Ensure that the diaphragm is correctly seated before installing the cover. Secure the cap with its screws.

0•14 Daily (pre-ride) checks

REAR BRAKE FLUID LEVEL

5 Remove the seat (see Chapter 7). The rear brake fluid level is visible through the reservoir body – it must be above the LOWER level line.

6 If the level is below the LOWER level line, remove the reservoir mounting screw and draw the reservoir from under the frame.

7 Unscrew the reservoir cap and remove the diaphragm plate and the diaphragm.

8 Top up with new clean DOT 4 hydraulic fluid, until the level is above the lower mark. Take care to avoid spills (see **Warning** on previous page).

9 Ensure that the diaphragm is correctly seated before installing the plate and cap. Tighten the cap securely, then mount the reservoir under the frame. Install the seat (see Chapter 7).

3 Suspension, steering and final drive checks

Suspension and steering:
- Check that the front and rear suspension operates smoothly without binding.
- Check that the suspension is adjusted as required.
- Check that the steering moves smoothly from lock-to-lock.

Final drive:
- Check that there is no sign of oil leakage around the final drive housing. If any is evident, check the final drive oil level (Chapter 1).

Daily (pre-ride) checks 0•15

4 Tyre checks

Tyre care:
● Check the tyres carefully for cuts, tears, embedded nails or other sharp objects and excessive wear. Operation of the motorcycle with excessively worn tyres is extremely hazardous, as traction and handling are directly affected.

● Check the condition of the tyre valve and ensure the dust cap is in place.

● Pick out any stones or nails which may have become embedded in the tyre tread. If left, they will eventually penetrate through the casing and cause a puncture.

● If tyre damage is apparent, or unexplained loss of pressure is experienced, seek the advice of a tyre fitting specialist without delay.

Tyre tread depth:
● At the time of writing UK law requires that tread depth must be at least 1 mm over 3/4 of the tread breadth all the way around the tyre, with no bald patches. Many riders, however, consider 2 mm tread depth minimum to be a safer limit. Yamaha recommend a minimum of 1.6 mm.

● Many tyres now incorporate wear indicators in the tread. Identify the triangular pointer or 'TWI' mark on the tyre sidewall to locate the indicator bar and replace the tyre with a new one if the tread has worn down to the bar.

Loading/speed	Front	Rear
Rider only	33 psi (2.25 Bar)	36 psi (2.50 Bar)
Rider and passenger, or high speed riding	36 psi (2.50 Bar)	42 psi (2.90 Bar)

The correct pressures:
● The tyres must be checked when **cold**, not immediately after riding. Note that low tyre pressures may cause the tyre to slip on the rim or come off. High tyre pressures will cause abnormal tread wear and unsafe handling.

● Use an accurate pressure gauge.

● Proper air pressure will increase tyre life and provide maximum stability and ride comfort.

1 Check the tyre pressures when the tyres are **cold** and keep them properly inflated.

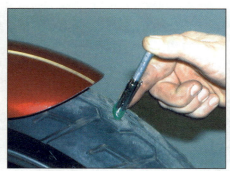

2 Measure tread depth at the centre of the tyre using a tread depth gauge.

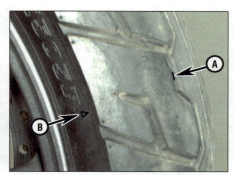

3 Tyre tread wear indicator bar (A) and its location marking (usually either an arrow, a triangle or the letters TWI) on the sidewall (B).

5 Legal and safety checks

Lighting and signalling:
● Take a minute to check that the headlight, tail light, brake light, instrument lights and turn signals all work correctly.
● Check that the horn sounds when operated.
● A working speedometer graduated in mph is a statutory requirement in the UK..

Safety:
● Check that the throttle grip rotates smoothly and snaps shut when released, in all steering positions. Also check for the correct amount of freeplay (see Section 15 of Chapter 1).
● Check that the engine shuts off when the kill switch is operated.
● Check that sidestand and centrestand return springs hold the stands securely up when retracted.

Fuel:
● This may seem obvious, but check that you have enough fuel to complete your journey. If you notice signs of fuel leakage – rectify the cause immediately (see Section 5 of Chapter 1, and also Chapter 3).
● Ensure you use the correct grade fuel – see Chapter 3 Specifications.

0•16 Notes

Chapter 1
Routine maintenance and Servicing

Contents

Air filter – cleaning and renewal	4
Alternator brushes – check and renewal	33
Battery – charging	see Chapter 9
Battery – check	10
Battery – removal, installation, inspection and maintenance	see Chapter 9
Brake hoses – renewal	27
Brake master cylinder and caliper seals – renewal	25
Brake pads – wear check	7
Brake system – check	8
Brakes – fluid change	26
Carburettors – synchronisation	3
Clutch – check and adjustment	9
Cylinder compression – check	29
Engine oil pressure – check	30
Engine/transmission – oil and oil filter change	19
Engine/transmission – oil change	6
Final drive – oil change	24
Final drive – oil level check	20
Front forks – oil change	32
Fuel hoses – renewal	31
Fuel system and air induction system (AIS) – check	5
Headlight aim – check and adjustment	28
Idle speed – check and adjustment	2
Nuts and bolts – tightness check	14
Sidestand and centrestand – check	13
Spark plug gap – check and adjustment	1
Stands, lever pivots and cables – lubrication	16
Steering head bearings – freeplay check and adjustment	18
Steering head bearings – re-greasing	22
Suspension – check	17
Swingarm and suspension linkage bearings – re-greasing	21
Throttle and choke cables – check	15
Valve clearances – check and adjustment	23
Wheel bearings – check	12
Wheels and tyres – general check	11

Degrees of difficulty

| Easy, suitable for novice with little experience | | Fairly easy, suitable for beginner with some experience | | Fairly difficult, suitable for competent DIY mechanic | 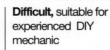 | Difficult, suitable for experienced DIY mechanic | | Very difficult, suitable for expert DIY or professional |

1•2 Specifications

Engine

Spark plugs	
Type	NGK DPR8EA-9 or Nippondenso X24EPR-U9
Electrode gap	0.8 to 0.9 mm
Engine idle speed	950 to 1050 rpm
Carburettor synchronisation	
Intake vacuum	230 to 250 mmHg
Max. difference between carburettors	10 mmHg
Valve clearances (COLD engine)	
Intake valves	0.11 to 0.15 mm
Exhaust valves	0.16 to 0.20 mm
Cylinder compression	
Standard	174 psi (12 Bar)
Maximum	203 psi (14 Bar)
Minimum	145 psi (10 Bar)
Max. difference between cylinders	14.5 psi (1.0 Bar)
Engine oil pressure	11.6 psi (0.8 Bar) @ 1000 rpm
Alternator brush length	
New	13.7 mm
Service limit	4.7 mm

Cycle parts

Rear brake pedal height (see text)	30 mm
Throttle cable freeplay	3 to 5 mm at twistgrip
Clutch cable freeplay	10 to 15 mm at lever end
Tyre pressures (cold)	see *Daily (pre-ride) checks*

Recommended lubricants and fluids

Engine/transmission

Type	see *Daily (pre-ride) checks*
Capacity	
Oil change	3.2 litres
Oil and filter change	3.4 litres
Following engine overhaul – dry engine, new filter	4.4 litres

Cycle parts

Brake fluid type	DOT 4
Final drive	
Oil type	SAE 80 API GL-4 Hypoid gear oil or SAE 80W90 Hypoid gear oil
Oil capacity	0.2 litres
Steering head bearings	Lightweight lithium-soap base grease
Wheel bearings	Lightweight lithium-soap base grease
Stands	Lightweight lithium-soap base grease
Swingarm pivot and bearings	Molybdenum disulphide grease
Suspension linkage bearings	Molybdenum disulphide grease
Gearchange lever/clutch lever/front brake lever/rear brake pedal	20W40 motor oil
Cables	20W40 motor oil
Throttle grip	Multi-purpose grease or dry film lubricant

Torque wrench settings

Spark plugs	18 Nm
Oil drain plug	43 Nm
Oil filter	17 Nm
Steering head bearing adjuster nut	
Initial setting	52 Nm
Final setting	18 Nm
Steering stem nut	110 Nm
Fork clamp bolts (top yoke)	30 Nm
Final drive oil filler cap	23 Nm
Final drive oil drain plug	23 Nm
Crankshaft end-cover screws/bolts	8 Nm
Oil gallery plug	8 Nm

Maintenance schedule 1•3

Note: *The daily (pre-ride) checks outlined in the owner's manual covers those items which should be inspected on a daily basis. Always perform the pre-ride inspection at every maintenance interval (in addition to the procedures listed). The intervals listed below are the intervals recommended by the manufacturer for each particular operation during the model years covered in this manual. Your owner's manual may have different intervals for your model.*

Daily (pre-ride)
☐ See *'Daily (pre-ride) checks'* at the beginning of this manual.

After the initial 600 miles (1000 km)
Note: *This check is usually performed by a Yamaha dealer after the first 600 miles (1000 km) from new. Thereafter, maintenance is carried out according to the following intervals of the schedule.*

Every 4000 miles (6000 km) or 6 months (whichever comes sooner)
☐ Check the spark plug gaps (Section 1)
☐ Check and adjust the idle speed (Section 2)
☐ Check/adjust the carburettor synchronisation (Section 3)
☐ Clean and check the air filter element (Section 4)
☐ Check the fuel system and air induction system (AIS) and hoses (Section 5)
☐ Change the engine transmission oil (Section 6)
☐ Check the brake pads (Section 7)
☐ Check the brake system and brake light switch operation (Section 8)
☐ Check and adjust the clutch (Section 9)
☐ Check the battery (Section 10)
☐ Check the condition of the wheels and tyres (Section 11)
☐ Check the wheel bearings (Section 12)
☐ Check the sidestand and centrestand (Section 13)
☐ Check the tightness of all nuts, bolts and fasteners (Section 14)
☐ Check and adjust the throttle and choke cables (Section 15)
☐ Lubricate the clutch lever/brake lever/gearchange pedal/brake pedal/sidestand/centrestand pivots and the throttle/choke/clutch cables (Section 16)
☐ Check the suspension (Section 17)

Every 8000 miles (12,000 km) or 12 months (whichever comes sooner)
Carry out all the items under the 4000 mile (6000 km) check, plus the following
☐ Check and adjust the steering head bearings (Section 18)
☐ Change the engine transmission oil and filter (Section 19)
☐ Check the final drive oil level (Section 20)

Every 16,000 miles (24,000 km) or two years (whichever comes sooner)
Carry out all the items under the 8000 mile (12,000 km) check, plus the following
☐ Re-grease the swingarm and suspension linkage bearings (Section 21)
☐ Re-grease the steering head bearings (Section 22)
☐ Check and adjust the valve clearances (Section 23)
☐ Change the final drive oil level (Section 24)

Every two years
☐ Renew the brake master cylinder and caliper seals (Section 25)
☐ Change the brake fluid (Section 26)

Every four years
☐ Renew the brake hoses (Section 27)

Non-scheduled maintenance
☐ Check and adjust the headlight aim (Section 28)
☐ Check the cylinder compression (Section 29)
☐ Check the engine oil pressure (Section 30)
☐ Renew the fuel hoses (Section 31)
☐ Change the front fork oil (Section 32)
☐ Check the alternator brushes (Section 33)

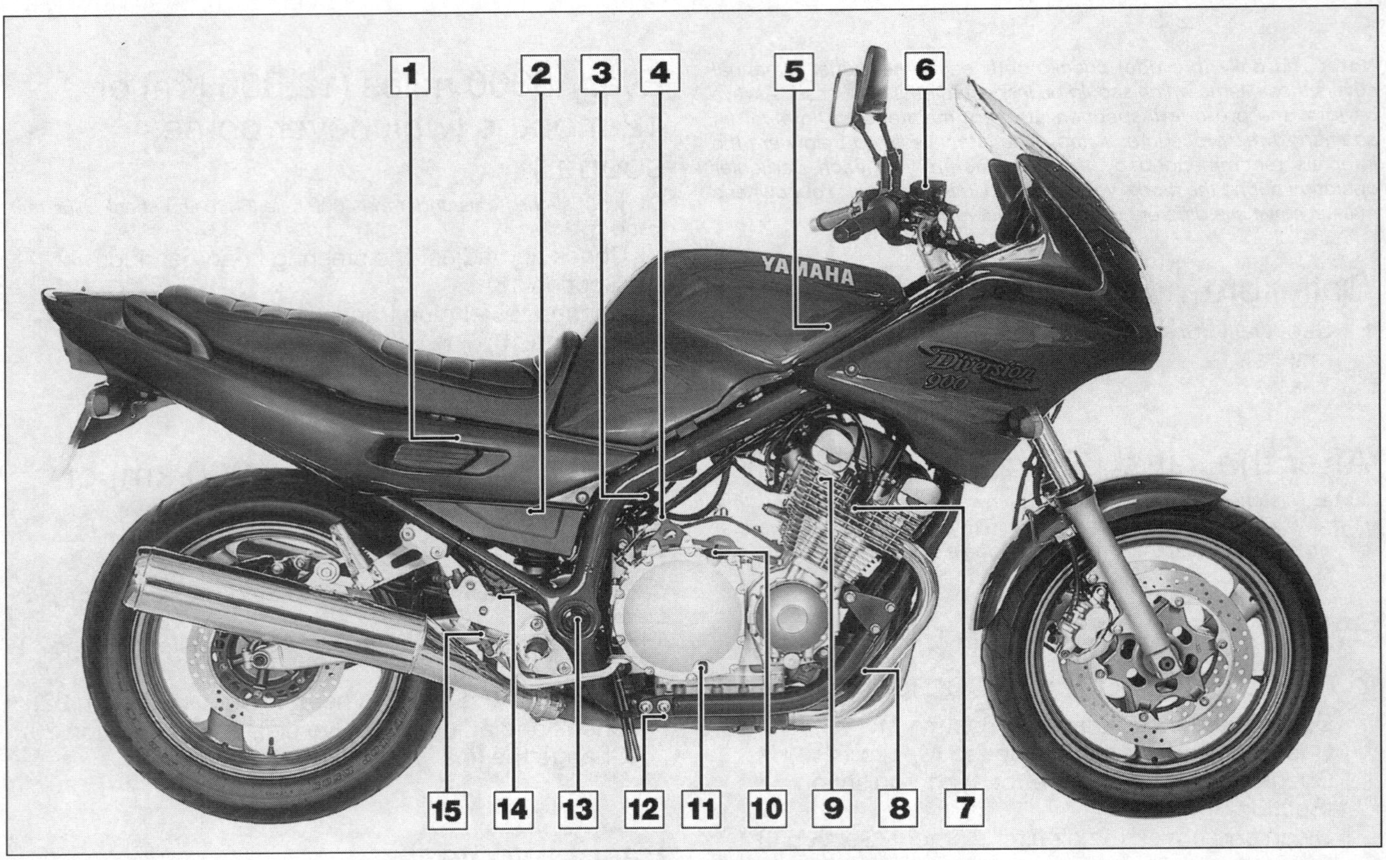

1•4 Component locations

Component locations on right-hand side

1 Rear brake fluid reservoir
2 Battery
3 Fuel tap and filter
4 Clutch cable lower adjuster
5 Air filter

6 Front brake fluid reservoir
7 Spark plugs and valves
8 Engine/transmission oil filter
9 Engine/transmission oil pressure plug
10 Engine/transmission oil filler cap

11 Engine/transmission oil level window
12 Engine/transmission oil drain plug
13 Swingarm pivot bearings
14 Rear brake light switch
15 Rear brake pedal height adjuster

Component locations 1•5

Component locations on left-hand side

1 Air cut-off valve and reed valves
2 Clutch cable upper adjuster
3 Steering head bearing adjuster
4 Idle speed adjuster
5 In-line fuel filter
6 Final drive oil level/filler plug
7 Final drive drain plug
8 Swingarm pivot bearings
9 Alternator
10 Engine turning bolt cover
11 Spark plugs and valves

Routine maintenance and servicing

Introduction

1 This Chapter is designed to help the home mechanic maintain his/her motorcycle for safety, economy, long life and peak performance.

2 Deciding where to start or plug into the routine maintenance schedule depends on several factors. If the warranty period on your motorcycle has just expired, and if it has been maintained according to the warranty standards, you may want to pick up routine maintenance as it coincides with the next mileage or calendar interval. If you have owned the machine for some time but have never performed any maintenance on it, then you may want to start at the beginning and include all frequent procedures to ensure that nothing important is overlooked. If you have just had a major engine overhaul, then you should start the engine maintenance routines from the beginning. If you have a used machine and have no knowledge of its history or maintenance record, you should combine all the checks into one large initial service and then settle into the maintenance schedule prescribed.

3 Before beginning any maintenance or repair, the machine should be cleaned thoroughly, especially around the oil filter, spark plugs, valve cover, side panels, carburettors, etc. Cleaning will help ensure that dirt does not contaminate the engine and will allow you to detect wear and damage that could otherwise easily go unnoticed.

4 Certain maintenance information is sometimes printed on decals attached to the motorcycle. If any information on the decals differs from that included here, use the information on the decal.

Every 4000 miles (6000 km) or 6 months

1 Spark plug gaps – check and adjustment

1 Make sure your spark plug socket is the correct size before attempting to remove the plugs – a suitable one is supplied in the motorcycle's tool kit which is stored under the seat.

2 Using compressed air if available, clean the area around the base of the spark plugs to prevent any dirt falling into the engine when the plugs are removed.

3 Check that the cylinder location is marked on each plug lead, then pull the spark plug cap off each spark plug **(see illustration)**. Using either the plug removing tool supplied in the bike's toolkit or a deep socket type wrench, unscrew the plugs from the cylinder head **(see illustration)**. Lay each plug out in relation to its cylinder; if any plug shows up a problem it will then be easy to identify the troublesome cylinder.

4 Inspect the electrodes for wear. Both the centre and side electrodes should have square edges and the side electrodes should be of uniform thickness. Look for excessive deposits and evidence of a cracked or chipped insulator around the centre electrode. Compare your spark plugs to the colour spark plug reading chart at the end of this manual. Check the threads, the washer and the ceramic insulator body for cracks and other damage.

5 If the electrodes are not excessively worn, and if the deposits can be easily removed with a wire brush, the plugs can be re-gapped and re-used (if no cracks or chips are visible in the insulator). If in doubt concerning the condition of the plugs, replace them with new ones, as the expense is minimal. Yamaha do not specify a replacement interval, but leave it to the discretion of the owner.

6 Cleaning spark plugs by sandblasting is permitted, provided you clean the plugs with a high flash-point solvent afterwards.

7 Before installing the plugs, make sure they are the correct type and heat range and check the gap between the electrodes **(see illustrations)**. Compare the gap to that specified and adjust as necessary. If the gap must be adjusted, bend the side electrodes only and be very careful not to chip or crack the insulator nose **(see illustration)**. Make sure the washer is in place on the plug before installing it.

1.3a Remove the spark plug cap . . .

1.3b . . . then unscrew the spark plug

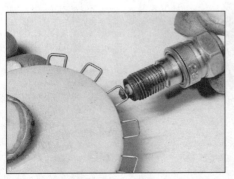
1.7a Using a wire type gauge to measure the spark plug electrode gap

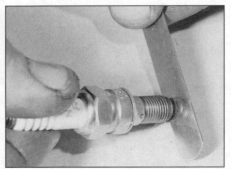
1.7b Using a feeler gauge to measure the spark plug electrode gap

1.7c Adjust the electrode gap by bending the side electrode only

Every 4000 miles (6000 km) 1•7

8 Since the cylinder head is made of aluminium, which is soft and easily damaged, thread the plugs into the heads by hand so that you can instantly tell if the plug is cross-threading **(see illustration)**. Once the plugs are finger-tight, the job can be finished with a spanner on the tool supplied or a socket drive **(see illustration 1.3b)**. If a torque wrench can be applied, tighten the spark plugs to the torque setting specified at the beginning of the Chapter. Otherwise tighten them by 1/4 to 1/2 turn after they have been fully hand tightened and have seated. Do not over-tighten them.

Stripped plug threads in the cylinder head can be repaired with a Heli-Coil insert – see 'Tools and Workshop Tips' in the Reference section.

9 Reconnect the spark plug caps, making sure they are securely connected to the correct cylinder **(see illustration 1.3a)**.

2 Idle speed – check and adjustment

1 The idle speed should be checked and adjusted before and after the carburettors are synchronised (balanced) and when it is obviously too high or too low. Before adjusting the idle speed, make sure the valve clearances and spark plug gaps are correct, and the air filter is clean. Also, turn the handlebars back-and-forth and see if the idle speed changes as this is done. If it does, the throttle cable may not be adjusted or routed correctly, or may be worn out. This is a dangerous condition that can cause loss of control of the bike. Be sure to correct this problem before proceeding.
2 The engine should be at normal operating temperature, which is usually reached after 10 to 15 minutes of stop-and-go riding. Make sure the transmission is in neutral, and place the motorcycle on its stand.
3 The idle speed adjuster knob is located on

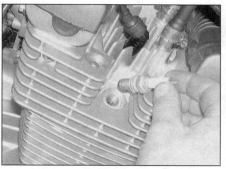

1.8 Thread the plug as far as possible by hand

the underside of the carburettors in the middle **(see illustration)**. With the engine idling, adjust the idle speed by turning the knob until the idle speed listed in this Chapter's Specifications is obtained. Turn the screw clockwise to increase idle speed, and anti-clockwise to decrease it.
4 Snap the throttle open and shut a few times, then recheck the idle speed. If necessary, repeat the adjustment procedure.
5 If a smooth, steady idle can't be achieved, the fuel/air mixture may be incorrect (check the pilot screw settings – see Chapter 3) or the carburettors may need synchronising (see Section 3), or the air induction system may not be working correctly (see Section 5). Also check the intake manifold rubbers for cracks which will cause an air leak, resulting in a weak mixture.

3 Carburettors – synchronisation

Warning: Petrol (gasoline) is extremely flammable, so take extra precautions when you work on any part of the fuel system. Don't smoke or allow open flames or bare light bulbs near the work area, and don't work in a garage where a natural gas-type appliance is present. If you spill any fuel on your skin, rinse it off immediately with soap and water. When you perform any kind of work on the fuel

2.3 Idle speed adjuster screw (arrowed)

system, wear safety glasses and have a fire extinguisher suitable for a Class B type fire (flammable liquids) on hand.

Warning: Take great care not to burn your hand on the hot engine unit when accessing the gauge take-off points on the intake manifolds. Do not allow exhaust gases to build up in the work area; either perform the check outside or use an exhaust gas extraction system.

1 Carburettor synchronisation is simply the process of adjusting the carburettors so they pass the same amount of fuel/air mixture to each cylinder. This is done by measuring the vacuum produced in each cylinder. Carburettors that are out of synchronisation will result in increased fuel consumption, increased engine temperature, less than ideal throttle response and higher vibration levels. Before synchronising the carburettors, make sure the valve clearances and idle speed are properly set.
2 To properly synchronise the carburettors you will need a set of vacuum gauges or a manometer. These instruments measure engine vacuum, and can be obtained from motorcycle dealers or mail order parts suppliers. The equipment used should be suitable for a four cylinder engine and come complete with the necessary adapters and hoses to fit the take-off points. **Note:** *Because of the nature of the synchronisation procedure and the need for special instruments, most owners leave the task to a Yamaha dealer.*
3 Start the engine and let it run until it reaches normal operating temperature, then shut it off.
4 Remove the fuel tank (see Chapter 3). Remove the blanking bolts (cylinders 1 and 2), cap (cylinder 3) and vacuum hose (cylinder 4) from the take-off points on the intake manifolds on the cylinder head **(see illustration)**. Thread suitable adapters into the bolt holes on cylinders 1 and 2, then attach the gauge or manometer hoses to them and to the cap and hose unions on cylinders 3 and 4 **(see illustration)**. Make sure the No. 1 gauge is attached to the hose from the No. 1 (left-hand) carburettor manifold, and so on.
5 Arrange a temporary fuel supply, either by using a small auxiliary tank with its hose attached to the fuel pump, or by using an extra long fuel hose to the now remote fuel

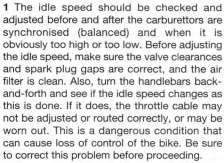

3.4a Remove the bolts (A), cap (B) and detach the hose (C)

3.4b Install adapters in place of the bolts, then connect the gauge hoses to all cylinders

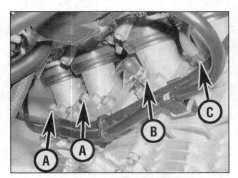

1•8 Every 4000 miles (6000 km)

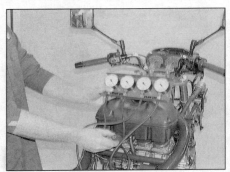

3.7a Carburettor synchronisation set-up

3.7b The screws for balancing 1 to 2 and 3 to 4 are located between the carburettors, and are accessed from the underside (arrowed)

3.7c The screw for balancing the pairs is accessed from the top as shown

tank. Alternatively, position the tank on a suitable base on the motorcycle, taking care not to scratch any paintwork, and making sure that the tank is safely and securely supported, and that access to the synchronising screws is not restricted.

6 Start the engine and let it idle. If the gauges are fitted with damping adjustment, set this so that the needle flutter is just eliminated but so that they can still respond to small changes in pressure.

7 The vacuum readings for all cylinders should be the same (see illustration). If the vacuum readings differ, balance the carburettors by turning the synchronising screws situated in the throttle linkage between the carburettors. Note: *Do not press on the screws whilst adjusting them, otherwise a false reading will be obtained.* First synchronise No. 1 carburettor to No. 2

using the left-hand synchronising screw until the readings are the same, then synchronise No. 3 carburettor to No. 4 using the right-hand screw (see illustration). Finally synchronise Nos. 1 and 2 carburettors to Nos. 3 and 4 using the centre screw (see illustration). When all the carburettors are synchronised, open and close the throttle quickly to settle the linkage, and recheck the gauge readings, readjusting if necessary.

8 When the adjustment is complete, recheck the vacuum readings, then adjust the idle speed (see Section 2) until the speed listed in this Chapter's Specifications is obtained. Remove the gauges and refit the blanking bolts and cap, and attach the vacuum hose (see illustration 3.4a). Detach the temporary fuel supply and install the fuel tank (see Chapter 3).

4 Air filter – cleaning and renewal

1 Remove the fuel tank (see Chapter 3).
2 Remove the screws securing the air intake to the filter housing, then remove the intake and withdraw the filter element from the housing (see illustrations).
3 Tap the element on a hard surface to dislodge any large particles of dirt. If compressed air is available, use it to clean the element, directing the air from the outside of the element in the opposite direction of normal airflow (see illustration).
Caution: If the machine is continually ridden in dusty conditions, the filter should be cleaned more frequently.
4 Check the element for signs of damage. If the element is damaged or torn or cannot be cleaned, or is obviously unsuitable for further use, replace it with a new one.
5 Install the filter element, making sure it is properly seated. Fit the air intake, making sure the rubber seal is in place in the groove, and check that it seats correctly (see illustration). Install the fuel tank (see Chapter 3).
6 Check that the collector in the drain hose coming out of the rear left-hand side of the filter housing has not become blocked. Also check that the collector in the underside of the housing is not full (see illustration). Detach them and clean or empty as required.

4.2a Remove the screws (arrowed) and lift the intake off . . .

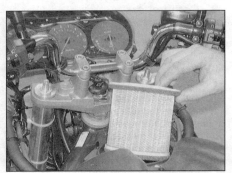

4.2b . . . then withdraw the element

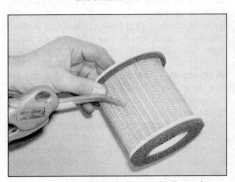

4.3 If compressed air is used, direct it as shown

4.5 Make sure the intake is properly seated

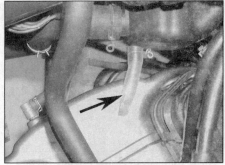

4.6 Empty the collector (arrowed) if it is full

Every 4000 miles (6000 km)

5.4 In-line fuel filter (arrowed)

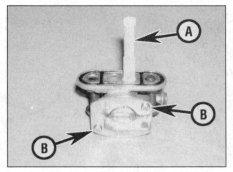

5.5 Fuel strainer (A), tap assembly screws (B)

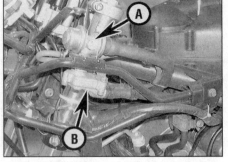

5.8 Check the air cut-off valves (A), the reed valves (B), and the interconnecting hoses and pipes as described

7 Check the crankcase breather hose between the engine and the air filter housing for loose connections, cracks and deterioration and replace it with a new one if necessary.

5 Fuel system and air induction system (AIS) – check

Warning: *Petrol (gasoline) is extremely flammable, so take extra precautions when you work on any part of the fuel system. Don't smoke or allow open flames or bare light bulbs near the work area, and don't work in a garage where a natural gas-type appliance is present. If you spill any fuel on your skin, rinse it off immediately with soap and water. When you perform any kind of work on the fuel system, wear safety glasses and have a fire extinguisher suitable for a Class B type fire (flammable liquids) on hand.*

Fuel system – check

1 Remove the fuel tank (see Chapter 3) and check the tank, the fuel tap, the filter, the fuel pump, and all the hoses and unions for signs of leakage, deterioration or damage; in particular check that there is no leakage from the fuel hoses. Replace any hoses which are cracked or deteriorated with new ones.

2 If the fuel tap is leaking, tighten the assembly screws **(see illustration 5.5)** and mounting screws. If leakage persists remove the tap (see Chapter 3) and disassemble it, noting how the components fit. Inspect all components and replace any that are worn or damaged with new ones, if available. Otherwise fit a new tap.

3 If the carburettor gaskets are leaking, the carburettors should be disassembled and rebuilt using new gaskets and seals (see Chapter 3).

Fuel filter cleaning and renewal

4 A fuel strainer is mounted in the tank and is integral with the fuel tap. An in-line fuel filter is fitted in the hose from the fuel tap to the fuel pump **(see illustration)**. Fitting a new in-line fuel filter is advised after a high mileage has been covered. It is also necessary if fuel starvation is suspected, or if the filter looks clogged or dirty. Yamaha do not specify a replacement interval. Check the condition of the inside of the tank – if the motorcycle is old and there is evidence of rust, remove, drain and clean the inside of the tank and tap strainer (see Chapter 3), and fit a new filter afterwards.

5 To clean the strainer, remove the fuel tank and the fuel tap (see Chapter 3). Clean the gauze strainer to remove all traces of dirt and fuel sediment **(see illustration)**. Check the gauze for holes. If any are found, a new tap should be fitted – the strainer is not available separately.

6 To renew the in-line filter, remove the fuel tank (see Chapter 3). Have a rag handy to soak up any residual fuel, then release the clamps and disconnect the hoses from the filter, noting which fits where **(see illustration 5.4)**. Release the filter from its holder and discard it. Install the new filter so that its arrow points in the direction of fuel flow (i.e. towards the pump). Fit the hoses to the unions on the filter and secure them with the clamps. The hose from the fuel tap goes on the inlet (lipped) end, and the hose to the pump goes on the outlet end. Install the fuel tank (see Chapter 3). Start the engine and check that there are no leaks.

Air induction system (AIS) – check

7 If the valves clearances are all correct and the carburettors have been synchronised, and have no other faults, and the idle speed cannot be set properly, it is possible the AIS is faulty. Further information on the function of the system is in Chapter 3.

8 Remove the fairing (see Chapter 7) and check the AIS hoses and pipes for signs of deterioration or damage, and check that they are all securely connected with the hoses clamped at each end **(see illustration)**. Replace any hoses which are cracked or deteriorated with new ones (see Chapter 3).

9 Check the air cut-off valves and the reed valves for signs of physical damage and replace them with new ones if necessary (see Chapter 3) **(see illustration 5.8)**.

10 If the AIS is suspected of being faulty, remove the reed valve and disassemble it (see Chapter 3). Check the reeds for cracks, warpage and any other damage or deterioration. Also check the contact areas between the reeds and the reed holders, and the holders themselves, for any signs of damage or deterioration. Any carbon deposits or other foreign particles can be cleaned off using a high flash-point solvent. Check that the maximum amount of bend in each reed is such that the gap between the end of each reed and the holder is 0.4 mm maximum – you can remove the reed from the valve and place it on a surface plate to check this (see Chapter 3).

11 Any further testing of the air induction system requires the use of exhaust gas analysers and temperature sensors. If the system is thought to be faulty, take the bike to a Yamaha dealer for assessment. Make sure that the idle speed, valve clearances and carburettor synchronisation have all been checked before assuming the AIS is faulty.

6 Engine/transmission – oil change

Warning: *Be careful when draining the oil, as the exhaust pipes, the engine, and the oil itself can cause severe burns.*

1 Consistent routine oil and filter changes are the single most important maintenance procedure you can perform on a motorcycle. The oil not only lubricates the internal parts of the engine, transmission and clutch, but it also acts as a coolant, a cleaner, a sealant, and a protectant. Because of these demands, the oil takes a terrific amount of abuse and should be replaced often with new oil of the recommended grade and type. Saving a little money on the difference in cost between a good oil and a cheap oil won't pay off if the engine is damaged. The oil filter should be changed with every second oil change.

2 Before changing the oil, warm up the engine so the oil will drain easily.

1•10 Every 4000 miles (6000 km)

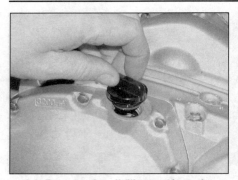

6.3 Remove the oil filler cap from the clutch cover

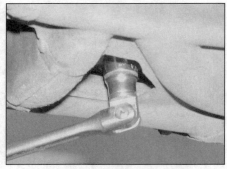

6.4a Unscrew the crankcase oil drain plug . . .

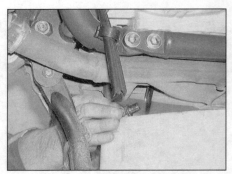

6.4b . . . and allow the oil to drain

3 Put the motorcycle on its centrestand, and position a clean drain tray below the engine. Unscrew the oil filler cap from the clutch cover to vent it and to act as a reminder that there is no oil in the engine (see illustration).

HAYNES HiNT *To help determine whether any abnormal or excessive engine wear is occurring, place a strainer between the engine and the drain tray so that any debris in the oil is filtered out and can be examined.*

4 Unscrew the oil drain plug from sump on the bottom of the engine and allow the oil to flow into the drain tray (see illustrations).

6.4c To remove the old sealing washer, cut it off

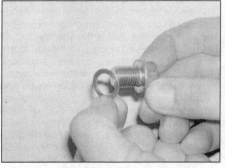

6.5a Install the drain plug, using a new sealing washer if necessary . . .

Check the condition of the sealing washer on the drain plug and discard it if it is damaged or worn – it will probably be necessary to cut the old one off using pliers (see illustration).
5 When the oil has completely drained, fit the drain plug into the sump, using a new sealing washer if required, and tighten it to the torque setting specified at the beginning of the Chapter **(see illustrations)**. Avoid overtightening, as damage to the crankcase will result.
6 Refill the engine to the proper level using the recommended type and amount of oil (see Daily (pre-ride) checks). With the motorcycle vertical, the oil level should lie between the maximum and minimum level lines on the inspection window (see Daily (pre-ride) checks). Install the filler cap. Start the engine and let it run for two or three minutes. Stop the engine, wait a few minutes, then check the oil level. If necessary, add more oil to bring the level up to the maximum level line on the window. Check around the drain plug for leaks.

HAYNES HiNT *Saving a little money on the difference between good and cheap oils won't pay off if the engine is damaged as a result.*

7 Every so often, and especially as Yamaha do not fit an oil pressure switch and warning light (the system fitted uses an oil level

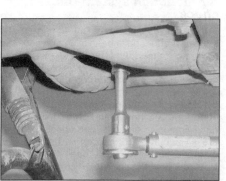

6.5b . . . and tighten it to the specified torque

sensor), it is advisable to perform an oil pressure check (see Section 30).
8 The old oil drained from the engine cannot be re-used and should be disposed of properly. Check with your local refuse disposal company, disposal facility or environmental agency to see whether they will accept the used oil for recycling. Don't pour used oil into drains or onto the ground.

HAYNES HiNT *Check the old oil carefully – if it is very metallic coloured, then the engine is experiencing wear from break-in (new engine) or from insufficient lubrication. If there are flakes or chips of metal in the oil, then something is drastically wrong internally and the engine will have to be disassembled for inspection and repair. If there are pieces of fibre-like material in the oil, the clutch is experiencing excessive wear and should be checked.*

Note: It is antisocial and illegal to dump oil down the drain. To find the location of your local oil recycling bank in the UK, call this number free.

In the USA, note that any oil supplier must accept used oil for recycling

7 Brake pads – wear check

1 Each brake pad has wear indicator grooves in the friction material that can be viewed without removing the pads from the caliper.

Every 4000 miles (6000 km)   1•11

7.1 Brake pad wear indicator groove (arrowed) – front caliper shown

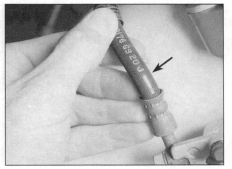

8.3 Flex the brake hose and check for cracks, bulges and leaking fluid

8.5 Rear brake light switch (arrowed)

The grooves are visible by looking up at the bottom edge of each pad **(see illustration)**.

2 When the grooves are only just visible the pads must be replaced with new ones, though it is advisable to renew the pads before they become this worn. If the grooves are no longer visible the pads are excessively worn, in which case check the brake discs (see Chapter 6).

Note: *Some after-market pads may use different indicators, such as turned in corners of the brake pad backing material or a coloured line, to those on the original equipment as shown. The pad is worn when the corner or line is almost contacting the brake disc.*

Caution: Do not allow the pads to wear to the extent that the indicators contact the disc itself as the disc will be damaged.

3 If the pads are worn to the limits, new ones must be installed. If the pads are dirty or if you are in doubt as to the amount of friction material remaining, remove them for inspection (see Chapter 6). If required, measure the amount of friction material remaining – the minimum is 0.8 mm.

4 Refer to Chapter 6 for details of pad renewal.

8 Brake system – check

1 A routine general check of the brake system will ensure that any problems are discovered and remedied before the rider's safety is jeopardised.

2 Check the brake lever and pedal for looseness, improper or rough action, excessive play, bends, and other damage. Replace any damaged parts with new ones (see Chapter 6). Clean and lubricate the lever and pedal pivots if their action is stiff or rough (see Section 16).

3 Make sure all brake fasteners are tight. Check the brake pads for wear (see Section 7) and make sure the fluid level in the reservoirs is correct (see *Daily (pre-ride) checks*). Look for leaks at the hose connections and check for cracks in the hoses themselves **(see illustration)**. If the lever or pedal is spongy, bleed the brakes (see Chapter 6). The brake fluid should be changed every two years (see Section 26), and the hoses replaced with new ones either if they deteriorate, or every four years irrespective of their condition (see Section 27). The master cylinder and caliper seals should be changed every two years, or if leakage from them is evident (see Section 25).

4 Make sure the brake light operates when the front brake lever is pulled in. The front brake light switch, mounted on the underside of the master cylinder, is not adjustable. If it fails to operate properly, check it (see Chapter 8).

5 Make sure the brake light is activated just before the rear brake takes effect. If adjustment is necessary, hold the switch and turn the adjuster nut on the switch body until the brake light is activated when required **(see illustration)**. If the brake light comes on too late, turn the nut clockwise. If the brake light comes on too soon or is permanently on, turn the nut anti-clockwise. If the switch doesn't operate the brake light, check it (see Chapter 8).

6 The front brake lever has a span adjuster which alters the distance of the lever from the handlebar. There are a number of settings, each identified when the notch in the adjuster ring aligns with the punchmark on the lever **(see illustration)**. Push the lever away from the handlebar and turn the adjuster ring until the span which best suits the rider is obtained, making sure the marks are aligned.

7 Check the height of the brake pedal. Yamaha recommend the distance between the brake pedal tip and the top of the rider's footrest should be as specified at the beginning of the Chapter **(see illustration)**. If the pedal height is incorrect, or if the rider's preference is different, slacken the clevis locknut on the master cylinder pushrod, then turn the pushrod using a spanner on the hex at the top of the rod until the pedal is at the correct or desired height **(see illustration)**. After adjustment check that the pushrod end is visible in the hole in the clevis. On completion tighten the locknut securely. Adjust the rear brake light switch after adjusting the pedal height (see Step 5).

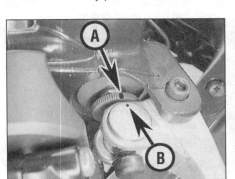

8.6 The notch in the adjuster ring (A) must align with the punchmark on the lever (B)

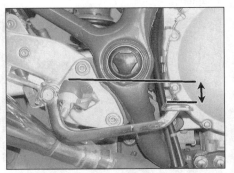

8.7a Measure the distance between the top of the footrest and the top of the brake pedal as shown

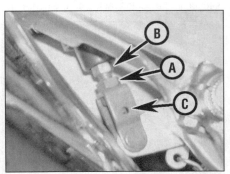

8.7b Slacken the locknut (A) and turn the pushrod using the hex (B) making sure the rod end is still visible in the hole (C)

1•12 Every 4000 miles (6000 km)

9.3 Checking clutch cable freeplay

9.4a Pull back the rubber boot ...

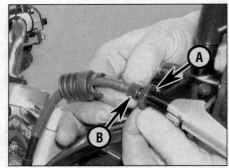
9.4b ... then slacken the lockring (A) and turn the adjuster (B) as required

9 Clutch – check and adjustment

1 Check that the clutch lever operates smoothly and easily.
2 If the lever operation is heavy or stiff, remove the cable (see Chapter 2) and lubricate it (see Section 16). If the cable is still stiff, replace it with a new one. Install the lubricated or new cable (see Chapter 2).
3 With the cable operating smoothly, check that the clutch lever is correctly adjusted. Periodic adjustment is necessary to compensate for wear in the clutch plates and stretch of the cable. Check that the amount of freeplay at the clutch lever end is within the specifications listed at the beginning of the Chapter **(see illustration)**.
4 If adjustment is required, pull back the rubber boot to expose the adjuster at the top of the cable, then loosen the adjuster lockring and turn the adjuster in or out until the required amount of freeplay is obtained **(see illustrations)**. To increase freeplay, turn the adjuster clockwise. To reduce freeplay, turn the adjuster anti-clockwise. Tighten the locking ring securely.
5 If all the adjustment has been taken up at the lever, reset the adjuster to give the maximum amount of freeplay (turn it in), then set the correct amount of freeplay using the adjuster nuts on each end of the threaded section in the cable bracket on the right-hand side of the engine. To increase freeplay, slacken the front nut and tighten the rear nut until the freeplay is as specified, then tighten the front nut **(see illustration)**. To reduce freeplay, slacken the rear nut and tighten the front nut until the freeplay is as specified, then tighten the rear nut. Subsequent adjustments can now be made using the lever adjuster only.

10 Battery – check

1 All models are fitted with a sealed battery which requires no maintenance. **Note:** *Do not attempt to remove the battery caps to check the electrolyte level or battery specific gravity. Removal will damage the caps, resulting in electrolyte leakage and battery damage.*
2 All that should be done is to check that the terminals are clean and tight and that the casing is not damaged or leaking. See Chapter 8 for further details.
Caution: Be extremely careful when handling or working around the battery. The electrolyte is very caustic and an explosive gas (hydrogen) is given off when the battery is charging.
3 If the machine is not in regular use, disconnect the battery and give it a refresher charge every month to six weeks (see Chapter 8).

11 Wheels and tyres – general check

Tyres
1 Check the tyre condition and tread depth thoroughly – see *Daily (pre-ride) checks*.

Wheels
2 Cast wheels are virtually maintenance free, but they should be kept clean and checked periodically for cracks and other damage. Also check the wheel runout and alignment (see Chapter 6). Never attempt to repair damaged cast wheels; they must be replaced with new ones. Check the valve rubber for signs of damage or deterioration and have it renewed if necessary. Also, make sure the valve cap is in place and tight.

12 Wheel bearings – check

1 Wheel bearings will wear over a period of time and result in handling problems.
2 Support the motorcycle on its centrestand, with the wheel to be checked raised off the ground. Check for any play in the bearings by pushing and pulling the wheel against the hub **(see illustration)**. Also rotate the wheel and check that it rotates smoothly.
3 If any play is detected in the hub, or if the wheel does not rotate smoothly (and this is not due to brake or transmission drag), the wheel bearings must be removed and inspected for wear or damage (see Chapter 6).

13 Sidestand and centrestand – check

1 The stand return springs must be capable of retracting the stands fully and holding them retracted when the motorcycle is in use. If a spring is sagged or broken it must be replaced with a new one.

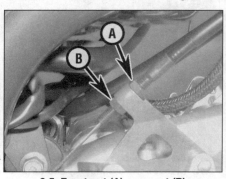
9.5 Front nut (A), rear nut (B)

12.2 Checking for play in the wheel bearings

Every 4000 miles (6000 km)

2 Lubricate the stand pivots regularly (see Section 16), and check the bolts are tight.
3 The sidestand switch prevents the motorcycle being started if the stand is extended. Check its operation by shifting the transmission into neutral, retracting the stand and starting the engine. Pull in the clutch lever and select a gear. Extend the sidestand. The engine should stop as the sidestand is extended. If the sidestand switch does not operate as described, check its circuit (see Chapter 8). The clutch switch is also part of the same circuit – to check it, retract the sidestand, then select a gear. With the clutch lever pulled in, start the engine – if the engine starts, the switch is good. Otherwise, check the circuit (see Chapter 8).

14 Nuts and bolts – tightness check

1 Since vibration of the machine tends to loosen fasteners, all nuts, bolts, screws, etc. should be periodically checked for proper tightness.
2 Pay particular attention to the following:
   Spark plugs
   Engine oil drain plug
   Final drive oil drain plug
   Gearchange lever, brake and clutch lever, and brake pedal bolts
   Footrest and stand bolts
   Engine mounting bolts
   Shock absorber and suspension linkage bolts and swingarm pivot bolts
   Handlebar clamp bolts
   Front axle bolt and axle clamp bolts
   Front fork clamp bolts (top and bottom yoke)
   Rear axle nut
   Brake caliper mounting bolts
   Brake hose banjo bolts and caliper bleed valves
   Brake disc bolts
   Exhaust system bolts/nuts
3 If a torque wrench is available, use it along with the torque specifications at the beginning of this and other Chapters.

15 Throttle and choke cables – check

Throttle cables

1 Make sure the throttle grip rotates easily from fully closed to fully open with the front wheel turned at various angles. The grip should return automatically from fully open to fully closed when released.
2 If the throttle sticks, this is probably due to a cable fault. Remove the cables (see Chapter 3) and lubricate them (see Section 16). Install the cables, making sure they are correctly routed. If this fails to improve the operation of the throttle, new cables must be installed. Note that in very rare cases the fault could lie in the carburettors rather than the cables, necessitating the removal of the carburettors and inspection of the throttle linkage (see Chapter 3).
3 With the throttle operating smoothly, check for a small amount of freeplay in the cables, measured in terms of the amount of twistgrip rotation before the throttle opens **(see illustration)**, and compare the amount to that listed in this Chapter's Specifications. If it's incorrect, adjust the cables to correct it.
4 Freeplay adjustments can be made at the throttle end of the cable. Pull back the rubber cover on the adjuster, then loosen the locknut **(see illustration)**. Turn the adjuster until the specified amount of freeplay is obtained (see this Chapter's Specifications), then retighten the locknut. Turn the adjuster in to increase freeplay and out to reduce it. Refit the rubber boot on completion.
5 If the adjuster has reached its limit of adjustment, reset it so that the freeplay is at a maximum, then adjust the cable at the carburettor end as follows: Remove the air filter housing (see Chapter 3). Fully slacken the locknut on the upper cable, then feed the cable down in the bracket until the captive nut is clear of the lug, and slip the cable out of the bracket **(see illustrations)**. Thread the captive nut up or down as required (threading it up the cable will increase freeplay, threading it down will decrease it) **(see illustration)**. Slip the cable back into the bracket and pull it up so the captive nut locates against the lug. Tighten the locknut down against the bracket. Further adjustments can now be made at the throttle end. If the cable cannot be adjusted as specified, renew the cable (see Chapter 3).

Warning: *Turn the handlebars all the way through their travel with the engine idling. Idle speed should not change. If it does, the cable may be routed incorrectly. Correct this condition before riding the bike.*

6 Check that the throttle twistgrip operates smoothly and snaps shut quickly when released.

Choke cable

7 If the choke does not operate smoothly this is probably due to a cable fault. Remove the cable (see Chapter 3) and lubricate it (see Section 16). Install the cable, routing it so it takes the smoothest route possible.
8 If this fails to improve the operation of the choke, a new cable must be installed. Note that in very rare cases the fault could lie in the carburettors rather than the cable, necessitating the removal of the carburettors and inspection of the choke plungers (see Chapter 3).
9 Make sure there is a small amount of freeplay in the cable before the plungers move. If there isn't, check that the cable is seating correctly at the carburettor end –

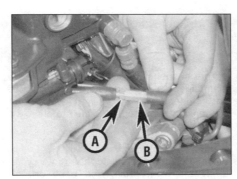

15.4 Throttle cable adjuster locknut (A) and adjuster (B)

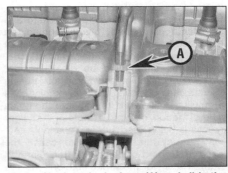

15.5a Slacken the locknut (A) and slide the cable down in the bracket . . .

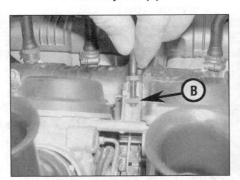

15.5b . . . until the bottom nut (B) is clear of the lug. Slip the cable out of the bracket . . .

15.5c . . . and thread the bottom nut up or down as required

1•14 Every 4000 miles (6000 km)

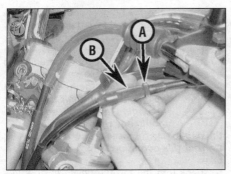

15.9 Choke cable adjuster locknut (A) and adjuster (B)

16.3a Lubricating a cable with a pressure lubricator. Make sure the tool seals around the inner cable

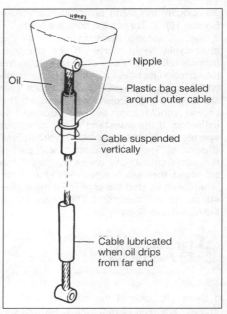

16.3b Lubricating a cable with a makeshift funnel and motor oil

remove the air filter housing for access (see Chapter 3). If it is, you can create some freeplay in the cable by slackening the locknut on the cable adjuster and turning the adjuster in **(see illustration)**. If there is to much freeplay, turn the adjuster out to reduce it. Otherwise, renew the cable.

16 Stands, lever pivots and cables – lubrication

1 Since the controls, cables and various other components of a motorcycle are exposed to the elements, they should be lubricated periodically to ensure safe and trouble-free operation.
2 The footrests, clutch and brake levers, brake pedal, gearchange lever linkage and sidestand/centrestand pivots should be lubricated frequently. In order for the lubricant to be applied where it will do the most good, the component should be disassembled. However, if chain and cable lubricant is being used, it can be applied to the pivot joint gaps and will usually work its way into the areas where friction occurs. If motor oil or light grease is being used, apply it sparingly as it may attract dirt (which could cause the controls to bind or wear at an accelerated rate). Refer to the Specifications at the beginning of the Chapter for the recommended lubricants. **Note:** *One of the best lubricants for the control lever pivots is a*

dry-film lubricant (available from many sources by different names).
3 To lubricate the throttle and choke cables, disconnect the relevant cable at its upper end, then lubricate the cable with a pressure adapter, or if one is not available, using the set-up shown **(see illustrations)**. See Chapter 3 for the throttle and choke cable removal procedures, and Chapter 2 for the clutch cable.
4 To lubricate the speedometer cable, remove it (see Chapter 8), then withdraw the inner cable from the outer cable and lubricate the inner cable with motor oil or cable lubricant. Do not lubricate the upper few inches of the cable as the lubricant may travel up into the instrument head.

17 Suspension – check

1 The suspension components must be maintained in top operating condition to ensure rider safety. Loose, worn or damaged suspension parts decrease the motorcycle's stability and control.

Front suspension

2 While standing alongside the motorcycle, apply the front brake and push on the handlebars to compress the forks several times. See if they move up-and-down smoothly without binding. If binding is felt, the

17.3 Lever off the dust seal and check underneath it for signs of oil leakage

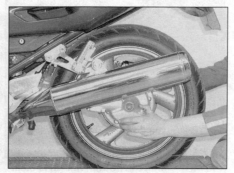

17.7a Checking for play in the swingarm bearings

forks should be disassembled and inspected (see Chapter 5).
3 Inspect the area around the dust seal for signs of oil leakage, then carefully lever off the dust seal using a flat-bladed screwdriver and inspect the area around the fork seal **(see illustration)**. If leakage is evident, new seals must be fitted (see Chapter 5). Check the fork tubes for scratches, corrosion and pitting as these will cause premature seal failure. If the damage is excessive new tubes should be installed (see Chapter 5).
4 Check the tightness of all suspension nuts and bolts to be sure none have worked loose, referring to the torque settings specified at the beginning of Chapter 5.

Rear suspension

5 Inspect the rear shock for fluid leakage and tightness of its mountings. If leakage is found, a new shock should be installed (see Chapter 5).
6 With the aid of an assistant to support the bike, compress the rear suspension several times. It should move up and down freely without binding. If any binding is felt, the worn or faulty component must be identified and renewed. The problem could be due to either the shock absorber, the suspension linkage components or the swingarm components.
7 Support the motorcycle on the centrestand so that the rear wheel is off the ground. Grab the swingarm and rock it from side to side – there should be no discernible movement at the rear (Yamaha specify a maximum of 1 mm) **(see illustration)**. If there's a little movement or a slight clicking can be heard, inspect the tightness of all the rear suspension mounting bolts and nuts, referring to the torque settings specified at the beginning of Chapter 5, and re-check for

Every 4000 miles (6000 km) 1•15

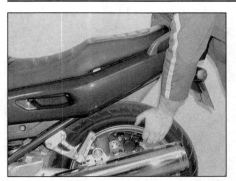

17.7b Checking for play in the suspension linkage bearings

movement. Next, grasp the top of the rear wheel and pull it upwards – there should be no discernible freeplay before the shock absorber begins to compress **(see illustration)**. Any freeplay felt in either check indicates worn bearings in the suspension linkage or swingarm, or worn shock absorber mountings. The worn components must be renewed (see Chapter 5).

8 To make an accurate assessment of the swingarm bearings, remove the rear wheel (see Chapter 6) and the bolt securing the suspension linkage rods to the swingarm (see Chapter 5). Grasp the rear of the swingarm with one hand and place your other hand at the junction of the swingarm and the frame.

Try to move the rear of the swingarm from side-to-side. Any wear (play) in the bearings should be felt as movement between the swingarm and the frame at the front. If there is any play the swingarm will be felt to move forward and backward at the front (not from side-to-side). Alternatively, measure the amount of freeplay at the swingarm end – Yamaha specify a maximum of 1 mm. Next, move the swingarm up and down through its full travel. It should move freely, without any binding or rough spots. If any play in the swingarm is noted or if the swingarm does not move freely, the bearings must be removed for inspection or renewal (see Chapter 5).

Every 8000 miles (12,000 km) or 12 months

Carry out all the items under the 4000 mile (6000 km) check, plus the following:

18 Steering head bearings – freeplay check and adjustment

1 This motorcycle is equipped with caged ball steering head bearings which can become dented, rough or loose during normal use of the machine. In extreme cases, worn or loose steering head bearings can cause steering wobble – a condition that is potentially dangerous.

Check

2 Support the motorcycle in an upright position using the centrestand. Raise the front wheel off the ground either by having an assistant push down on the rear, or by placing a support under the engine.
3 Point the front wheel straight-ahead and slowly move the handlebars from side-to-side. Any dents or roughness in the bearing races will be felt and the bars will not move smoothly and freely.
4 Next, grasp the fork sliders and try to pull and push them forward and backward **(see illustration)**. Any looseness in the steering

head bearings will be felt as front-to-rear movement of the forks. If play is felt in the bearings, adjust the steering head as follows:

 Freeplay in the fork due to worn fork bushes can be misinterpreted for steering head bearing play – do not confuse the two.

Adjustment

5 Remove the fuel tank (see Chapter 3). Remove the fairing (see Chapter 7). **Note:** *Although it is not strictly necessary to remove the fairing, doing so will prevent the possibility of damage should a tool slip.*
6 Displace the handlebars from the top yoke (see Chapter 5). Support them so the master cylinder is upright to prevent the possibility of fluid leakage. There is no need to remove the handlebar assemblies from the handlebars. Unscrew the bolt securing the cable guide to the underside of the top yoke and displace it. On 1994 and 1995 models, unscrew the bolt securing the choke knob holder to the top yoke and displace it.

7 Slacken the fork clamp bolts in the top yoke **(see illustration)**.
8 Unscrew the steering stem nut and remove it along with its washer, where fitted (1998-on models) **(see illustration)**.
9 Gently ease the top yoke upwards off the fork tubes and position it clear, using a rag to protect the other components **(see illustration)**.
10 Remove the tabbed lockwasher, noting

18.4 Checking for play in the steering head bearings

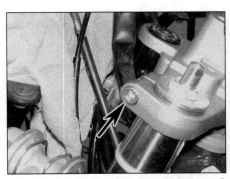

18.7 Slacken the fork clamp bolt (arrowed) on each side

18.8 Unscrew the steering stem nut (arrowed)

18.9 Ease the top yoke up off the steering stem and forks

1•16 Every 8000 miles (12,000 km)

18.10a Remove the tabbed lockwasher...

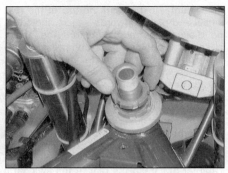
18.10b ...then unscrew the locknut...

18.10c ...and remove the rubber washer

how it fits, then unscrew and remove the locknut using either a C-spanner, a peg spanner or a drift located in one of the notches **(see illustrations)**. Remove the rubber washer **(see illustration)**.

11 To adjust the bearings as specified by Yamaha, a special service tool (Pt. No. 90890-01403) and a torque wrench are required. If the tool is available, first slacken the adjuster nut, then tighten it to the initial torque setting specified at the beginning of the Chapter, making sure the torque wrench handle is at right angles (90°) to the line between the adjuster nut and the wrench socket in the special tool **(see illustration)**. Now slacken the nut so that it is loose, then tighten it to the final torque setting specified. Check that the steering is still able to move freely from side to side, but that all freeplay is eliminated.

12 If the Yamaha tool is not available, using either a C-spanner, a peg spanner or a drift located in one of the notches, slacken the adjuster nut slightly until pressure is just released, then tighten it until all freeplay is removed, then tighten it a little more **(see illustration)**. This pre-loads the bearings. Now slacken the nut, then tighten it again, setting it so that all freeplay is just removed yet the steering is able to move freely from side to side. To do this tighten the nut only a little at a time, and after each tightening repeat the check outlined above (Step 4) until the bearings are correctly set. The object is to set the adjuster nut so that the bearings are under a very light loading, just enough to remove any freeplay.

Caution: Take great care not to apply excessive pressure because this will cause premature failure of the bearings.

13 With the bearings correctly adjusted, install the rubber washer and the locknut **(see illustrations 18.10c and b)**. Tighten the locknut finger-tight, then tighten it further until its notches align with those in the adjuster nut. If necessary, counter-hold the adjuster nut and tighten the locknut using a C-spanner or drift until the notches align, but make sure the adjuster nut does not turn as well. Install the tabbed lockwasher so that the tabs fit into the notches in both the locknut and adjuster nut **(see illustration 18.10a)**.

14 Fit the top yoke onto the steering stem **(see illustration 18.9)**, then install the washer (where fitted) and steering stem nut and tighten it to the torque setting specified at the beginning of the Chapter **(see illustrations)**. Now tighten both the fork clamp bolts to the specified torque setting **(see illustration)**.

15 Fit the cable guide onto the underside of the top yoke and tighten the bolt securely. On 1994 and 1995 models, fit the choke knob holder onto the top yoke.

16 Install the handlebars (see Chapter 5).

17 Re-check the bearing adjustment as described above and re-adjust if necessary.

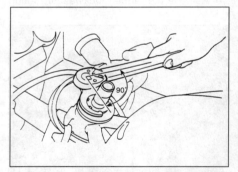
18.11 Make sure the torque wrench arm is at right angles (90°) to the tool

18.12 If the tool is not available, adjust the bearings as described

18.14a Fit the steering stem nut and washer (where applicable)...

18.14b ...and tighten it to the specified torque

18.14c Now tighten the fork clamp bolts to the specified torque

Every 8000 miles (12,000 km) 1•17

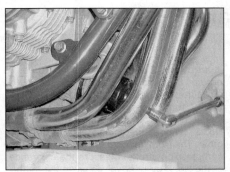

19.2 Unscrew the filter and drain it into the tray

19.3a Smear some clean oil onto the seal...

19.3b ...then thread the filter onto the cooler...

19 Engine/transmission – oil and oil filter change

Warning: *Be careful when draining the oil, as the exhaust pipes, the engine, and the oil itself can cause severe burns.*

1 Drain the engine oil as described in Section 6, Steps 1 to 5.

2 Now place the drain tray below the oil filter, which is on the front of the engine. Unscrew the oil filter using a filter removal adapter and socket or a strap/chain wrench and tip any residue oil into the drain tray **(see illustration)**. Wipe any oil off the exhaust pipes to prevent too much smoke when you start it.

3 Smear clean engine oil onto the rubber seal on the new filter, then manoeuvre it into position and screw it onto the engine until the seal just seats **(see illustrations)**. If a filter adapter is available, tighten the filter to the torque setting specified at the beginning of the Chapter **(see illustration)**. Otherwise, tighten the filter as tight as possible by hand, or by the number of turns specified on the filter or its packaging. **Note:** *Do not use a strap or chain-type filter removing tool to tighten the filter as you will damage it.*

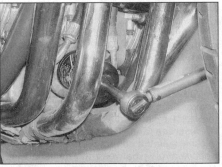

19.3c ...and tighten it as described

4 Refill the engine to the proper level as described in Section 6, Steps 6 to 8.

20 Final drive – oil level check

1 Place the motorcycle on its centrestand, making sure it is on level ground. The check should be made after the machine has been standing for a few hours.

2 Unscrew the oil filler cap and check that the

20.2a Unscrew the oil filler cap

oil is up to the edge of the filler hole **(see illustrations)**. If the level is below this, look for signs of leakage, such as oil staining on the underside of the casing. If leakage is evident, the problem must be rectified to avoid the possibility of damage to the final drive and oil contaminating the rear tyre (see Chapter 5).

3 Replenish the oil if necessary to the correct level **(see illustration)** using the type and grade specified at the beginning of the Chapter, then install the filler cap, using a new sealing washer if necessary, and tighten it to the torque setting specified at the beginning of the Chapter.

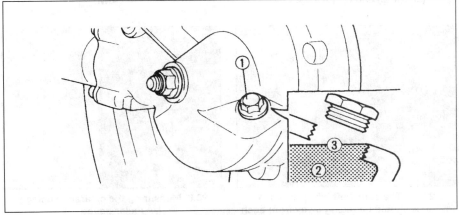

20.2b The oil should come up to the edge of the filler hole (arrowed)
1 Oil filler bolt   2 Oil   3 Correct oil level

20.3 Top up with the specified oil if required

1•18 Routine maintenance and servicing

Every 16,000 miles (24,000 km) or two years

Carry out all the items under the 4000 mile (6000 km) and 8000 mile (12,000 km) checks:

21 Swingarm and suspension linkage bearings – re-greasing

1 Over a period of time the grease will harden or dirt will penetrate the bearings.
2 The rear suspension components are not equipped with grease nipples. Remove the swingarm and the suspension linkage as described in Chapter 5 for greasing of the bearings.

22 Steering head bearings – re-greasing

1 Over a period of time the grease will harden or may be washed out of the bearings by incorrect use of jet washes.
2 Disassemble the steering head for re-greasing of the bearings. Refer to Chapter 5 for details.

23 Valve clearances – check and adjustment

1 The engine must be completely cool for this maintenance procedure, so let the machine sit overnight before beginning.
2 Remove the valve cover (see Chapter 2). Each cylinder is referred to by a number. They are numbered 1 to 4 from left to right.
3 Make a chart or sketch of all valve positions so that a note of each clearance can be made against the relevant valve.
4 Remove the left-hand crankshaft end-cover, secured by four screws or bolts (according to model) **(see illustration)**. The engine can be turned using a 14 mm spanner or socket on the timing rotor bolt, turning it in an anti-clockwise direction only **(see illustration)**. Alternatively, place the motorcycle on an auxiliary stand so that the rear wheel is off the ground, select a high gear and rotate the rear wheel by hand in its normal direction of rotation.
5 Turn the engine until the line next to the 'T' mark on the rotor aligns with the mark on the timing plate **(see illustration)**, and the camshaft lobes for the No. 1 (left-hand) cylinder face away from each other **(see illustration)**. If the cam lobes are facing towards each other, rotate the engine anti-clockwise 360° (one full turn) so that the line next to the 'T' mark again aligns with the mark on the timing plate. The camshaft lobes will now be facing away from each other, meaning the No. 1 cylinder is at TDC (top dead centre) on the compression stroke.
6 With No. 1 cylinder at TDC on the compression stroke, check the clearances on the No. 1 cylinder intake and exhaust valves by inserting a feeler gauge of the same thickness as the correct valve clearance (see *Specifications*) between the camshaft lobe and follower of each valve and check that it is a firm sliding fit – you should feel a slight drag when the you pull the gauge out **(see illustration)**. If not, use the feeler gauges to obtain the exact clearance. Record the measured clearance on the chart.
7 Now turn the engine anti-clockwise 180° (half a turn) so that the camshaft lobes for the No. 2 cylinder are facing away from each other. The No. 2 cylinder is now at TDC on the compression stroke. Measure the clearances of the No. 2 cylinder valves using the method described in Step 6.
8 Now turn the engine anti-clockwise 180° (half a turn) so that the line next to the 'T' mark on the rotor again aligns with the mark on the timing plate, and the camshaft lobes for the No. 4 cylinder are facing away from each other. The No. 4 cylinder is now at TDC on the compression stroke. Measure the clearances of the No. 4 cylinder valves using the method described in Step 6.
9 Now turn the engine anti-clockwise 180° (half a turn) so that the camshaft lobes for the No. 3 cylinder are facing away from each other. The No. 3 cylinder is now at TDC on the compression stroke. Measure the clearances of the No. 3 cylinder valves using the method described in Step 6.
10 When all clearances have been measured and charted, identify whether the clearance

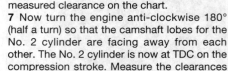

23.4a Unscrew the four screws or bolts (arrowed) and remove the cover

23.4b Turn the engine anti-clockwise as shown

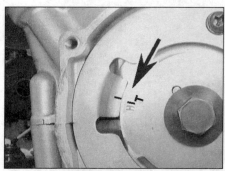

23.5a Turn the engine until the line next to the 'T' mark aligns with the mark on the timing plate (arrowed)

23.5b The camshaft lobes for no. 1 cylinder should be facing away from each other (intake pointing back, exhaust pointing forward) as shown

23.6 Measuring the clearance using a feeler gauge

Every 16,000 miles (24,000 km)

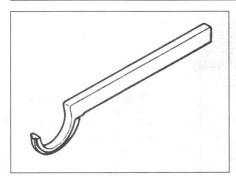

23.11 The Yamaha shim replacement tool

23.12 Turn the follower so that its notch faces either forwards (exhaust) or backwards (intake)

23.13 Removing the shim using a magnet

on any valve falls outside that specified. If it does, the shim on the top of the cam follower must be replaced with one of a thickness which will restore the correct clearance.

11 Shim replacement requires the use of a Yamaha special tool, Pt. No. 90890-04125, or a suitable commercially available equivalent **(see illustration)**.

12 Rotate the cam follower of the valve in question so that its shim removal slot faces backwards (exhaust valve) or forwards (inlet valve) **(see illustration)**. Place a rag over the cam chain tunnel to prevent a shim from dropping into the engine on removal.

13 Fit the tool, making sure it contacts only the rim of the follower and not the shim. Push down on the handle of the tool so that it depresses the cam follower. If it is difficult to depress the follower, remove the tool and turn the engine until the camshaft lobe depresses it. Refit the tool and hold it in place, then turn the engine so that the lobe moves off the follower. Pick the shim out of the top of the valve using either a magnet, a screwdriver with a dab of grease on it (the shim will stick to the grease), or a small screwdriver and a pair of pliers **(see illustration)**. Do not allow

23.14a Note the size marking on the shim face

the shim to fall into the engine.

14 A size mark should be stamped on the upper face of the shim – a shim marked 250 is 2.5 mm thick, 245 is 2.45 mm **(see illustration)**. If the mark is not visible the shim thickness will have to be measured. It is recommended that the shim is measured anyway to check that it has not worn **(see illustration)**.

15 Using the appropriate shim selection chart, find where the measured valve

23.14b Measure the shim using a micrometer

clearance and existing shim thickness values intersect and read off the shim size required **(see illustrations, below and overleaf)**. *Note: If the existing shim is marked with a number not ending in 0 or 5, round it up or down as appropriate to the nearest number ending in 0 or 5 so that the chart can be used.* Shims are available in 0.05 mm increments from 2.00 to 3.20 mm. *Note: If the required replacement shim is greater than 3.20 mm (the largest available), the valve is probably not*

23.15a Shim selection chart – Intake camshaft

Standard valve clearance (cold): 0.11 to 0.15 mm
Example of reading off:
　　Installed pad is 250
　　Measured clearance is 0.23
　　Replace 250 pad with 260 pad
Pad numbers (example)
　　250 is 2.50 mm thick
　　255 is 2.55 mm thick

1•20 Every 16,000 miles (24,000 km)

MEASURED CLEARANCE	INSTALLED PAD NUMBER*																								
	200	205	210	215	220	225	230	235	240	245	250	255	260	265	270	275	280	285	290	295	300	305	310	315	320
0.00 ~ 0.05					200	205	210	215	220	225	230	235	240	245	250	255	260	265	270	275	280	285	290	295	300	305
0.06 ~ 0.10			200	205	210	215	220	225	230	235	240	245	250	255	260	265	270	275	280	285	290	295	300	305	310
0.11 ~ 0.15		200	205	210	215	220	225	230	235	240	245	250	255	260	265	270	275	280	285	290	295	300	305	310	315
0.16 ~ 0.20																									
0.21 ~ 0.25	205	210	215	220	225	230	235	240	245	250	255	260	265	270	275	280	285	290	295	300	305	310	315	320	
0.26 ~ 0.30	210	215	220	225	230	235	240	245	250	255	260	265	270	275	280	285	290	295	300	305	310	315	320		
0.31 ~ 0.35	215	220	225	230	235	240	245	250	255	260	265	270	275	280	285	290	295	300	305	310	315	320			
0.36 ~ 0.40	220	225	230	235	240	245	250	255	260	265	270	275	280	285	290	295	300	305	310	315	320				
0.41 ~ 0.45	225	230	235	240	245	250	255	260	265	270	275	280	285	290	295	300	305	310	315	320					
0.46 ~ 0.50	230	235	240	245	250	255	260	265	270	275	280	285	290	295	300	305	310	315	320						
0.51 ~ 0.55	235	240	245	250	255	260	265	270	275	280	285	290	295	300	305	310	315	320							
0.56 ~ 0.60	240	245	250	255	260	265	270	275	280	285	290	295	300	305	310	315	320								
0.61 ~ 0.65	245	250	255	260	265	270	275	280	285	290	295	300	305	310	315	320									
0.66 ~ 0.70	250	255	260	265	270	275	280	285	290	295	300	305	310	315	320										
0.71 ~ 0.75	255	260	265	270	275	280	285	290	295	300	305	310	315	320											
0.76 ~ 0.80	260	265	270	275	280	285	290	295	300	305	310	315	320												
0.81 ~ 0.85	265	270	275	280	285	290	295	300	305	310	315	320													
0.86 ~ 0.90	270	275	280	285	290	295	300	305	310	315	320														
0.91 ~ 0.95	275	280	285	290	295	300	305	310	315	320															
0.96 ~ 1.00	280	285	290	295	300	305	310	315	320																
1.01 ~ 1.05	285	290	295	300	305	310	315	320																	
1.06 ~ 1.10	290	295	300	305	310	315	320																		
1.11 ~ 1.15	295	300	305	310	315	320																			
1.16 ~ 1.20	300	305	310	315	320																				
1.21 ~ 1.25	305	310	315	320																					
1.26 ~ 1.30	310	315	320																						
1.31 ~ 1.35	315	320																							
1.36 ~ 1.40	320																								

23.15b Shim selection chart – Exhaust camshaft

Standard valve clearance (cold):
 0.16 to 0.20 mm
Example of reading off:
 Installed pad is 250
 Measured clearance is 0.32 mm
 Replace 250 pad with 265 pad
 Pad numbers (example)
  250 is 2.50 mm thick
  255 is 2.55 mm thick

seating correctly due to a build-up of carbon deposits and should be checked and cleaned or resurfaced as required (see Chapter 2).
16 Obtain and install the replacement shim, noting that its size marking should be installed downwards and that the shim should be lubricated with engine oil. Check that the shim is correctly seated. Lift the shim replacement tool handle so that the cam follower rises and remove the tool when it is free. Alternatively turn the camshaft until the lobe is holding the follower, then remove the tool. Check the clearance again, then repeat the process for any other valves until the clearances are correct.
17 Rotate the crankshaft several turns to seat the new shim(s), then check the clearances again.
18 Install all disturbed components in a reverse of the removal sequence. Tighten the crankshaft end-cover screws to the torque setting specified at the beginning of the Chapter.

24 Final drive – oil change

1 Place the motorcycle on its centre stand, making sure it is on level ground.
2 Place an oil drain pan under the drain plug in the bottom of the final drive housing. Unscrew the filler cap (see illustration 20.2a) and the drain plug, and allow the oil to drain into the pan (see illustration).
3 Check the condition of the drain plug sealing washer and replace it with a new one if necessary (it is advisable to renew it as a matter of course). Install the drain plug and tighten it to the torque setting specified at the beginning of the Chapter.
4 Fill the housing using the amount and type of oil specified at the beginning of the Chapter (see illustration 20.3). The oil should come up to the edge of the filler hole (see illustration 20.2b).
5 Install the filler cap, using a new sealing washer if necessary, and tighten it to the specified torque setting.

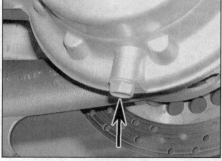

24.2 Final drive oil drain plug (arrowed)

Every two years

25 Brake master cylinder and caliper seals – renewal

1 The seals will deteriorate over a period of time and lose their effectiveness, leading to sticky operation or fluid loss, or allowing the ingress of air and dirt. Refer to Chapter 6 and dismantle the components for seal renewal every two years.

26 Brakes – fluid change

1 The brake fluid should be renewed every two years or whenever a master cylinder or caliper overhaul is carried out. Refer to the brake bleeding section in Chapter 6, noting that all old fluid must be pumped from the fluid reservoir and hydraulic line before filling with new fluid.

HAYNES HiNT *Old brake fluid is invariably much darker in colour than new fluid, making it easy to see when all old fluid has been expelled from the system.*

Routine maintenance and servicing 1•21

Every four years

27 Brake hoses – renewal

1 The hoses will deteriorate with age and should be replaced with new ones every four years regardless of their apparent condition.

2 Refer to Chapter 6 and disconnect the hoses from the master cylinders and calipers. Always replace the banjo union sealing washers with new ones.

Non-scheduled maintenance

28 Headlight aim – check and adjustment

Note: *An improperly adjusted headlight may cause problems for oncoming traffic or provide poor, unsafe illumination of the road ahead. Before adjusting the headlight aim, be sure to consult with local traffic laws and regulations – for UK models refer to MOT Test Checks in the Reference section.*

1 The headlight beam can adjusted both horizontally and vertically. Before making any adjustment, check that the tyre pressures are correct and the suspension is adjusted as required. Make any adjustments to the headlight aim with the machine on level ground, with the fuel tank half full and with an assistant sitting on the seat. If the bike is usually ridden with a passenger on the back, have a second assistant to do this.

2 Vertical adjustment is made by turning the adjuster screw on the bottom left corner of the headlight unit **(see illustration)**. Turn it clockwise to raise the beam, and anti-clockwise to lower it.

3 Horizontal adjustment is made by turning the adjuster screw on the bottom right corner of the headlight unit. Turn it clockwise to move the beam to the right, and anti-clockwise to move it to the left.

29 Cylinder compression – check

1 Among other things, poor engine performance may be caused by leaking valves, incorrect valve clearances, a leaking head gasket, or worn pistons, rings and/or cylinder walls. A cylinder compression check will help pinpoint these conditions and can also indicate the presence of excessive carbon deposits in the cylinder heads.

2 The only tools required are a compression gauge and a spark plug wrench. A compression gauge with a threaded end for the spark plug hole is preferable to the type which requires hand pressure to maintain a tight seal. Depending on the outcome of the initial test, a squirt-type oil can may also be needed.

3 Make sure the valve clearances are correctly set (see Section 23) and that the cylinder head nuts are tightened to the correct torque setting (see Chapter 2).

4 Refer to *Fault Finding Equipment* in the Reference section for details of the compression test. Refer to the specifications at the beginning of the Chapter for compression figures.

30 Engine oil pressure – check

1 None of the models covered in this manual are fitted with an oil pressure switch and warning light, only an oil level sensor and warning light (see Chapter 8 for further information). If a lubrication problem is suspected, first check the oil level (see *Daily (pre-ride) checks*).

2 If the oil level is correct, an oil pressure check must be carried out. The check provides useful information about the condition of the engine's lubrication system.

3 To check the oil pressure, slacken the oil gallery plug in the right-hand side of the cylinder head – there is no need to remove it **(see illustration)**. Start the engine and allow it to idle. After a short while oil should begin to seep out from the oil gallery plug. If no oil has appeared after one minute, stop the engine immediately; either the pressure regulator is stuck open, the oil pump is faulty, the oil strainer or filter is blocked, or there is other engine damage. Begin diagnosis by checking the oil filter, strainer and regulator, then the oil pump (see Chapter 2). If those items check out okay, chances are the bearing oil clearances are excessive and the engine needs to be overhauled. If the oil appears very

28.2 Vertical adjuster (A), horizontal adjuster (B)

30.3 Oil gallery plug (arrowed)

1•22 Non-scheduled maintenance

quickly and spurts out, the pressure may be too high, meaning either an oil passage is clogged, the regulator is stuck closed or the wrong grade of oil is being used. Rectify any problems before running the engine again.

4 Tighten the oil gallery plug to the torque setting specified at the beginning of the Chapter.

5 If the oil pressure and oil level are both good, then the oil level sensor or its warning light may be faulty. Check them and the circuit and replace with a new one if necessary (see Chapter 8).

31 Fuel hoses – renewal

Warning: Petrol (gasoline) is extremely flammable, so take extra precautions when you work on any part of the fuel system. Don't smoke or allow open flames or bare light bulbs near the work area, and don't work in a garage where a natural gas-type appliance is present. If you spill any fuel on your skin, rinse it off immediately with soap and water. When you perform any kind of work on the fuel system, wear safety glasses and have a fire extinguisher suitable for a Class B type fire (flammable liquids) on hand.

1 The fuel delivery hoses between the fuel tank and the carburettors should be renewed after a few years regardless of their condition.

2 Remove the fuel tank (see Chapter 3). Disconnect the fuel hoses from the fuel tap, filter, fuel pump and from the carburettors, noting the routing of each hose and where it connects (see Chapter 3 if required). It is advisable to make a sketch of the various hoses before removing them to ensure they are correctly installed.

3 Secure each new hose to its unions using new clamps. Run the engine and check for leaks before taking the machine out on the road.

32 Front forks – oil change

1 Fork oil degrades over a period of time and loses its damping qualities. Refer to Chapter 5 for front fork removal, oil draining and refilling, following the relevant steps. The forks do not need to be completely disassembled.

33 Alternator brushes – check and renewal

1 The brushes will wear down with use. They should be checked and replaced with new ones if necessary. Refer to Chapter 8 for details.

Chapter 2
Engine, clutch and transmission

Contents

Alternator drive shaft and starter clutch assembly – removal, inspection and installation	26
Alternator/regulator/rectifier – removal and installation	see Chapter 8
Cam chain and tensioner blade – removal, inspection and installation	25
Cam chain tensioner and guides – removal, inspection and installation	9
Camshafts and followers – removal, inspection and installation	10
Clutch – check	see Chapter 1
Clutch – removal, inspection and installation	17
Clutch cable – removal and installation	18
Connecting rods – removal, inspection and installation	29
Crankcase halves – inspection and servicing	24
Crankcase – separation and reassembly	23
Crankshaft and main bearings – removal, inspection and installation	28
Cylinder block – removal, inspection and installation	14
Cylinder head – removal and installation	11
Cylinder head and valves – disassembly, inspection and reassembly	13
Engine – compression check	see Chapter 1
Engine – removal and installation	5
Engine disassembly and reassembly – general information	6
Gearchange mechanism – removal, inspection and installation	19
General information	1
Idle speed – check and adjustment	see Chapter 1
Initial start-up after overhaul	33
Main and connecting rod bearings – general information	27
Major engine repair – general information	4
Middle gear shafts – removal, inspection and installation	20
Neutral switch – check, removal and installation	see Chapter 8
Oil and filter – change	see Chapter 1
Oil cooler and oil filter housing – removal, inspection and installation	7
Oil level – check	see Daily (pre-ride) checks
Oil pressure – check	see Chapter 1
Oil pump and pressure relief valve – removal, inspection and installation	22
Oil sump – removal and installation	21
Operations possible with the engine in the frame	2
Operations requiring engine removal	3
Pick-up coil assembly – removal and installation	see Chapter 4
Piston rings – inspection and installation	16
Pistons – removal, inspection and installation	15
Recommended running-in procedure	34
Selector drum and forks – removal, inspection and installation	32
Spark plug gap – check and adjustment	see Chapter 1
Starter clutch and idle gear – removal, inspection and installation	26
Starter motor – removal and installation	see Chapter 8
Transmission shafts – disassembly, inspection and reassembly	31
Transmission shafts – removal and installation	30
Valve clearances – check and adjustment	see Chapter 1
Valve cover – removal and installation	8
Valves/valve seats/valve guides – servicing	12

Degrees of difficulty

| Easy, suitable for novice with little experience | | Fairly easy, suitable for beginner with some experience | | Fairly difficult, suitable for competent DIY mechanic | | Difficult, suitable for experienced DIY mechanic | | Very difficult, suitable for expert DIY or professional | |

2•2 Engine, clutch and transmission

Specifications

General
Type	Four-stroke in-line four cylinder, air cooled
Capacity	892 cc
Bore	68.5 mm
Stroke	60.5 mm
Compression ratio	10 to 1
Cylinder numbering	1 to 4 from left to right
Clutch	Wet multi-plate
Transmission	Five-speed constant mesh
Final drive	Shaft

Camshafts
Lobe height	
Standard	36.85 mm
Service limit (min)	36.75 mm
Journal diameter	24.967 to 24.980 mm
Holder diameter	25.000 to 25.021 mm
Journal oil clearance	0.020 to 0.054 mm
Runout (max)	0.03 mm

Cylinder head
Warpage (max)	0.03 mm

Valves, guides and springs
Valve clearances	see Chapter 1
Intake valve	
Stem diameter	5.975 to 5.990 mm
Guide bore diameter	6.000 to 6.012 mm
Stem-to-guide clearance	
Standard	0.010 to 0.037 mm
Service limit (max)	0.08 mm
Head diameter	33.9 to 34.1 mm
Face width	2.3 mm
Seat width	0.9 to 1.1 mm
Margin thickness	1.0 mm
Valve lift	8.75 to 8.85 mm
Exhaust valve	
Stem diameter	5.960 to 5.975 mm
Guide bore diameter	6.000 to 6.012 mm
Stem-to-guide clearance	
Standard	0.025 to 0.052 mm
Service limit (max)	0.10 mm
Head diameter	27.9 to 28.1 mm
Face width	2.3 mm
Seat width	0.9 to 1.1 mm
Margin thickness	1.0 mm
Valve lift	8.75 to 8.85 mm
Valve stem runout (max)	0.01 mm
Valve spring free length (intake and exhaust)	
Inner spring	37.40 mm
Outer spring	39.85 mm
Valve spring bend (max)	
Inner spring	1.6 mm
Outer spring	1.7 mm

Cylinder block
Bore	
Standard	68.49 to 68.54 mm
Service limit	68.60 mm
Warpage (max)	0.03 mm
Ovality (out-of-round) (max)	0.01 mm
Taper (max)	0.05 mm
Cylinder compression	see Chapter 1

Pistons
Piston diameter (measured 5.5 mm up from skirt, at 90° to piston pin axis)	68.45 to 68.50 mm

Engine, clutch and transmission 2•3

Piston-to-bore clearance
    Standard . . . . 0.03 to 0.05 mm
    Service limit (max) . . . . 0.1 mm
Piston pin diameter . . . . 15.990 to 16.000 mm
Piston pin bore diameter in piston . . . . 16.002 to 16.013 mm
Piston pin-to-piston pin bore clearance
    Standard . . . . 0.002 to 0.023 mm
    Service limit . . . . 0.070 mm

Piston rings
Top ring
    Ring width . . . . 2.5 mm
    Ring thickness . . . . 1.2 mm
    Ring end gap (installed) . . . . 0.10 to 0.25 mm
    Piston ring-to-groove clearance . . . . 0.025 to 0.080 mm
2nd ring
    Ring width . . . . 3.1 mm
    Ring thickness . . . . 1.21 mm
    Ring end gap (installed) . . . . 0.30 to 0.45 mm
    Piston ring-to-groove clearance . . . . 0.02 to 0.06 mm
Oil ring
    Ring width . . . . 2.8 mm
    Ring thickness . . . . 2.5 mm
    Side-rail end gap (installed) . . . . 0.2 to 0.7 mm

Clutch
Friction plates
    Quantity 8
    Thickness
        Standard . . . . 2.9 to 3.1 mm
        Service limit (min) . . . . 2.8 mm
Plain plates
    Quantity 7
    Thickness . . . . 1.9 to 2.1 mm
    Warpage (max) . . . . 0.05 mm
Clutch springs
    Quantity 6
    Spring free length
        Standard . . . . 51.8 mm
        Service limit (min) . . . . 50.0 mm

Lubrication system
Oil pressure . . . . see Chapter 1
Relief valve opening pressure . . . . 78.3 to 95.7 psi
Oil pump
    Inner rotor tip-to-outer rotor clearance . . . . 0.03 to 0.09 mm
    Outer rotor-to-body clearance . . . . 0.03 to 0.08 mm

Connecting rods
Big-end side clearance . . . . 0.160 to 0.262 mm
Big-end oil clearance . . . . 0.026 to 0.055 mm

Crankshaft and bearings
Main bearing oil clearance . . . . 0.020 to 0.052 mm
Runout (max) . . . . 0.03 mm

Transmission
Gear ratios (No. of teeth)
    Primary reduction . . . . 1.672 to 1 (97/58T)
    Final reduction (overall) . . . . 3.717 to 1 (46/38 x 19/18 x 32/11T)
        Secondary reduction . . . . 1.210 to 1 (46/38T)
        Middle gear . . . . 1.055 to 1 (19/18T)
        Final drive . . . . 2.909 to 1 (32/11T)
    1st gear . . . . 2.188 to 1 (35/16T)
    2nd gear . . . . 1.500 to 1 (30/20T)
    3rd gear . . . . 1.154 to 1 (30/26T)
    4th gear . . . . 0.933 to 1 (28/30T)
    5th gear . . . . 0.813 to 1 (26/32T)
Shaft runout (max) . . . . 0.08 mm
Middle gear backlash . . . . 0.1 to 0.2 mm

2•4 Engine, clutch and transmission

Torque wrench settings

Engine mounting bolts

Mounting bracket bolt nuts	30 Nm
Lower rear mounting bolt nut	48 Nm
Upper rear mounting bolt nut	48 Nm
Frame downtube bolts	89 Nm
Front mounting bolt nuts	48 Nm
Oil filter housing bolt	50 Nm
Oil pipe banjo bolts	32 Nm
Oil hose union bolts	12 Nm
Valve cover bolts	10 Nm
Cam chain tensioner mounting bolts	10 Nm
Cam chain tensioner cap bolt	20 Nm
Crankshaft end-cover screws/bolts	8 Nm
Camshaft holder bolts	10 Nm
Camshaft sprocket bolts	24 Nm
Valve cover holder bolts	10 Nm
Cylinder head domed nuts	32 Nm
Cylinder head front and rear nuts	10 Nm
Cylinder block nut	20 Nm
Clutch nut	70 Nm
Clutch spring bolts	8 Nm
Clutch cover bolts	12 Nm
Gearchange mechanism cover bolts	12 Nm
Middle gear drive shaft nut	110 Nm
Middle gear driven shaft nut	90 Nm
Middle gear drive shaft bearing retainer plate Torx screws	25 Nm
Middle gear driven shaft bearing housing bolts	25 Nm
Oil sump bolts	12 Nm
Oil pump assembly screw	12 Nm
Oil pump sprocket bolt	12 Nm
Oil pump mounting bolts	12 Nm
Crankcase 8 mm bolts	24 Nm
Crankcase 6 mm bolts	12 Nm
Timing rotor bolt	45 Nm
Cam chain tensioner blade bolt	20 Nm
Hy-Vo chain guide bolts	10 Nm
Alternator drive shaft bearing retainer bolts	10 Nm
Idle gear shaft retainer bolt	10 Nm

Connecting rod cap nuts

Initial setting (see Text)	30 Nm
Final setting	37 Nm
Transmission output shaft bearing housing bolts	12 Nm
Selector drum retainer plate screws	10 Nm

1 General information

The engine/transmission unit is an air-cooled in-line four cylinder with two valves per cylinder. The valves are operated by double overhead camshafts which are chain driven off the crankshaft. The engine/transmission assembly is constructed from aluminium alloy. The crankcase is divided horizontally.

The crankcase incorporates a wet sump, pressure-fed lubrication system which uses a chain-driven, dual-rotor oil pump, an oil filter and by-pass valve assembly, a relief valve and an oil level switch. The pump is driven by a chain off the back of the clutch housing. The oil is cooled by a cooler.

A Hy-Vo chain running off the crankshaft drives a shaft which has the alternator on its left-hand end and the starter clutch on its right-hand end.

Power from the crankshaft is routed to the transmission via the clutch. The clutch is of the wet, multi-plate type and is gear-driven off the crankshaft. The transmission is a five-speed constant-mesh unit. Drive is turned through 90° via middle gear shafts. Final drive to the rear wheel is by shaft.

2 Operations possible with the engine in the frame

The components and assemblies listed below can be removed without having to remove the engine/transmission assembly from the frame. If however, a number of areas require attention at the same time, removal of the engine is recommended.

Valve cover
Camshafts
Cam chain tensioner
Cylinder head
Cylinder block, pistons and piston
  rings
Clutch
Gearchange mechanism
Alternator
Pick-up coil assembly
Oil filter and cooler
Oil sump
Oil pump
Starter motor
Middle gear shafts

Engine, clutch and transmission 2•5

3 Operations requiring engine removal

It is necessary to remove the engine/transmission assembly from the frame to gain access to the following components.
Transmission shafts
Selector drum and forks
Starter clutch
Connecting rods and bearings
Crankshaft and bearings

4 Major engine repair – general information

1 It is not always easy to determine when or if an engine should be completely overhauled, as a number of factors must be considered.
2 High mileage is not necessarily an indication that an overhaul is needed, while low mileage, on the other hand, does not preclude the need for an overhaul. Frequency of servicing is probably the single most important consideration. An engine that has regular and frequent oil and filter changes, as well as other required maintenance, will most likely give many miles of reliable service. Conversely, a neglected engine, or one which has not been run in properly, may require an overhaul very early in its life.
3 Exhaust smoke and excessive oil consumption are both indications that piston rings and/or valve guides are in need of attention, although make sure that the fault is not due to oil leakage.
4 If the engine is making obvious knocking or rumbling noises, the connecting rods and/or main bearings are probably at fault.
5 Loss of power, rough running, excessive valve train noise and high fuel consumption rates may also point to the need for an overhaul, especially if they are all present at the same time. If a complete tune-up does not remedy the situation, major mechanical work is the only solution.
6 An engine overhaul generally involves restoring the internal parts to the specifications of a new engine. The piston rings and main and connecting rod bearings are usually renewed and the cylinder walls honed or, if necessary, re-bored, during a major overhaul. Generally the valve seats are re-ground, since they are usually in less than perfect condition at this point. The end result should be a like new engine that will give as many trouble-free miles as the original.
7 Before beginning the engine overhaul, read through the related procedures to familiarise yourself with the scope and requirements of the job. Overhauling an engine is not all that difficult, but it is time consuming. Plan on the motorcycle being tied up for a minimum of two weeks. Check on the availability of parts and make sure that any necessary special tools, equipment and supplies are obtained in advance.
8 Most work can be done with typical workshop hand tools, although a number of precision measuring tools are required for inspecting parts to determine if they must be renewed. Often a dealer will handle the inspection of parts and offer advice concerning reconditioning and renewal. As a general rule, time is the primary cost of an overhaul so it does not pay to install worn or substandard parts.
9 As a final note, to ensure maximum life and minimum trouble from a rebuilt engine, everything must be assembled with care in a spotlessly clean environment.

5 Engine – removal and installation

Caution: The engine is very heavy. Engine removal and installation should be carried out with the aid of at least one assistant. Personal injury or damage could occur if the engine falls or is dropped. An hydraulic or mechanical floor jack should be used to support and lower or raise the engine if possible.
Note: *Although not strictly necessary, it is advisable to remove the final drive housing and driveshaft to avoid having to disengage and engage the engine from it at the same time as manoeuvring the engine in or out of the frame. It is too easy to damage the frame, especially if you only have one assistant, and the extra work involved is not considerable (see Chapter 5).*

Removal

1 Support the motorcycle securely in an upright position using the centrestand. Work can be made easier by raising the machine to a suitable working height on an hydraulic ramp or a suitable platform. Make sure the motorcycle is secure and will not topple over (see Section 1 in *Tools and Workshop Tips* in the *Reference* section). When disconnecting any wiring, cables and hoses, it is advisable to mark or tag them as a reminder to where they connect.
2 If the engine is dirty, particularly around its mountings, wash it thoroughly before starting any major dismantling work. This will make work much easier and rule out the possibility of caked-on lumps of dirt falling into some vital component.
3 Remove the seat, side panels and right-hand side cover, and the fairing (see Chapter 7). Note: *The fairing can stay on the bike, though it is wiser to remove it as it could get in the way and be damaged – if its not there, it can't do either!*
4 Remove the fuel tank (see Chapter 3).
5 Drain the engine oil and remove the oil filter (see Chapter 1). Remove the oil cooler, the oil filter housing and the oil cooler hoses (see Section 7).
6 Remove the battery (see Chapter 8). Disconnect the wiring connector joining the negative wire to the negative lead **(see illustration)**. Feed the lead through to the engine, noting its routing, and coil it on the crankcase so that it does not impede engine removal.
7 Remove the carburettors (see Chapter 3). Plug the intake manifolds with clean rag. Detach the vacuum hose from the No. 4 cylinder intake manifold.
8 Disconnect the spark plug caps from the spark plugs, then detach the leads from the clips on the back of the engine and secure them clear **(see illustrations)**. Detach the air

5.6 Disconnect the negative wire connector (arrowed)

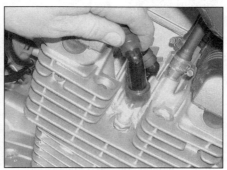
5.8a Pull the caps off the spark plugs . . .

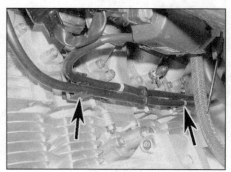
5.8b . . . and free the leads from the clips (arrowed)

2•6 Engine, clutch and transmission

5.10 Disconnect the alternator wiring connector

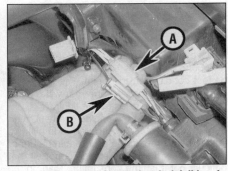

5.11 Pick-up coil/neutral switch/oil level sensor wiring connector (A), sidestand switch wiring connector (B)

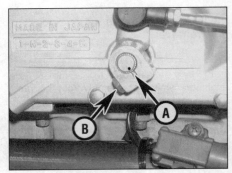

5.13 Note the alignment of the punchmark with the slit (A), then unscrew the pinchbolt (B)

induction system (AIS) hoses/pipes from the engine (see Chapter 3).
9 Remove the exhaust system (see Chapter 3).
10 Trace the alternator wiring from the alternator and disconnect it at the connector **(see illustration)**. Release the wiring from any clips or ties, noting its routing, and coil it so that it does not impede engine removal.
11 Trace the ignition pick-up coil, neutral switch and oil level sensor wiring from the right-hand side of the engine and disconnect it at the connector **(see illustration)**. Release the wiring from any clips or ties, noting its

5.14 Unscrew the nut (arrowed) and detach the starter motor lead

routing, and coil it so that it does not impede engine removal.
12 Trace the sidestand switch wiring from the stand and disconnect it at the connector **(see illustration 5.11)**. Release the wiring from any clips or ties, noting its routing, and feed it down to the switch.
13 Unscrew the gearchange lever linkage arm pinch bolt and slide the arm off the shaft, noting how the punchmark on the shaft end aligns with the split in the arm **(see illustration)**. If no marks are visible, make your own before removing the arm so that it can be correctly aligned with the shaft on installation.
14 Pull back the rubber cover on the starter motor terminal, then unscrew the nut and detach the lead **(see illustration)**. Secure it clear of the engine.
15 Detach the clutch cable from the release mechanism on the clutch cover (see Section 18).
16 Pull back the rubber boot covering the universal joint for the driveshaft **(see illustration)**. If required, remove the final drive housing and driveshaft (see **Note** at the beginning of the Section). If required, detach the crankcase breather hose from the crankcase and remove it.
17 At this point, position an hydraulic or

mechanical jack under the engine with a block of wood between the jack head and crankcase. Make sure the jack is centrally positioned so the engine will not topple in any direction when the last mounting bolt is removed. Take the weight of the engine on the jack. It is also advisable to place a block of wood between the rear wheel and the ground, or under the swingarm, in case the bike tilts back when the engine is removed. Check around the engine and frame to make sure that all wiring, cables and hoses that need to be disconnected have been disconnected, and that any remaining connected to the engine are not retained by any clips, guides or brackets connected to the frame. Check that any protruding mounting brackets will not get in the way and remove them if possible.
18 Unscrew the nuts and remove the upper and lower front mounting bolts on each side **(see illustration)**.
19 Unscrew the nuts and remove the bolts securing the upper front mounting bolt brackets and frame cross-piece to the frame downtubes and remove the bracket and cross-piece, noting which way round they fit **(see illustration)**.
20 Unscrew the nuts and remove the bolts securing the right-hand frame downtube section to the frame and remove the

5.16 Pull the rubber boot back off the crankcase

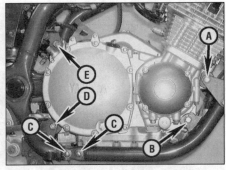

5.18 Upper front mounting bolt (A), lower front mounting bolt (B), frame downtube rear bolts (C), lower rear mounting bolt (D), upper rear mounting bolt (E)

5.19 Remove the brackets and the frame cross-piece, noting how they fit

Engine, clutch and transmission 2•7

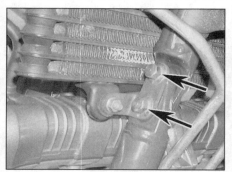

5.20a Remove the top bolts (arrowed), noting the bracket . . .

5.20b . . . and the bottom bolts (arrowed), noting the washers, and remove the downtube

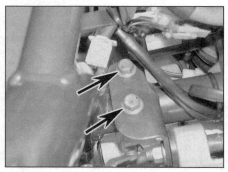

5.22 Unscrew the bolts (arrowed) and remove the bracket

downtube, noting the oil cooler bracket held by the top bolts and the washers with the bottom bolts **(see illustrations)**.
21 Unscrew the nut on the lower rear mounting bolt but do not yet withdraw the bolt **(see illustration 5.18)**. Unscrew the nut on the upper rear mounting bolt, but do not yet withdraw the bolt **(see illustration 5.18)**.

 Tie some rags around the frame tubes to protect their paint finish from damage in case the engine knocks them during removal. Remember, the engine is very heavy and difficult to manoeuvre.

22 Make sure the engine is properly supported on the jack, and have an assistant support it as well, then withdraw the upper and lower rear mounting bolts **(see illustration 5.18)**. Unscrew the two bolts securing the upper rear mounting bolt bracket and remove the bracket, noting how it fits **(see illustration)**. Carefully manoeuvre the engine forward slightly so that the output driveshaft from the engine disengages from the final driveshaft (if not removed), then manoeuvre it out from the right-hand side of the frame.

Installation

23 Installation is the reverse of removal, noting the following points:
a) Check that all the engine mounting dampers and the bolt collars for the rear

bolts are in place. If any of the dampers are damaged or deteriorated, replace them with new ones **(see illustrations)**.
b) Make sure no wires, cables or hoses become trapped between the engine and the frame when installing the engine.
c) Many of the engine mounting bolts are of different size and length. Make sure the correct bolt is installed in its correct location, with its washer if fitted. Install all of the bolts and nuts finger-tight only until they are all located, then tighten them in the order given in the relevant Step below to their torque settings as specified at the beginning of the Chapter.
d) With the aid of an assistant place the engine unit on top of the jack and block of wood and carefully raise the engine into position in the frame, making sure the output driveshaft from the engine engages with the final driveshaft (if not removed), and that all the mounting bolt holes align. Also make sure no wires, cables or hoses become trapped between the engine and the frame. Locate all the brackets, frame sections and mounting bolts, not forgetting the washers and oil cooler bracket with the frame downtube bolts, and tighten them finger-tight. First tighten the bolts for the upper rear mounting bolt bracket. Now tighten the upper and lower rear mounting bolt nuts, then the frame downtube and front bracket bolts, then the front mounting bolts, tightening them all to their specified

torque settings **(see illustrations 5.18, 5.19, 5.20a and b and 5.22)**.
e) Use new gaskets on the exhaust pipe connections.
f) Make sure all wires, cables and hoses are correctly routed and connected, and secured by any clips or ties.
g) Refill the engine with oil (see Chapter 1).
h) Adjust the throttle and clutch cable freeplay and engine idle speed (see Chapter 1).
i) Start the engine and check for any oil leaks before installing the body panels.

6 Engine disassembly and reassembly – general information

Disassembly

1 Before disassembling the engine, the external surfaces of the unit should be thoroughly cleaned and degreased. This will prevent contamination of the engine internals, and will also make working a lot easier and cleaner. A high flash-point solvent, such as paraffin (kerosene) can be used, or better still, a proprietary engine degreaser such as Gunk. Use old paintbrushes and toothbrushes to work the solvent into the various recesses of the engine casings. Take care to not to get solvent or water in the electrical components, breather unions, oil filter feed and intake and exhaust ports.

 Warning: The use of petrol (gasoline) as a cleaning agent should be avoided because of the risk of fire.

2 When clean and dry, arrange the unit on the workbench, leaving suitable clear area for working. Gather a selection of small containers and plastic bags so that parts can be grouped together in an easily identifiable manner. Some paper and a pen should be on hand so that notes can be made and labels attached where necessary. A supply of clean rag is also required.
3 Before commencing work, read through the appropriate section so that some idea of the necessary procedure can be gained. When

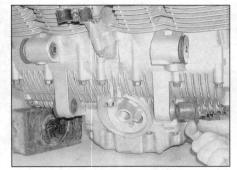

5.23a Check the mounting dampers for the front mounts . . .

5.23b . . . and the rear mounts, not forgetting the bolt collars

2•8 Engine, clutch and transmission

6.4 An engine support made from pieces of 2 x 4 inch wood

7.2a Unscrew the banjo bolts, counter-holding the base hex as shown

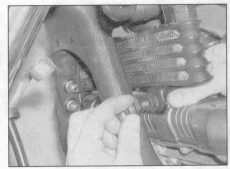

7.2b Unscrew the cooler mounting bolts and remove the cooler . . .

removing components it should be noted that great force is seldom required, unless specified. In many cases, a component's reluctance to be removed is indicative of an incorrect approach or removal method – if in any doubt, re-check with the text.

4 An engine support stand can be made from short lengths of 2 x 4 inch wood bolted together into a rectangle to help support the engine if required **(see illustration)**, though the engine will sit nicely on the flat bottom of the sump, and there are two pegs at the front to keep it stable. The perimeter of the mount should be just big enough to accommodate the sump within it so that the engine rests on its crankcase.

5 When disassembling the engine, keep 'mated' parts together (including gears, cylinders, pistons, connecting rods, valves, etc. that have been in contact with each other during engine operation). These 'mated' parts must be reused or renewed as an assembly.

6 A complete engine/transmission disassembly should be done in the following general order with reference to the appropriate Sections.

  Remove the valve cover
  Remove the camshafts
  Remove the cylinder head
  Remove the cylinder block
  Remove the pistons
  Remove the clutch
  Remove the pick-up coil assembly (see Chapter 4)
  Remove the alternator (see Chapter 8)
  Remove the starter motor (see Chapter 8)
  Remove the gearchange mechanism.
  Remove the middle gear shafts
  Remove the oil sump
  Remove the oil pump
  Separate the crankcase halves
  Remove the crankshaft
  Remove the transmission shafts
  Remove the selector drum and forks
  Remove the starter clutch and idle/reduction gears

Reassembly

7 Reassembly is accomplished by reversing the general disassembly sequence.

7 Oil cooler and oil filter housing – removal, inspection and installation

Note: *The oil cooler and its hoses can be removed with the engine in the frame. If the engine has been removed, ignore the steps which do not apply.*

Removal

1 Drain the engine oil (see Chapter 1). Remove the fairing (see Chapter 7).

2 To remove the cooler, unscrew the banjo bolt securing each hose to its union on the cooler, counter-holding the base hex as you do, and detach the hoses **(see illustration)**. Discard the sealing washers as new ones must be used. Unscrew the two bolts securing the bottom of the cooler to the frame, then carefully remove the cooler, noting how it locates at the top **(see illustrations)**.

3 To remove the oil filter housing, first remove the filter (see Chapter 1). Unscrew the housing bolt and remove the base plate and the collar, noting which way round it fits **(see illustrations)**. Discard the base plate O-ring as a new one should be used. Draw the housing forward to access the oil hose union bolts, then unscrew them and detach the

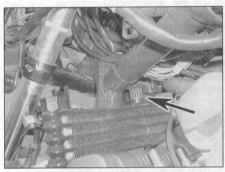

7.2c . . . noting how the rubber bush (arrowed) locates in the bracket

7.3a Unscrew the bolt . . .

7.3b . . . and remove the base plate . . .

7.3c . . . and collar

Engine, clutch and transmission 2•9

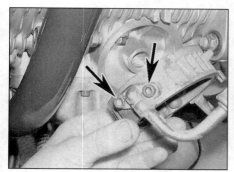

7.3d Each hose union is secured by two bolts (arrowed)

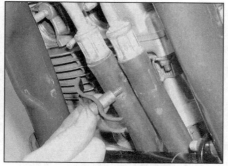

7.4 Unscrew the bolt and remove the clamp, noting the spacer

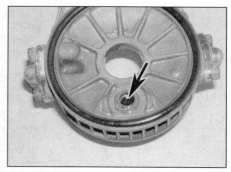

7.6a Press down on the plunger (arrowed) and check its operation

hoses (see illustration). Discard the union O-rings and the housing O-ring as new ones should be used.

4 To remove the hoses, detach them from the cooler and filter housing as described above. Unscrew the bolt securing the hose clamp cap and draw the hoses out from between the engine and frame (see illustration).

Inspection

5 Check the cooler for leaks and other damage. If any are noted, have it repaired or replace it with a new one. Check the cooler fins for mud, dirt and insects, which may impede the flow of air. If the fins are dirty,

clean the cooler using water or low pressure compressed air directed through the fins from the backside. If the fins are bent or distorted, straighten them carefully with a screwdriver. If the air flow is restricted by bent or damaged fins over more than 30% of the surface area, install a new cooler.

6 Check the operation of the by-pass valve in the filter housing by pressing on the plunger from the inside (see illustration). If it is stuck or does not move smoothly against the pressure of its spring, remove the circlip from the outside of the housing and remove the washer, spring and plunger (see illustration). Clean and inspect all components, and check

the sliding surfaces of the plunger and its bore in the housing.

Installation

7 Installation is the reverse of removal. Fit new O-rings on the filter housing and base plate (see illustrations). Align the projections on the housing and the base plate with the tabs on the engine (see illustration). Fit the shouldered side of the collar into the housing (see illustration 7.3c). Always use new sealing washers and O-rings when installing the hoses (see illustration). Tighten the various bolts to the torque settings specified at the beginning of the Chapter (see illustration). Fit a new filter and fill the engine with oil (see Chapter 1).

7.6b Remove the circlip (arrowed) to release the valve components

7.7a Use a new O-ring between the housing and the engine . . .

7.7b . . . and between the base plate and the housing

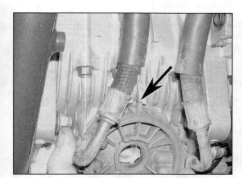

7.7c Fit the projection on the housing between the tabs on the engine (arrowed). Similarly align the base plate

7.7d Use new sealing washers on each side of the banjo union

7.7e Counter-hold the base hex when torquing the banjo bolt

2•10 Engine, clutch and transmission

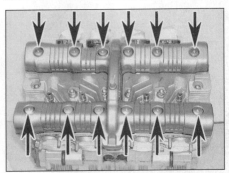

8.4 Unscrew the cover bolts (arrowed) and remove the cover

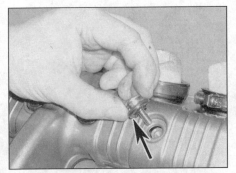

8.5 Check the rubber grommet (arrowed) on each bolt and use new ones if necessary

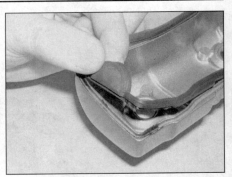

8.7 Make sure the gasket locates in the groove in the cover

8 Valve cover – removal and installation

Note: *The valve cover can be removed with the engine in the frame. If the engine has been removed, ignore the steps which do not apply.*

Removal

1 Remove the seat and the fairing (see Chapter 7), and the fuel tank and the air filter housing (see Chapter 3).
2 Detach the air induction system (AIS) hoses/pipes from the engine (see Chapter 3).
3 Remove the oil cooler (see Section 7). Pull off the spark plug caps.
4 Unscrew the bolts securing the valve cover and remove it **(see illustration)**. If the cover is stuck, do not try to lever it off with a screwdriver. Tap it gently around the sides with a rubber hammer or block of wood to dislodge it.

Installation

5 Examine the valve cover gasket for signs of damage or deterioration and fit a new one if necessary. Similarly check the rubber grommets on the cover bolts for cracks, hardening and deterioration **(see illustration)**.
6 Clean the mating surfaces of the cylinder head and the valve cover with solvent.
7 Fit the gasket into the valve cover, making sure it locates correctly into the groove **(see illustration)**. Use a few dabs of grease to keep the gasket in place while the cover is fitted.
8 Apply a suitable sealant to the cut-outs in the cylinder head where the gasket half-circles fit **(see illustration)**. Position the valve cover on the cylinder head, making sure the gasket stays in place **(see illustration)**. Install the cover bolts and tighten them to the torque setting specified at the beginning of the Chapter.
9 Install the remaining components in the reverse order of removal.

9 Cam chain tensioner and guides – removal, inspection and installation

Note 1: *The cam chain tensioner and guides can be removed with the engine in the frame.*
Note 2: *Refer to Section 25 for removal of the cam chain and tensioner blade.*
Caution: Once you start to remove the tensioner bolts, you must remove the tensioner all the way and reset it before tightening the bolts. The tensioner extends itself and locks in place, so if you loosen the bolts partway and then retighten them, the tensioner or cam chain will be damaged.

Cam chain tensioner

Removal

1 Unscrew the tensioner cap bolt and withdraw the springs from the tensioner body **(see illustrations)**.
2 Unscrew the two tensioner mounting bolts and withdraw the tensioner from the back of the cylinder block, noting which way up it fits **(see illustration)**.

8.8a Apply the sealant to the cutouts in the head

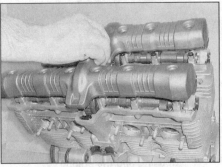

8.8b Make sure the gasket stays in place and seats correctly

9.1a Unscrew the cap bolt (arrowed) . . .

9.1b . . . and withdraw the springs (one fits inside the other)

9.2 Unscrew the tensioner bolts (arrowed) and remove the tensioner

Engine, clutch and transmission 2•11

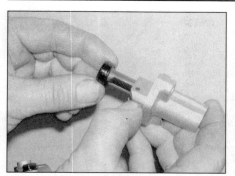

9.5 Release the ratchet mechanism to free the plunger

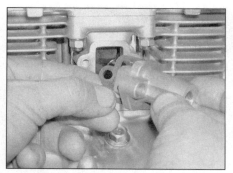

9.8 Install the tensioner with the ratchet mechanism at the bottom, and use a new gasket

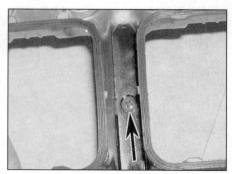

9.13 Remove the screw (arrowed) and lift the top cam chain guide out of the valve cover

3 Discard the tensioner body gasket as a new one must be used.

Inspection

4 Examine the tensioner components for signs of wear or damage.
5 Release the ratchet mechanism from the tensioner plunger and check that the plunger moves freely in and out of the tensioner body (see illustration).
6 If the tensioner or any of its components are worn or damaged, or if the plunger is seized in the body, the tensioner must be renewed. Individual internal components are not available.

Installation

7 Release the ratchet mechanism and press the tensioner plunger all the way into the tensioner body (see illustration 9.5).
8 Fit a new gasket onto the tensioner body, then fit the tensioner into the engine, making sure the ratchet release lever is on the bottom (see illustration). Tighten the bolts to the torque setting specified at the beginning of the Chapter.
9 Check the condition of the sealing washer on the cap bolt and replace it with a new one if it is worn or damaged. Install the springs and cap bolt and tighten the bolt to the specified torque setting (see illustration 9.1b). It should be possible to hear the plunger sliding out over the ratchet as the spring pressure forces it out against the chain.

10 Refer to Section 10, Step 2 and remove the left-hand crankshaft end-cover, then turn the crankshaft anti-clockwise through two full turns using the method described (see illustrations 10.2a and b). This will allow the tensioner to set itself properly. Install the cover and tighten the screws or bolts (according to model) to the specified torque setting.
11 It is advisable to remove the valve cover (see Section 8) and check that the cam chain is tensioned and all the timing marks are in alignment (see Section 10). If the chain is slack, the tensioner plunger did not release when the spring and cap bolt were installed. Remove the tensioner again and re-check it. Again check the timing marks (see Section 10), then install the valve cover (see Section 8).

Cam chain guides

Removal

12 Remove the valve cover (see Section 8).
13 To remove the cam chain top guide, remove the screw securing it to the valve cover (see illustration). Note which way round the guide fits.
14 To remove the cam chain front guide, lift it out of the front of the cam chain tunnel, noting which way round it fits and how it locates (see illustration).

Inspection

15 Check the sliding surfaces of the guides

for excessive wear, deep grooves, cracking and other obvious damage, and renew them if necessary.

Installation

16 Fit the front guide blade into the front of the cam chain tunnel (see illustration 9.14), making sure it locates correctly onto its seat and its lugs locate in their cut-outs (see illustration).
17 Fit the top guide onto the valve cover and tighten the screw securely (see illustration 9.13).
18 Install the valve cover (see Section 8).

10 Camshafts and followers – removal, inspection and installation

Note: *The camshafts can be removed with the engine in the frame. Place rags in the spark plug holes and cam chain tunnel to prevent any component from dropping into the engine.*

Removal

1 Remove the valve cover (see Section 8).
2 Remove the left-hand crankshaft end-cover, secured by four screws or bolts (depending on model) (see illustration). The engine can be turned using a 14 mm spanner or socket on the timing rotor bolt, turning it in an anti-clockwise direction only (see

9.14 Lift the front guide out of the engine noting how the lugs locate in the cutouts

9.16 Make sure the lugs fit into the cutouts (arrowed)

10.2a Unscrew the bolts (arrowed) and remove the cover

2

2•12 Engine, clutch and transmission

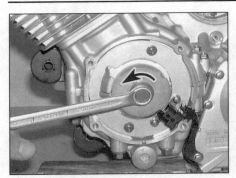

10.2b Turn the engine anti-clockwise as shown

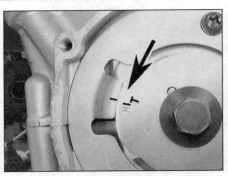

10.3a Turn the engine until the line next to the 'T' mark aligns with the mark on the timing plate (arrowed) . . .

10.3b . . . the camshaft lobes for no. 1 cylinder are facing away from each other (intake pointing back, exhaust pointing forward) as shown . . .

illustration). Alternatively, place the motorcycle on an auxiliary stand so that the rear wheel is off the ground, select a high gear and rotate the rear wheel by hand in its normal direction of rotation.

3 Turn the engine until the line next to the 'T' mark on the rotor aligns with the mark on the timing plate (see illustration), and the camshaft lobes for the No. 1 (left-hand) cylinder face away from each other, and the punchmark on the right-hand end of each camshaft is visible in the hole in the top of the camshaft caps (see illustrations). If the cam lobes are facing towards each other and the punchmarks aren't visible, rotate the engine anti-clockwise 360° (one full turn) so that the line next to the 'T' mark again aligns with the mark on the timing plate. The camshaft lobes will now be facing away from each other and the punchmarks will be visible in the holes, meaning the No. 1 cylinder is at TDC (top dead centre) on the compression stroke.

4 Before disturbing the camshafts, make a note of the timing markings described above and how they align. Also note the markings on the sprockets. If you are in any doubt as to the alignment of the markings, or if they are not visible, make your own alignment marks between all components, and also between a tooth on each sprocket and its corresponding link on the chain, before disturbing them. These markings ensure that the valve timing can be correctly set up on assembly without difficulty. As it is easy to be a tooth out on installation, marking between a tooth on each sprocket and its link in the chain is especially useful, but note that if the engine is being completely disassembled it will only be of use if similar marks are made between the chain and the crankshaft sprocket, and you are careful not to let the chain go slack around the crankshaft sprocket and slip by a tooth before the marks are made.

5 Remove the cam chain tensioner (see Section 9).

6 Remove the cam chain front guide (see Section 9).

7 Before removing the camshaft holders, make a note of which fits where – all the holders are marked with a letter and a number to denote their location, although these marks are difficult to see, so it is advisable to make your own (it is essential the holders are returned to their original locations on installation) (see illustration). Also note the arrow or triangle on each holder which points to the right-hand side of the engine. Note that the four central holders (two for each camshaft on each side of the sprocket) are not camshaft holders, but are for the valve cover bolts. These do not have to be installed in their original location, but the arrow on each one must point away from the sprocket. Do not mix up the camshaft holders with the cover bolt holders. Also mark each camshaft to denote whether it is the intake or exhaust – the camshafts are identical, even to the point of being stamped with both an I and an E, so don't rely on these marks for identification as it could lead to confusion. Like the holders, it is essential each camshaft is installed in its original location. When removing the camshafts, remove the intake camshaft first, then the exhaust camshaft.

8 Unscrew the two bolts securing each valve cover bolt holder and remove the holders (see illustration). Unscrew the camshaft holder bolts, slackening them evenly and a little at a time in a criss-cross pattern, starting from the outside and working towards the centre, slackening the bolts above any lobes that are pressing onto a valve last in the sequence so that the pressure from the open valves cannot cause the camshaft to bend (see illustration 10.7).

Caution: *A camshaft could break if the holder bolts are not slackened as described and the pressure from a depressed valve causes the shaft to bend. Also, if the holder does not come squarely away from the head, the holder is likely to break. If this happens the camshaft case must be renewed; the holders are matched to the case and cannot be renewed separately.*

Remove the bolts, then lift off the camshaft

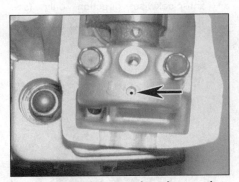

10.3c . . . and the punchmark on each camshaft right-hand end aligns with the hole in the holder (arrowed)

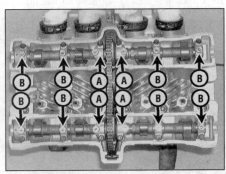

10.7 Valve cover bolt holders (A), camshaft holders (B)

10.8 Valve cover holder bolts (arrowed)

Engine, clutch and transmission 2•13

10.9a Pick the shim out of the top of the follower . . .

10.9b . . . then lift out the follower

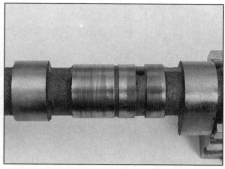
10.10 Inspect the bearing surfaces in the camshaft case and holder and the journal surfaces of the camshaft for scratches or wear

holders, noting how they fit **(see illustration 10.26b)**. Retrieve the dowels from either the holder or the camshaft case if they are loose **(see illustration 10.26a)**. Remove the camshafts, rotating them towards the centre of the engine as you do. Keep all mated parts together. While the camshafts are out, don't allow the cam chain to go slack and do not rotate the crankshaft – the chain may drop down and bind between the crankshaft and case, which could damage these components. Wire the chain to another component or secure it using a rod of some sort to prevent it from dropping.

9 If the shims and followers are being removed from the cylinder head, obtain a container which is divided into eight compartments, and label each compartment with the location of its corresponding valve in the cylinder head and whether it belongs with an intake or an exhaust valve. If a container is not available, use labelled plastic bags (egg cartons also do very well!). Pick each shim out of the top of its cam follower using either a magnet or a small screwdriver, then remove the follower **(see illustrations)**. Do not allow the shim to fall into the engine.

Inspection

10 Inspect the bearing surfaces of the camshaft holders and cylinder head and the corresponding journals on the camshaft **(see illustration)**. Look for score marks, deep scratches and evidence of spalling (a pitted appearance). If damage is noted or wear is excessive, the components must be replaced with new ones.

11 Check the camshaft lobes for heat discoloration (blue appearance), score marks, chipped areas, flat spots and spalling **(see illustration)**. Measure the height of each lobe with a micrometer **(see illustration)** and compare the results to the minimum lobe height listed in this Chapter's Specifications. If damage is noted or wear is excessive, the camshaft must be replaced with a new one. Also, be sure to check the condition of the followers.

12 Check the amount of camshaft runout by supporting each end of the camshaft on V-blocks, and measuring any runout using a dial gauge. If the runout exceeds the specified limit the camshaft must be renewed.

HAYNES HiNT *Refer to Section 3 in Tools and Workshop Tips in the Reference section for details of how to read a micrometer and dial gauge.*

13 Next, check the camshaft journal oil clearances. Check each camshaft in turn rather than at the same time. Clean the camshaft and the bearing surfaces in the cylinder head and camshaft holders with a clean lint-free cloth, then lay the camshaft in its correct location in the cylinder head.

14 Cut some strips of Plastigauge and lay one piece on each journal, parallel with the camshaft centreline **(see illustration)**. Make sure the camshaft holder dowels are installed **(see illustration 10.26a)**. Lay the holders in their correct place in the cylinder head (see Step 7) **(see illustration 10.26b)**. Install the holder bolts and tighten them evenly and a little at a time in a criss-cross pattern, working from the centre of the camshaft outwards, (i.e. starting with the bolts that are above valves that will be opened when the camshaft is tightened down), to the torque setting specified at the beginning of the Chapter. Whilst tightening the bolts, make sure the holders are being pulled squarely down and are not binding on the dowels. While doing this, don't let the camshaft rotate.

15 Now unscrew the bolts evenly and a little at a time in a criss-cross pattern, starting from the outside and working towards the centre, and carefully lift off the camshaft holders.

16 To determine the oil clearance, compare the crushed Plastigauge (at its widest point) on each journal to the scale printed on the

10.11a Check the lobes of the camshaft for wear – here's an example of damage requiring camshaft repair or renewal

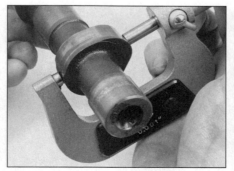
10.11b Measure the height of the camshaft lobes with a micrometer

10.14 Lay a strip of Plastigauge across each bearing journal, parallel with the camshaft centreline

2•14 Engine, clutch and transmission

10.16a Compare the width of the crushed Plastigauge to the scale printed on the Plastigauge container

10.16b Measure the cam bearing journals with a micrometer

10.21 Install the follower then fit the shim into the top of it

Plastigauge container **(see illustration)**. Compare the results to this Chapter's Specifications. If the oil clearance is greater than specified, measure the diameter of the camshaft journal with a micrometer **(see illustration)**. If the journal diameter is less than the specified limit, replace the camshaft with a new one and recheck the clearance. If the clearance is still too great, or if the camshaft journal is within its limit, replace the cylinder head and holders with new ones.

 Before renewing the camshafts, cylinder head or holders because of damage, check with local machine shops specialising in motorcycle engine work. In the case of the camshafts, it may be possible for cam lobes to be welded, reground and hardened, at a cost far lower than that of a new camshaft. If the bearing surfaces in the case or holders are damaged, it may be possible for them to be bored out to accept bearing inserts. Due to the cost of new components it is recommended that all options be explored.

17 Except in cases of oil starvation, the cam chain should wear very little. If the chain has stretched excessively, which makes it difficult to maintain proper tension, or if it is stiff or the links are binding or kinking, replace it with a new one. Refer to Section 25 for renewal.
18 Check the sprockets for wear, cracks and other damage. If the sprockets are worn, the cam chain is also worn, and so probably is the sprocket on the crankshaft. If severe wear is apparent, the entire engine should be disassembled for inspection.
19 Inspect the cam chain guides and tensioner blade (see Sections 9 and 25).
20 Inspect the outer surfaces of the cam followers for evidence of scoring or other damage. If a follower is in poor condition, it is probable that the bore in which it works is also damaged. Check for clearance between the followers and their bores. Whilst no specifications are given, if slack is excessive, renew the followers. If the bores are seriously out-of-round or tapered, the cylinder head and the followers must be renewed.

Installation

21 If removed, lubricate each shim and its follower with molybdenum disulphide oil (a 50/50 mixture of molybdenum disulphide grease and engine oil) then install each follower, making sure it fits squarely in its bore **(see illustration 10.9b)**. Fit each shim into its recess in the top of the follower, with the size marking facing down, making sure it is correctly seated **(see illustration)**. Note: *It is most important that the shims and followers are returned to their original valves otherwise the valve clearances will be inaccurate.*
22 Make sure the bearing surfaces on the camshafts and in the cylinder head are clean, then apply molybdenum disulphide oil (a 50/50 mixture of molybdenum disulphide grease and engine oil) to each of them. Also apply it to the camshaft lobes.
23 Check that the line next to the 'T' mark on the rotor still aligns with the mark on the timing plate (see Step 3) **(see illustration 10.3a)**.
24 Fit the exhaust camshaft through the cam chain and onto the front of the head, making sure the No. 1 (left-hand) cylinder lobe is facing forwards and the punchmark on the right-hand end is facing up **(see illustration)**. Fit the cam chain around the exhaust sprocket, aligning the marks between sprocket tooth and link if made. When fitting the chain, pull up on the front run to remove all slack from it.
25 Now fit the intake camshaft through the cam chain and onto the back of the head, making sure the No. 1 cylinder lobes are facing back and the punchmark on the right-hand end is facing up **(see illustration)**. Fit the cam chain around the intake sprocket, aligning the marks between sprocket tooth and link if made. When fitting the chain, pull it tight to make sure there is no slack between the two camshaft sprockets.
26 Fit the camshaft holder dowels into the cylinder head **(see illustration)**. Make sure

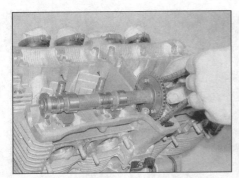

10.24 Install the exhaust camshaft first, keeping the front run of the chain taut . . .

10.25 . . . then install the intake camshaft, making sure the chain is tight between the sprockets

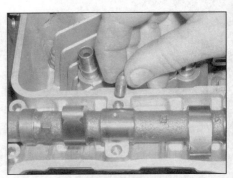

10.26a Make sure all the dowels are installed . . .

Engine, clutch and transmission 2•15

10.26b ... and make sure the holders locate correctly onto them

the bearing surfaces in the holders are clean, then apply molybdenum disulphide oil (a 50/50 mixture of molybdenum disulphide grease and engine oil) to them. Lay the holders in their correct place in the case (see Step 7) **(see illustration)**. Install the holder bolts and tighten them evenly and a little at a time in a criss-cross pattern, working from the centre of the camshaft outwards, (i.e. starting with the bolts that are above valves that will be opened when the camshaft is tightened down), to the torque setting specified at the beginning of the Chapter. Whilst tightening the bolts, make sure the holders are being pulled squarely down and are not binding on the dowels.

Caution: The camshaft is likely to break if it is tightened down onto the closed valves before the open valves. The holders are likely to break if they are not tightened down evenly and squarely.

27 Using a piece of wooden dowel, press on the back of the cam chain tensioner blade via the tensioner bore in the cylinder block to ensure that any slack in the cam chain between the crankshaft and the intake camshaft, and between the two camshafts, is taken up and transferred to the rear run of the chain (where it will later be taken up by the tensioner). At this point check that all the timing marks are still in **exact** alignment as described in Steps 3 and 4. Note that it is easy to be slightly out (one tooth on the sprocket) without the marks appearing drastically out of alignment. If the marks are out, verify which sprocket is misaligned, then unscrew its bolts and slide it off the camshaft, then disengage it from the chain. Move the camshaft round as required, then fit the sprocket back into the chain and onto the camshaft, and check the marks again. With everything correctly aligned, tighten the sprocket bolts to the torque setting specified at the beginning of the Chapter. Now install the valve cover bolt holders, making sure the arrow on each points away from the sprocket, and tighten the bolts to the specified torque **(see illustration 10.8)**.

Caution: If the marks are not aligned exactly as described, the valve timing will be incorrect and the valves may strike the pistons, causing extensive damage to the engine.

28 Install the cam chain front guide (see Section 9).
29 Install the cam chain tensioner (see Section 9). Turn the engine anti-clockwise through two full turns and check again that all the timing marks still align (see Steps 3 and 4).
30 Check the valve clearances and adjust them if necessary (see Chapter 1).
31 Install the left-hand crankshaft end-cover and tighten the screws or bolts (according to model) to the specified torque setting.
32 Install the valve cover (see Section 7).

11 Cylinder head – removal and installation

Caution: *The engine must be completely cool before beginning this procedure or the cylinder head may become warped.*
Note: *The cylinder head can be removed with the engine in the frame. If the engine has been removed, ignore the steps which don't apply.*

Removal

1 Remove the exhaust system (see Chapter 3). Plug the exhaust ports with clean rag.
2 Remove the carburettors (see Chapter 3). Plug the intake manifolds with clean rag.
3 Remove the valve cover (see Section 8) and the camshafts and followers (see Section 10).
4 The cylinder head is secured by sixteen nuts. First unscrew the two nuts on the front of the cylinder head and displace the oil hose clamp (or remove it if the oil hoses have been removed, noting which way up it fits), then unscrew the two nuts on the back and remove the washers **(see illustration)**. Now slacken the twelve domed nuts in the top of the head, slackening them evenly and a little at a time in a **reverse** of the numerical tightening sequence shown until they are all slack, then remove the nuts and their washers, using either a magnet, a screwdriver, or a piece of wire hooked over at the end to lift them out where necessary **(see illustration)**. Note that the two washers for the nuts on the right-hand end of the head are copper, while the rest are steel.
5 Pull the cylinder head up off the block **(see illustration)**. If it is stuck, tap around the joint faces of the cylinder head with a soft-faced mallet to free the head. Do not attempt to free the head by inserting a screwdriver between the head and cylinder block – you'll damage the sealing surfaces. Remove the old cylinder head gasket and discard it as a new one must be used **(see illustration 11.9b)**.
6 If they are loose, remove the dowels from the cylinder block, along with the O-rings fitted with the right-hand end dowels **(see illustration 11.9a)**. If they appear to be missing they are probably stuck in the underside of the cylinder head.
7 Check the cylinder head gasket and the mating surfaces on the cylinder head and block for signs of leakage, which could indicate warpage. Refer to Section 13 and check the flatness of the cylinder head.

Installation

8 Clean all traces of old gasket material from the cylinder head and block. If a scraper is used, take care not to scratch or gouge the soft aluminium. Be careful not to let any of the gasket material fall into the crankcase, the cylinder bores or the oil passages. Lubricate the cylinder bores with new engine oil.

> **HAYNES HINT** *Refer to Section 7 in Tools and Workshop Tips in the Reference section for details of gasket removal methods.*

11.4a Unscrew the nuts on the front and back of the cylinder head (arrowed)

11.4b Cylinder head nut TIGHTENING sequence – slacken the nuts in reverse order

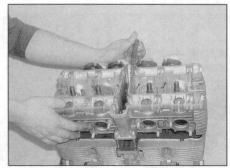

11.5 Carefully lift the head up off the block

2•16 Engine, clutch and transmission

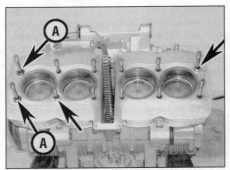

11.9a Cylinder head dowels (arrowed). Note O-rings (A)

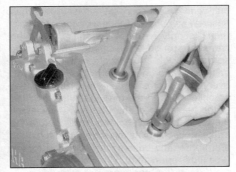

11.9b Fit new O-rings around the right-hand end dowels

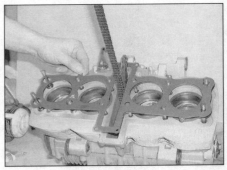

11.9c Lay the new gasket over the dowels and onto the head

9 Ensure both cylinder head and block mating surfaces are clean. If removed, fit the dowels into the cylinder block, and fit new O-rings around the dowels on the right-hand end **(see illustrations)**. Lay the new head gasket in place on the block with the longer middle section at the front, making sure it locates correctly over the dowels, and all the holes are correctly aligned **(see illustration)**. Never re-use the old gasket.

10 Carefully fit the cylinder head onto the block, making sure it locates correctly onto the dowels **(see illustration 11.5)**.

11 Lubricate the threads of the domed cylinder head nuts with clean engine oil. Install the nuts with their washers, fitting the two copper washers with the right-hand end nuts, and tighten them finger-tight **(see illustration)**. Now tighten the nuts evenly and a little at a time and in the correct numerical sequence **(see illustration 11.4b)** to the torque setting specified at the beginning of the Chapter **(see illustration)**.

12 Install the two front nuts with the oil hose clamp and two rear nuts with their washers and tighten them to the specified torque setting **(see illustration 11.4a)**. Fit the hose clamp so that the cups for the hoses are below the mounting bracket.

13 Install the remaining components in a reverse of their removal sequence, referring to the relevant Sections or Chapters (see Steps 1, 2 and 3).

12 Valves/valve seats/valve guides – servicing

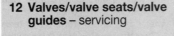

1 Because of the complex nature of this job and the special tools and equipment required, most owners leave servicing of the valves, valve seats and valve guides to a professional. However, you can make an initial assessment of whether the valves are seating, and therefore sealing, correctly by pouring a small amount of solvent into each of the valve ports. If the solvent leaks past any valve into the combustion chamber area the valve is not seating and sealing correctly.

2 You can also remove the valves from the cylinder head, clean the components, check them for wear to assess the extent of the work needed, and, unless a valve service is required, grind in the valves (see Section 13). The head can then be reassembled.

3 The dealer service department will remove the valves and springs, renew the valves and guides, recut the valve seats, check and renew the valve springs, spring retainers and collets (as necessary), replace the valve seals with new ones and reassemble the valve components.

4 After the valve service has been performed, the head will be in like-new condition. When the head is returned, be sure to clean it again very thoroughly before installation on the engine to remove any metal particles or abrasive grit that may still be present from the valve service operations. Use compressed air, if available, to blow out all the holes and passages.

13 Cylinder head and valves – disassembly, inspection and reassembly

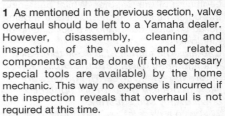

1 As mentioned in the previous section, valve overhaul should be left to a Yamaha dealer. However, disassembly, cleaning and inspection of the valves and related components can be done (if the necessary special tools are available) by the home mechanic. This way no expense is incurred if the inspection reveals that overhaul is not required at this time.

2 To disassemble the valve components without the risk of damaging them, a valve spring compressor is absolutely essential. Make sure it is suitable for motorcycle work.

Disassembly

3 Before proceeding, arrange to label and store the valves along with their related components in such a way that they can be returned to their original locations without getting mixed up **(see illustration opposite)**. A good way to do this is to use the same container as the followers and shims are stored in (see Section 10), or to obtain a separate container which is divided into eight compartments, and to label each compartment with the identity of the valve which will be stored in it (i.e. number of cylinder, intake or exhaust side). Alternatively, labelled plastic bags will do just as well.

4 Clean all traces of old gasket material from the cylinder head. If a scraper is used, take care not to scratch or gouge the soft aluminium.

 Refer to Section 7 in Tools and Workshop Tips in the Reference section for details of gasket removal methods.

11.11a Fit the nuts with their washers ...

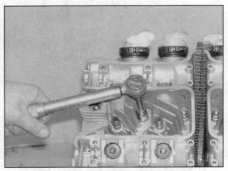

11.11b ... and tighten them to the specified torque

Engine, clutch and transmission 2•17

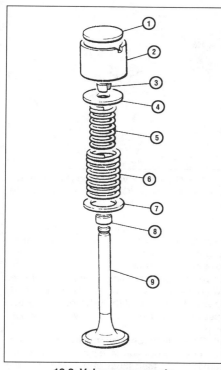

13.3 Valve components

1	Shim	6	Outer spring
2	Follower	7	Spring seat
3	Collets	8	Valve stem oil
4	Spring retainer		seal
5	Inner spring	9	Valve

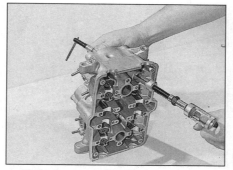

13.5a Compressing the valve springs using a valve spring compressor

13.5b Remove the collets with needle-nose pliers, tweezers, a magnet or a screwdriver with a dab of grease on it

5 Compress the valve spring on the first valve with a spring compressor, making sure it is correctly located onto each end of the valve assembly **(see illustration)**. On the underside of the head make sure the plate on the compressor only contacts the valve and not the soft aluminium of the head – if the plate is too big for the valve, use a spacer between them. Do not compress the springs any more than is absolutely necessary. Remove the collets, using either needle-nose pliers, tweezers, a magnet or a screwdriver with a dab of grease on it **(see illustration)**. Carefully release the valve spring compressor and remove the spring retainer, noting which way up it fits, the outer and inner springs and the spring seat from the top of the head, and the valve from the underside of the head **(see illustration 13.3)**. If the valve binds in the guide (won't pull through), push it back into the head and deburr the area around the collet groove with a very fine file or whetstone **(see illustration)**.

6 Repeat the procedure for the remaining valves. Remember to keep the parts for each valve together and in order so they can be reinstalled in the same location.

7 Once the valves have been removed and labelled, pull the valve stem seals off the top of the valve guides with pliers and discard them (the old seals should never be reused).

8 Next, clean the cylinder head with solvent and dry it thoroughly. Compressed air will speed the drying process and ensure that all holes and recessed areas are clean.

9 Clean all of the valve springs, collets, retainers and spring seats with solvent and dry them thoroughly. Do the parts from one valve at a time so that no mixing of parts between valves occurs.

10 Scrape off any deposits that may have formed on the valve, then use a motorised wire brush to remove deposits from the valve heads and stems. Again, make sure the valves do not get mixed up.

Inspection

11 Inspect the head very carefully for cracks and other damage. If cracks are found, a new head will be required. Check the cam bearing surfaces for wear and evidence of seizure. Check the camshafts for wear as well (see Section 10).

12 Using a precision straight-edge and a feeler gauge set to the warpage limit listed in the specifications at the beginning of the Chapter, check the head gasket mating surface for warpage. Refer to Section 3 in *Tools and Workshop Tips* in the *Reference* section for details of how to use the straight-edge.

13 Examine the valve seats in the combustion chamber. If they are pitted, cracked or burned, the head will require work beyond the scope of the home mechanic. Measure the valve seat width and compare it to this Chapter's Specifications **(see illustration)**. If it exceeds the service limit, or if it varies around its circumference, valve overhaul is required. If available, use Prussian blue to determine the extent of valve seat wear. Uniformly coat the seat with the Prussian blue, then install the valve and rotate it back and forth using a lapping tool. Remove the valve and check whether the ring of blue on the valve is uniform and continuous around the valve, and of the correct width as specified.

14 Measure the valve stem diameter **(see illustration)**. Clean the valve guides to remove any carbon build-up, then measure

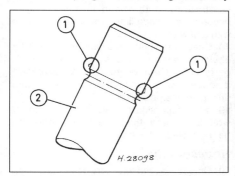

13.5c If the valve stem (2) won't pull through the guide, deburr the area above the collet groove (1)

13.13 Measure the valve seat width with a ruler (or for greater precision use a vernier caliper)

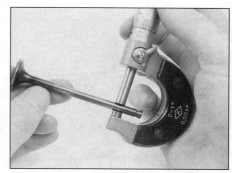

13.14a Measure the valve stem diameter with a micrometer

2•18 Engine, clutch and transmission

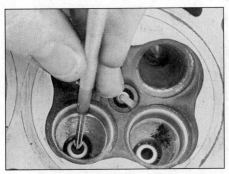

13.14b Insert a small hole gauge into the valve guide and expand it so there's a slight drag when it's pulled out

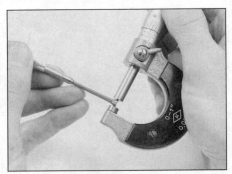

13.14c Measure the small hole gauge with a micrometer

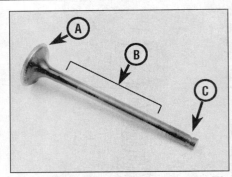

13.15a Check the valve face (A), stem (B) and collet groove (C) for signs of wear and damage

the inside diameters of the guides (at both ends and the centre of the guide) with a small hole gauge and micrometer **(see illustrations)**. The guides are measured at the ends and at the centre to determine if they are worn in a bell-mouth pattern (more wear at the ends). Subtract the stem diameter from the valve guide diameter to obtain the valve stem-to-guide clearance. If the stem-to-guide clearance is greater than listed in this Chapter's Specifications, renew whichever components are worn beyond their specification limits. If the valve guide is within specifications, but is worn unevenly, it should be renewed.

15 Carefully inspect each valve face, stem and collet groove area for cracks, pits and burned spots **(see illustration)**. Measure the valve margin thickness and compare it to the specifications **(see illustrations)**. If it is thinner than specified, replace the valve with a new one. The margin is the portion of the valve head which is below the valve seat.

16 Rotate the valve and check for any obvious indication that it is bent. Using V-blocks and a dial gauge if available, measure the valve stem runout and compare the results to the specifications **(see illustration)**. If the measurement exceeds the service limit specified, the valve must be replaced with a new one.

17 Check the end of each valve spring for wear and pitting. Measure the spring free lengths and compare them to the specifications **(see illustration)**. If any spring is shorter than specified it has sagged and must be replaced with a new one. Also place the spring upright on a flat surface and check it for bend by placing a ruler against it **(see illustration)**. If the bend in any spring is beyond the service limit, it must be replaced with a new one.

18 Check the spring retainers and collets for obvious wear and cracks. Any questionable parts should not be reused, as extensive damage will occur in the event of failure during engine operation.

19 If the inspection indicates that no overhaul work is required, the valve components can be reinstalled in the head.

Reassembly

20 Unless a valve service has been performed, before installing the valves in the head they should be ground in (lapped) to ensure a positive seal between the valves and

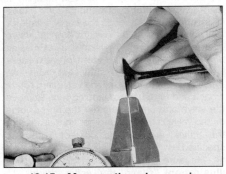

13.15b Valve head measurement points

A Head diameter   B Face width   C Seat width   D Margin thickness

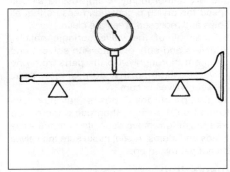

13.16 Check the valve stem for runout using V-blocks and a dial gauge

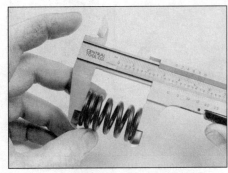

13.15c Measure the valve margin thickness as shown

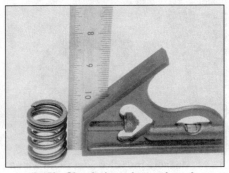

13.17a Measure the free length of the valve springs

13.17b Check the valve springs for squareness

Engine, clutch and transmission 2•19

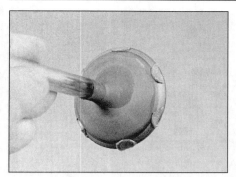

13.21 Apply the lapping compound very sparingly, in small dabs, to the valve face only

13.22a Rotate the valve grinding tool back and forth between the palms of your hands

13.22b The valve face and seat should show a uniform unbroken ring . . .

seats. This procedure requires coarse and fine valve grinding compound and a valve grinding tool. If a grinding tool is not available, a piece of rubber or plastic hose can be slipped over the valve stem (after the valve has been installed in the guide) and used to turn the valve.

21 Apply a small amount of coarse grinding compound to the valve face and some molybdenum disulphide oil (a 50/50 mixture of molybdenum disulphide grease and engine oil) to the valve stem, then slip the valve into the guide (see illustration). Note: *Make sure each valve is installed in its correct guide and be careful not to get any grinding compound on the valve stem.*

22 Attach the grinding tool (or hose) to the valve and rotate the tool between the palms of your hands. Use a back-and-forth motion (as though rubbing your hands together) rather than a circular motion (i.e. so that the valve rotates alternately clockwise and anti-clockwise rather than in one direction only) (see illustration). Lift the valve off the seat and turn it at regular intervals to distribute the grinding compound properly. Continue the grinding procedure until the valve face and seat contact area is of uniform width and unbroken around the entire circumference of the valve face and seat (see illustrations).

23 Carefully remove the valve from the guide and wipe off all traces of grinding compound.

Use solvent to clean the valve and wipe the seat area thoroughly with a solvent soaked cloth.

24 Repeat the procedure with fine valve grinding compound, then repeat the entire procedure for the remaining valves.

25 Working on one valve at a time, lay the spring seat in place in the cylinder head (if the seat is shouldered, fit it with its shouldered side up so that it fits into the spring) (see illustration).

26 Using an appropriate size deep socket, fit a new valve stem seal onto the guide, using the socket to push the seal over the end of the valve guide until it is felt to clip into place (see illustration). Don't twist or cock the seal, or it will not seal properly against the valve stem.

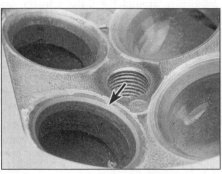

13.22c . . . and the seat (arrowed) should be the specified width all the way round

Also, don't remove it again or it will be damaged.

27 Coat the valve stem with molybdenum disulphide oil (a 50/50 mixture of molybdenum disulphide grease and engine oil), then install it into its guide, rotating it slowly to avoid damaging the seal (see illustration). Check that the valve moves up and down freely in the guide.

28 Next, install the inner and outer springs, with their closer-wound coils facing down into the cylinder head, followed by the spring retainer, with its shouldered side facing down so that it fits into the top of the spring (see illustrations).

29 Apply a small amount of grease to the collets to help hold them in place as the pressure is released from the spring (see

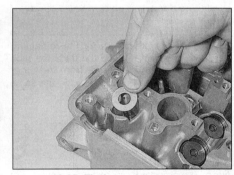

13.25 Fit the spring seat . . .

13.26 . . . then press the valve stem seal into position using a suitable deep socket

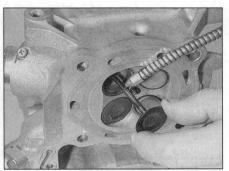

13.27 Lubricate the stem and slide the valve into its correct location

13.28a Fit the valve spring with its closer wound coils facing down. . .

2•20 Engine, clutch and transmission

13.28b ... then fit the spring retainer

13.29a A small dab of grease will help to keep the collets in place on the valve while the spring is released

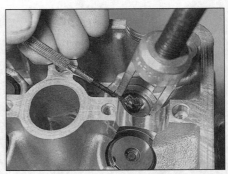

13.29b Compress the springs and install the collets, making sure they locate in the groove

illustration). Compress the spring with the valve spring compressor and install the collets (see illustration). When compressing the spring, do so only as far as is necessary to slip the collets into place. Make certain that the collets are securely locked in the retaining groove.

30 Support the cylinder head on blocks so the valves can't contact the workbench top, then very gently tap the valve stem with a soft-faced hammer. This will help seat the collets in the groove.

 Check for proper sealing of the valves by pouring a small amount of solvent into each of the valve ports. If the solvent leaks past any valve into the combustion chamber area the valve grinding operation on that valve should be repeated.

31 Repeat the procedure for the remaining valves. Remember to keep the parts for each valve together and separate from the other valves so they can be reinstalled in the same location.

14 Cylinder block – removal, inspection and installation

Note: *The cylinder block can be removed with the engine in the frame.*

Removal

1 Remove the cylinder head (see Section 11).
2 Unscrew the nut securing the front of the cylinder block to the crankcase and remove the washer (see illustration).
3 Hold the cam chain up and lift the cylinder block off the crankcase, then pass the cam chain down through the tunnel (see illustration). Do not let the chain fall into the crankcase – secure it with a piece of wire or metal bar to prevent it from doing so. If the block is stuck, tap around the joint faces of the block with a soft-faced mallet to free it from the crankcase. Don't attempt to free the block by inserting a screwdriver between it and the crankcase – you'll damage the sealing surfaces. When the block is removed, stuff clean rags around the pistons to prevent anything falling into the crankcase.
4 Remove the gasket and the four large O-rings from the base of each cylinder and clean all traces of old gasket material from the cylinder block and crankcase mating surfaces. If a scraper is used, take care not to scratch or gouge the soft aluminium. Be careful not to let any of the gasket material fall into the crankcase or the oil passages.
5 Remove the dowels from the mating surface of the crankcase or the underside of the block if they are loose (see illustration 14.16a). Be careful not to drop them into the engine. Note which fits where as they are different.

Inspection

Caution: *Do not attempt to separate the liners from the cylinder block.*

6 Check the cylinder walls carefully for scratches and score marks.
7 Using a precision straight-edge and a feeler gauge set to the warpage limit listed in the specifications at the beginning of the Chapter, check the block gasket mating surface for warpage. Refer to Section 3 in *Tools and Workshop Tips* in the *Reference* section for details of how to use the straight-edge. If warpage is excessive the block must be replaced with a new one.
8 Using telescoping gauges and a micrometer (see Section 3 in *Tools and Workshop Tips* in the *Reference* section), check the dimensions of each cylinder to assess the amount of wear, taper and ovality. Measure near the top (but below the level of the top piston ring at TDC), centre and bottom (but above the level of the oil ring at BDC) of the bore, both parallel to and across the crankshaft axis (see illustration). Compare the results to the specifications at the beginning of the Chapter.
9 If the precision measuring tools are not available, take the block to a Yamaha dealer or specialist motorcycle repair shop for assessment and advice.
10 If the cylinders are worn beyond the service limits, or badly scratched, scuffed or scored, the cylinder block must be either be

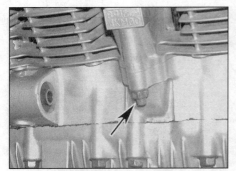

14.2 Unscrew the nut (arrowed) and remove the washer

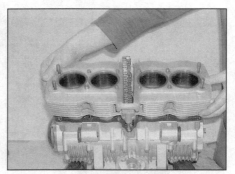

14.3 Lift the block up off the studs

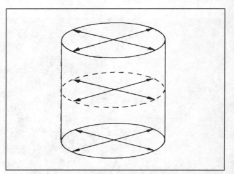

14.8 Measure the cylinder bore in the directions shown with a telescoping gauge, then measure the gauge with a micrometer

Engine, clutch and transmission 2•21

14.15 Check the cylinder base O-rings (arrowed) and replace them with new ones if necessary

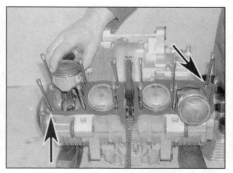

14.16 Make sure the dowels (arrowed) are installed, then fit the gasket

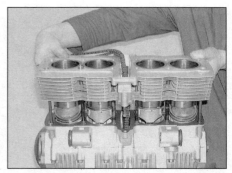

14.19 Carefully feed the rings in using a screwdriver and/or fingernails as you lower the block

replaced with a new one, or it can be rebored by a Yamaha dealer or specialist motorcycle repair shop. Yamaha supply two oversize piston and ring sets, +0.5 mm and +1.0 mm.
11 If the block and cylinders are in good condition and the piston-to-bore clearance is within specifications (see Section 15), the cylinders should be honed (de-glazed). To perform this operation you will need the proper size flexible hone with fine stones (see *Specialist Tools* in *Tools and Workshop Tips* in the *Reference* section), or a bottle-brush type hone, plenty of light oil or honing oil, some clean rags and an electric drill.
12 Hold the block sideways (so that the bores are horizontal rather than vertical) in a vice with soft jaws or cushioned with wooden blocks. Mount the hone in the drill motor, compress the stones and insert the hone into the cylinder. Thoroughly lubricate the cylinder, then turn on the drill and move the hone up and down in the cylinder at a pace which produces a fine cross-hatch pattern on the cylinder wall with the lines intersecting at an angle of approximately 60 degrees. Be sure to use plenty of lubricant and do not take off any more material than is necessary to produce the desired effect. Do not withdraw the hone from the cylinder while it is still turning. Switch off the drill and continue to move it up and down in the cylinder until it has stopped turning, then compress the stones and withdraw the hone. Wipe the oil from the cylinder and repeat the procedure on the other cylinder. Remember, do not take too much material from the cylinder wall.
13 Wash the cylinders thoroughly with warm soapy water to remove all traces of the abrasive grit produced during the honing operation. Be sure to run a brush through the bolt holes and flush them with running water. After rinsing, dry the cylinders thoroughly and apply a thin coat of light, rust-preventative oil to all machined surfaces.
14 If you do not have the equipment or desire to perform the honing operation, take the block to a Yamaha dealer or specialist motorcycle repair shop.

Installation

15 Check the condition of the O-rings fitted around the base of each cylinder and replace them with new ones if necessary **(see illustration)**. Check that the mating surfaces of the cylinder block and crankcase are free from oil or pieces of old gasket.
16 If removed, fit the dowels into the crankcase **(see illustration)**. Remove the rags from around the pistons. Lay the new base gasket in place on the crankcase, making sure it locates correctly over the dowels and all the holes are correctly aligned. Never re-use the old gasket.
17 If required, install piston ring clamps onto the pistons to ease their entry into the bores as the block is lowered. This is not essential as each cylinder has a good lead-in enabling the piston rings to be hand-fed into the bore.

If possible, have an assistant to support the block while this is done.

> **HAYNES HiNT** *Rotate the crankshaft until the inner pistons (2 and 3) are uppermost and feed them into the block first. Access to the lower pistons (1 and 4) is easier since they are on the outside.*

18 Lubricate the cylinder bores, pistons and piston rings, and the connecting rod big- and small-ends, with clean engine oil, then fit the block down over the studs until the uppermost piston crowns fit into the bores. At this stage feed the cam chain up through the block and secure it in place with a piece of wire to prevent it from falling back down.
19 Gently push down on the cylinder block, making sure the pistons enter the bores squarely and do not get cocked sideways. If piston ring clamps are not being used, carefully compress and feed each ring into the bore as the block is lowered **(see illustration)**. If necessary, use a soft mallet to gently tap the block down, but do not use force if the block appears to be stuck as the pistons and/or rings will be damaged. If clamps are used, remove them once the pistons are in the bore.
20 When the pistons are correctly installed in the cylinders, press the block down onto the base gasket, making sure it locates correctly onto the dowels.
21 Install the front nut with its washer and tighten it to the torque setting specified at the beginning of the Chapter **(see illustrations)**.
22 Install the cylinder head (see Section 11).

15 Pistons – removal, inspection and installation

Note: *The pistons can be removed with the engine in the frame.*

Removal

1 Remove the cylinder block (see Section 14).
2 Before removing a piston from its

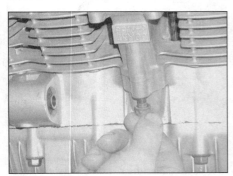

14.21a Fit the nut with its washer . . .

14.21b . . . and tighten it to the specified torque

2•22 Engine, clutch and transmission

15.3a Prise out the circlip ...

15.3b ... then push out the pin and remove the piston

15.5 Removing the piston rings using a ring removal and installation tool

connecting rod, and if not already done, stuff a clean rag into the hole around the rod to prevent the circlips or anything else from falling into the crankcase. Use a sharp scriber or felt marker pen to write the cylinder identity on the crown of each piston (or on the inside of the skirt if the piston is dirty and going to be cleaned) as it must be installed in its original cylinder. Each piston should also have an arrow on its crown which should point to the exhaust (front) side of the bore. If this is not visible, mark the piston accordingly so that it can be installed the correct way round.

3 Carefully prise out the circlip on one side of the piston using needle-nose pliers or a small flat-bladed screwdriver inserted into the notch **(see illustration)**. Push the piston pin out from the other side to free the piston from the connecting rod **(see illustration)**. Remove the other circlip and discard them as new ones must be used. When the piston has been removed, install its pin back into its bore so that related parts do not get mixed up. Rotate the crankshaft so that the best access is obtained for each piston.

 To prevent the circlip from pinging away, pass a rod or screwdriver, whose diameter is greater than the gap between the circlip ends, through the piston pin. This will trap the circlip if it springs out.

 If a piston pin is a tight fit in the piston bosses, soak a rag in boiling water then wring it out and wrap it around the piston – this will expand the alloy piston sufficiently to release its grip on the pin. If the piston pin is particularly stubborn, extract it using a drawbolt tool, but be careful to protect the piston's working surfaces.

Inspection

4 Before the inspection process can be carried out, the pistons must be cleaned and the old piston rings removed.
5 Using your thumbs or a piston ring removal and installation tool, carefully remove the rings from the pistons **(see illustration)**. Do not nick or gouge the pistons in the process. Carefully note which way up each ring fits and in which groove as they must be installed in their original positions if being re-used. The upper surface of each ring should have a manufacturer's mark or letter at one end.

6 Scrape all traces of carbon from the tops of the pistons. A hand-held wire brush or a piece of fine emery cloth can be used once most of the deposits have been scraped away. Do not, under any circumstances, use a wire brush mounted in a drill motor to remove deposits from the pistons; the piston material is soft and will be eroded away by the wire brush.

7 Use a piston ring groove cleaning tool to remove any carbon deposits from the ring grooves. If a tool is not available, a piece broken off an old ring will do the job. Be very careful to remove only the carbon deposits. Do not remove any metal and do not nick or gouge the sides of the ring grooves.

8 Once the deposits have been removed, clean the pistons with solvent and dry them thoroughly. If the identification previously marked on the piston is cleaned off, be sure to re-mark it with the correct identity. Make sure the oil return holes below the oil ring groove are clear.

9 Carefully inspect each piston for cracks around the skirt, at the pin bosses and at the ring lands. Normal piston wear appears as even, vertical wear on the thrust surfaces of the piston and slight looseness of the top ring in its groove. If the skirt is scored or scuffed, the engine may have been suffering from overheating and/or abnormal combustion, which caused excessively high operating temperatures. The oil pump should be checked thoroughly. Also check that the circlip grooves are not damaged.

10 A hole in the piston crown, an extreme to be sure, is an indication that abnormal combustion (pre-ignition) was occurring. Burned areas at the edge of the piston crown are usually evidence of spark knock (detonation). If any of the above problems exist, the causes must be corrected or the damage will occur again.

11 Measure the piston ring-to-groove clearance by laying each piston ring in its groove and slipping a feeler gauge in beside it **(see illustration)**. Make sure you have the correct ring for the groove (see Step 5). Check the clearance at three or four locations around the groove. If the clearance is greater than specified, renew both the piston and rings as a set. If new rings are being used, measure the clearance using the new rings. If the clearance is greater than that specified, the piston is worn and must be renewed.

12 Check the piston-to-bore clearance by measuring the bore (see Section 14) and the piston diameter. Make sure each piston is matched to its correct cylinder. Measure the piston 5.5 mm up from the bottom of the skirt and at 90° to the piston pin axis **(see illustration)**. Subtract the piston diameter from the bore diameter to obtain the clearance. If it is greater than the specified figure, the piston must be renewed (assuming the bore itself is within limits, otherwise the

15.11 Measure the piston ring-to-groove clearance with a feeler gauge

15.12 Measure the piston diameter with a micrometer at the specified distance from the bottom of the skirt

Engine, clutch and transmission 2•23

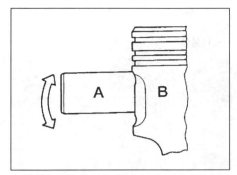

15.13a Slip the pin (A) into the piston (B) and try to rock it back and forth. If it's loose, renew the piston and pin

15.13b Measure the external diameter of the pin . . .

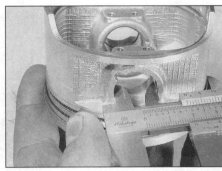

15.13c . . . and the internal diameter of the bore in the piston

cylinder block must be rebored – Yamaha supply two oversize piston and ring sets, +0.5 mm and +1.0 mm).

13 Apply clean engine oil to the piston pin, insert it into the piston and check for any freeplay between the two **(see illustration)**. Measure the pin external diameter, and the pin bore in the piston **(see illustrations)**. Calculate the difference to obtain the piston pin-to-piston pin bore clearance. Compare the result to the specifications at the beginning of the Chapter. If the clearance is greater than specified, renew the components that are worn beyond their specified limits. Repeat the checks between the pin and the connecting rod small-end (see Section 29).

14 Remove the two small-end oil jets – they are a push-fit **(see illustration)**. Discard their O-rings as new ones must be used. Clean the jets in solvent and blow them through, using compressed air if available, to ensure they are not blocked. Fit a new O-ring onto each jet and press them back into the crankcase **(see illustration)**.

Installation

15 Inspect and install the piston rings (see Section 16).
16 Lubricate the piston pin, the piston pin

15.14a Pull the two oil jets out of the crankcase

bore and the connecting rod small-end bore with clean engine oil.

17 Install a **new** circlip in the inner side of the piston (do not re-use old circlips). Line up the piston on its correct connecting rod, making sure the arrow on the piston crown points forwards, and insert the piston pin from the other side **(see illustration)**. Secure the pin with the other **new** circlip. When installing the circlips, compress them only just enough to fit them in the piston, and make sure they are properly seated in their grooves with the open end away from the removal notch **(see illustration)**.

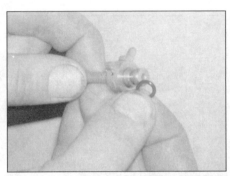

15.14b Remove the old O-rings and fit new ones

18 Install the cylinder block (see Section 14).

16 Piston rings – inspection and installation

1 It is good practice to renew the piston rings when an engine is being overhauled. Before installing the new piston rings, the ring end gaps must be checked with the rings installed in the cylinder.

15.17a Align the piston with the rod, making sure the arrow points forward, and insert the pin

15.17b Do not over-compress the circlips and make sure they seat in the groove

2•24 Engine, clutch and transmission

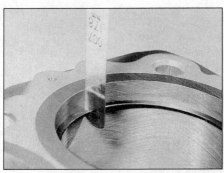

16.3 Measuring piston ring installed end gap

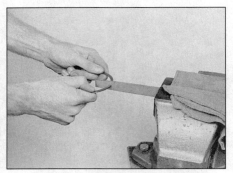

16.5 Ring end gap can be enlarged by clamping a file in a vice and filing the ring ends

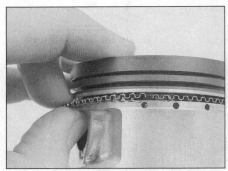

16.9a Install the oil ring expander in its groove . . .

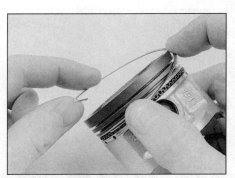

16.9b . . . and fit the side rails each side of it. The oil ring must be installed by hand

2 Lay out the pistons and the new ring sets so the rings will be matched with the same piston and cylinder during the end gap measurement procedure and engine assembly.
3 To measure the installed ring end gap, insert the top ring into the top of the first cylinder and square it up with the cylinder walls by pushing it in with the top of the piston. The ring should be about 20 mm below the top edge of the cylinder. To measure the end gap, slip a feeler gauge between the ends of the ring and compare the measurement to the specifications at the beginning of the Chapter (see illustration).
4 If the gap is larger or smaller than specified, double check to make sure that you have the correct rings before proceeding.
5 If the gap is too small, it must be enlarged or the ring ends may come in contact with each other during engine operation, which can cause serious damage. The end gap can be increased by filing the ring ends very carefully with a fine file. When performing this operation, file only from the outside in (see illustration).
6 Excess end gap is not critical unless it exceeds the service limit. Again, double-check to make sure you have the correct rings for your engine and check that the bore is not worn.
7 Repeat the procedure for each ring that will be installed in the cylinders. When checking the oil ring, only the side-rails can be checked as the ends of the expander ring should contact each other. Remember to keep the rings, pistons and cylinders matched up.
8 Once the ring end gaps have been checked/corrected, the rings can be installed on the pistons.
9 The oil control ring (lowest on the piston) is installed first. It is composed of three separate components, namely the expander and the upper and lower side rails. Slip the expander into the groove, then install the upper side rail (see illustration). Do not use a piston ring installation tool on the oil ring side rails as they may be damaged. Instead, place one end of the side rail into the groove between the expander and the ring land (see illustration). Hold it firmly in place and slide a finger around the piston while pushing the rail into the groove. Next, install the lower side rail in the same manner. Make sure the ends of the expander do not overlap.
10 After the three oil ring components have been installed, check to make sure that both the upper and lower side rails can be turned smoothly in the ring groove.
11 The upper surface of each compression ring should have a mark or letter at one end which must face up when the ring is installed on the piston. The first and second rings are distinguishable from each other by their different profiles (see illustration).
12 Fit the second ring into the middle groove in the piston. Do not expand the ring any more than is necessary to slide it into place. To avoid breaking the ring, use a piston ring installation tool (see illustration 15.5), or pieces of old feeler gauge blades (see illustration).
13 Finally, install the top ring in the same manner into the top groove in the piston.
14 Once the rings are correctly installed, check they move freely without snagging and stagger their end gaps as shown (see illustration).

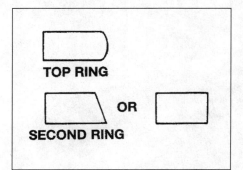

16.11 The rings can be identified by their different profiles

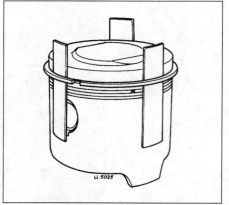

16.12 Old pieces of feeler gauge blade can be used to guide the ring over the piston

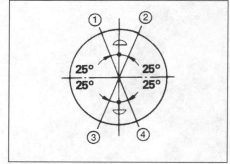

16.14 Stagger the ring end gaps as shown

1 Top compression ring
2 Oil ring lower rail
3 Oil ring upper rail
4 Second compression ring

Engine, clutch and transmission 2•25

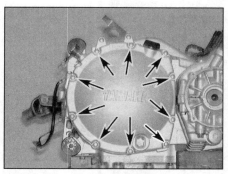

17.3 Unscrew the bolts (arrowed) and remove the cover

17 Clutch – removal, inspection and installation

Note: *The clutch can be removed with the engine in the frame. If the engine has been removed, ignore the steps which don't apply.*

Removal

1 Drain the engine oil (see Chapter 1).
2 Detach the clutch cable from the release lever on the clutch cover (see Section 18).
3 Working evenly in a criss-cross pattern, unscrew the clutch cover bolts **(see illustration)**. Lift the cover away from the engine, being prepared to catch any residual oil which may be released as the cover is removed.
4 Remove the gasket and discard it. Note the positions of the two locating dowels fitted to the crankcase and remove them for safekeeping if they are loose – if they are not in the crankcase they will be in the cover.
5 Working in a criss-cross pattern, gradually slacken the clutch pressure plate bolts until spring pressure is released **(see illustrations)**. Counter-hold the clutch housing to prevent it turning. Remove the bolts and springs, then lift out the clutch pressure plate complete with its pull-rod, thrust bearing and plate washer **(see illustration)**.
6 Grasp the complete set of clutch plates and remove them as a pack **(see illustration)**. Unless the plates are being replaced with new ones, keep them in their original order.

17.5b Unscrew the pressure plate bolts (arrowed) and remove the springs . . .

17.5c . . . then remove the pressure plate

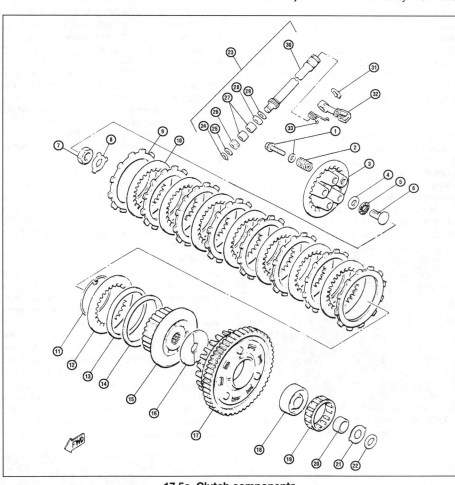

17.5a Clutch components

1 Pressure plate bolts and washers	12 Plain plate	23 Clutch release assembly
2 Clutch spring	13 Anti-judder spring	24 E-clip
3 Pressure plate	14 Spring seat	25 Washer
4 Washer	15 Clutch centre	26 Pinion
5 Thrust bearing	16 Thrust plate	27 Needle roller bearings
6 Pull-rod	17 Clutch housing	28 Oil seal
7 Clutch nut	18 Sleeve	29 Washer
8 Lockwasher	19 Needle roller bearing	30 Actuating shaft
9 Friction plate	20 Collar	31 E-clip
10 Plain plate	21 Oil pump drive sprocket	32 Clutch release lever
11 Wire retainer ring	22 Thrust washer	33 Return spring

17.6 Draw off the clutch plates as a pack

2•26 Engine, clutch and transmission

17.7a Bend back the lockwasher tabs . . .

17.7b . . . then unscrew the clutch nut as described and remove the lockwasher

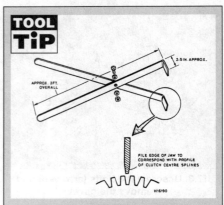

A clutch centre holding tool can easily be made using two strips of steel with the ends bent over, and bolted together in the middle

7 Bend back the tabs on the clutch nut lockwasher **(see illustration)**. To remove the clutch nut the transmission input shaft must be locked. This can be done in several ways. If the engine is in the frame, engage 1st gear and have an assistant hold the rear brake on hard with the rear tyre in firm contact with the ground. Alternatively, the Yamaha service tool (Pt. No. 90890-04086), or a similar commercially available or home-made tool (made from two strips of steel bent at the ends and bolted together in the middle – see **Tool tip**), can be used to stop the clutch centre from turning whilst the nut is slackened **(see illustration)**. Unscrew the nut and remove the lockwasher from the mainshaft, noting how it fits. Discard the lockwasher as a new one must be used on installation.

8 Remove the clutch centre and the thrust plate from the shaft **(see illustrations 17.27a and 17.26)**.
9 Support the clutch housing and remove the large sleeve from its centre **(see illustration)**. To get a grip on the sleeve, grasp the housing and wiggle it out and in – it should draw the sleeve out far enough to grip it. If difficulty is experienced in getting a grip on the sleeve, install a 6 mm bolt (a clutch cover bolt is the correct size) into one or both of the threaded holes and pull the sleeve from the housing.
10 Remove the caged needle roller bearing from the housing if it didn't come away with the sleeve, and then remove the housing from the engine **(see illustrations 17.25a and 17.24b)**.
11 Note the two tabs on the oil pump drive sprocket behind the clutch housing which must locate in the slots in the housing on reassembly. Remove the collar from the centre of the oil pump drive sprocket, then disengage the pump drive chain and remove the sprocket **(see illustrations 17.23c and b)**. Remove the thrust washer from behind the sprocket **(see illustration 17.23a)**.
12 If required, remove the oil deflector plate, noting how it fits **(see illustration)**.
13 The clutch centre anti-judder assembly can be left intact unless the clutch has been chattering (juddering) excessively. If it is necessary to remove it, remove the wire retainer ring, plain plate, anti-judder spring and spring seat, noting how they fit **(see illustration)**.

Inspection

14 After an extended period of service the clutch friction plates will wear and promote clutch slip. Measure the thickness of each friction plate using a vernier caliper **(see illustration)**. If any plate has worn to or beyond the service limit given in the Specifications at the beginning of the Chapter, the friction plates must be renewed as a set. Also, if any of the plates smell burnt or are glazed, they must be renewed as a set.
15 The plain plates should not show any signs of excess heating (bluing). Check for warpage using a flat surface and feeler gauges **(see illustration)**. If any plate exceeds

17.9 Remove the inner sleeve and bearing as described

17.12 Note how the deflector plate locates before removing it

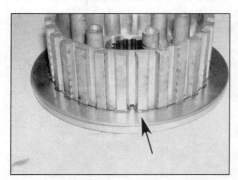

17.13 The anti-judder assembly is held by the wire retainer (arrowed)

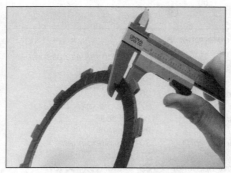

17.14 Measuring clutch friction plate thickness

17.15 Check the plain plates for warpage

Engine, clutch and transmission 2•27

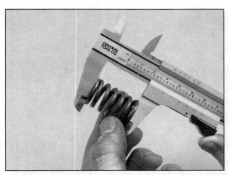

17.16 Measure the free length of the springs as shown

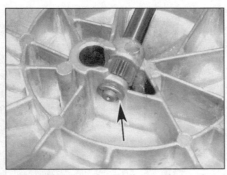

17.21 Remove the E-clip to release the shaft

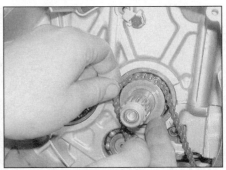

17.23a Slide on the thrust washer . . .

the maximum permissible amount of warpage, or shows signs of bluing, all plain plates must be renewed as a set.

16 Measure the free length of each clutch spring using a vernier caliper **(see illustration)**. If any spring is below the service limit specified, renew all the springs as a set.

17 Inspect the clutch assembly for burrs and indentations on the edges of the protruding tangs of the friction plates and/or slots in the edge of the housing with which they engage. Similarly check for wear between the inner tongues of the plain plates and the slots in the clutch centre. Wear of this nature will cause clutch drag and slow disengagement during gear changes, since the plates will snag when the pressure plate is lifted. With care a small amount of wear can be corrected by dressing with a fine file, but if this is excessive the worn components should be replaced with new ones.

18 Inspect the sleeve and caged needle roller bearing in conjunction with the clutch housing's internal bearing surface. If there are any signs of wear, pitting or other damage the affected parts must be replaced with new ones.

19 Check the pressure plate, thrust bearing and plate washer for signs of roughness, wear or damage, and renew any parts as necessary.

20 If removed, check the clutch centre anti-judder assembly components (consisting of the wire retainer ring, plain plate, anti-judder spring and spring seat) for wear or damage, and renew any parts as necessary.

21 Check the clutch release mechanism in the clutch cover for smooth operation. Check the pinion and pull-rod teeth for signs of damage. If necessary, prise off the E-clip securing the pinion to the actuating shaft, and withdraw the shaft from the cover **(see illustration)**. Check the two needle roller bearings for roughness, wear or damage. If they need to be renewed, heat the cover in very hot water to ease removal and drift them out. If the shaft is removed, lever out the oil seal and replace it

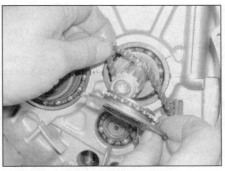

17.23b . . . then engage the chain with the oil pump drive sprocket . . .

with a new one. Clean all components and lubricate the seal and bearings with grease.

Installation

22 Remove all traces of old gasket from the crankcase and clutch cover surfaces. If disassembled, reassemble the clutch centre anti-judder assembly components, fitting the spring seat, the anti-judder spring, the plain plate and the wire retainer ring in that order **(see illustration 17.13)**. Make sure that both ends of the wire retainer ring fit into the hole in the clutch centre.

23 Install the oil pump drive sprocket thrust

17.24a Align the housing so the drive tabs (A) fit into the holes (B) . . .

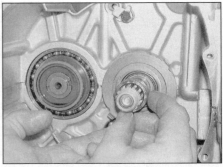

17.23c . . . and fit the collar into the centre of the sprocket

washer against the shaft bearing, then install the drive sprocket and engage it with the oil pump drive chain **(see illustrations)**. Slide the collar into the centre of the drive sprocket **(see illustration)**.

24 Lubricate the needle roller bearing and sleeve with clean engine oil. Install the clutch housing, without its needle roller bearing and sleeve, and support it in position, making sure it is engaged correctly with the primary drive gear on the crankshaft, and that the drive tabs on the oil pump sprocket locate in the holes in the back of the housing **(see illustrations)**.

25 Install the needle bearing and the sleeve into the middle of the clutch housing, making

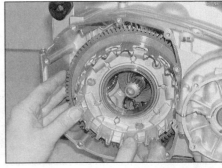

17.24b . . . then install the housing

2

2•28 Engine, clutch and transmission

17.25a Fit the needle bearing . . .

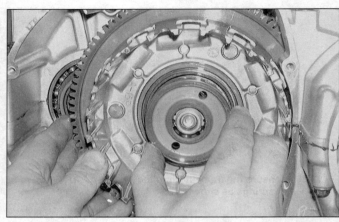

17.25b . . . and the sleeve into the middle of the housing

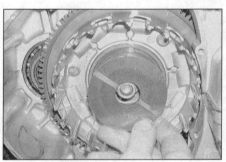

17.26 Slide the thrust plate onto the shaft . . .

sure the bolt holes in the sleeve face out **(see illustrations)**.

26 Lubricate the thrust plate with clean engine oil and fit it onto the shaft **(see illustration)**.

27 Install the clutch centre onto the shaft splines, then install the new lockwasher, engaging its tabs with the slots **(see illustrations)**. Install the clutch nut and, using the method employed on dismantling to lock the input shaft, tighten the nut to the torque setting specified at the beginning of the Chapter **(see illustrations)**. **Note:** *Check that the clutch centre rotates freely after tightening.* Bend up the tabs of the lockwasher to secure the nut **(see illustration)**.

28 Build up the clutch plates, starting with a friction plate, then a plain plate and alternating friction and plain plates until all are installed **(see illustrations)**. Coat each plate with engine oil prior to installation.

29 Lubricate the clutch release thrust bearing and washer with molybdenum disulphide oil (a 50/50 mixture of molybdenum disulphide grease and engine oil). Install the thrust bearing and plate washer onto the pull-rod, then install the pull-rod assembly in through

17.27a . . . then install the clutch centre

17.27b Install the lockwasher, fitting the smaller bent tabs into the slots in the centre (arrows)

17.27c Fit the nut . . .

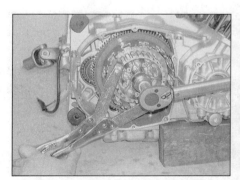

17.27d . . . and tighten it to the specified torque . . .

17.27e . . . then bend up the washer tabs

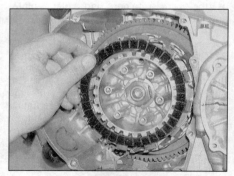

17.28a Fit a friction plate first . . .

Engine, clutch and transmission 2•29

17.28b . . . then a plain plate and so on

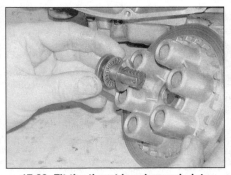

17.29 Fit the thrust bearing and plate washer onto the pull-rod, then fit the pull-rod assembly into the pressure plate

17.30a Install the pressure plate, aligning the dots

the back of the clutch pressure plate (see illustration).
30 Install the pressure plate onto the clutch, aligning the punchmark on the plate with that on the clutch centre (see illustration). Install the springs and the bolts with their washers, and tighten the bolts evenly in a criss-cross sequence to the specified torque setting (see illustrations). Counter-hold the clutch housing to prevent it turning. Check that the clutch release pull-rod rotates freely.
31 Install the oil deflector plate, making sure it is correctly fitted (see illustrations).
32 If disassembled, install the clutch release mechanism in the clutch cover. Align the shaft

so that the release lever is facing back but angled in slightly.
33 Insert the dowels in the crankcase, then set the pull-rod so that the teeth point towards the rear and are angled down at roughly 45°. Install the clutch cover using a new gasket and tighten its bolts evenly in a criss-cross sequence to the specified torque setting – the two long bolts go where the dowels are (see illustrations).
34 Push the clutch release lever forward until all the freeplay in the release mechanism has been taken up. At this point the mark on the lever should align with the mark on the cover (see illustration). If the marks do not align,

17.30b Install the springs and bolts . . .

17.30c . . . and tighten them as described to the specified torque

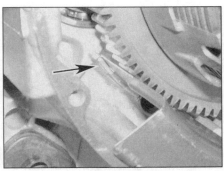

17.31a Make sure the deflector plate locates correctly at the back (arrowed) . . .

17.31b . . . and at the front (arrowed)

17.33a Fit the new gasket onto the dowels (arrowed) . . .

17.33b . . . then install the cover

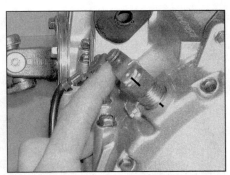

17.34 With the lever pushed forward, the marks should align

2•30 Engine, clutch and transmission

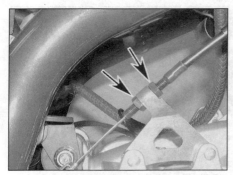

18.1a Slacken the nuts (arrowed) . . .

18.1b . . . and slip the cable out of the bracket

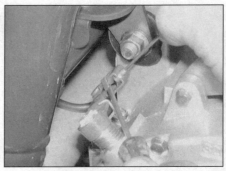

18.2a Bend up the retaining tab . . .

remove the E-clip and the lever, noting how the spring fits, and move the lever around on the splines of the shaft until they do. Make sure the spring is correctly set on the lever and install the E-clip.
35 Fit the clutch cable onto the lever (see Section 18).
36 Refill the engine with oil (see Chapter 1).

18 Clutch cable – removal and installation

1 Fully slacken the adjuster nuts on the threaded section in the cable bracket on the right-hand side of the engine and slip the adjuster out of the bracket **(see illustrations)**.
2 Bend back the retaining tab securing the cable end in the clutch release mechanism lever and disconnect the cable, noting how it fits **(see illustrations)**.
3 Pull back the rubber boot covering the adjuster at the handlebar end of the cable **(see illustration)**. Fully slacken the lockring on the adjuster then screw the adjuster fully in **(see illustration)**. This resets it to the beginning of its adjustment span.
4 Align the slots in the adjuster and lockwheel with that in the lever bracket, then pull the outer cable end from the socket in the adjuster and release the inner cable from the lever **(see illustrations)**. Remove the cable from the machine, noting its routing and any guides or clips.

HAYNES HINT Before removing the cable from the bike, tape the lower end of the new cable to the upper end of the old cable. Slowly pull the lower end of the old cable out, guiding the new cable down into position. Using this method will ensure the cable is routed correctly.

5 Installation is the reverse of removal. Apply grease to the cable ends. Make sure the cable is correctly routed. Secure the cable end in the release lever by bending the tab against it. Adjust the amount of clutch lever freeplay (see Chapter 1).

19 Gearchange mechanism – removal, inspection and installation

Note: *The gearchange mechanism can be removed with the engine in the frame. If the engine has been removed, ignore the steps which don't apply.*

Removal

1 Make sure the transmission is in neutral. Drain the engine oil (see Chapter 1). Release the clamp securing the breather hose to the top of the gearchange mechanism cover and detach the hose.
2 Unscrew the gearchange lever linkage arm pinch bolt and slide the arm off the shaft,

18.2b . . . then detach the cable end from the release arm

18.3a Pull back the rubber boot . . .

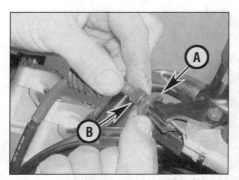

18.3b . . . then slacken the lockring (A) and thread the adjuster (B) in

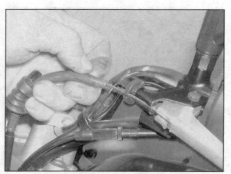

18.4a Align the slots and slip the cable out of the bracket . . .

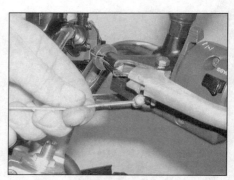

18.4b . . . and the cable nipple from the lever

Engine, clutch and transmission 2•31

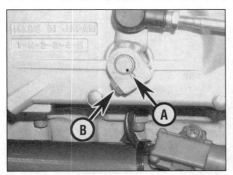

19.2 Note the alignment of the punchmark with the slit (A), then unscrew the pinchbolt (B)

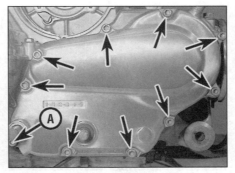

19.3a Unscrew the bolts (arrowed) and remove the cover, noting the position of the wiring guide (A)

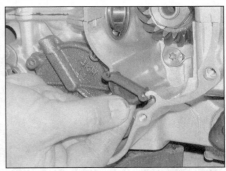

19.3b Remove the rubber fillet if required

noting any alignment marks **(see illustration)**. If no marks are visible, make your own before removing the arm so that it can be correctly aligned with the shaft on installation.

HAYNES HiNT *Apply some insulating tape to the splines on the gearchange shaft before removing the crankcase cover to avoid damaging the oil seal.*

3 Working in a criss-cross pattern, slacken the gearchange mechanism/middle gear shaft cover bolts, noting the positions of the longer ones and of the pick-up coil wiring guide **(see illustration)**. Lift the cover away from the engine, being prepared to catch any residual oil which may be released as the cover is removed. Remove the gasket and discard it. Note the positions of the two locating dowels fitted to the crankcase and remove them for safe-keeping if they are loose **(see illustration 19.14a)**. If required, remove the half-moon shaped rubber fillet from the cutout in the crankcase in the front lower wall of the middle gear housing **(see illustration)**.

4 Withdraw the centralising arm assembly from its recess in the crankcase, noting how the centralising spring ends fit on each side of the locating pin **(see illustration)**. Retrieve the washer if it didn't come away on the shaft.

5 Carefully note the locations of the selector arm, the stopper arm and their return springs, then lift the selector arm and stopper arm away from their positions on the selector drum end and withdraw the gearchange shaft assembly from its recess in the crankcase **(see illustration)**.

Inspection

6 Inspect the selector arm and the stopper arm return springs and the centralising arm spring. If they are worn or damaged they must be replaced with new ones. To remove the selector arm return spring, unhook it from its locating holes **(see illustration)**. Note which way round the stopper arm return spring fits, then slide the stopper arm off the gearchange shaft and install the new spring. To remove the centralising arm spring, prise off the E-clip and slide the spring off the shaft, noting how the spring ends locate on each side of the lug **(see illustration)**.

7 Check the gearchange shaft for straightness and damage to the splines. If the shaft is bent you can attempt to straighten it, but if the splines are damaged the shaft must be replaced with a new one.

8 Inspect the selector arm claw and the stopper arm roller and their contacts on the selector drum end **(see illustration)**. If they are worn or damaged they must be renewed.

9 Inspect the teeth where the gearchange shaft pawl meshes with the centralising arm. If they are worn or damaged they must be renewed.

19.4 Withdraw the centralising arm assembly, noting how it fits

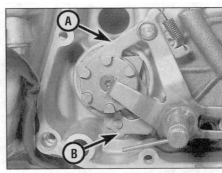

19.5 Gearchange mechanism selector arm (A) and stopper arm (B)

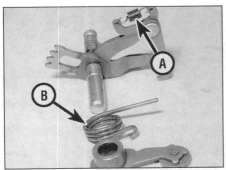

19.6a Selector arm spring (A) and stopper arm spring (B)

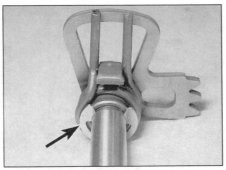

19.6b Prise off the E-clip to remove the spring

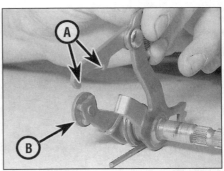

19.8 Selector arm claw (A) and stopper arm roller (B)

2•32 Engine, clutch and transmission

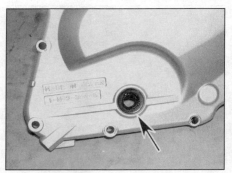

19.10 Check the oil seal (arrowed) and replace it with a new one if necessary

19.11a Install the gearchange shaft . . .

19.11b . . . making sure the stopper arm and spring ends locate as shown

10 Check the condition of the oil seal in the crankcase cover (see illustration). If it is worn or shows any signs of leakage, lever it out using a flat-bladed screwdriver and press in a new one.

Installation

11 Install the gearchange shaft assembly into its recess in the crankcase, lifting the selector arm and the stopper arm into position on the selector drum end, and making sure the return spring ends locate correctly (see illustrations).
12 Install the centralising arm with its washer into its recess in the crankcase, making sure that the spring ends fit on each side of the locating pin (see illustration). Make sure that

the teeth of the centralising arm mesh symmetrically with those of the gearchange arm pawl (see illustration).
13 Temporarily install the gearchange lever linkage arm and linkage and check that the mechanism works correctly before installing the cover.
14 If removed, fit the half-moon shaped rubber fillet in the cutout in the crankcase in the front lower wall of the middle gear housing (see illustration 19.3b). Fit the dowels into the crankcase, then fit the new gasket onto them (see illustration). Install the gearchange mechanism/middle gear shaft cover and tighten its bolts evenly in a criss-cross sequence to the torque setting specified at the beginning of the Chapter, making sure the

longer bolts are located with the dowels, and not forgetting the pick-up coil wiring clamp with the front one (see illustration).
15 Slide the gearchange linkage arm onto the shaft, aligning the marks, and tighten the pinch bolt (see illustration 19.2). Fit the breather hose onto its union on the cover and secure it with its clamp.
16 Refill the engine with oil (see Chapter 1).

20 Middle gear shafts – removal, inspection and installation

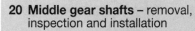

Note: *The middle gear assembly shafts can be removed with the engine in the frame. If work is being carried out with the engine removed ignore the preliminary steps.*

Removal

1 Drain the engine oil (see Chapter 1).
2 Remove the swingarm and the driveshaft (see Chapter 5).
3 Remove the gearchange mechanism/middle gear shaft cover (see Section 19).
4 Unscrew the four bolts securing the middle gear driven shaft housing to the rear of the crankcase (see illustration). Carefully note the positions of the shims between the housing and the crankcase as these must be installed in the same locations.
5 Grasp the shaft output flange or the

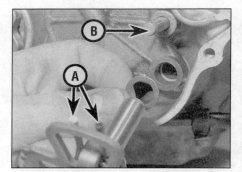

19.12a The spring ends (A) must locate either side of the pin (B)

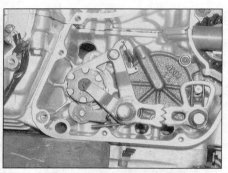

19.12b The installed assembly should be as shown

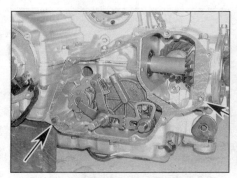

19.14a Install the dowels (arrowed) and a new gasket . . .

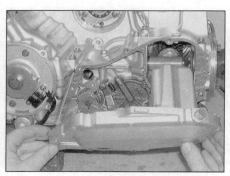

19.14b . . . then fit the cover

20.4 Unscrew the bolts (arrowed) . . .

Engine, clutch and transmission 2•33

20.5 ... and withdraw the shaft – slacken the crankcase bolts (arrowed) if the shaft is tight

20.6 Remove the Torx screws (arrowed) and withdraw the shaft

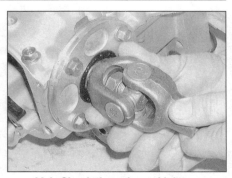

20.9 Check the universal joint as described

universal joint and withdraw the driven shaft assembly from the crankcase **(see illustration)**. If removal is difficult, slacken the two crankcase bolts on either side of the assembly and, if necessary, tap around the housing using a soft mallet. Discard the O-ring as a new one must be used.

6 Unscrew the four Torx screws securing the middle gear drive shaft bearing retainer plates to the crankcase **(see illustration)**. Note that these screws are staked into indentations in the retainer plates, which could make removal difficult. To avoid having to use too much force and possibly stripping the heads of the screws, it may be necessary to carefully drill out the staked areas of the screws, taking care not to drill into the retainer plates. Discard the Torx screws whether they have been drilled or not as new ones must be used on installation.

7 Withdraw the middle gear drive shaft from the sleeve gear assembly in the crankcase, noting the shim(s) **(see illustration 20.12b and a)**. The remainder of the middle gear assembly, namely the sleeve gear (which drives the middle gear drive shaft), and the drive gear on the transmission output shaft (which drives the sleeve gear), can only be removed after the crankcases have been split, and consequently are dealt with in Sections 23 and 24. **Note:** *If difficulty is experienced in withdrawing the drive shaft from the sleeve gear, the crankcases will have to be separated and the drive shaft removed with the sleeve gear).*

Inspection

8 During the normal course of events the middle gear shaft assemblies should last throughout the life of the motorcycle without the need for overhaul or component renewal.
9 Inspect the drive and driven shaft bevel gears for signs of wear or damage. Check that the shafts rotate freely in their bearings. Also check the universal joint on the driven shaft – there should be no noticeable play in the bearings, and the joint should move smoothly and freely with no signs of roughness, stiffness or notchiness **(see illustration)**. If any wear or damage is evident, or if the bearings show signs of roughness or play, take the shafts to a Yamaha dealer or specialist repair shop for overhaul as dismantling the damper assembly and/or universal joint assembly requires specialist equipment and is a potentially dangerous operation. **Note:** *The drive and driven shaft bevel gears are only available as a matched pair. If one is renewed, the other must also be renewed. It is not possible to separate the driven shaft bearing from its housing as individual components are not available, so the entire housing must be renewed.*
10 Check the drive shaft damper assembly for signs of wear or damage. In particular, check the damper spring and the damper cam surfaces. If any wear or damage is evident, the unit should be taken to a Yamaha dealer or specialist repair shop for overhaul as dismantling the damper assembly requires specialist equipment and is a potentially dangerous operation.

Installation

11 If either the drive and driven shaft bevel gears, the driven shaft bearing housing or the crankcase have been renewed, it is necessary to check the thickness of shim required for the middle gear drive shaft before installing it and to renew the existing shim if necessary. The shim size required is calculated using the formula $A=c-a-b$, where A is the unknown shim size, c is the bottom of the three numbers etched into the upper crankcase half **(see illustration)** which must be added to 60, a is a number (pre-fixed either by a + (plus) sign or a – (minus) sign) etched into the end of the drive shaft bevel gear which must be added to or subtracted from 43 (depending on whether it has a + (plus) sign or a – (minus) sign in front of it), and b is a constant 16.94. Shims are available in 0.05 mm increments from 0.15 to 0.50 mm. If the shim size A required does not end in 5 or zero, then it must be rounded up or down according to the table:

Last digit of shim size A	Round off to
0, 1, 2	0
3, 4, 5, 6, 7	5
8, 9	10

12 If none of the components mentioned in Step 11 have been renewed, install the middle gear drive shaft assembly with its original shim(s) into the sleeve gear in the crankcase, making sure it is firmly seated **(see illustrations)**. Install the bearing retainer plates and secure them in place with new

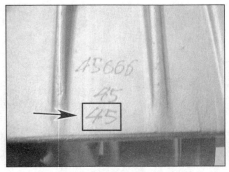

20.11 Number represented by 'c' when calculating shim size (arrowed)

20.12a Fit the shims into the bearing housing ...

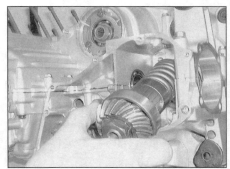

20.12b ...then install the shaft

2•34 Engine, clutch and transmission

20.12c Install the retainer plates and tighten the Torx screws . . .

20.12d . . . and stake them in place

20.14a Fit a new O-ring onto the shaft . . .

Torx screws **(see illustration)**. Tighten the screws to the torque setting specified at the beginning of the Chapter, and stake them into the indentations in the retainer plates using a centre punch **(see illustration)**.

13 If either the drive and driven shaft bevel gears, the driven shaft bearing housing or the crankcase have been renewed, or any of the drive or driven shaft components have been disturbed, it is necessary to check the amount of backlash between the bevel gears and to install new shims if necessary. If none of the components have been renewed or disturbed, the amount of backlash should not have changed, though it is advisable to check it as a matter of course.

14 Fit a new O-ring onto the middle gear driven shaft bearing housing **(see illustration)**. Install the driven shaft assembly in the crankcase with the shims in the same position as they were on removal **(see illustrations)**. Install the housing bolts and tighten them to the specified torque setting. If slackened on removal, also tighten the two crankcase bolts on either side of the housing to the specified torque setting.

15 To check the amount of backlash, a dial gauge mounted on a stand and a method of securing the middle gear drive shaft so that it does not rotate are required. A Yamaha special tool, Pt. No. 90890-04080 can be obtained for securing the drive shaft. Alternatively it should be possible to secure it using either a piece of steel strip wedged in between two of the gear teeth and the crankcase, or by using a spanner with a shortened grip on the gear nut, with the grip wedged against the crankcase.

16 Set up the dial gauge, using the stand to position the gauge end against the edge of one of the arms on the universal joint yoke that is attached to the shaft. With the middle gear drive shaft locked, rotate the universal joint gently back and forward between the extremes of its free movement. Note the reading on the gauge. Remove the drive shaft holding tool and turn the driven shaft through 90° and repeat the measurement. Do this two more times, so that in all four measurements are taken, each 90° apart.

17 If the amount of backlash measured exceeds the limit specified at the beginning of the Chapter, the driven shaft must be re-shimmed to bring it back within limits.

18 To re-shim the driven shaft, unscrew the four bolts securing the shaft housing to the rear of the crankcase. Withdraw the housing from the crankcase just far enough to remove the existing shims **(see illustration 20.14c)**. Slacken the two crankcase bolts on either side of the housing to ease removal if necessary.

19 Set the housing so that there is a gap of about 2 mm between it and the crankcase, then install two of the housing bolts 180° apart and screw them in until their shoulders just contact the housing face.

20 Using the dial gauge arrangement and with the drive shaft locked (see Steps 15 and 16), repeatedly check the amount of backlash whilst screwing in the housing bolts a fraction at a time. When the amount of backlash is 0.2 mm, measure the clearance between the housing and the crankcase using feeler gauges. The clearance measured indicates the shim thickness required.

21 Shims are available in 0.05 mm increments from 0.1 to 0.5 mm. Install the correct shims, then tighten the housing bolts to the specified torque setting. Re-check the backlash.

22 When the amount of backlash is correct, remove the housing bolts and apply a suitable non-permanent thread locking compound, then install them and tighten them to the specified torque setting. If slackened, also tighten the two crankcase bolts on either side of the housing to the specified torque setting.

23 Install the gearchange mechanism/middle gear shaft cover (see Section 19).

21 Oil sump – removal and installation

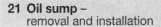

Removal

1 Remove the exhaust system (see Chapter 3).
2 Drain the engine oil (see Chapter 1).
3 Release the oil level sensor wiring from its clip and disconnect it at the connector **(see illustration)**.

20.14b . . . then install the shaft . . .

20.14c . . . and fit the shims

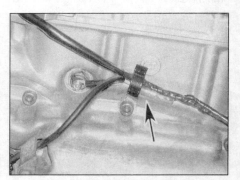

21.3 Release the wiring from the clip and disconnect the connector (arrowed)

Engine, clutch and transmission 2•35

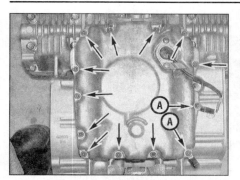

21.4 Oil sump bolts (arrowed) – note the wiring clamps (A)

21.7 Locate the gasket over the dowels (arrowed) . . .

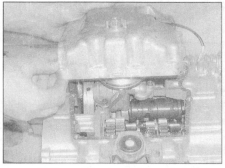

21.8 . . . then install the sump

4 Unscrew the sump bolts, slackening them evenly in a criss-cross sequence to prevent distortion, noting the positions of any wiring clips and of the different length bolts **(see illustration)**. Remove the sump and its gasket. Remove the dowels from either the sump or the crankcase if they are loose, noting their positions.
5 If required, unscrew the baffle plate screws and remove the plate from the sump.

Installation

6 Remove all traces of gasket from the sump and crankcase mating surfaces. If removed, fit the baffle plate into the sump.
7 If removed, fit the dowels into either the sump or crankcase, then lay a new gasket onto the sump (if the engine is in the frame) or onto the crankcase (if the engine has been removed and is positioned upside down on the work surface) **(see illustration)**.
8 Position the sump on the crankcase and install the bolts, not forgetting any wiring clips **(see illustration 21.4)**, and tighten them evenly in a criss-cross pattern to the torque setting specified at the beginning of the Chapter **(see illustration)**.
9 Connect the oil level sensor wiring at the connector and secure it in the clip **(see illustration 21.3)**.
10 Install the exhaust system (see Chapter 3).
11 Fill the engine with oil (see Chapter 1).

Start the engine and check for leaks around the sump.

22 Oil pump and pressure relief valve – removal, inspection and installation

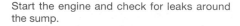

Removal

1 Remove the sump (see Section 21).
2 Unscrew the three bolts securing the pump assembly to the crankcase **(see illustration)**. Remove the plate and the shroud, then tilt the pump to create slack in the chain and slip the chain off the sprocket **(see illustrations)**. If not enough slack can be created, unscrew the

22.2a Unscrew the bolts (arrowed) . . .

bolt securing the sprocket to the pump shaft, using a screwdriver inserted through one of the holes in the sprocket to lock it, and slide the sprocket off the shaft.
3 Remove the pump, noting how it fits **(see illustration)**. Remove the O-ring from the pump outlet and discard it as a new one must be used **(see illustration 22.13a)**.

Inspection

4 If the sprocket has not been removed, unscrew the bolt securing it to the pump and slide it off the shaft **(see illustration)**. If necessary, insert a screwdriver through a hole in the sprocket and lock it against the pump body to prevent it from turning.
5 Remove the four screws securing the pump

22.2b . . . and remove the plate . . .

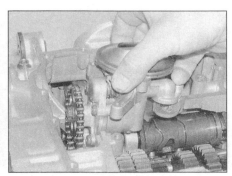

22.2c . . . and the shroud . . .

22.3 . . . then remove the pump

22.4 Unscrew the bolt and remove the sprocket

2•36 Engine, clutch and transmission

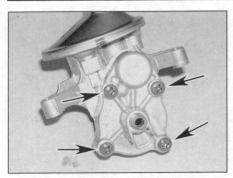

22.5 Remove the screws (arrowed) and the cover

22.6a Remove the spring . . .

22.6b . . . and check the plunger as described

cover **(see illustration)**. The cover will be displaced by the pressure of the relief valve spring. Note the pin in the pump body which locates in the hole in the cover and take care not to lose it.

6 Remove the spring and check that the relief valve plunger moves freely in the body **(see illustrations)**. Inspect it for wear or damage.

7 Measure the clearance between the inner rotor tip and the outer rotor with a feeler gauge and compare it to the maximum clearance listed in the specifications at the beginning of the Chapter **(see illustration)**. If the clearance measured is greater than the maximum listed, replace the pump with a new one.

8 Measure the clearance between the outer rotor and the pump body with a feeler gauge and compare it to the maximum clearance listed in the specifications at the beginning of the Chapter **(see illustration)**. If the clearance measured is greater than the maximum listed, replace the pump with a new one.

9 Remove the shaft and inner rotor from the pump, then remove the outer rotor, noting which way round they fit **(see illustrations)**. If required, slide the inner rotor off the shaft and remove the drive pin **(see illustration)**. Inspect the pump body and rotors for scoring and wear **(see illustration)**. If any damage, scoring or uneven or excessive wear is evident, replace the pump (individual components are not available) with a new one.

10 If the pump is good, reassemble it. Make sure the pin in the rotor shaft is centred so that it aligns and fits into the slot in the inner face of the inner rotor **(see illustration 22.9c)**. Make sure the locating pin is installed in the pump cover **(see illustration)**. Hold the cover

22.7 Measure inner rotor tip to outer rotor clearance

22.8 Measure outer rotor to body clearance

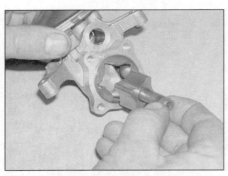

22.9a Remove the shaft and inner rotor . . .

22.9b . . . and the outer rotor

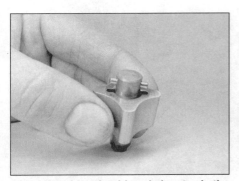

22.9c Note how the drive pin locates in the slots in the inner rotor

22.9d Look for scoring and wear, such as on this outer rotor

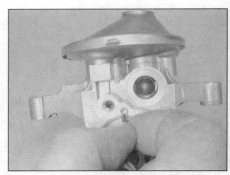

22.10 Do not forget the locating pin

Engine, clutch and transmission 2•37

22.11 Tighten the sprocket bolt to the specified torque

22.13a Fit a new O-ring onto the pump

22.13b Make sure the rubber fillet (arrowed) is on the shroud

down against the spring pressure while installing the screws.

11 Fit the sprocket onto the pump shaft and tighten the bolt to the torque setting specified at the beginning of the Chapter, using a screwdriver as shown to prevent the sprocket turning **(see illustration)**.

Installation

12 Before installing the pump, prime it by pouring oil into the outlet and turning the shaft by hand. This ensures that oil is being pumped as soon as the engine is turned over. Make sure the strainer is clean and free of any debris.

13 Installation is the reverse of removal, noting the following:
   a) Fit a new O-ring between the pump outlet and the crankcase **(see illustration)**.
   b) Make sure the rubber fillet is installed on the shroud, and make sure the shroud locates correctly **(see illustration)**.
   c) Tighten the pump mounting bolts to the torque specified at the beginning of the Chapter.

23 Crankcase – separation and reassembly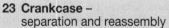

Separation

1 To access the crankshaft and connecting rods, bearings, transmission components, alternator/starter clutch drive and starter clutch assembly, the crankcase must be split into two parts.

2 To enable the crankcases to be separated, the engine must be removed from the frame (see Section 5). If the crankcases are being separated for removal of the crankshaft or connecting rod assemblies, the camshafts, cylinder head, cylinder block, clutch, gearchange mechanism, middle gear shafts, oil pump, ignition pick-up coil and timing plate, alternator and starter motor must be removed. If the crankcases are being separated for removal of the transmission or alternator/starter clutch components only, then there is no need to disassemble the camshafts, cylinder head, and cylinder block. See the relevant Sections or Chapters for details.

23.3a The cover is secured by four screws or bolts (arrowed)

3 Remove the screws or bolts (depending on model) securing the right-hand crankshaft end-cover and remove the cover **(see illustration)**. Unscrew the bolt securing the timing rotor to the left-hand end of the crankshaft and remove it, noting the locating pin that fits between them **(see illustrations)**.

4 The crankcase halves are secured by a total of 39 bolts, the locations of which are identified by a number which is stamped into the crankcase close to the bolt hole **(see illustration)**. The numbers form the sequence in which the bolts must be slackened and tightened.

5 Starting with the upper crankcase half, slacken each bolt in sequence starting at number 39 and working backwards to number 24. Slacken each bolt 1/2 a turn at a time until they are all finger tight, then remove

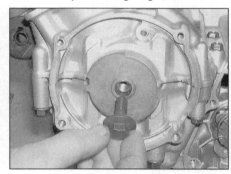

23.3b Unscrew the bolt . . .

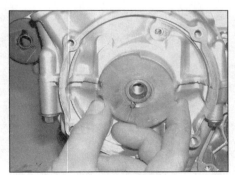

23.3c . . . and remove the rotor . . .

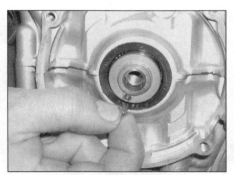

23.3d . . . and its locating pin

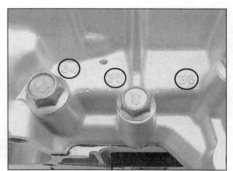

23.4 The bolt numbers (circled) are stamped into the crankcases

2

2•38 Engine, clutch and transmission

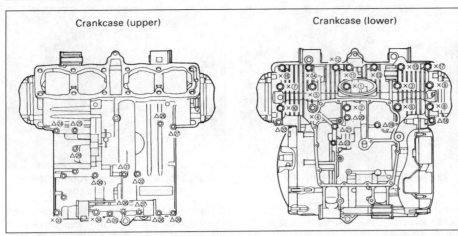

23.5 Crankcase bolt locations – 8 mm bolts are marked by a cross, 6 mm bolts by a triangle

23.7 Carefully lift the lower half off the upper half

the bolts **(see illustration)**. *Note: As each bolt is removed, store it in its relative position in a cardboard template of the crankcase halves. This will ensure all bolts are installed in the correct location on reassembly. Take note of the earth cables attached to bolts 35 and/or 37 (depending on model) and store them with the bolts to ensure correct reassembly.*

6 Turn the engine upside down and slacken each lower crankcase bolt in sequence, starting at number 23 and working backwards to number 1. Note that the number 1 bolt is located inside the oil filter housing, and that numbers 2, 19, 20, 21 and 23 are located within the crankcase sump area. Slacken each bolt 1/2 a turn at a time until they are all finger tight, then remove the bolts. *Note: As each bolt is removed, store it in its relative position in a cardboard template of the crankcase halves. This will ensure all bolts are installed in the correct location on reassembly.*

7 Carefully lift the lower crankcase half off the upper half **(see illustration)**. The gearbox output shaft, selector drum and selector forks will come away with the lower half, leaving the crankshaft, transmission input shaft and middle sleeve gear in the upper half. As the lower half is lifted away take care not to dislodge or lose any main bearing inserts. *Note: If the halves do not separate easily, make sure all fasteners have been removed. Do not try and separate the halves by levering against the mating surfaces as they are easily scored and will leak oil. Initial separation can be achieved by tapping gently around the joint with a soft-faced mallet.*

8 Remove the four locating dowels from the crankcase if they are loose, noting their locations **(see illustration 23.13a)**. Remove the O-ring from the central dowel and discard it as a new one must be fitted **(see illustration 23.13b)**. Remove the crankshaft end-plug and oil seal and discard them as new ones should be used.

Reassembly

9 Remove all traces of sealant from the crankcase mating surfaces.

10 Ensure that all components and their bearings are in place in the upper and lower crankcase halves. Do not forget the middle driven shaft bearing and its half-ring retainer **(see illustrations)**. Make sure the retainer is properly seated in its groove and positioned so it bridges both crankcase halves. Fit a new crankshaft end-plug and oil seal, applying a smear of grease to their lips **(see illustration)**. *Note: The old-type end-plug and oil seal were lipped, the lip fitting into the groove in the crankcase. These have been superseded by unlipped parts, and they should fit flush with the crankcase walls.*

11 Generously lubricate the transmission shafts, selector drum and forks, and the crankshaft, particularly around the bearings, with clean engine oil, then use a rag soaked in high flash-point solvent to wipe over the gasket surfaces of both halves to remove all traces of oil.

12 Apply a small amount of suitable sealant to the mating surface of the upper crankcase half **(see illustration)**. **Caution:** *Do not apply an excessive amount of sealant, as it will ooze out when the case halves are assembled and may obstruct oil passages and prevent the bearings from seating. Make sure that sealant is applied around the main bearing cap bolt holes but not within 2 to 3 mm of the main*

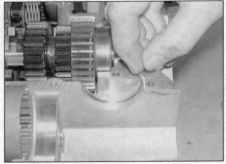

23.10a Fit the middle driven shaft bearing retainer into the groove ...

23.10b ... then fit the bearing

23.10c Fit a new oil seal and end-plug onto the crankshaft

23.12 Apply the sealant as described ...

Engine, clutch and transmission 2•39

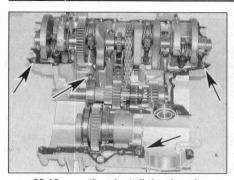

23.13a ... then install the dowels (arrowed)

23.13b Fit a new O-ring round the central dowel

24.8 The breather separators are on the inside of the cover

bearing shells. Also do not apply the sealant within 2 to 3 mm of the central oil feed dowel and O-ring.

13 Install the four locating dowels in the upper crankcase half (see illustration). Fit a new O-ring around the central dowel (see illustration).

14 Make sure the gear selector drum is in the neutral position.

15 Make sure that the main bearing shells are in position in the lower case, then carefully fit the lower case onto the upper case (see illustration 23.7). Make sure the centre gear selector fork engages with the slot in the 2nd/3rd pinion as the halves are joined. Make sure the dowels, the lips of the crankshaft oil seal and end-plug, and the transmission bearing retainers fit properly into their recesses – if the unlipped oil seal and plug are installed, make sure they do not get cocked sideways, and that they fit flush with the crankcase walls.

16 Check that the lower crankcase half is correctly seated. **Note:** *The crankcase halves should fit together without being forced. If the casings are not correctly seated, remove the lower crankcase half and investigate the problem. Do not attempt to pull them together using the crankcase bolts as the casing will crack and be ruined.*

17 Check that the transmission shafts rotate freely and independently in neutral, then rotate the selector drum by hand and select each gear in turn whilst rotating the input shaft. Check that all gears can be selected and that the shafts rotate freely in every gear.

18 Clean the threads of the lower crankcase bolts, then insert them in their original locations and tighten them finger-tight (see illustration 23.5). Now tighten the bolts evenly and progressively and in the correct numerical sequence (starting at No. 1) to the torque settings specified at the beginning of the Chapter. When torquing the bolts, be sure to distinguish correctly between the 8 mm bolts and the 6 mm bolts.

19 Turn the engine over so that it is upright. Clean the threads of the upper crankcase bolts, then insert them in their original locations and tighten them finger-tight (see illustration 23.5). Do not forget to install the

earth cables on bolts 35 and/or 37 (according to model). Now tighten the bolts evenly and progressively to the torque settings specified at the beginning of the Chapter. When torquing the bolts, be sure to distinguish correctly between the 8 mm bolts and the 6 mm bolts.

20 With all crankcase fasteners tightened, check that the crankshaft and transmission shafts rotate smoothly and easily. If the top-end has been removed, keep the cam chain taut when rotating the crankshaft to prevent it from jamming around the crankshaft sprocket. Check the operation of the transmission in each gear (see Step 17). If there are any signs of undue stiffness, tight or rough spots, or of any other problem, the fault must be rectified before proceeding further.

21 Install all other removed assemblies in the reverse of the sequence given in Steps 3 and 2. Tighten the timing rotor bolt and the crankshaft end-cover screws or bolts (according to model) to the specified torque setting.

24 Crankcase halves – inspection and servicing

1 After the crankcases have been separated, remove the crankshaft and bearings, cam chain tensioner blade, transmission shafts, selector drum and forks, Hy-Vo chain guide blade, starter clutch and alternator drive shaft and bearings, and any other components or assemblies not already removed, referring to the relevant Sections of this and other Chapters (see Step 2, Section 23).

2 Remove any oil gallery plugs that haven't already been removed.

3 The crankcases should be cleaned thoroughly with new solvent and dried with compressed air. All oil passages, pipes and oil nozzles should be blown out with compressed air.

4 All traces of old gasket sealant should be removed from the mating surfaces. Minor damage to the surfaces can be cleaned up with a fine sharpening stone or grindstone.

Caution: Be very careful not to nick or gouge the crankcase mating surfaces or oil leaks will result. Check both crankcase halves very carefully for cracks and other damage.

5 Small cracks or holes in aluminium castings may be repaired with an epoxy resin adhesive as a temporary measure. Permanent repairs can only be effected by argon-arc welding, and only a specialist in this process is in a position to advise on the economy or practical aspect of such a repair. If any damage is found that can't be repaired, renew the crankcase halves as a set.

6 Damaged threads can be economically reclaimed by using a diamond section wire insert, of the Heli-Coil type, which is easily fitted after drilling and re-tapping the affected thread.

7 Sheared studs or screws can usually be removed with screw extractors, which consist of a tapered, left thread screw of very hard steel. These are inserted into a pre-drilled hole in the stud, and usually succeed in dislodging the most stubborn stud or screw.

> **HAYNES HINT** *Refer to Section 2 in Tools and Workshop Tips in the Reference section for details of installing a thread insert and using screw extractors.*

8 The crankcase ventilation system is fully automatic in operation and will require no attention during normal use. Only in unusual circumstances, where the machine is used only for short journeys in a cold, damp climate is there a risk of the oil separator becoming clogged with emulsified oil. Should this be noted during oil changes, in the form of a thick creamy white scum, it is advisable to remove the separator castings from the inside of the left-hand crankcase cover and clean them out (see illustration).

9 Install the crankshaft and bearings, cam chain and tensioner blade, transmission shafts, selector drum and forks, Hy-Vo chain, starter clutch and alternator drive shaft and bearings, before reassembling the crankcase halves.

2•40 Engine, clutch and transmission

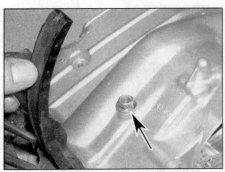

25.4a Unscrew the bolt (arrowed) and remove the tensioner blade . . .

25.4b . . . noting how it fits inside

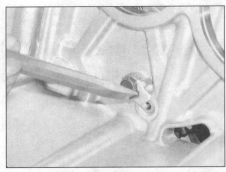

26.3a Bend back the tab, then unscrew the bolt and remove the plate

25 Cam chain and tensioner blade – removal, inspection and installation

Removal

Cam chain

1 Remove the crankshaft (see Section 28).
2 Remove the cam chain from around its sprocket.

Tensioner blade

3 Remove the crankshaft (see Section 28).
4 Unscrew the bolt securing the tensioner blade base to the crankcase and remove the blade **(see illustrations)**.

26.3b Withdraw the shaft and remove the gear (arrowed)

Inspection

Cam chain

5 Check the chain for binding, kinks and any obvious damage and replace it with a new one if necessary. Check the camshaft and crankshaft sprocket teeth for wear and renew the cam chain, camshaft sprockets and crankshaft as a set if necessary.

Tensioner blade

6 Check the sliding surface and edges of the blade for excessive wear, deep grooves, cracking and other obvious damage, and replace it with a new one if necessary. Also check the condition of the pivot hardware on the base.

Installation

7 Installation of the chain and blade is the reverse of removal. Apply a suitable non-permanent thread locking compound to the tensioner blade bolt and tighten it to the torque setting specified at the beginning of the Chapter **(see illustrations 25.4b and a)**.

26 Alternator drive shaft and starter clutch assembly – removal, inspection and installation

Note: *These components can only be accessed after separation of the crankcase halves.*

Removal

1 Separate the crankcase halves (see Section 23). The alternator drive shaft, starter clutch and idle gear assembly are all located in the upper half of the crankcase.
2 Remove the transmission input shaft (see Section 30).
3 Bend back the tabs on the idle gear shaft retaining bolt lockwasher, then unscrew the bolt and remove the washer and retainer **(see illustration)**. Support the idle gear from inside the crankcase, then withdraw the shaft from the crankcase and remove the gear, noting which way round it fits **(see illustration)**.
4 Unscrew the three bolts securing the alternator drive shaft bearing retainer plate to the crankcase and remove the plate **(see illustration)**.
5 Support the starter clutch, then withdraw the bearing and the drive shaft from the crankcase. If the bearing or shaft is a tight fit, use a slide hammer with suitable end-adapter threaded into the middle of the shaft, or a suitable bolt and a pair of pliers or grips, to withdraw the shaft and bring the bearing with it **(see illustration)**.
6 Disengage the Hy-Vo chain from the starter clutch and remove the starter clutch from the crankcase **(see illustration)**. If the Hy-Vo chain is later to be removed from the crankshaft mark one of the chain side plates to indicate whether it points to the left or right side of the engine (remembering to account

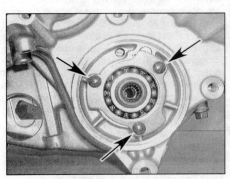

26.4 Unscrew the bolts (arrowed) and remove the plate

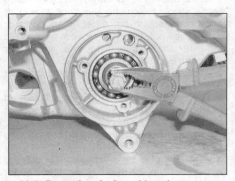

26.5 Draw the shaft and bearing out as described

26.6 Disengage the chain and remove the starter clutch

Engine, clutch and transmission 2•41

26.7 Withdraw the oil nozzle (arrowed)

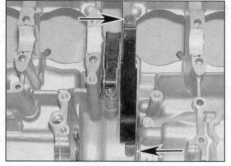

26.8 The Hy-Vo chain guide is secured by two bolts (arrowed)

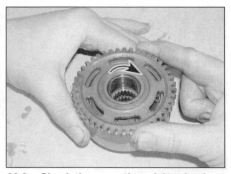

26.9a Check the operation of the clutch as described

for the engine being upside down at this stage). This is to ensure that the chain is replaced with its direction of travel unchanged, otherwise noise and vibration can occur.

7 Remove the oil spray nozzle from its recess in the crankcase face of the bearing housing mating surfaces **(see illustration)**. Discard the O-ring as a new one must be used.

8 If required, remove the crankshaft (see Section 28) and disengage the Hy-Vo chain. Unscrew the bolts securing the chain guide to the crankcase and remove the guide, noting which way round it fits **(see illustration)**.

Inspection

9 With the clutch face down on a workbench, check that the gear rotates freely in a clockwise direction and locks against the rotor in an anti-clockwise direction **(see illustration)**. If it doesn't, the gear and sprag assembly must be replaced with new ones. Withdraw the starter clutch gear and its sleeve from the starter clutch **(see illustration)**. If the gear appears stuck, rotate it anti-clockwise as you withdraw it to free it.

10 Inspect the bearing surface of the starter clutch gear hub and the condition of the sprags inside the clutch body **(see illustration)**. If the bearing surface shows signs of excessive wear or the sprags are damaged, marked or flattened at any point, they should be replaced with new ones. The sprag assembly is secured in the clutch body by a circlip **(see illustration)**.

11 Examine the teeth of the starter idler gear and the corresponding teeth of the starter clutch gear and starter motor gear. Renew the gears as a set if worn or chipped teeth are discovered.

12 Inspect the alternator drive shaft and its bearings (one in the housing or on the shaft, the other in the crankcase). If the shaft splines are worn or damaged the shaft must be replaced with a new one. Check also the corresponding splines in the starter clutch. If the bearings do not rotate freely or have rough spots or excessive play, they must be replaced with new ones. Heat the area around the bearing in the crankcase to ease its removal.

13 Remove the circlip securing the drive sprocket to the starter clutch **(see illustration)**. Separate the sprocket and cush drive housing and inspect the cush drive rubbers **(see illustrations)**. If compacted or deteriorated they should be replaced with new ones.

26.9b Remove the sleeve and the gear and check the components as described

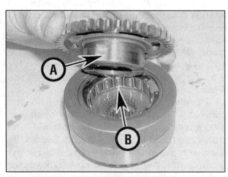

26.10a Check the hub (A) and the sprags (B) as described

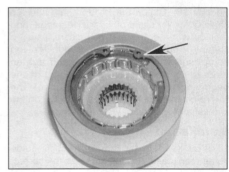

26.10b The sprag assembly is secured by a circlip (arrowed)

26.13a Remove the circlip . . .

26.13b . . . and lift off the sprocket

26.13c Check the rubbers as described

2•42 Engine, clutch and transmission

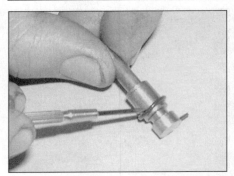

26.17 Fit a new O-ring onto the oil nozzle

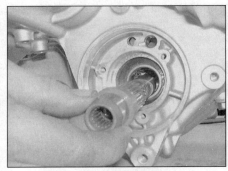

26.18a Install the shaft . . .

26.18b . . . and the bearing . . .

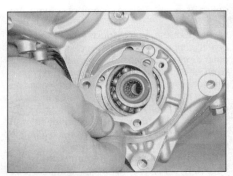

26.18c . . . and secure them with the retainer plate

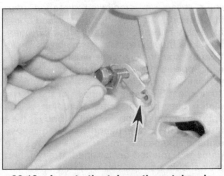

26.19a Locate the tab on the retainer in the hole in the shaft (arrowed)

26.19b Bend up the lockwasher tabs to secure the bolt

14 The Hy-Vo chain and its guide in the crankcase can only be inspected properly after the crankshaft has been removed (see Section 28). Check the Hy-Vo chain and the chain guide for signs of wear or damage, and replace with new ones if necessary. Apply a suitable non-permanent thread locking compound to the bolt threads and tighten them to the torque setting specified at the beginning of the Chapter. Also check the Hy-Vo chain sprocket and the sprocket on the crankshaft for signs of wear or damage.

Installation

15 If removed, install the Hy-Vo chain guide in the crankcase, making sure it is the correct way round. Apply a suitable non-permanent thread locking compound to the bolts and tighten them to the torque setting specified at the beginning of the Chapter (see illustration 26.8). Fit the Hy-Vo chain onto the crankshaft, making sure it is the correct way round (see Step 5), then install the crankshaft (see Section 28).

16 Insert the reassembled starter clutch in the crankcase and engage the Hy-Vo chain on the sprocket (see illustration 26.6). Lay the starter clutch down in the crankcase.

17 Fit a new O-ring onto the oil spray nozzle (see illustration). Install the nozzle in its recess, making sure the locating pin on the nozzle fits into its slot (see illustration 26.7).

18 Lubricate the alternator drive shaft, then, supporting the starter clutch, insert the shaft through the assembly from the outside of the crankcase until it seats fully into the bearing in the crankcase (see illustration). Slide the bearing onto the end of the shaft and push it into its housing (see illustration). Apply a suitable non-permanent thread locking compound to the retainer plate bolts and tighten them to the torque setting specified at the beginning of the Chapter (see illustration).

19 Position the starter idle gear in the crankcase. Lubricate the idle gear shaft and slide it fully into place from the outside of the crankcase (see illustration 26.3b). Secure the shaft with the retainer, locating the tab in the shaft centre, then install a new lockwasher and tighten the bolt to the specified torque setting (see illustration). Bend up the tabs of the lockwasher to secure the bolt (see illustration).

20 Install the transmission shaft (see Section 30) and reassemble the crankcase halves (see Section 23).

27 Main and connecting rod bearings – general information

1 Even though main and connecting rod bearings are generally replaced with new ones during an engine overhaul, the old bearings should be retained for close examination as they may reveal valuable information about the condition of the engine.

2 Bearing failure occurs mainly because of lack of lubrication, the presence of dirt or other foreign particles, overloading the engine and/or corrosion. Regardless of the cause of bearing failure, it must be corrected before the engine is reassembled to prevent it from happening again.

3 When examining the connecting rod bearings, remove them from the connecting rods and caps and lay them out on a clean surface in the same general position as their location on the crankshaft journals. This will enable you to match any noted bearing problems with the corresponding crankshaft journal.

4 Dirt and other foreign particles get into the engine in a variety of ways. It may be left in the engine during assembly or it may pass through filters or breathers. It may get into the oil and from there into the bearings. Metal chips from machining operations and normal engine wear are often present. Abrasives are sometimes left in engine components after reconditioning operations, especially when parts are not thoroughly cleaned using the proper cleaning methods. Whatever the source, these foreign objects often end up imbedded in the soft bearing material and are easily recognised. Large particles will not imbed in the bearing and will score or gouge the bearing and journal. The best prevention for this cause of bearing failure is to clean all

Engine, clutch and transmission 2•43

parts thoroughly and keep everything spotlessly clean during engine reassembly. Frequent and regular oil and filter changes are also recommended.

5 Lack of lubrication or lubrication breakdown has a number of interrelated causes. Excessive heat (which thins the oil), overloading (which squeezes the oil from the bearing face) and oil leakage or throw off (from excessive bearing clearances, worn oil pump or high engine speeds) all contribute to lubrication breakdown. Blocked oil passages will also starve a bearing and destroy it. When lack of lubrication is the cause of bearing failure, the bearing material is wiped or extruded from the steel backing of the bearing. Temperatures may increase to the point where the steel backing and the journal turn blue from overheating.

 HAYNES HiNT *Refer to Section 5 in Tools and Workshop Tips in the Reference section for bearing fault finding*

6 Riding habits can have a definite effect on bearing life. Full throttle low speed operation, or labouring the engine, puts very high loads on bearings, which tend to squeeze out the oil film. These loads cause the bearings to flex, which produces fine cracks in the bearing face (fatigue failure). Eventually the bearing material will loosen in pieces and tear away from the steel backing. Short trip riding leads to corrosion of bearings, as insufficient engine heat is produced to drive off the condensed water and corrosive gases produced. These products collect in the engine oil, forming acid and sludge. As the oil is carried to the engine bearings, the acid attacks and corrodes the bearing material.

7 Incorrect bearing installation during engine assembly will lead to bearing failure as well. Tight fitting bearings which leave insufficient bearing oil clearances result in oil starvation. Dirt or foreign particles trapped behind a bearing insert result in high spots on the bearing which lead to failure.

8 To avoid bearing problems, clean all parts thoroughly before reassembly, double check all bearing clearance measurements and lubricate the new bearings with clean engine oil during installation.

28 Crankshaft and main bearings – removal, inspection and installation

Removal

1 Remove the engine (see Section 5) and separate the crankcase halves (see Section 23).
2 Remove the alternator drive shaft and starter clutch (see Section 26). Unscrew the bolt securing the timing rotor to the left-hand end of the crankshaft and remove it, noting the locating pin that fits between them.
3 Mark one of the Hy-Vo chain side plates to indicate whether it points to the left or right side of the engine (remembering to account for the engine being upside down at this stage) **(see illustration)**. This is to ensure that the chain is replaced with its direction of travel unchanged, otherwise noise and vibration can occur. If you made timing alignment marks between the cam chain and sprockets when removing the camshafts, make a similar alignment mark between the chain and the sprocket on the crankshaft, but only if you are sure the chain has not slipped round the sprocket since the first marks were made.
4 Lift the crankshaft out of the upper crankcase half **(see illustration)**. If it appears stuck, tap it gently using a soft-faced mallet. Take care not to snag either the cam chain or the Hy-Vo chain when lifting the crankshaft clear. Note how the crankshaft oil seal and end-plug fit and take care not to lose them. Disengage the chains from the crankshaft if required.
5 The main bearing shells can be removed from the crankcase halves by pushing their centres to the side, then lifting them out **(see illustration)**. Keep the bearing shells in order as they must be installed in their original positions if they are being re-used.
6 If required, separate the connecting rods from the crankshaft (see Section 29).

28.3 Make a mark on the Hy-Vo chain so that it is installed the same way round

28.4 Carefully lift the crankshaft out of the crankcase

Inspection

7 Clean the crankshaft with solvent, using a rifle-cleaning brush to scrub out the oil passages. Remove the three oil nozzles from the passages in the lower crankcase half for cleaning, then install them back in their holes and tighten them securely. If available, blow the crank dry with compressed air. Check the primary drive gear, cam chain and Hy-Vo chain sprockets for wear or damage **(see illustration)**. If any of the sprocket teeth are excessively worn, chipped or broken, the crankshaft must be replaced with a new one. If wear or damage is found on the primary drive gear, check the driven gear on the clutch housing.
8 Refer to Section 27 and examine the main bearing shells. If they are scored, badly scuffed or appear to have been seized, new bearings must be installed. Always renew the main bearings as a set. If they are badly damaged, check the corresponding crankshaft journals. Evidence of extreme heat, such as discoloration, indicates that lubrication failure has occurred. Be sure to thoroughly check the oil pump and pressure relief valve as well as all oil holes and passages before reassembling the engine.
9 Place the crankshaft on V-blocks and check the runout at the main bearing journals using a dial gauge. Compare the reading to the maximum specified at the beginning of the Chapter. If the runout exceeds the limit, the crankshaft must be replaced with a new one.

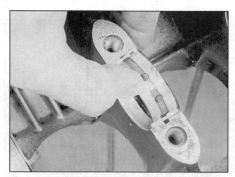

28.5 To remove a main bearing shell, push it sideways and lift it out

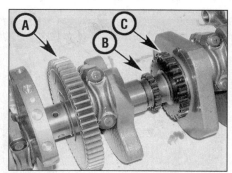

28.7 Check the primary drive gear (A), the cam chain sprocket (B) and the Hy-Vo chain sprocket (C) as described

2•44 Engine, clutch and transmission

28.14 Lay a strip of Plastigauge on each journal parallel to the crankshaft centreline

28.18 Measure the width of the crushed Plastigauge (be sure to use the correct scale – metric and imperial are included)

Oil clearance check

10 Whether new bearing shells are being fitted or the original ones are being re-used, the main bearing oil clearance should be checked before the engine is reassembled. Main bearing oil clearance is measured with a product known as Plastigauge.
11 If not already done, remove the bearing shells from the crankcase halves (see Step 5). Clean the backs of the shells and the bearing housings in both crankcase halves, and the main bearing journals on the crankshaft.
12 Press the bearing shells into their cut-outs, ensuring that the tab on each shell engages in the notch in the crankcase (see illustration 28.25). Make sure the bearings are fitted in the correct locations and take care not to touch any shell's bearing surface with your fingers.
13 Ensure the shells and crankshaft are clean and dry. Lay the crankshaft in position in the upper crankcase (see illustration 28.4).
14 Cut several lengths of the appropriate size Plastigauge (they should be slightly shorter than the width of the crankshaft journals). Place a strand of Plastigauge on each journal, making sure it will be clear of the oil holes in the shells when the lower crankcase is installed (see illustration). Make sure the crankshaft does not turn.
15 Install the four locating dowels in the upper crankcase half (see illustration 23.13a). Fit the O-ring around the central dowel (see illustration 23.13b).

16 Carefully fit the lower crankcase half onto the upper half (see illustration 23.7). Make sure that the selector forks (if installed) engage with their respective slots in the transmission gears as the halves are joined. Check that the lower crankcase half is correctly seated. **Note:** *Do not tighten the crankcase bolts if the casing is not correctly seated.* Clean the threads of the lower crankcase bolts numbers 1 to 10 and apply new engine oil to their threads. Install the bolts in their original locations and tighten them evenly and in the correct numerical sequence to the torque setting specified at the beginning of the Chapter (see illustration 23.5). Make sure that the crankshaft does not turn as the bolts are tightened.
17 Slacken each bolt in reverse sequence starting at number 10 and working backwards to number 1. Slacken each bolt 1/2 a turn at a time until they are all finger tight, then remove the bolts. Carefully lift off the lower crankcase half, making sure the Plastigauge is not disturbed.
18 Compare the width of the crushed Plastigauge on each crankshaft journal to the scale printed on the Plastigauge envelope to obtain the main bearing oil clearance (see illustration). Compare the reading to the specifications at the beginning of the Chapter.
19 On completion carefully scrape away all traces of the Plastigauge material from the crankshaft journal and bearing shells; use a fingernail or other object which is unlikely to score them.
20 If the oil clearance falls into the specified range, no bearing shell renewal is required (provided they are in good condition). If the clearance is beyond the service limit, refer to the marks on the case and the marks on the crankshaft and select new bearing shells (see Steps 22 and 23). Install the new shells and check the oil clearance once again (the new shells may bring bearing clearance within the specified range). Always renew all of the shells at the same time.
21 If the clearance is still greater than the service limit listed in this Chapter's Specifications (even with replacement shells), the crankshaft journal is worn and the crankshaft should be renewed.

Bearing shell selection

22 Replacement bearing shells for the main bearings are supplied on a selected fit basis. Code numbers stamped on various components are used to identify the correct replacement bearings. The crankshaft journal size numbers are stamped on the outside of the crankshaft left-hand web. The block of five numbers on the left are for the main bearing journals (the block of four numbers on the right are for the big-end bearing journals) (see illustration). The main bearing housing numbers are stamped into the rear of the upper crankcase half (see illustration). Note that if there is only one number stamped into the crankcase, it means that all the journals are the same number.
23 A range of bearing shells is available. To select the correct bearing for a particular journal, subtract the main bearing journal number (stamped on the crank web) from the main bearing housing number (stamped on the crankcase). For example, from the illustrations shown (see Step 22), the number 5 journal on the right end of the crankshaft would require a replacement bearing number 4. Compare the bearing number calculated with the table below to find the colour coding of the replacement bearing required. In the example, a green coded bearing is required.

Number	Colour
1	Blue
2	Black
3	Brown
4	Green
5	Yellow

Installation

24 Clean the backs of the bearing shells and the bearing recesses in both crankcase halves. If new shells are being fitted, ensure that all traces of the protective grease are cleaned off using paraffin. Wipe the shells and crankcase halves dry with a lint-free cloth. Make sure all the oil passages and holes are clear, and blow them through with compressed air if it is available.
25 Press the bearing shells into their

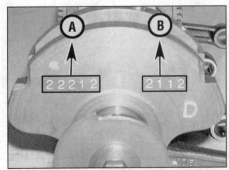

28.22a Main journal size numbers (A), big-end journal size numbers (B)

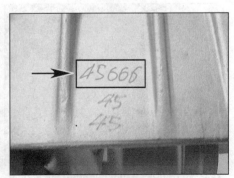

28.22b Main bearing housing numbers (arrowed)

Engine, clutch and transmission 2•45

28.25 Make sure the tabs on the shells locate in the notches in the cutouts

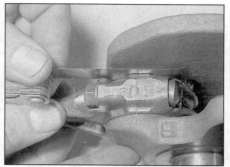

29.2 Measure the connecting rod side clearance using a feeler gauge

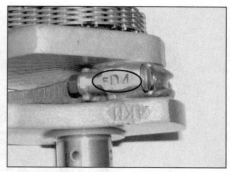

29.3 Note the marks across the rod and cap

locations. Note that the shells for the upper crankcase half are solid, while the lower crankcase shells have holes in them. Make sure the tab on each shell engages in the notch in the casing and lubricate the shell with clean engine oil **(see illustration)**. Make sure the bearings are fitted in the correct locations and take care not to touch any shell's bearing surface with your fingers.

26 If removed, fit the connecting rods onto the crankshaft (see Section 29).
27 If removed, install the Hy-Vo chain guide in the crankcase (see Section 26).
28 Engage the Hy-Vo chain (making sure it is the correct way round) (see Step 3) and the cam chain (making sure your alignment marks align, if you made any) onto their sprockets on the crankshaft **(see illustration 28.3)**.
29 Lower the crankshaft into position in the upper crankcase, feeding the cam chain down through its tunnel and the Hy-Vo chain onto is guide **(see illustration 28.4)**.
30 Reassemble the crankcase halves (see Section 23).

29 Connecting rods – removal, inspection and installation

Note: *To remove the connecting rods the engine must be removed from the frame and the crankcases separated.*

Removal

1 Remove the engine from the frame (see Section 5) and separate the crankcase halves (see Section 23). Remove the crankshaft (see Section 28).
2 Before removing the rods from the crankshaft, measure the side clearance on each rod with a feeler gauge **(see illustration)**. If the clearance between any rod is greater than the service limit listed in this Chapter's Specifications, replace that rod with a new one.
3 Using paint or a felt marker pen, mark the relevant cylinder identity on each connecting rod and cap. Mark across the cap-to-connecting rod join, and note the 'Y' mark on each connecting rod which must face to the

left-hand side of the engine, to ensure that the cap and rod are fitted the correct way around on reassembly **(see illustration)**. Note that the number and letter already across the rod and cap indicate rod size and weight grade respectively, not cylinder number.
4 Unscrew the connecting rod cap nuts and separate the cap from the crankpin **(see illustration)**. Do not remove the bolts from the caps. Immediately install the relevant bearing shells (if removed), bearing cap, and nuts on each piston/connecting rod assembly so that they are all kept together as a matched set to ensure correct installation. Having done that, note that Yamaha specify that new bolts and nuts should be used on reassembly, and if required, for the oil clearance check, as the bolts are of the stretch type which can only be used once. Using the old bolts for the clearance check could lead to inaccurate results.

Inspection

5 Check the connecting rods for cracks and other obvious damage.
6 Apply clean engine oil to the piston pin, insert it into its connecting rod small-end and check for any freeplay between the two **(see illustration)**. If freeplay is excessive, measure the pin external diameter **(see illustration 15.13b)**. Compare the result to the specifications at the beginning of the Chapter. Replace the pin with a new one if it is worn beyond its specified limits. If the pin diameter

is within specifications, replace the connecting rod with a new one. Repeat the measurements for all the rods.
7 Refer to Section 27 and examine the connecting rod bearing shells. If they are scored, badly scuffed or appear to have seized, new shells must be installed. Always renew the shells in the connecting rods as a set. If they are badly damaged, check the corresponding crankpin. Evidence of extreme heat, such as discoloration, indicates that lubrication failure has occurred. Be sure to thoroughly check the oil pump and pressure regulator as well as all oil holes and passages before reassembling the engine.
8 Have the rods checked for twist and bend by a Yamaha dealer if you are in doubt about their straightness.

Oil clearance check

9 Whether new bearing shells are being fitted or the original ones are being re-used, the connecting rod (big-end) bearing oil clearance should be checked prior to reassembly. Obtain new bolts and nuts for the connecting rods and discard the old ones.
10 Remove the bearing shells from the rods and caps, keeping them in order. Clean the backs of the shells and the bearing locations in both the connecting rod and cap, and the crankpin journal.
11 Press the bearing shells into their locations, ensuring that the tab on each shell engages the notch in the connecting rod/cap

29.4 Unscrew the nuts (arrowed) and remove the connecting rods

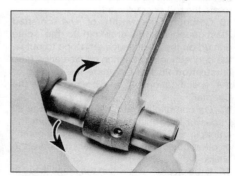

29.6 Slip the piston pin into the rod's small-end and rock it back and forth to check for looseness

2•46 Engine, clutch and transmission

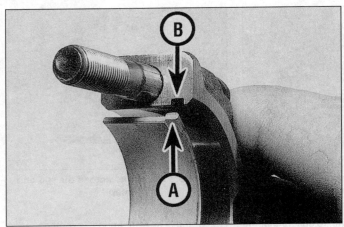

29.24 Make sure the tab (A) locates in the notch (B)

29.26 Tighten the nuts as described, first to the initial torque, then to the final torque

(see illustration 29.24). Make sure the bearings are fitted in the correct locations and take care not to touch any shell's bearing surface with your fingers.

12 Cut a length of the appropriate size Plastigauge (it should be slightly shorter than the width of the crankpin). Place a strand of Plastigauge on the crankpin journal.

13 Apply molybdenum disulphide grease to the bolt shanks and threads and to the seats of the nuts, then fit the bolts into the cap. Fit the connecting rod and cap onto the crankshaft. Make sure the cap is fitted the correct way around so the previously made markings align, and that the rod is facing the right way (see Step 3). Fit the nuts and tighten them finger-tight, making sure the connecting rod does not rotate on the crankshaft.

14 Tighten the cap nuts to the initial torque setting specified at the beginning of the Chapter, making sure the connecting rod does not rotate on the crankshaft. Now tighten each nut in turn and in one continuous movement to the final torque setting specified. If tightening is paused between the initial and final settings, slacken the nut to below the initial setting and repeat the procedure.

15 Slacken the cap nuts and remove the connecting rod, again taking great care not to rotate the rod or crankshaft.

16 Compare the width of the crushed Plastigauge on the crankpin to the scale printed on the Plastigauge envelope to obtain the connecting rod bearing oil clearance **(see illustration 28.18)**. Compare the reading to the specifications at the beginning of the Chapter.

17 On completion carefully scrape away all traces of the Plastigauge material from the crankpin and bearing shells using a fingernail or other object which is unlikely to score the shells.

18 If the clearance is within the range listed in this Chapter's Specifications and the bearings are in perfect condition, they can be reused. If the clearance is beyond the service limit,

replace the bearing shells with new ones (see Steps 21 and 22). Check the oil clearance once again (the new shells may be thick enough to bring bearing clearance within the specified range). Always renew all of the inserts at the same time.

19 If the clearance is still greater than the service limit listed in this Chapter's Specifications, the big-end bearing journal is worn and the crankshaft should be replaced with a new one.

20 Repeat the bearing selection procedure for the remaining connecting rods.

Bearing shell selection

21 Replacement bearing shells for the big-end bearings are supplied on a selected fit basis. Code numbers stamped on various components are used to identify the correct replacement bearings. The crankshaft journal size numbers are stamped on the outside of the crankshaft left-hand web **(see illustration 28.22a)**. The block of four numbers on the right are for the big-end bearing journals (the block of five numbers on the left are for the main bearing journals). The connecting rod numbers are marked in ink on the flat face of the connecting rod and cap **(see illustration 29.3)**.

22 A range of bearing shells is available. To select the correct bearing for a particular connecting rod, subtract the big-end bearing journal number (stamped on the crank web) from the connecting rod number (marked on the rod). For example, from the illustrations shown, cylinder No. 1's connecting rod on the left end of the crankshaft would require a replacement bearing number 2. Compare the bearing number calculated with the table below to find the colour coding of the replacement bearing required. In the example, a black coded bearing is required.

Number	Colour
1	Blue
2	Black
3	Brown
4	Green

Installation

Note: *New connecting rod bolts and nuts should be used whenever the rods have been disassembled.*

23 Clean the backs of the bearing shells and the bearing locations in both the connecting rod and cap.

24 Press the bearing shells into their locations, making sure the tab on each shell locates in the notch in the connecting rod/cap **(see illustration)**. Make sure the bearings are fitted in their correct locations and take care not to touch any shell's bearing surface with your fingers. Lubricate the shells with clean engine oil.

25 Obtain new bolts and nuts for the connecting rods and discard the old ones. Apply molybdenum disulphide grease to the bolt shanks and threads and to the seats of the nuts, then fit the bolts into the cap. Assemble the connecting rod and cap on the crankpin. Make sure the cap is fitted the correct way around so the previously made markings align, and that the rod is facing the right way (see Step 3). Fit the nuts and tighten them finger-tight. Check again to make sure all components have been returned to their original locations using the marks made on disassembly.

26 Tighten the cap nuts to the initial torque setting specified at the beginning of the Chapter **(see illustration)**. Now tighten each nut in turn and in one continuous movement to the final torque setting specified. If tightening is paused between the initial and final settings, slacken the nut to below the initial setting and repeat the procedure.

27 Check that the rods rotate smoothly and freely on the crankpin. If there are any signs of roughness or tightness, remove the rods and re-check the bearing clearance. Sometimes tapping the bottom of the connecting rod cap will relieve tightness, but if in doubt, recheck the clearances.

28 Install the crankshaft (see Section 28).

Engine, clutch and transmission 2•47

30.2a Remove the middle sleeve gear . . .

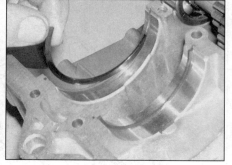

30.2b . . . and its bearing retainers

30.3 Lift the input shaft out of the crankcase

30 Transmission shafts – removal and installation

Note: *To remove the transmission shafts the engine must be removed from the frame and the crankcase halves separated.*

Removal

1 Remove the engine from the frame (see Section 5) and separate the crankcase halves (see Section 23).
2 Lift the middle sleeve gear assembly out of the upper crankcase half **(see illustration)**. Remove the half-ring retainers from each bearing, noting how they fit **(see illustration)**. If the middle gear drive shaft is still inside the sleeve gear, withdraw it.
3 Note how the locating pin on the transmission input shaft right-hand end bearing fits against the crankcase face, pointing forward towards the crankshaft, then lift the shaft out of the upper crankcase half **(see illustration)**. Remove the bearing half ring retainers from the right-hand end, noting how they fit.
4 Remove the selector forks (see Section 32).
5 Remove the bolts securing the transmission output shaft bearing housing to the crankcase **(see illustration)**. Remove the housing, noting how the oil feed nozzle locates into the centre of the shaft. Discard the O-ring as a new one must be used.
6 Remove the bearing from the end of the shaft if it did not come away with the housing. It should be a sliding fit on the shaft and in the housing. If necessary, displace it by sliding the gear cluster onto it. Slide the 5th gear pinion off the end of the shaft and remove it via the bearing aperture **(see illustration)**.
7 Manoeuvre the output shaft towards the left side of the engine so that its right-hand end can be lifted up and out through the bottom of the lower crankcase half **(see illustration)**. If necessary, remove the shaft's right-hand end bearing from its housing in the crankcase.
8 If necessary, the transmission shafts can be disassembled and inspected for wear or damage as described in Section 31.

Installation

9 If the output shaft right-hand bearing was removed from the crankcase, install it in its housing. Manoeuvre the transmission output shaft, without the 5th gear pinion or bearing on its left-hand end, through the underside of the lower crankcase half and into position so that the right-hand end of the shaft locates in its bearing in the casing **(see illustration 30.7)**.
10 Slide the 5th gear pinion onto the left-hand end of the shaft with its selector fork groove facing out **(see illustration 30.6)**.
11 Fit a new O-ring into the output shaft bearing housing, then install the housing, making sure it is correctly fitted, and tighten its bolts to the torque setting specified at the beginning of the Chapter **(see illustrations)**.
12 Install the selector forks in (see Section 32.)

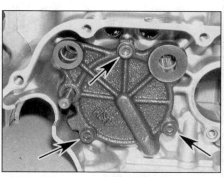

30.5 Unscrew the bolts (arrowed) and remove the housing

30.6 Remove the 5th gear pinion via the bearing aperture . . .

30.7 . . . then manoeuvre the shaft out of the bottom of the crankcase

30.11a Fit a new O-ring to the housing . . .

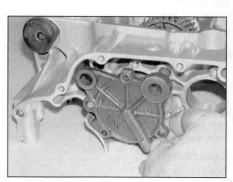

30.11b . . . and install the housing

2•48 Engine, clutch and transmission

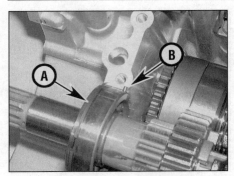

30.13 Make sure the bearing retainers (A) and locating pin (B) are correctly positioned

13 Locate the bearing half-ring retainers in the bearing housing groove in the right-hand end of the input shaft. Install the shaft into the upper crankcase half, with the bearing retainers positioned so that they bridge both casing halves when reassembled **(see illustration 30.3)**. Make sure they locate correctly in their grooves. Make sure the locating pin on the right-hand end bearing fits against the crankcase face and points forward towards the crankshaft **(see illustration)**.

14 Install the middle sleeve gear assembly in the upper crankcase half with the bearing half-ring retainers (one for each bearing) positioned so that they bridge both casing halves when reassembled **(see illustrations 30.2b and a)**. Make sure they locate correctly in their grooves. Note that the middle gear drive shaft is installed into the sleeve gear after the crankcase halves have been reassembled.

15 Make sure both transmission shafts are correctly seated and their related pinions are correctly engaged.

Caution: If the ball bearing locating pins and half-ring retainers are not correctly engaged, the crankcase halves will not seat correctly.

16 Position the gears in the neutral position and check the shafts are free to rotate easily and independently (i.e. the input shaft can turn whilst the output shaft is held stationary) before proceeding further.

17 Reassemble the crankcase halves (see Section 23).

31 Transmission shafts – disassembly, inspection and reassembly

1 Remove the transmission shafts from the crankcase halves (see Section 30). Always disassemble the transmission shafts separately to avoid mixing up the components **(see illustration)**.

Input shaft
Disassembly

2 Remove the bearing from the left end of the shaft. If the bearing is a tight fit on the shaft,

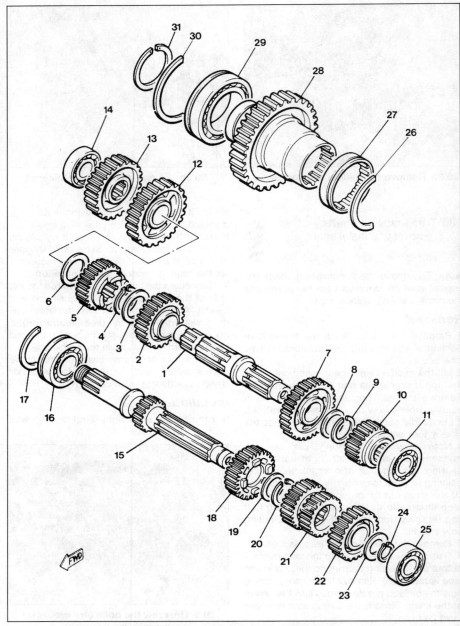

31.1 Transmission components

1 Output shaft
2 Output 3rd gear pinion
3 Thrust washer
4 Circlip
5 Output 4th gear pinion
6 Thrust washer
7 Output 2nd gear pinion
8 Thrust washer
9 Circlip
10 Output 5th gear pinion
11 Bearing
12 Output 1st gear pinion
13 Middle sleeve gear
14 Bearing
15 Input shaft
16 Bearing
17 Bearing half-ring retainer
18 Input 4th gear pinion
19 Thrust washer
20 Circlip
21 Input 2nd and 3rd gear pinion
22 Input 5th gear pinion
23 Thrust washer
24 Circlip
25 Bearing
26 Bearing half-ring retainer
27 Needle roller bearing
28 Middle sleeve gear
29 Bearing
30 Bearing half-ring retainer
31 Circlip

Engine, clutch and transmission 2•49

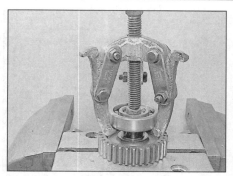

31.2a Using a bearing puller to remove the bearing

31.2b The bearing can also be levered off

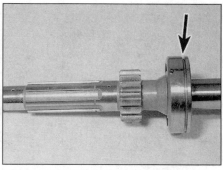

31.14 Install the bearing with its groove (arrowed) facing the clutch end

use a bearing puller. If one is not available, carefully lever it off using a pair of tyre levers **(see illustrations)**.

3 Remove the circlip from the shaft **(see illustration 31.17c)**. Slide the thrust washer and the 5th gear pinion off the shaft, followed by the combined 2nd/3rd gear pinion **(see illustrations 31.17b and a and 31.16)**.

 When disassembling the transmission shafts, place the parts on a long rod or thread a wire through them to keep them in order and facing the proper direction.

4 Remove the circlip securing the 4th gear pinion, then slide the thrust washer and the pinion off the shaft **(see illustrations 31.15d, c, b and a)**.

5 The 1st gear pinion is integral with the shaft **(see illustration 31.14)**. If the bearing on the right (clutch) end of the shaft is to be renewed, remove it from the shaft using a bearing puller if necessary. Note the position of the locating groove in the outer race of the bearing prior to removing it and ensure that the new bearing is fitted with the groove in the same position.

Inspection

6 Wash all of the components in clean solvent and dry them off.

7 Check the gear teeth for cracking, chipping, pitting and other obvious wear or damage. Any pinion that is damaged as such must be replaced with a new one.

8 Inspect the dogs and the dog holes in the gears for cracks, chips, and excessive wear especially in the form of rounded edges. Make sure mating gears engage properly. Replace the paired gears with new ones as a set if necessary.

9 Check for signs of scoring or bluing on the pinions and shaft. This could be caused by overheating due to inadequate lubrication. Check that all the oil holes and passages are clear. Replace any damaged pinions with new ones.

10 Check that each mobile pinion moves freely on the shaft but without undue freeplay.

11 The shaft is unlikely to sustain damage unless the engine has seized, placing an unusually high loading on the transmission, or the machine has covered a very high mileage. Check the surface of the shaft, especially where a pinion turns on it, and renew the shaft if it has scored or picked up, or if there are any cracks. Place the shaft on V-blocks and check the runout at the shaft centre using a dial gauge. Compare the reading to the maximum specified at the beginning of the Chapter. Damage of any kind can only be cured by renewal.

12 Referring to Section 5 in *Tools and Workshop Tips* in the *Reference* section, check the bearings and replace them with new ones if necessary.

13 Check the circlips and thrust washers and renew any that are bent or appear weakened or worn. It is a good idea to use new circlips as a matter of course.

Reassembly

14 During reassembly, apply molybdenum disulphide oil (a 50/50 mixture of molybdenum disulphide grease and new engine oil) to the mating surfaces of the shaft and pinions. When installing the circlips, do not expand the ends any further than is necessary. Install the stamped circlips so that their chamfered side faces the pinion it secures (see *Correct fitting of a stamped circlip* illustration in Section 2 in *Tools and Workshop Tips* of the *Reference* section). If removed, fit the bearing onto the right-hand end of the shaft, making sure the retainer grooves are on the outside **(see illustration)**.

15 Slide the 4th gear pinion onto the left-hand end of the shaft with its dogs facing away from the integral 1st gear **(see illustration)**. Install the thrust washer and

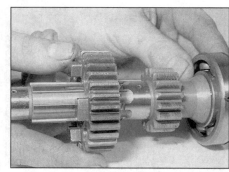

31.15a 4th gear pinion dogs must face away from the integral 1st gear pinion

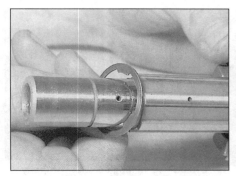

31.15b Slide on the thrust washer . . .

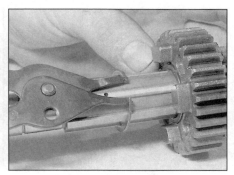

31.15c . . . and circlip . . .

31.15d . . . making sure it is properly seated in its groove and with its ends positioned as shown

2•50 Engine, clutch and transmission

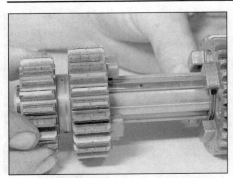

31.16 Install the combined 2nd/3rd gear pinion with the larger 3rd gear dogs facing the 4th gear dogs

31.17a Install the 5th gear pinion with its toothed inner edge facing the 2nd/3rd gear pinion

31.17b Slide on the thrust washer . . .

circlip, making sure that the circlip locates in the groove in the shaft **(see illustrations)**.

16 Slide the combined 2nd/3rd gear pinion onto the shaft so that the larger (3rd) gear faces the 4th gear **(see illustration)**.

17 Slide the 5th gear pinion and then its thrust washer onto the shaft **(see illustrations)**. Secure them in place with the circlip, making sure that the circlip locates in the groove in the shaft **(see illustration)**.

18 Fit the bearing onto the shaft end, using a press if necessary **(see illustration)**.

Output shaft
Disassembly

19 The left-hand bearing and 5th gear pinion have already been removed during removal of the shaft from the crankcase (see Section 30).

20 Remove the circlip from the left end of the shaft, then slide off the thrust washer and the 2nd gear pinion **(see illustrations 31.29c, b and a)**.

21 Slide the middle drive gear and the 1st gear pinion off the shaft, followed by the thrust washer and the 4th gear pinion **(see illustrations 31.28c, b and a, and 31.27)**.

22 Remove the circlip securing the 3rd gear pinion, then slide the thrust washer and pinion off the shaft **(see illustrations 31.26d, c, b and a)**.

23 Remove the bearing for the right-hand end of the shaft from the crankcase if required.

Inspection

24 Refer to Steps 6 to 13 above.

Reassembly

25 During reassembly, apply molybdenum disulphide oil (a 50/50 mixture of molybdenum disulphide grease and new engine oil) to the mating surfaces of the shaft and pinions. When installing the circlips, do not expand the ends any further than is necessary. Install the stamped circlips so that their chamfered side faces the pinion it secures (see *Correct fitting of a stamped circlip* illustration in Section 2 of *Tools and Workshop Tips* of the *Reference* section).

26 Slide the 3rd gear pinion onto the right-hand end of the shaft, followed by its thrust washer, and secure them in place with the circlip, making sure it is properly seated in its groove **(see illustrations)**.

31.17c . . . and the circlip, making sure it is properly seated in its groove

31.18 Install the bearing onto the shaft end

31.26a Install the 3rd gear pinion onto the right-hand end of the shaft . . .

31.26b . . . followed by its thrust washer . . .

31.26c . . . and secure them with their circlip . . .

31.26d . . . making sure it is properly seated in its groove and with its ends positioned as shown (arrowed)

Engine, clutch and transmission 2•51

31.27 4th gear pinion selector fork groove must face the 3rd gear pinion

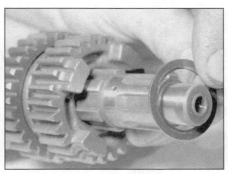

31.28a Slide on the thrust washer . . .

31.28b . . . followed by the 1st gear pinion . . .

27 Slide the 4th gear pinion onto the shaft with its selector fork groove facing the 3rd gear pinion **(see illustration)**.
28 Slide the thrust washer onto the shaft, followed by the 1st gear pinion and then the middle drive gear **(see illustrations)**.
29 Slide the 2nd gear pinion onto the left-hand end of the shaft, followed by its thrust washer, and secure them in place with the circlip, making sure it is properly seated in its groove **(see illustrations)**.
30 The 5th gear pinion and left-hand bearing are installed after the shaft has been installed in the crankcase (see Section 30).

Middle sleeve gear

Disassembly

31 Remove the circlip securing the caged bearing on the right-hand end of the sleeve and slide the bearing off the sleeve, noting that the groove in the bearing faces away from the sleeve pinion **(see illustration)**.
32 Slide the needle roller bearing off the left-hand end of the sleeve, noting that the groove in the bearing faces away from the sleeve pinion **(see illustration)**.

Inspection

33 Inspect the sleeve both internally and externally for any signs of wear or damage. Check the internal splines and the pinion teeth for cracks or broken edges. Replace the sleeve with a new one if it is worn or damaged.
34 Check the bearings for any signs of wear or damage. Check that they rotate freely on the sleeve with no rough spots or excessive play. Replace the bearings with new ones if they are worn or damaged.

Reassembly

35 Slide the needle roller bearing onto the left-hand end of the sleeve with its groove facing away from the pinion.

31.28c . . . and the middle drive gear

31.29a Install the 2nd gear pinion . . .

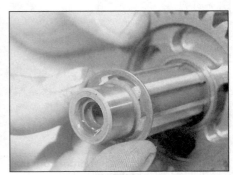

31.29b . . . followed by its thrust washer . . .

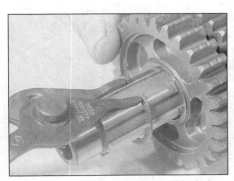

31.29c . . . and secure them with their circlip, making sure it is properly seated in its groove

31.31 Remove the circlip securing the bearing to the sleeve

31.32 Slide the needle roller bearing off the left-hand end of the sleeve

2•52 Engine, clutch and transmission

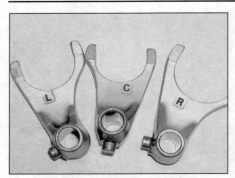

32.2a Note the letter on each fork denoting its position

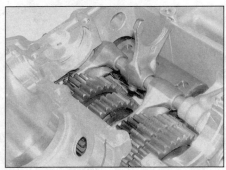

32.2b Withdraw the shaft and remove the forks

32.3 Remove the screws (arrowed) and the retainer plates

36 Slide the caged bearing onto the right-hand end of the sleeve with its groove facing away from the pinion and secure it with its circlip. Make sure the circlip is properly seated in its groove.

32 Selector drum and forks – removal, inspection and installation

Removal

1 Separate the crankcase halves (see Section 23).
2 Before removing the selector forks, note

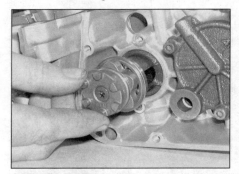

32.5 Withdraw the selector drum from the crankcase

that each fork is lettered for identification. The right-hand fork has an 'R', the centre fork a 'C', and the left-hand fork an 'L' **(see illustration)**. These letters face the right-hand side of the engine. If no letters are visible, mark them yourself using a felt pen. Withdraw the gear selector fork shaft from the lower crankcase half and remove the forks **(see illustration)**. Install the forks back on the shaft in their correct positions as a reminder for installation.
3 Remove the screw securing each selector drum bearing retainer plate and remove the plates, noting how they fit **(see illustration)**.
4 Remove the neutral switch (see Chapter 8).
5 Withdraw the selector drum from the crankcase **(see illustration)**.

Inspection

6 Inspect the selector forks for any signs of wear or damage, especially around the fork ends where they engage with the groove in the pinion. Check that each fork fits correctly in its pinion groove. Check closely to see if the forks are bent. If the forks are in any way damaged they must be replaced with new ones.
7 Check that the forks fit correctly on the shaft. They should move freely with a light fit but no appreciable freeplay. Check that the fork shaft holes in the casing are not worn or damaged.

8 The selector fork shaft can be checked for trueness by rolling it along a flat surface. A bent shaft will cause difficulty in selecting gears and make the gearchange action heavy. Replace the shaft with a new one if bent.
9 Inspect the selector drum grooves and selector fork guide pins for signs of wear or damage. If either show signs of wear or damage they must be replaced with new ones.
10 Check that the selector drum bearing rotates freely and has no signs of roughness or excessive freeplay between it and the drum or crankcase (when installed) (see Section 5 in *Tools and Workshop Tips* in the *Reference* section for more information on bearings). Renew the bearing if necessary. It is retained by the selector cam which is secured by a single central screw **(see illustration)**. Remove the screw, then draw off the cam and remove the pins and the collar. Note the locating pin which fits between the drum and the cam.

Installation

11 Align the selector drum so that the neutral detent for the stopper arm and the contact for the neutral switch point to the bottom of the engine, and slide the drum into the crankcase, locating the inner end in its bore in the crankcase **(see illustration)**. Fit the bearing retainer plates and tighten the screws to the

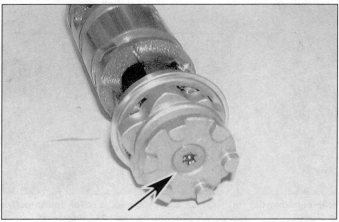

32.10 Remove the screw (arrowed) and draw off the cam

32.11 Slide the drum into the crankcase

Engine, clutch and transmission 2•53

torque setting specified at the beginning of the Chapter **(see illustration 32.3)**.
12 Install the neutral switch (see Chapter 8).
13 Refer to Step 2 for the correct location of each fork. Lubricate the selector fork shaft with clean engine oil. Engage forks R and L in their grooves in the pinions on the output shaft, then slide the selector fork shaft through the forks, locating the guide pin on the end of each fork in its groove in the drum as you do **(see illustrations)**. Make sure the forks are positioned according to their letter (Left, Centre and Right) and with the letters facing the right-hand side of the engine.
14 Check that the selector drum and selector forks all rotate or move freely, and position the selector drum in the neutral position.
15 Assemble the crankcase halves (see Section 23).

33 Initial start-up after overhaul

1 Make sure the engine oil level is correct (see *Daily (pre-ride) checks*).
2 Make sure there is fuel in the tank, then set the choke.
3 As no oil pressure warning light is fitted, an oil pressure check must be carried out. Slacken the oil gallery bolt in the left-hand side of the cylinder head (there is no need to remove it) **(see illustration)**.
4 Start the engine and allow it to idle. After a short while oil should begin to seep out from the oil gallery plug. If no oil has appeared after one minute, stop the engine immediately and investigate the problem (see Chapter 1).
5 After the oil has appeared, allow the engine

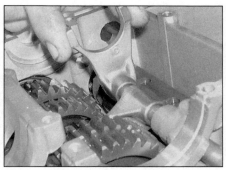

32.13a Slide the shaft through each fork in turn . . .

to run at a moderately fast idle until it reaches operating temperature.
6 Check carefully for oil leaks and make sure the transmission and controls, especially the brakes, function properly before road testing the machine. Refer to Section 34 for the recommended running-in procedure.
7 Upon completion of the road test, and after the engine has cooled down completely, recheck the valve clearances (see Chapter 1) and check the engine oil level (see *Daily (pre-ride) checks*).

34 Recommended running-in procedure

1 Treat the machine gently for the first few miles to make sure oil has circulated throughout the engine and any new parts installed have started to seat.
2 Even greater care is necessary if the engine has been extensively overhauled – the bike

32.13b . . . locating the guide pin on each fork into its groove in the drum

will have to be run in as when new. This means greater use of the transmission and a restraining hand on the throttle until at least 600 miles (1000 km) have been covered. There's no point in keeping to any set speed limit – the main idea is to keep from labouring the engine and to gradually increase performance up to the 600 mile (1000 km) mark. These recommendations can be lessened to an extent when only a partial overhaul has been done, though it does depend to an extent on the nature of the work carried out and which components have been renewed. Experience is the best guide, since it's easy to tell when an engine is running freely. If in any doubt, consult a Yamaha dealer. The maximum engine speed limitations shown in the table below, which Yamaha provide for new motorcycles, can be used as a guide.
3 If a lubrication failure is suspected, stop the engine immediately and try to find the cause. If an engine is run without oil, even for a short period of time, severe damage will occur.

Up to 300 miles (500 km)	4000 rpm max	Vary throttle position/speed. Do not use full throttle
300 to 600 miles (500 to 1000 km)	5000 rpm max	Vary throttle position/speed. Do not use full throttle. Higher revs can be used for short periods, as long as the engine is not laboured
Over 600 miles (1000 km)		Do not exceed tachometer red line

2•54 Engine, clutch and transmission

Notes

Chapter 3
Fuel and exhaust systems

Contents

Air filter – cleaning and renewal . . . . .see Chapter 1	Exhaust system – removal and installation 14
Air filter housing – removal and installation 4	Fuel gauge, warning light and sensor – check and renewal 16
Air induction system (AIS) – function, disassembly and reassembly . . 17	Fuel hoses – renewal . . . . .see Chapter 1
Air induction system (AIS) – check . . . . .see Chapter 1	Fuel pump and relay – check and renewal 15
Air/fuel mixture adjustment – general information 5	Fuel system – check . . . . .see Chapter 1
Carburettor heater system – check 13	Fuel tank – cleaning and repair 3
Carburettor overhaul – general information 6	Fuel tank and fuel tap – removal and installation 2
Carburettor synchronisation . . . . .see Chapter 1	General information and precautions 1
Carburettors – disassembly, cleaning and inspection 8	Idle speed – check . . . . .see Chapter 1
Carburettors – reassembly and fuel level check 10	Throttle and choke cables – check and adjustment . . . .see Chapter 1
Carburettors – removal and installation 7	Throttle cables – removal and installation 11
Carburettors – separation and joining 9	Throttle position sensor – check and adjustment . . . . . . .see Chapter 4
Choke cable – removal and installation 12	

Degrees of difficulty

Easy, suitable for novice with little experience	Fairly easy, suitable for beginner with some experience	Fairly difficult, suitable for competent DIY mechanic	Difficult, suitable for experienced DIY mechanic	Very difficult, suitable for expert DIY or professional

Specifications

Fuel
Grade	Unleaded, minimum 91 RON (Research Octane Number)
Fuel tank capacity (including reserve)	24.0 litres
Reserve	5.0 litres

Carburettors
Type	Mikuni BDSR34/4
Fuel level (see text)	6.0 to 7.0 mm below float chamber line
Idle speed	see Chapter 1
Pilot screw setting (turns out)	1 $\frac{1}{2}$
Main jet	100
Main air jet	72.5
Jet needle	5DT3-2
Needle jet	0-2
Pilot air jet	120
Pilot jet	12.5
Starter jet	30

Carburettor heater system
Resistance	6 to 10 ohms @ 20°C

Fuel pump
Resistance	4 to 30 ohms @ 20°C

Fuel level sensor
Resistance
Full	4 to 10 ohms @ 20°C
Empty	90 to 100 ohms @ 20°C

3•2 Fuel and exhaust systems

Torque settings

Fuel tap screws	7 Nm
Carburettor heaters	3 Nm
Silencer-to-collector box clamp bolts	20 Nm
Silencer mounting bolts	25 Nm
Downpipe-to-collector box clamp bolts	20 Nm
Downpipe assembly nuts	20 Nm
Collector box bolt	25 Nm
Fuel level sensor bolts	4 Nm

1 General information and precautions

General information

The fuel system consists of the fuel tank with internal level sensor, fuel tap, fuel filter, fuel pump, fuel hoses, carburettors and control cables. The fuel tap has an integral strainer, and the fuel pump is mounted externally with an in-line filter.

The carburettors used are CV types. There is a carburettor for each cylinder. For cold starting, a choke knob or lever is connected to the carburettors by a cable. On 1994 and 1995 models, the knob is mounted on the top yoke. On all other models, the lever is housed in the left-hand switch housing on the handlebar.

Air is drawn into the carburettors via an air filter which is housed under the fuel tank.

The exhaust system is a four-into-two design.

Many of the fuel system service procedures are considered routine maintenance items and for that reason are included in Chapter 1.

Precautions

⚠ **Warning: Petrol (gasoline) is extremely flammable, so take extra precautions when you work on any part of the fuel system. Don't smoke or allow open flames or bare light bulbs near the work area, and don't work in a garage where a natural gas-type appliance is present. If you spill any fuel on your skin, rinse it off immediately with soap and water. When you perform any kind of work on the fuel system, wear safety glasses and have a fire extinguisher suitable for a class B type fire (flammable liquids) on hand.**

Always perform service procedures in a well-ventilated area to prevent a build-up of fumes.

Never work in a building containing a gas appliance with a pilot light, or any other form of naked flame. Ensure that there are no naked light bulbs or any sources of flame or sparks nearby.

Do not smoke (or allow anyone else to smoke) while in the vicinity of petrol (gasoline) or of components containing it. Remember the possible presence of vapour from these sources and move well clear before smoking.

Check all electrical equipment belonging to the house, garage or workshop where work is being undertaken (see the Safety first! section of this manual). Remember that certain electrical appliances such as drills, cutters etc. create sparks in the normal course of operation and must not be used near petrol (gasoline) or any component containing it. Again, remember the possible presence of fumes before using electrical equipment.

Always mop up any spilt fuel and safely dispose of the rag used.

Any stored fuel that is drained off during servicing work must be kept in sealed containers that are suitable for holding petrol (gasoline), and clearly marked as such; the containers themselves should be kept in a safe place. Note that this last point applies equally to the fuel tank if it is removed from the machine; also remember to keep its filler cap closed at all times.

Read the Safety first! section of this manual carefully before starting work.

2 Fuel tank and fuel tap – removal and installation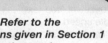

⚠ **Warning: Refer to the precautions given in Section 1 before starting work.**

Fuel tank

Removal

1 Make sure the fuel cap is secure. Remove the seat (see Chapter 7).
2 Unscrew the bolt securing the rear of the tank and remove the plate and rubber seat **(see illustration)**. Unscrew the bolt securing the front of the tank **(see illustration)**.
3 Turn the fuel tap OFF **(see illustration)**.
4 Release the clamp securing the fuel hose to the fuel tap and detach the hose, being prepared to catch the residual fuel from the hose and the fuel filter with a rag **(see illustration 2.3)**. Disconnect the fuel level sensor wiring connector

2.2a Unscrew the rear bolt (arrowed) and remove the plate . . .

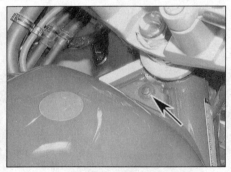

2.2b . . . then unscrew the front bolt (arrowed)

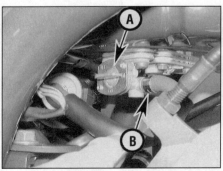

2.3 Turn the fuel tap (A) OFF, then release the clamp and detach the fuel hose (B)

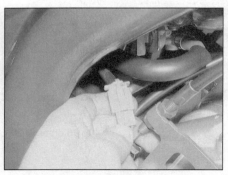

2.4 Disconnect the wiring connector

Fuel and exhaust systems 3•3

2.5 Carefully remove the tank

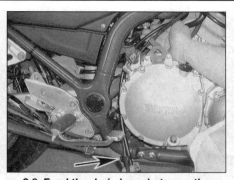

2.6 Feed the drain hose between the engine and frame and through the guide (arrowed)

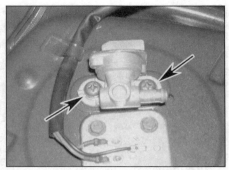

2.10a Remove the screws (arrowed) . . .

5 Carefully lift the tank off the frame and remove it, bringing the drain hose with it (see illustration). Inspect the tank mounting rubbers for signs of damage or deterioration and replace them with new ones if necessary.

Installation

6 Installation is the reverse of removal, noting the following:
   a) Feed the drain hose between the upper rear engine mounting bolt and the frame and through its guide on the right-hand side of the bike (see illustration).
   b) Make sure the fuel hose is properly attached and secured by its clamp (see illustration 2.3). Make sure the wiring connector is securely connected (see illustration 2.4).
   c) Turn the fuel tap ON (see illustration 2.3).
   d) Tighten the mounting bolts securely.
   e) Start the engine and check that there is no sign of fuel leakage.

Fuel tap

Removal

7 Remove the fuel tank as described above.
8 Connect a drain hose to the fuel outlet union on the tap and insert its end in a container suitable and large enough for storing the fuel. Turn the fuel tap to the 'ON'

position and allow the tank to drain. When the tank has drained, turn the tap to the 'OFF' position.
9 If the fuel tap has been leaking, tightening the assembly screws on the tap face may help (see illustration 2.11). Slacken the screws a little first, then tighten them evenly and a little at a time to ensure the cover seats properly on the tap body. If leakage persists, the tap should be replaced with a new one, however nothing is lost by dismantling the tap for further inspection. Remove the screws on the face of the tap and disassemble it, noting how the components fit. Inspect all components for wear or damage, and replace them with new ones as necessary, if available. If any of the components are worn or damaged beyond repair and are not available individually, a new tap must be fitted.
10 Remove the screws securing the tap to the tank and withdraw the tap assembly (see illustrations). Discard the O-ring as a new one must be used.
11 Clean the gauze strainer to remove all traces of dirt and fuel sediment (see illustration). Check the gauze for holes. If any are found, a new tap should be fitted as the strainer is not available individually.

Installation

12 Installation is the reverse of removal.
13 Use a new O-ring on the tap, and tighten the screws to the torque setting specified at

the beginning of the Chapter (see illustration).
14 Install the fuel tank (see above).

3 Fuel tank – cleaning and repair

1 All repairs to the fuel tank should be carried out by a professional who has experience in this critical and potentially dangerous work. Even after cleaning and flushing of the fuel system, explosive fumes can remain and ignite during repair of the tank.
2 If the fuel tank is removed from the bike, it should not be placed in an area where sparks or open flames could ignite the fumes coming out of the tank. Be especially careful inside garages where a natural gas-type appliance is located, because the pilot light could cause an explosion.

4 Air filter housing – removal and installation

Removal

1 Remove the fuel tank (see Section 2).
2 Release the clamps securing the crankcase

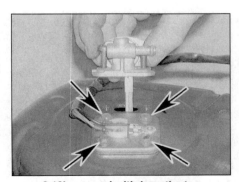

2.10b . . . and withdraw the tap

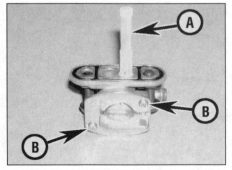

2.11 Fuel strainer (A), tap assembly screws (B)

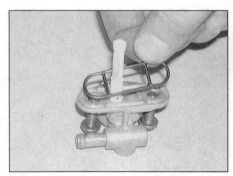

2.13 Always use a new O-ring when installing the tap

3•4 Fuel and exhaust systems

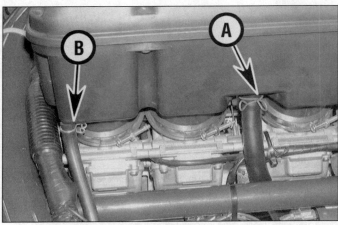

4.2a Detach the breather hose (A) and the drain hose (B)

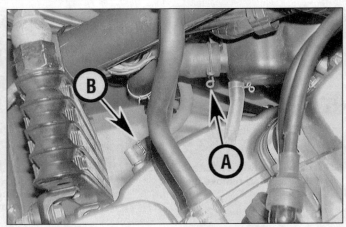

4.2b Detach the AIS hose (A) and the breather hose (B)

breather hose and the drain hose to the back of the air filter housing and detach the hoses **(see illustration)**. Release the clamps securing the AIS system hose to the front of the air filter housing and the valve cover breather hose to the valve cover and detach the hoses **(see illustration)**.

3 Unscrew the bolt securing the front of the housing to the frame **(see illustration)**. Slacken the clamp screws securing the housing to the carburettor intakes on the underside **(see illustration)**.

4 Lift the housing up off the carburettors and remove it **(see illustration)**.

Installation

5 Installation is the reverse of removal. Check the condition of the various hoses and their clamps and replace them with new ones if necessary.

5 Air/fuel mixture adjustment – general information

Adjustment – UK

1 If the engine runs extremely rough at idle or continually stalls, and if a carburettor overhaul does not cure the problem, the pilot screws probably require adjustment to achieve a smooth idle and restore low speed performance. It is worth noting at this point that unless you have the skill to carry this out on a multi-cylinder machine it is best to entrust the task to a motorcycle dealer, tuner or fuel systems specialist. Note that you will need a long thin screwdriver with an angled end to access the pilot screws.

2 Before adjusting the pilot screws **(see illustration 8.8)**, the engine must be warmed up to normal working temperature. Stop the engine and screw in all four pilot screws until they seat lightly, then back them out to the number of turns specified (see this Chapter's Specifications). This is the base position for adjustment.

3 Start the engine and reset the idle speed to the correct level (see Chapter 1). Working on one carburettor at a time, turn the pilot screw by a small amount either side of this position to find the point at which the highest consistent idle speed is obtained. When you've reached this position, reset the idle speed to the specified amount (see Chapter 1). Repeat on the other three carburettors in turn.

Other markets

4 Due to the increased emphasis on controlling exhaust emissions in certain world markets, regulations have been formulated which prevent adjustment of the air/fuel mixture. On such models the pilot screw positions are pre-set at the factory and in some cases have a limiter cap fitted to prevent tampering. Where adjustment is possible, it can only be made in conjunction with an exhaust gas analyser to ensure that the machine does not exceed the emissions regulations.

6 Carburettor overhaul – general information

1 Poor engine performance, hesitation, hard starting, stalling, flooding and backfiring are all signs that major carburettor maintenance may be required.

2 Keep in mind that many so-called carburettor problems are really not carburettor problems at all, but mechanical problems within the engine, or ignition system malfunctions. Try to establish for certain that

4.3a Unscrew the bolt (arrowed) . . .

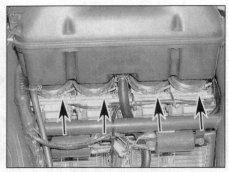

4.3b . . . and slacken the four carburettor clamp screws (arrowed)

4.4 Lift the housing up off the carburettors

Fuel and exhaust systems 3•5

7.2 Detach the fuel hose from its union (arrowed)

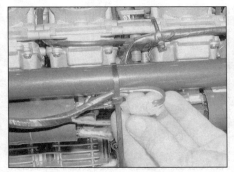

7.3a Disconnect the heater system wiring connector...

7.3b ... and the throttle position sensor wiring connector

the carburettors are in need of maintenance before beginning a major overhaul.

3 Check the fuel tap and filter, the fuel hoses, the fuel pump, the intake manifold joint clamps, the air filter, the ignition system, the spark plugs and carburettor synchronisation before assuming that a carburettor overhaul is required.

4 Most carburettor problems are caused by dirt particles, varnish and other deposits which build up in and block the fuel and air passages. Also, in time, gaskets and O-rings shrink or deteriorate and cause fuel and air leaks which lead to poor performance.

5 When overhauling the carburettors, disassemble them completely and clean the parts thoroughly with a carburettor cleaning solvent and dry them with filtered, unlubricated compressed air. Blow through the fuel and air passages with compressed air to force out any dirt that may have been loosened but not removed by the solvent. Once the cleaning process is complete, reassemble the carburettor using new gaskets and O-rings.

6 Before disassembling the carburettors, make sure you have all necessary O-rings and other parts, some carburettor cleaner, a supply of clean rags, some means of blowing out the carburettor passages and a clean place to work. It is recommended that only one carburettor be overhauled at a time to avoid mixing up parts.

7 Carburettors – removal and installation

Warning: Refer to the precautions given in Section 1 before starting work.

Removal

1 Remove the fuel tank (see Section 2) and the air filter housing (see Section 4).
2 Release the clamp securing the fuel supply hose to the carburettors and detach the hose, being prepared to catch any residual fuel with a rag **(see illustration)**.
3 Trace the wiring from the carburettor heaters and disconnect it at the connector **(see illustration)**. Also disconnect the throttle position sensor wiring connector **(see illustration)**.
4 Detach the choke cable from the carburettors (see Section 12).
5 Detach the throttle cables from the carburettors (see Section 11).
6 Fully slacken the clamp screws on the cylinder head intake rubbers **(see illustration)**.
7 Ease the carburettors off the intakes and remove them **(see illustration)**. **Note:** *Keep the carburettors level to prevent fuel spillage from the float chambers and the possibility of the piston diaphragms being damaged.*
Caution: Stuff clean rag into each cylinder

head intake after removing the carburettors to prevent anything from falling in.
8 Place a suitable container below the float chambers, then slacken the drain screw on each chamber in turn and drain all the fuel from the carburettors **(see illustration)**. Tighten the drain screws securely once all the fuel has been drained.

Installation

9 Installation is the reverse of removal, noting the following.
a) Check for cracks or splits in the cylinder head intake rubbers, and replace them with new ones if necessary.
b) Make sure the carburettors are fully engaged with the cylinder head and air intake rubbers and the clamps are securely tightened.
c) Do not forget to connect the heater system and TPS wiring connectors.
d) Make sure all hoses are correctly routed and secured and not trapped or kinked.
e) Refer to Section 11 for installation of the throttle cables, and Section 12 for the choke cable. Check the operation of the cables and adjust them as necessary (see Chapter 1).
f) Check idle speed and carburettor synchronisation and adjust as necessary (see Chapter 1).

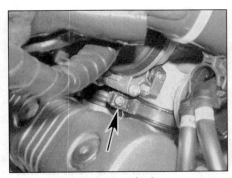

7.6 Fully slacken each clamp screw (arrowed) ...

7.7 ... then ease the carburettors off the intakes and remove them

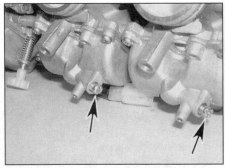

7.8 Carburettor drain screws (arrowed)

3•6 Fuel and exhaust systems

8.2a Remove the screws (arrowed) and lift off the cover

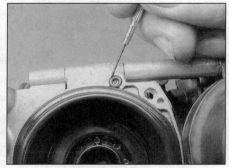

8.2b Remove the air passage O-ring

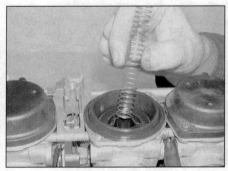

8.3a Remove the spring . . .

8 Carburettors – disassembly, cleaning and inspection

Warning: Refer to the precautions given in Section 1 before starting work.

Disassembly

1 Remove the carburettors from the machine as described in the previous Section. **Note:** *Do not separate the carburettors unless absolutely necessary; each carburettor can be dismantled sufficiently for all normal cleaning and adjustments while in place on the mounting brackets. Dismantle the carburettors separately to avoid interchanging parts* **(see illustration 9.2)**.

2 Unscrew and remove the top cover retaining screws and remove the cover **(see illustration)**. Remove the air passage O-ring **(see illustration)**.

3 Remove the spring from inside the piston **(see illustration)**. Carefully peel the diaphragm away from its sealing groove in the carburettor and withdraw the diaphragm and piston assembly **(see illustration)**. Using a pair of thin-nosed pliers, carefully withdraw the jet needle holder from inside the piston – it is a press fit, held by an O-ring **(see illustration)**. Note the spring fitted into the bottom of the holder. Push the jet needle up from the bottom of the piston and withdraw it from the top, noting the washer on the top of the needle **(see illustration)**. If the E-clip and spacer are removed from the needle, note which notch the clip is fitted into.

Caution: Do not use a sharp instrument to displace the diaphragm as it is easily damaged.

4 Remove the screws securing the float chamber to the base of the carburettor and remove the float chamber, noting how it fits **(see illustration)**. Remove the rubber gasket and discard it as a new one must be used.

5 Remove the screw retaining the float pivot pin **(see illustration)**. Remove the float assembly, noting how it fits **(see illustration 10.7e)**. Withdraw the pivot pin **(see illustration 10.7d)**. Unhook the needle valve from the tab on the float, noting how it fits **(see illustration 10.7c)**. Remove the

8.3b . . . and withdraw the piston/diaphragm assembly

8.3c Remove the needle holder . . .

8.3d . . . then push the needle up from the bottom and withdraw it

8.4 Float chamber screws (arrowed)

8.5a Remove the screw (arrowed) and lift off the float assembly

8.5b Remove the screw (arrowed) . . .

Fuel and exhaust systems 3•7

8.5c ... and withdraw the needle valve seat

8.6a Unscrew the main jet (arrowed) ...

8.6b ... then remove the sealing washer

screw securing the needle valve seat and draw out the seat **(see illustrations)**. Discard its O-ring as a new one must be used.

6 Unscrew and remove the main jet **(see illustration)**. Remove the sealing washer that fits between the jet and the jet holder **(see illustration)**. Unscrew the jet holder and remove the main jet nozzle **(see illustrations)**.

7 Unscrew the holder securing the needle jet, then draw the jet out from the carburettor venturi using a long pair of thin-nosed pliers **(see illustrations)**.

8 Unscrew and remove the pilot jet **(see illustration)**.

9 The pilot screw can be removed from the carburettor, but note that its setting will be disturbed (see **Haynes Hint**). Unscrew and remove the pilot screw along with its spring, washer and O-ring **(see illustration 8.8)**. Discard the O-ring as a new one must be used.

8.6c Unscrew the main jet holder ...

8.6d ... then remove the nozzle

 To record the pilot screw's current setting, turn the screw in until it seats lightly, counting the number of turns necessary to achieve this, then fully unscrew it. On installation, the screw is simply backed out the number of turns you've recorded.

10 A throttle position sensor is mounted on the outside of the left-hand carburettor. Do not remove the sensor from the carburettor unless it is known to be faulty and is being replaced with a new one. Refer to Chapter 4 for check and adjustment of the sensor.

11 If required, release the spring clamp securing the intake duct to the holder and remove the duct, then remove the screws securing the duct holder and remove the holder **(see illustrations)**.

8.7a Unscrew the needle jet holder (arrowed) ...

8.7b ... then draw the jet out of the carburettor body

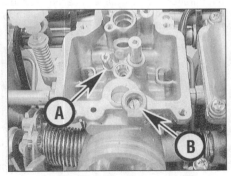

8.8 Pilot jet (A), pilot screw (B)

8.11a Release the spring and lift the duct off the holder ...

8.11b ... then remove the screws (arrowed) securing the holder

3•8 Fuel and exhaust systems

8.15a Release the clips . . .

8.15b . . . and remove the linkage bar, noting how it fits (arrowed)

8.16a Unscrew the plunger nut and withdraw the spring and plunger

Cleaning

Caution: Use only a petroleum based solvent for carburettor cleaning. Don't use caustic cleaners.

12 Submerge the metal components in the solvent for approximately thirty minutes (or longer, if the directions recommend it).
13 After the carburettor has soaked long enough for the cleaner to loosen and dissolve most of the varnish and other deposits, use a nylon-bristled brush to remove the stubborn deposits. Rinse it again, then dry it with compressed air.
14 Use a jet of compressed air to blow out all of the fuel and air passages in the main and upper body. Do not forget to blow through the air jets and passages in the intake side of the carburettor. The jets can be removed if required.
Caution: Never clean the jets or passages with a piece of wire or a drill bit, as they will be enlarged, causing the fuel and air metering rates to be upset.

Inspection

15 Check the operation of the choke plunger assembly. If it doesn't move smoothly, release and push out the clips securing the choke linkage bar to the carburettors, noting how they fit **(see illustration)**. Lift off the bar, noting how it locates into the choke activator and onto the end of each choke plunger **(see illustration)**.
16 Check the operation of each plunger individually. If the action on any is stiff, unscrew the choke plunger nut, using a pair of thin nosed pliers if access is too restricted for a spanner, and withdraw the plunger assembly from the carburettor body **(see illustration)**. Inspect the needle on the end of the choke plunger, the spring and the plunger linkage bar **(see illustration)**. Replace the assembly with a new one if any component is worn, damaged or bent – individual parts are not available. Note that only the plungers for Nos. 1 and 3 carburettors can be removed with the carburettors joined – to remove the No. 2 and 4 plungers, the carburettors must be separated (see Section 9).
17 If removed from the carburettor, check the tapered portion of the pilot screw and the spring and O-ring for wear or damage **(see illustration)**. Replace the assembly with a new one if necessary – individual parts are not available.
18 Check the carburettor body, float chamber and top cover for cracks, distorted sealing surfaces and other damage. If any defects are found, replace the faulty component with a new one, although replacement of the entire carburettor may be necessary (check with a Yamaha dealer on the availability of separate components).
19 Check the piston diaphragm for splits, holes and general deterioration. Holding it up to a light will help to reveal problems of this nature.
20 Insert the piston in the carburettor body and check that it moves up-and-down smoothly. Check the surface of the piston or slide for wear. If it's worn excessively or doesn't move smoothly in the guide, replace the components with new ones as necessary.
21 Check the jet needle for straightness by rolling it on a flat surface such as a piece of glass. Replace it with a new one if it's bent or if the tip is worn.
22 Check the tip of the float needle valve and the valve seat. If either has grooves or scratches in it, or is in any way worn, they must be renewed as a set **(see illustration)**.
23 Operate the throttle shaft to make sure the throttle butterfly valve opens and closes smoothly. If it doesn't, clean the throttle linkage, and also check the butterfly for distortion, or for any debris caught between its edge and the carburettor. Also check that the butterfly is central on the shaft – if the screws securing it to the shaft have come loose it may be catching. Otherwise, replace the carburettor with a new one.
24 Check the float for damage. This will usually be apparent by the presence of fuel inside the float. If it is damaged, replace it with a new one.

9 Carburettors – separation and joining

Warning: Refer to the precautions given in Section 1 before proceeding.

Separation

1 The carburettors do not need to be separated for normal overhaul. If you need to separate them (to renew a carburettor body, for example), refer to the following procedure.
2 Remove the carburettors from the machine (see Section 7). Mark the body of each carburettor with its cylinder location to ensure that it is positioned correctly on reassembly **(see illustration)**.

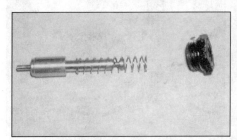

8.16b Check the choke components as described

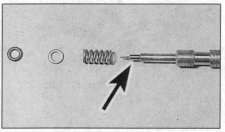

8.17 Check the tapered portion of the pilot screw (arrowed) for wear

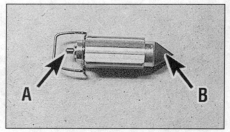

8.22 Check the valve's spring loaded rod (A) and tip (B) for wear or damage

Fuel and exhaust systems 3•9

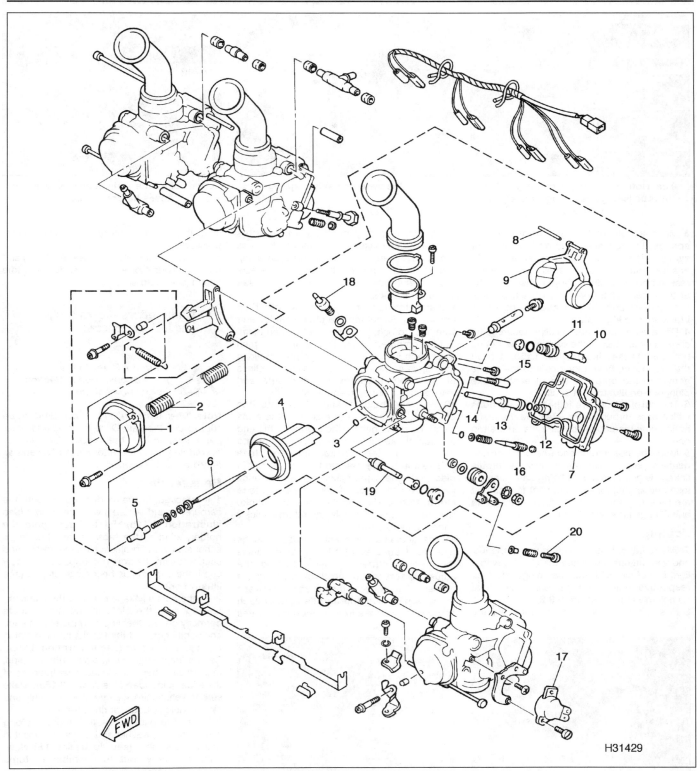

9.2 Carburettor assembly

1 Top cover
2 Spring
3 Air passage O-ring
4 Piston/diaphragm
5 Jet holder
6 Jet needle
7 Float chamber
8 Float pivot pin
9 Float
10 Needle valve
11 Needle valve seat
12 Main jet
13 Jet holder
14 Main nozzle
15 Pilot jet
16 Pilot screw
17 Throttle position sensor
18 Heater
19 Choke plunger
20 Synchronising screw

3•10 Fuel and exhaust systems

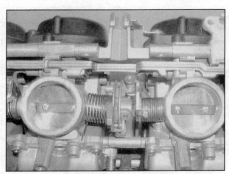

9.3a Note the correct assembly of the throttle linkage assembly and return springs, . . .

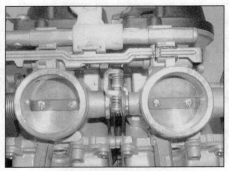

9.3b . . . the synchronisation springs . . .

9.3c . . . and the various collars joints and hoses before separation

3 Make a note of how the throttle return springs, linkage assembly and carburettor synchronisation springs are arranged to ensure that they are fitted correctly on reassembly (see illustrations). Also note the arrangement of the various hoses, unions, joint pieces and collars, and of the cable brackets (see illustration).

4 Release and push out the clips securing the choke linkage bar to the carburettors, noting how they fit (see illustration 8.15a). Lift off the bar, noting how it locates into the choke activator and onto the end of each choke plunger (see illustration 8.15b).

5 The carburettors are joined by long bolts which pass through them. Remove the bolts, noting how the choke activator fits on the top one.

6 Mark the position of each carburettor and gently separate them, noting how the throttle linkage is connected, and being careful not to lose any springs or fuel and vent fittings that are present between the carburettors, noting any O-rings fitted with them.

Joining

7 Where fitted, install new O-rings on the fuel and vent fittings. Lubricate the O-rings with a light film of oil and install the fittings into their respective holes, making sure they seat completely (see illustration 9.2).

8 Position the coil springs between the carburettors, gently push the carburettors together, then make sure the throttle linkages are correctly engaged (see illustration 9.3a). Check the fuel and vent fittings to make sure they engage properly also (see illustration 9.3c).

9 Install the long through-bolts with their collars, not forgetting the choke cable lever with the top bolt, but do not yet tighten them. Set the carburettors on a sheet of glass, then align them with a straight-edge placed along the edges of the bores. When the centrelines of the carburettors are all in horizontal and vertical alignment, tighten the bolts.

10 Fit the choke linkage bar onto the plungers, making sure the slots in the arms locate correctly behind the nipple on the end of each choke plunger, and the tab fits into the slot in the choke activator (see illustration 8.15b). Secure the linkage bar in place with the clips, making sure their ends locate over the ends of the slide guide (see illustration 8.15a). Make sure the choke linkage operates smoothly and returns quickly under spring pressure.

11 Install the throttle synchronisation springs (see illustration 9.3b). Visually synchronise the throttle butterfly valves, turning the adjusting screws on the throttle linkage, if necessary, to equalise the clearance between the butterfly valve and throttle bore of each carburettor. Make sure the throttle operates smoothly and returns quickly under spring pressure.

12 Install the carburettors (see Section 7) and check carburettor synchronisation and idle speed (see Chapter 1).

10 Carburettors – reassembly and fuel level check

 Warning: Refer to the precautions given in Section 1 before proceeding.

Note: *When reassembling the carburettors, be sure to use the new O-rings, seals and other parts supplied in the rebuild kit. Do not overtighten the carburettor jets and screws as they are easily damaged.*

Reassembly

1 If removed, fit the air duct holder onto the carburettor and secure it with the screws (see illustration 8.11b). Fit the duct onto the holder, aligning the tabs so they locate on either side of the projection on the holder, and secure it with the spring clamp, using a new one if the original has become stretched (see illustration).

2 Fit the choke linkage bar onto the plungers, making sure the slots in the arms locate correctly behind the nipple on the end of each choke plunger, and the tab fits into the slot in the choke activator (see illustration 8.15b). Secure the linkage bar in place with the clips, making sure their ends locate over the ends of the slide guide (see illustration 8.15a). Make sure the choke linkage operates smoothly and returns quickly under spring pressure.

3 Install the pilot screw (if removed) along with its spring, washer and O-ring, turning it in until it seats lightly (see illustration 8.8). Now, turn the screw out the number of turns previously recorded, or as specified at the beginning of the Chapter – see Section 5 for more information.

4 Install the pilot jet (see illustration).

5 Fit the needle jet down through the carburettor (see illustration 8.7b), aligning the cutout in its base with the projection in the

10.1 Align the tabs on the duct with the projection (arrowed) on the holder

10.4 Install the pilot jet

Fuel and exhaust systems 3•11

10.5a Align the cutout in the jet with the projection (arrowed)

10.5b Install the needle jet holder

10.6a Install the nozzle with the grooved end out

bore (see illustration). Install the needle jet holder (see illustration).

6 Install the main jet nozzle with its grooved end on the outside (see illustration 8.6d). Install the main jet holder (see illustration). Insert the sealing washer into the top of the holder (see illustration 8.6b), then screw the main jet into the holder (see illustration).

7 Fit a new O-ring onto the needle valve seat, then press it into place and secure it with the screw (see illustrations). Hook the float needle valve onto the tab on the float assembly, then insert the pivot pin (see illustrations). Position the float assembly onto the carburettor, making sure the needle valve locates in the seat (see illustration). Install the pivot pin retaining screw (see illustration 8.5a).

8 Fit a new rubber gasket onto the float chamber, making sure it is seated properly in

its groove, then fit the chamber onto the carburettor and tighten its screws securely (see illustrations).

10.6b Thread the main jet into the holder

9 If removed, fit the spacer and E-clip onto the needle, making sure the clip is in the same groove from which it was removed, then fit the

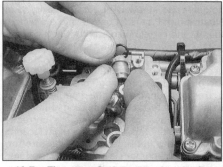

10.7a Fit a new O-ring onto the needle valve seat . . .

10.7b . . . and press it into place

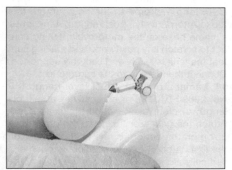

10.7c Hook the needle valve onto the tab on the float . . .

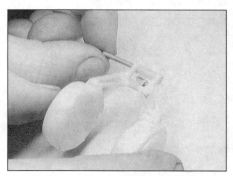

10.7d . . . then insert the pivot pin

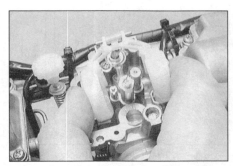

10.7e Install the float assembly, making sure the valve locates in the seat and the pin ends locate in their cutouts

10.8a Make sure the gasket is in its groove . . .

10.8b . . . then install the float chamber

3•12 Fuel and exhaust systems

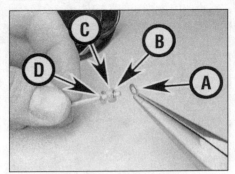

10.9a There should be an upper washer (A), E-clip (B), spacer (C) and lower washer (D) on the needle

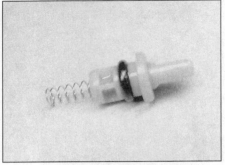

10.9b Needle holder assembly

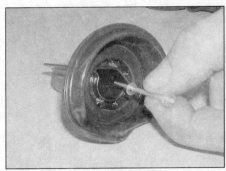

10.9c Fit the needle into the piston . . .

washers on top of the clip and underneath the spacer **(see illustration)**. Check that the spring and O-ring are fitted to the needle holder – use a new O-ring if necessary **(see illustration)**. Fit the jet needle into the piston, then fit the needle holder onto it and press it gently down until it is secure **(see illustrations)**. Fit the piston/diaphragm assembly into the carburettor and lightly push the piston down, making sure the needle is correctly aligned with the needle jet **(see illustration)**. Press the diaphragm outer edge into its groove, making sure it is correctly seated with the tab on the diaphragm locating correctly into the recess in the carburettor. Check the diaphragm is not creased, and that the piston moves smoothly up and down in the guide.

10 Fit the air passage O-ring **(see**

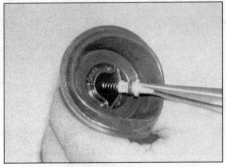

10.9d . . . and secure it with the holder

10.9e Insert the piston/diaphragm assembly into the carburettor

illustration 8.2b). Fit the spring into the diaphragm assembly, making sure it locates correctly onto the needle holder, then fit the top cover onto the carburettor, locating the peg into the top of the spring, and tighten its screws securely **(see illustration)**.

11 Install the carburettors (see Section 7), but if the fuel level (float height) is to be checked do not yet install the air filter housing or fuel tank.

Fuel level check

12 To check the fuel level, position the motorcycle on level ground and support it using the centrestand so that it is vertical. Remove the fuel tank and the air filter housing (see Sections 2 and 4).

13 Arrange a temporary fuel supply, either by using a small temporary tank or by using an extra long fuel pipe to the now remote fuel tank. Alternatively, position the tank on a suitable base on the motorcycle, taking care not to scratch any paintwork, and making sure that the tank is safely and securely supported. Connect the fuel line to the carburettors.

14 Yamaha provide a fuel level gauge (Pt. No. 90890-01312), or alternatively a suitable length of clear plastic tubing can be used. Attach the gauge or tubing to the drain hose union on the bottom of the float chamber on the first carburettor and position its open end vertically alongside and above the level of the carburettors **(see illustration)**.

15 If the bike's fuel tank is being used, turn

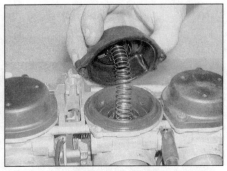

10.10 Fit the top cover, making sure the spring is correctly located top and bottom

the tap ON. Slacken the drain screw and allow the fuel to flow into the tube. The level at which the fuel stabilises in the tubing indicates the level of the fuel in the float chamber. Refer to the Specifications at the beginning of the Chapter and measure the level relative to the reference line on the float chamber **(see illustration 10.14)**. If the bike's fuel tank is being used, turn the tap OFF. Tighten the drain screw, then detach the fuel supply.

16 If the level was incorrect, drain the carburettors, then remove the float from the chamber (see Section 8), and adjust the float height by carefully bending the float tab a little at a time until the correct height is obtained. Repeat the procedure for the other carburettors. **Note:** *Bending the tab up lowers the fuel level – bending it down raises the fuel level.*

11 Throttle cables – removal and installation

Warning: *Refer to the precautions given in Section 1 before proceeding.*

Removal

1 Remove the fuel tank and the air filter housing (see Sections 2 and 4).

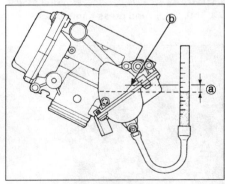

10.14 Fuel level check

a *Distance between fuel level and reference line*
b *Reference line on float chamber*

Fuel and exhaust systems 3•13

11.3a Slacken the locknut . . .

11.3b . . . then free the cable from the bracket . . .

11.3c . . . and detach the cable nipple from the carburettor

2 Mark each cable according to its location at both ends. If new cables are being fitted, match them to the old cables to ensure they are correctly installed.
3 Slacken the accelerator (opening) cable top nut and thread it up the elbow, then slide the cable down in the bracket until the bottom nut is clear of the small lug on the bracket **(see illustration)**. Slip the cable out of the bracket and detach the nipple from the carburettors **(see illustrations)**. Repeat the procedure for the decelerator (closing) cable.
4 Pull the rubber boot back off the throttle housing on the handlebar **(see illustration)**. Remove the throttle housing screws and separate the halves – unless an angled screwdriver is available you may have to remove the front brake lever to get a good line on the bottom screw (see Chapter 5) **(see illustration)**. Displace the cable elbows from the housing, noting how they fit, and detach the cable nipples from the pulley **(see illustrations)**. Mark each cable to ensure it is connected correctly on installation. Withdraw the cables from the machine noting the correct routing of each cable.

Installation

5 Lubricate the cable nipples with multi-purpose grease and install them into the throttle pulley at the handlebar **(see illustration 11.4d)**. Fit the cable elbows into the housing, making sure they locate correctly **(see illustration 11.4c)**. Join the housing halves, making sure the pin locates in the hole in the handlebar **(see illustration)**, and tighten the screws **(see illustration 11.4b)**. Fit the rubber boot **(see illustration 11.4a)**. If removed, install the front brake lever (see Chapter 5).
6 Feed the cables through to the carburettors, making sure they are correctly routed. The cables must not interfere with any other component and should not be kinked or bent sharply.
7 Lubricate the decelerator cable nipple with multi-purpose grease and fit it into the lower socket on the carburettor throttle cam **(see illustration)**. Fit the decelerator cable into the bracket and draw it up into the bracket so that the bottom nut becomes captive against the

11.4a Pull the boot back off the housing . . .

11.4b . . . and remove the housing screws (arrowed)

11.4c Separate the housing halves and detach the cable elbows . . .

11.4d . . . and free the cable nipples from the throttle pulley

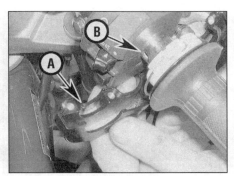

11.5 Locate the pin (A) in the hole (B)

11.7a Fit the cable nipple into the throttle cam . . .

3•14 Fuel and exhaust systems

11.7b ... then locate the cable in the bracket

12.2a Slacken the clamp screw (arrowed) ...

12.2b ... then free the outer cable from the bracket ...

small lug **(see illustration)**. Tighten the nut down onto the bracket. Lubricate the accelerator cable nipple with multi-purpose grease and fit it into the upper socket on the carburettor throttle cam **(see illustration 11.3c)**. Fit the accelerator cable into the upper bracket and adjust is described in Chapter 1 to obtain the correct amount of freeplay **(see illustrations 11.3b and a)**.

8 Operate the throttle to check that it opens and closes freely. Turn the handlebars back and forth to make sure the cable doesn't cause the steering to bind.

9 Install the air filter housing and the fuel tank (see Sections 4 and 2).

10 Start the engine and check that the idle speed does not rise as the handlebars are turned. If it does, the throttle cable is routed incorrectly. Correct the problem before riding the motorcycle.

12 Choke cable – removal and installation

Removal

1 Remove the fuel tank and the air filter housing (see Sections 2 and 4).

2 Slacken the choke outer cable clamp screw and free the cable from the bracket on the front of the carburettors, then detach the inner cable nipple from the choke activator **(see illustrations)**.

3 On 1994 and 1995 models, unscrew the nut securing the choke knob in its holder on the top yoke. Slip the cable out of the holder.

4 On all other models, unscrew the two handlebar switch/choke lever housing screws and separate the two halves **(see illustration)**. Lift the cable elbow and lever out of the housing, noting how they fit, and detach the cable nipple from the lever **(see illustrations)**.

Installation

5 Install the cable making sure it is correctly routed. The cable must not interfere with any other component and should not be kinked or bent sharply.

6 On 1994 and 1995 models, fit the choke knob into its holder and tighten the nut to secure it.

7 On all other models, lubricate the cable nipple with multi-purpose grease and attach it to the choke lever **(see illustrations 12.4c)**. Fit the lever and cable elbow into the housing **(see illustration 12.4b)**, then fit the two halves of the housing onto the handlebar, making sure the lever fits correctly, and the pin in the front half locates in the hole in the front of the handlebar **(see illustration)**. Install the screws and tighten them securely **(see illustration 12.4a)**.

8 Lubricate the cable nipple with multi-purpose grease and attach it to the choke activator on the carburettor **(see illustration 12.2c)**. Fit the outer cable into its bracket, making sure there is a small amount

12.2c ... and the cable nipple from the linkage bar

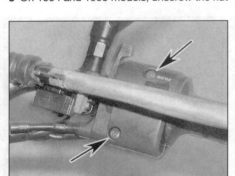

12.4a Remove the housing screws (arrowed) and separate the halves

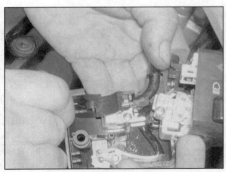

12.4b Remove the choke lever and cable elbow from the housing ...

12.4c ... and free the cable nipple from the lever

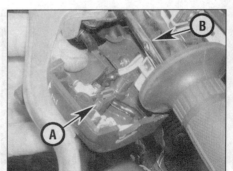

12.7 Make sure the pin (A) in the housing locates in the hole (B) in the handlebar

Fuel and exhaust systems 3•15

13.3 Disconnect the wiring connectors (arrowed) from the heater

13.5 Carburettor heater relay (arrowed)

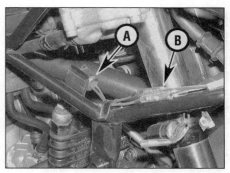

13.6 Thermo switch (A) and its wiring connectors (B)

of freeplay in the inner cable, and tighten the screw **(see illustrations 12.2b and a)**.
9 Check the operation of the choke cable (see Chapter 1).
10 Install the air filter housing and the fuel tank (see Sections 4 and 2).

13 Carburettor heater system – check

Warning: Refer to the precautions given in Section 1 before starting work.

1 Each carburettor has a heater unit threaded into its body. The heaters are controlled by a thermo-switch and a relay. Before checking the system, check the fuse and all the connectors, referring to the *Wiring Diagrams* at the end of Chapter 8.
2 To access the heaters, remove the fuel tank (see Section 2). To access the relay, remove the left-hand side panel (see Chapter 7). To access the thermo switch, remove the fairing (see Chapter 7).
3 To test a heater, disconnect the wiring connectors **(see illustration)**. Using an ohmmeter or multi-meter set to the ohms x 1 scale, connect the positive (+ve) probe to the tip of the heater and the negative (–ve) probe to the earth terminal or to the hex on the base of each heater. The resistance of each heater should be as specified at the beginning of the Chapter. If not, replace the heater with a new one.
4 To replace a heater, disconnect its wiring connectors and unscrew it from the carburettor **(see illustration 13.3)**. Note that depending on the tools available, access to some of the heaters is very restricted and may necessitate removal and possibly separation of the carburettors, though access can be improved by removing the choke linkage bar and holding the throttle open – refer to Sections 7, 8, 9 and 10 of this Chapter as required. Apply a smear of a suitable sealant such as 'Heat Sinker' to the threads of the new heater, then thread it into the carburettor and tighten it to the torque setting specified at the beginning of the Chapter.
5 To check the relay, disconnect its wiring connector **(see illustration)**. Using an ohmmeter or continuity tester, connect the positive (+ve) probe to the relay's brown wire terminal (the one that is above the black/yellow wire terminal), and the negative (–ve) probe to the relay's black/yellow wire terminal. There should be no continuity. Leaving the meter connected, now connect a fully charged 12 volt battery using two insulated jumper wires, connecting the positive (+ve) terminal of the battery to the relay's brown terminal (the one that is above the light green wire terminal), and the negative (–ve) terminal of the battery to the relay's light green wire terminal. There should now be continuity. If the relay does not behave as described, replace it with a new one.
6 To check the thermo switch, unplug the wiring connectors and remove it from its mounting **(see illustration)**. Fill a small heatproof container with cold water and place it on a stove. Using a continuity tester or multi-meter, insert the probes into the switch wiring connectors. Using some wire or other support suspend the switch in the water, leaving the exit points of the wires above the surface. Also place a thermometer capable of reading temperatures up to 60°C in the water so that its bulb is close to the switch. **Note:** *None of the components should be allowed to directly touch the container.* Initially there should be continuity, showing the switch is closed (ON). Heat the water, stirring it gently.

Warning: This must be done very carefully to avoid the risk of personal injury.

When the temperature reaches around 20 to 26°C the meter reading should show no continuity, indicating that the switch has opened (OFF). Now turn the heat off. As the temperature falls, the meter should continue to show no continuity until the temperature drops to 16 to 8°C, whereupon it should close and show continuity (ON). If the meter readings are obtained at different temperatures, then the switch is faulty and must be replaced with a new one.
7 If the heaters, the relay and the switch are all good, turn the ignition switch ON and check for battery voltage at each heater wiring connector, and at the switch wiring connector in the loom. If there is none, refer to the *Wiring Diagrams* at the end of Chapter 8 and check the circuits for damaged or broken wiring.

14 Exhaust system – removal and installation

Warning: If the engine has been running the exhaust system will be very hot. Allow the system to cool before carrying out any work.

Silencers

Removal

1 Slacken the clamp bolt securing the silencer pipe to the collector box. Unscrew and remove the silencer mounting bolt, then release the silencer from the collector box **(see illustrations)**. Remove the sealing ring

14.1a Unscrew the bolt . . .

14.1b . . . and remove the silencer

3•16 Fuel and exhaust systems

14.2 Use a new sealing ring

14.5 Unscrew the nuts and displace the flanges

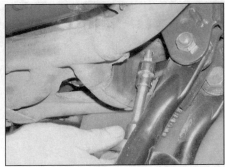

14.6a Unscrew the collector box bolt . . .

from the end of the silencer or collector box and discard it as a new one should be used **(see illustration 14.2)**.

Installation

2 Fit the new sealing ring into the silencer **(see illustration)**. Fit the silencer into the collector box, making sure it is pushed fully home **(see illustration 14.1b)**. Align the silencer mounting bracket at the rear and install the bolt, aligning the captive nut in the bracket with it, and tighten it finger-tight **(see illustration 14.1a)**. Tighten the clamp bolt to the torque setting specified at the beginning of the Chapter, then tighten the silencer mounting bolt to the specified torque.

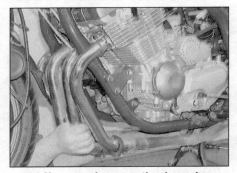

14.6b . . . and remove the downpipe assembly

3 Run the engine and check the system for leaks.

Downpipe/collector box assembly

Removal

4 Remove the silencers (see above).
5 Unscrew the eight downpipe flange nuts and draw the flanges off the studs **(see illustration)**.
6 Supporting the system, unscrew the bolt securing the rear of the collector box, then detach the downpipes from the cylinder head and remove the system **(see illustrations)**.

14.7 Remove the old gasket from each port

7 Remove the gasket from each port in the cylinder head and discard them as new ones must be fitted **(see illustration)**.
8 If required, slacken the clamp bolts securing the downpipes in the collector box and separate them **(see illustration)**. Discard the sealing rings as new ones must be used.

Installation

9 If separated, fit new sealing rings into the collector box, then fit the downpipes into the box, making sure they are pushed full home **(see illustration 14.8)**. Align them so they are roughly in the correct position. Do not tighten the clamp bolts yet.
10 Fit a new gasket into each of the cylinder head ports **(see illustration)**. Apply a smear of grease to the gaskets to keep them in place whilst fitting the downpipes if necessary.
11 Manoeuvre the assembly into position so that the head of each downpipe is located in its port in the cylinder head **(see illustration 14.6b)**, then install the collector box bolt, but do not yet tighten it fully **(see illustration 14.6a)**.
12 Locate the downpipe flanges onto the studs, then fit the nuts and tighten them to the torque setting specified at the beginning of the Chapter **(see illustration 14.5)**. Now tighten the rear bolt to the specified torque. If the downpipes were separated from the

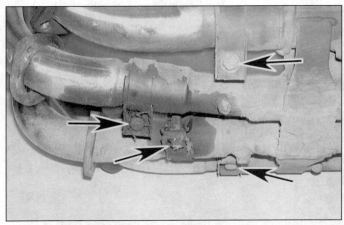

14.8 Separate the downpipes from the collector box by slackening the clamp bolts (arrowed)

14.10 Fit a new gasket into each port

Fuel and exhaust systems 3•17

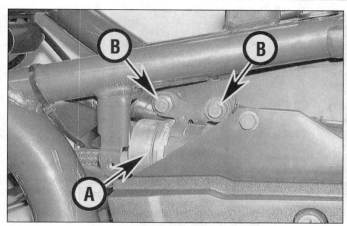

15.1a Fuel pump (A), mounting bolts (B)

15.1b Relay assembly (arrowed)

collector box, also tighten the clamp bolts to the specified torque.
13 Install the silencers (see above).
14 Run the engine and check the system for leaks.

15 Fuel pump and relay – check, removal and installation

Warning: Refer to the precautions given in Section 1 before starting work.

Check

1 The fuel pump is mounted behind the left-hand side panel **(see illustration)** – remove the side panel (see Chapter 7) and fuel tank (see Section 2) to access it. The fuel pump relay is integrated in the relay assembly, mounted behind the left-hand side panel **(see illustration)** – remove the panel to access it (see Chapter 7).
2 The fuel pump is controlled through the starter circuit cut-off relay so that it runs whenever the ignition is switched ON and the ignition is operative (i.e., only when the engine is turning over). As soon as the ignition is killed, the relay will cut off the fuel pump's electrical supply (so that there is no risk of fuel being sprayed out under pressure in the event of an accident).
3 It should be possible to hear or feel the fuel pump running whenever the engine is turning over – either place your ear close beside the fuel pump or feel it with your fingertips. If you can't hear or feel anything, check that the battery is fully charged and the fuses are good (see Chapter 8). Then check the pump and relay for loose or corroded connections or physical damage and rectify as necessary.
4 If the circuit is fine so far, switch the ignition OFF. Unplug the relay's wiring connector **(see illustration 15.1b)**. Using an ohmmeter or continuity tester, connect the positive (+ve) probe to the relay's red/black terminal, and the negative (–ve) probe to the relay's

blue/black terminal. There should be no continuity. Leaving the meter connected, now connect a fully charged 12 volt battery using two insulated jumper wires, connecting the positive (+ve) terminal of the battery to the relay's red/black terminal, and the negative (–ve) terminal of the battery to the relay's blue/red terminal. There should now be continuity. If the relay does not behave as described, replace it with a new one.
5 If the pump still does not work, trace the wiring from the pump and disconnect it at the connector **(see illustration)**. Using an ohmmeter, connect the positive (+ve) probe to the pump's black/blue terminal, and the negative (–ve) probe to the black terminal, and measure the resistance. If the reading is not as specified at the beginning of the Chapter, replace the pump with a new one.

Removal

6 Make sure the ignition is switched OFF.
7 To access the fuel pump, remove the left-hand side panel (see Chapter 7) and the fuel tank (see Section 2). Trace the wiring from the pump and disconnect it at the connector **(see illustration 15.5)**. Make a note or sketch of which fuel hose fits where as an aid to installation. Using a rag to mop up any spilled fuel, disconnect the two fuel hoses from the fuel pump **(see illustration)**. Unscrew the

bolts securing the pump holder to the frame and remove the pump with its holder **(see illustration 15.1a)**. Slacken the screw on the bottom of the holder and separate the pump from it.
8 To access the relay, remove the left-hand side panel (see Chapter 7). Disconnect the relay wiring connector and remove the relay from its mounting **(see illustration 15.1b)**.

Installation

9 Installation is a reverse of the removal procedure. Make sure the fuel hoses are correctly and securely fitted to the pump – the hose from the in-line filter attaches to the curved union marked 'INLET'; the hose to the carburettors attaches to the straight union **(see illustration 15.7)**. Start the engine and check carefully that there are no leaks at the pipe connections.

16 Fuel gauge, warning light and sensor – check and renewal

Check

1 The circuit consists of the sensor mounted in the fuel tank and the gauge and warning light mounted in the instrument panel. If the

15.5 Fuel pump wiring connector

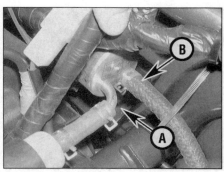

15.7 Disconnect the inlet hose (A) and the outlet hose (B)

3•18 Fuel and exhaust systems

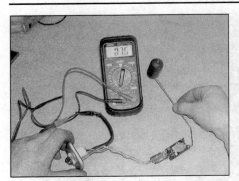

16.3a Testing the sensor in the 'FULL' position

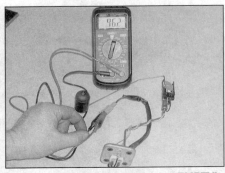

16.3b Testing the sensor in the 'EMPTY' position

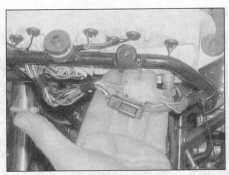

16.4 Disconnect the black instrument cluster wiring connector

system malfunctions check first that the battery is fully charged and that the bulb and fuses are good (see Chapter 8). If they are, remove the fuel tank and drain it (see Section 2).

2 Using an ohmmeter or continuity tester, check for continuity between the green/red and black wire terminals on the sensor side of the wiring connector coming from the fuel tank, with the fuel tank positioned as it would be on the bike. There should be continuity. If not, replace the sensor with a new one (see below).

3 If continuity is shown, remove the sensor (see below). Connect the positive (+ve) probe of an ohmmeter to the green terminal on the sensor connector, and the negative (–ve) probe to the black terminal. Check the resistance of the sensor in both the 'FULL' and 'EMPTY' positions and compare the readings to those specified at the beginning of the Chapter **(see illustrations)**. If the readings are not as specified, replace the sensor with a new one.

4 If the resistances are correct, connect the sensor wiring connector and turn the ignition switch ON. With the sensor in the 'FULL' position, the gauge should read 'FULL', and with the sensor in the empty position the gauge should read 'EMPTY' (the gauge needle may not respond immediately – leave it in the position being tested for at least three minutes to accurately check the system). If not, remove the fairing (see Chapter 7) and disconnect the black instrument cluster wiring connector **(see illustration)**. Check for voltage to the gauge by connecting the positive (+ve) probe of a voltmeter to the brown terminal on the loom side of the instrument cluster wiring connector, and the negative (–ve) probe to the black terminal. If no voltage is present, check all the relevant wiring and wiring connectors between the sensor and the gauge, referring to the *Wiring Diagrams* at the end of Chapter 8. If the wiring and connectors are good, there could be an internal fault in the instrument cluster wiring between the connector and the gauge. If not, replace the gauge with a new one.

5 To check the warning light, remove and drain the fuel tank, then connect the fuel level sensor wiring connector. Remove the fairing (see Chapter 7) and disconnect the black instrument cluster wiring connector **(see illustration 16.4)**. With the fuel tank positioned as it would be on the bike and the ignition ON, check for voltage by connecting the positive (+ve) probe of a voltmeter to the brown wire terminal on the loom side of the connector, and the negative (–ve) probe to the green/red terminal. If no voltage is present, the fault lies in the wiring. Check all the relevant wiring and wiring connectors (see Chapter 8), referring to the *Wiring Diagrams* at the end of Chapter 8. If all the wiring and connectors are good, there could be an internal fault in the instrument cluster wiring between the connector and the bulb.

Renewal

6 See Chapter 8 for fitting a new fuel gauge and warning light.
7 To fit a new sensor, remove the fuel tank and drain it (see Section 2).
8 Remove the bolts securing the sensor and draw it out of the tank **(see illustrations)**. Discard the gasket.
9 Fit a new gasket onto the sensor and install it in the tank **(see illustration)**. Tighten the bolts to the torque setting specified at the beginning of the Chapter.
10 Install the tank (see Section 2), and check carefully for leaks around the sensor before using the bike.

17 Air induction system (AIS) – function, disassembly and reassembly

Function

1 The air induction system uses exhaust gas pulses to suck fresh air into the exhaust ports,

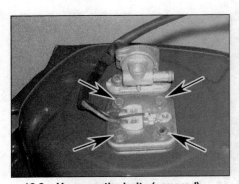

16.8a Unscrew the bolts (arrowed) . . .

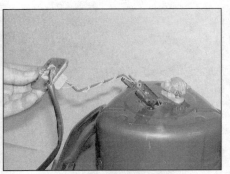

16.8b . . . and carefully withdraw the sensor

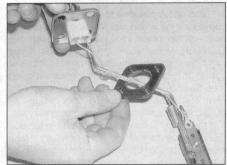

16.9 Use a new gasket, locating the raised sections in the mounting bolt holes

Fuel and exhaust systems 3•19

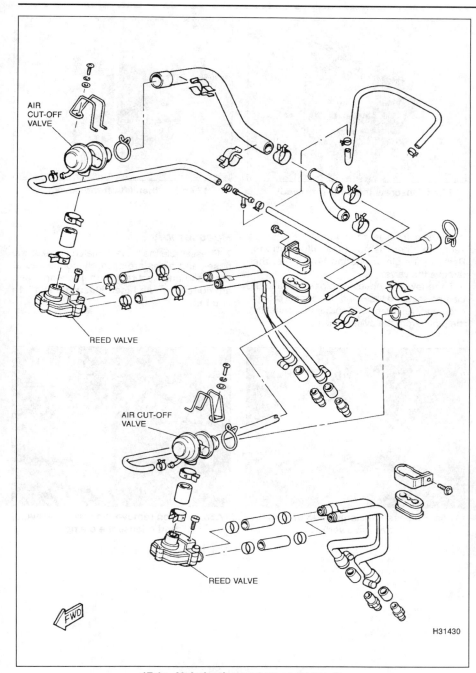

17.1a Air induction system components

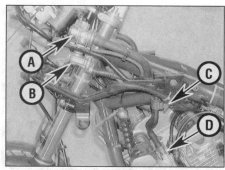

17.1b Air cut-off valve (A), reed valve (B), pipe clamp bolt (C), pipe unions on cylinder head (D)

17.3a Release the clamps and detach the pipes from the reed valve (arrows)

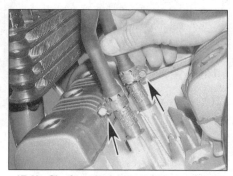

17.3b Slacken the clamps (arrowed) and pull the pipes off the unions

17.3c Replace the sealing collars with new ones if necessary

where it mixes with hot combustion gases **(see illustrations)**. The extra oxygen causes continued combustion, allowing unburnt hydrocarbons to burn off, thereby reducing emissions. Reed valves control the flow of air into the ports and prevent exhaust gases flowing back into the AIS. Air cut-off valves shut off the flow of air during deceleration, preventing backfiring.

2 Refer to Chapter 1 for a check of the system.

Disassembly

3 When removing the engine or valve cover, remove the bolt securing the pipe clamp and release the pipes **(see illustration 17.1b)**. Release the clamps and detach the pipes from the reed valves, then slacken the clamps and detach the pipes from the unions on the cylinder head **(see illustrations)**. Remove the sealing collars and replace them with new ones if they are deformed or damaged **(see illustration)**.

3•20 Fuel and exhaust systems

17.4a Detach the reed valve from the hoses

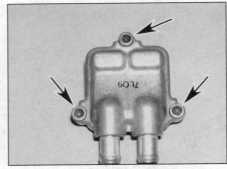

17.4b Unscrew the bolts (arrowed) . . .

17.4c . . . then lift off the cover . . .

4 To renew a reed valve, release the clamps and detach it from the three hoses that hold it **(see illustration)**. To disassemble the valve, remove its assembly bolts and separate the housing, then remove the bolts securing the reed itself and remove the reed, noting how it fits **(see illustrations)**.

5 To renew an air cut-off valve, disconnect the hoses from it, then remove the screw securing the clamp **(see illustrations)**. Remove the clamp, noting how it fits, then remove the valve.

6 To renew any hoses or pipes, release the clamps securing them and disconnect them at each end, referring to Step 3 if disconnecting the pipes from the cylinder head.

Reassembly

7 Reassemble the system, making sure all the hoses and pipes are securely connected at each end and secured by their clamps, and are correctly routed **(see illustrations 17.1a and b)**.

17.4d . . . and remove the valve assembly

17.5a Release the clamps and detach the hoses (arrowed) . . .

17.5b . . . then remove the screw (arrowed) and release the clamp

Chapter 4
Ignition system

Contents

Clutch switch – check and renewal .... see Chapter 8	Ignition timing – general information and check 6
General information 1	Neutral switch – check and renewal .... see Chapter 8
Ignition (main) switch – check, removal and installation .see Chapter 8	Pick-up coil – check and renewal 4
Ignition control unit – check, removal and installation 5	Sidestand switch – check and renewal .... see Chapter 8
Ignition HT coils – check, removal and installation 3	Spark plugs – gap check and renewal .... see Chapter 1
Ignition system – check 2	Throttle position sensor – check, adjustment and renewal 7

Degrees of difficulty

| Easy, suitable for novice with little experience | | Fairly easy, suitable for beginner with some experience | | Fairly difficult, suitable for competent DIY mechanic | | Difficult, suitable for experienced DIY mechanic | | Very difficult, suitable for expert DIY or professional | |

Specifications

General information
Cylinder numbering	1 to 4 from left to right
Spark plugs	see Chapter 1

Ignition timing
At idle	5° BTDC @ 1000 rpm
At full advance	40° BTDC @ 5000 rpm

Pick-up coil
Resistance	446 to 545 ohms @ 20°C

Ignition HT coils
Primary winding resistance	1.87 to 2.53 ohms @ 20°C
Secondary winding resistance (without plug cap)	12 to 18 K-ohms @ 20°C
Spark plug cap resistance	10 K-ohms @ 20°C
Minimum spark gap (see Section 2)	6 mm

Throttle position sensor
Maximum resistance	5.0 ± 1.5 K-ohms
Resistance range	Zero to 5.0 ± 1.5 K-ohms

Torque wrench settings
Pick-up coil mounting plate screws	8 Nm
Crankshaft end-cover screws	8 Nm

4•2 Ignition system

1 General information

All models are fitted with a fully transistorised electronic ignition system, which due to its lack of mechanical parts is totally maintenance free. The system comprises a rotor, pick-up coil, ignition control unit and ignition HT coils (refer to the wiring diagrams at the end of Chapter 8 for details). All models are fitted with two HT coils. A throttle position sensor provides information for the ignition control unit.

The ignition triggers, which are on the rotor on the left-hand end of the crankshaft, magnetically operate the pick-up coil as the crankshaft rotates. The pick-up coil sends a signal to the ignition control unit which then supplies the ignition HT coils with the power necessary to produce a spark at the plugs.

The system incorporates an electronic advance system controlled by signals from the ignition triggers, the pick-up coil and the throttle position sensor.

The system incorporates a safety interlock circuit which will cut the ignition if the sidestand is put down whilst the engine is running and in gear, or if a gear is selected whilst the engine is running and the sidestand is down. It also prevents the engine from being started if the engine is in gear unless the clutch lever is pulled in.

Because of their nature, the individual ignition system components can be checked but not repaired. If ignition system troubles occur, and the faulty component can be isolated, the only cure for the problem is to replace the part with a new one. Keep in mind that most electrical parts, once purchased, cannot be returned. To avoid unnecessary expense, make very sure the faulty component has been positively identified before buying a replacement part.

Note that there is no provision for adjusting the ignition timing on these models.

2 Ignition system – check

Warning: The energy levels in electronic systems can be very high. On no account should the ignition be switched on whilst the plugs or plug caps are being held. Shocks from the HT circuit can be most unpleasant. Secondly, it is vital that the engine is not turned over or run with any of the plug caps removed, and that the plugs are soundly earthed (grounded) when the system is checked for sparking. The ignition system components can be seriously damaged if the HT circuit becomes isolated.

1 As no means of adjustment is available, any failure of the system can be traced to failure of a system component or a simple wiring fault. Of the two possibilities, the latter is by far the most likely. In the event of failure, check the system in a logical fashion, as described below.

2 Disconnect the cap from one spark plug **(see illustration)**. Connect the lead to a spare spark plug that is known to be good, and lay the plug on the engine with the threads contacting the engine **(see illustration)**. If necessary, hold the spark plug with an insulated tool.

Warning: Do not remove any of the spark plugs from the engine to perform this check – atomised fuel being pumped out of the open spark plug hole could ignite, causing severe injury!

3 Check that the kill switch is in the 'RUN' position and the transmission is in neutral, then turn the ignition switch ON and turn the engine over on the starter motor. If the system is in good condition a regular, fat blue spark should be evident at the plug electrode. If the spark appears thin or yellowish, or is non-existent, further investigation will be necessary. Turn the ignition off and repeat the test for each spark plug in turn.

2.2a Pull the cap off the spark plug

2.2b Ground (earth) the spark plug and operate the starter – bright blue sparks should be visible

4 The ignition system must be able to produce a spark which is capable of jumping a particular size gap. Yamaha specify that a healthy system should produce a spark capable of jumping at least 6 mm. A simple testing tool can be made to test the minimum gap across which the spark will jump (see **Tool Tip**) or alternatively it is possible to buy an ignition gap tester tool, and some of those tools are adjustable to alter the spark gap.

5 Connect one of the spark plug HT leads from one coil to the protruding electrode on the test tool, and clip the tool to a good earth (ground) on the engine or frame **(see illustration)**. Check that the kill switch is in the RUN position, turn the ignition switch ON and turn the engine over on the starter motor. If the system is in good condition a regular, fat blue spark should be seen to jump the gap between the nail ends. Repeat the test for the other coil. If the test results are good the entire ignition system can be considered good. If the spark appears thin or yellowish, or is non-existent, further investigation will be necessary.

6 Ignition faults can be divided into two categories, namely those where the ignition system has failed completely, and those which are due to a partial failure. The likely faults are listed below, starting with the most probable source of failure. Work through the list systematically, referring to the subsequent sections for full details of the necessary checks and tests. **Note:** *Before checking the*

TOOL TIP
A simple spark gap testing tool can be made from a block of wood, a large alligator clip and two nails, one of which is fashioned so that a spark plug cap or bare HT lead end can be connected to its end. Make sure the gap between the two nail ends is the same as specified

2.5 Connect the tester as shown – when the starter is operated sparks should jump between the nails

Ignition system 4•3

following items ensure that the battery is fully charged and that all fuses are in good condition.
a) Loose, corroded or damaged wiring connections, broken or shorted wiring between any of the component parts of the ignition system (see Chapter 8).
b) Faulty HT lead or spark plug cap, faulty spark plug, dirty, worn or corroded plug electrodes, or incorrect gap between electrodes.
c) Faulty ignition (main) switch or engine kill switch (see Chapter 8).
d) Faulty neutral, clutch or sidestand switch (see Chapter 8).
e) Faulty diode or starter circuit cut-off relay (see Chapter 8).
f) Faulty pick-up coil or damaged trigger.
g) Faulty ignition HT coil(s).
h) Faulty ignition control unit.

7 If the above checks don't reveal the cause of the problem, have the ignition system tested by a Yamaha dealer. Yamaha produce a tester which can perform a complete diagnostic analysis of the ignition system.

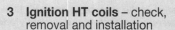

3 Ignition HT coils – check, removal and installation

Check

1 Check the coil visually for cracks and other damage.
2 The primary and secondary coil resistance can be measured with a multimeter. If the coil is undamaged, and if the resistance readings are as specified at the beginning of the Chapter, it is probably capable of proper operation.
3 Remove the seat (see Chapter 7). Disconnect the battery negative (–ve) lead.
4 The coils are mounted on the frame cross-member – remove the fuel tank and the air filter housing for access (see Chapter 3).
5 Disconnect the primary circuit electrical connectors from the coil (see illustration). Disconnect the spark plug caps from the spark plugs (see illustration 2.2a). Mark the

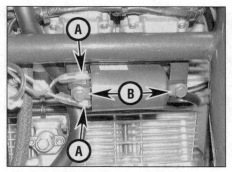

3.5 Primary circuit wiring connectors (A), mounting bolts (B)

locations of all wires and leads before disconnecting them.
6 Set the meter to the ohms x 1 scale and measure the resistance between the primary circuit terminals on the coil (see illustration). This will give a resistance reading of the primary windings of the coil and should be consistent with the value given in the Specifications at the beginning of the Chapter.
7 To check the condition of the secondary windings, unscrew the spark plug caps from the HT leads and set the meter to the K-ohm scale. Connect one meter probe to one HT lead end and the other probe to the other lead end (see illustration). If the reading obtained is not within the range shown in the Specifications, it is likely that the coil is defective.
8 If the reading is as specified, measure the resistance of the spark plug cap by connecting the meter probes between the HT lead socket in the cap and the spark plug contact in the cap (see illustration). If the reading obtained is not as specified, replace the spark plug caps with new ones.
9 Should any of the above checks not produce the expected result the coil must be replaced with a new one; the coil is a sealed unit and cannot be repaired.

Removal

10 Remove the seat (see Chapter 7). Disconnect the battery negative (–ve) lead.

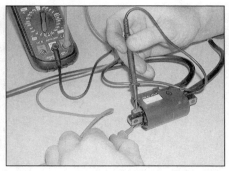

3.6 To test the coil primary resistance, connect the multimeter leads between the primary circuit terminals

11 The coils are mounted on the frame cross-member – remove the fuel tank and the air filter housing for access (see Chapter 3).
12 Disconnect the primary circuit electrical connectors from the coil (see illustration 3.5). Disconnect the caps from the spark plugs (see illustration 2.2a). Mark the locations of all wires and leads before disconnecting them.
13 Unscrew the bolts securing the coil and remove the coil (see illustration 3.5). Note the routing of the HT leads.

Installation

14 Installation is the reverse of removal. Make sure the wiring connectors and HT leads are securely connected.

4 Pick-up coil – check and renewal

Check

1 Remove the seat (see Chapter 7). Disconnect the battery negative (–ve) lead.
2 Remove the fuel tank (see Chapter 3).
3 Trace the wiring from the pick-up coil on the left-hand side of the engine and disconnect it at the connector (see illustration). Using a multimeter set to the ohms x 100 scale, measure the resistance between the white/red and white/green wire

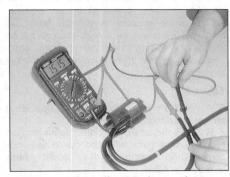

3.7 To test the coil secondary resistance, connect the multimeter leads between the spark plug leads

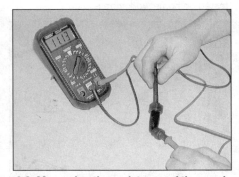

3.8 Measuring the resistance of the spark plug cap

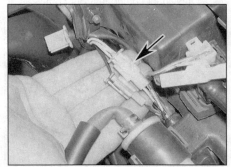

4.3 Disconnect the pick-up coil wiring connector (arrowed)

4•4 Ignition system

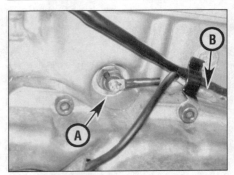

4.8 Detach the wire from the neutral switch (A) and disconnect the bullet connector (B)

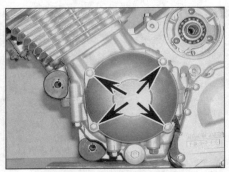

4.9a Undo the screws or bolts (arrowed) and remove the cover

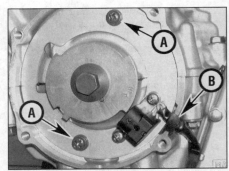

4.9b Remove the mounting plate screws (A) and pull the fillet (B) out of its notch

terminals on the pick-up coil side of the connector.

4 Compare the reading obtained with that given in the Specifications at the beginning of this Chapter. The pick-up coil must be replaced with a new one if the reading obtained differs greatly from that given, particularly if the meter indicates a short circuit (no measurable resistance) or an open circuit (infinite, or very high resistance).

5 If the pick-up coil is thought to be faulty, first check that this is not due to a damaged or broken wire between the coil and the connector; pinched or broken wires can usually be repaired.

Renewal

6 Remove the seat (see Chapter 7). Disconnect the battery negative (–ve) lead.
7 Remove the fuel tank (see Chapter 3).
8 Trace the wiring from the pick-up coil on the right-hand side of the engine and disconnect it at the connector **(see illustration 4.3)**. Slacken the screw securing the wiring connector to the neutral switch and detach the wire, then disconnect the oil level sensor wire at the bullet connector **(see illustration)**. Feed the wiring back to the coil, noting its routing and releasing it from any clips or ties.
9 Remove the screws or bolts (depending on models) securing the left-hand crankshaft end-cover and remove the cover **(see illustration)**. The pick-up coil is not available as an individual component but comes as an assembly with its mounting plate. Remove the screws securing the plate to the engine and remove it, drawing the wiring fillet from the case as you do **(see illustration)**.
10 Install the new pick-up coil and mounting plate and tighten the screws to the torque setting specified at the beginning of the chapter **(see illustration 4.9b)**. Fit the wiring fillet into its notch. Feed the wiring through to the connector, securing it with any clips or ties and making sure it is correctly routed, and reconnect it **(see illustration 4.3)**. Also connect the neutral switch and oil level sensor wiring **(see illustration 4.8)**.
11 Install the crankshaft left-hand end-cover and tighten its screws or bolts (according to models) to the specified torque setting **(see illustration 4.9a)**.
12 Install the fuel tank (see Chapter 3) and seat (see Chapter 7).

5 Ignition control unit – check, removal and installation

Check

1 If the tests shown in the preceding or following Sections have failed to isolate the cause of an ignition fault, it is possible that the ignition control unit itself is faulty. No test details are available with which the unit can be tested on home workshop equipment.

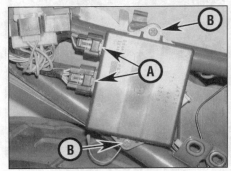

5.3 Ignition control unit wiring connectors (A) and mounting screws (B)

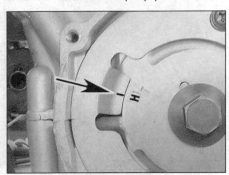

6.5 Timing marks

Removal

2 Remove the seat and the right-hand side panel (see Chapter 7). Disconnect the battery negative (–ve) lead.
3 Disconnect the wiring connectors from the ignition control unit **(see illustration)**.
4 Remove the screws securing the ignition control unit and remove the unit.

Installation

5 Installation is the reverse of removal. Make sure the wiring connectors are correctly and securely connected.

6 Ignition timing – general information and check

General information

1 Since no provision exists for adjusting the ignition timing and since no component is subject to mechanical wear, there is no need for regular checks; only if investigating a fault such as a loss of power or a misfire should the ignition timing be checked.
2 The ignition timing is checked dynamically (engine running) using a stroboscopic lamp. The inexpensive neon lamps should be adequate in theory, but in practice may produce a pulse of such low intensity that the timing mark remains indistinct. If possible, one of the more precise xenon tube lamps should be used, powered by an external source of the appropriate voltage. **Note:** *Do not use the machine's own battery as an incorrect reading may result from stray impulses within the machine's electrical system.*

Check

3 Warm the engine up to normal operating temperature then stop it.
4 Remove the screws or bolts (depending on model) securing the left-hand crankshaft end-cover and remove the cover **(see illustration 4.9a)**.
5 The mark on the timing plate which indicates the firing point at idle speed for the No. 1 cylinder is an 'H' mark **(see illustration)**.

Ignition system 4•5

The static timing mark with which this should align is the line on the pick-up coil mounting plate.

 HAYNES HiNT *The timing marks can be highlighted with white paint to make them more visible under the stroboscope light.*

6 Connect the timing light to the No. 1 cylinder HT lead as described in the manufacturer's instructions.
7 Start the engine and aim the light at the static timing mark.
8 With the machine idling at the specified speed, the static timing mark should point between the uprights of the 'H'.
9 Slowly increase the engine speed whilst observing the 'H' mark. The mark should move clockwise, increasing in relation to the engine speed until it reaches full advance (no identification mark).
10 As already stated, there is no means of adjustment of the ignition timing on these machines. If the ignition timing is incorrect, or suspected of being incorrect, one of the ignition system components is at fault, and the system must be tested as described in the preceding Sections of this Chapter.
11 When the check is complete, install the crankshaft end-cover and tighten the screws or bolts (according to models) to the torque setting specified at the beginning of the Chapter.

7 Throttle position sensor – check, adjustment and renewal

1 The throttle position sensor (TPS) is mounted on the outside of the left-hand carburettor and is keyed to the throttle shaft. The sensor provides the ignition control unit with information on throttle position and rate of opening or closing.
2 When the ignition is first switched ON, or while the engine is running, the throttle position sensor performs its own self-diagnosis in the event of failure or faulty wiring. When a fault occurs, the tachometer will be seen to display zero rpm for 3 seconds, then 10,000 rpm for 2.5 seconds, then the actual engine speed for 3 seconds, whereupon it will repeat the cycle until the engine is switched off.

Check

3 The throttle sensor is mounted on the outside of the left-hand carburettor.
4 Make sure the ignition is switched OFF, then disconnect the sensor's wiring connector **(see illustration)**. Using an ohmmeter or multimeter set to the K-ohms range, measure the sensor maximum resistance by connecting the meter probes between the blue and black/blue wire terminals on the sensor side of the connector. Now measure the resistance range by connecting the meter probes between the yellow and black/blue wire terminals on the connector, and slowly opening the throttle from fully closed to fully open. If the readings obtained differ from those specified at the beginning of the Chapter, replace the sensor with a new one.
5 If the readings were as specified, using a multimeter set to resistance or a continuity tester, check for continuity between the terminals on the wiring loom side of the sensor wiring connector and the corresponding terminals on the ignition control unit connector, referring to the *Wiring Diagrams* at the end of Chapter 8 (first disconnect it). There should be continuity between each terminal. If not, this is probably due to a damaged or broken wire between the connectors; pinched or broken wires can usually be repaired. Also check the connectors for loose or corroded terminals, and check the sensor itself for cracks and other damage. If the wiring and connectors are good, check the adjustment of the sensor as described below.
6 If the sensor is suspected of being faulty, take it to a Yamaha dealer for further testing. If it is confirmed to be faulty, it must be replaced with a new one; the sensor is a sealed unit and cannot therefore be repaired. If the sensor is good, have the ignition control unit checked by the dealer.

Adjustment

7 Before adjusting the sensor, check the idle speed and carburettor synchronisation (see Chapter 1).
8 Turn the ignition switch ON, then disconnect and reconnect the sensor wiring connector **(see illustration 7.4)**. This sets the ignition control unit to sensor adjustment mode.
9 Slacken the sensor mounting screws and rotate the sensor until the tachometer needle reads 5000 rpm **(see illustration)**. If the tachometer reads either 0 rpm or 10,000 rpm, the angle of the sensor is either too narrow or too wide. Adjust it as required until the reading is 5000 rpm, then tighten the screws evenly and a little at a time. Unless an angled tool is available, it may be necessary to displace the carburettors to access the screws (see Chapter 3). If it cannot be adjusted to within the range, or if no reading is obtained, check it as described above. Start the engine or turn the ignition switch OFF to reset the mode.

Renewal

10 The throttle sensor is mounted on the outside of the left-hand carburettor.
11 Disconnect the wiring connector, then unscrew the sensor mounting screws and remove the sensor, noting how it fits **(see illustration 7.4 and 7.9)**. Unless an angled screwdriver is available, it may be necessary to displace the carburettors to access the screws (see Chapter 3).
12 Install the sensor and lightly tighten the screws, then connect the wiring connector and adjust the sensor as described above until the correct reading is obtained. On completion, tighten the screws evenly and a little at a time.

7.4 Disconnect the TPS wiring connector

7.9 Throttle position sensor mounting screws (arrowed)

4•6 Ignition system

Notes

Chapter 5
Frame, suspension and final drive

Contents

Driveshaft and final drive – removal, inspection and installation . . .	15
Final drive oil change . . . . .see Chapter	1
Final drive oil level check . . . . .see Chapter	1
Footrest, brake pedal and gearchange lever – removal and installation	3
Forks – disassembly, inspection and reassembly	7
Forks – oil change . . . . .see Chapter	1
Forks – removal and installation	6
Frame – inspection and repair	2
General information	1
Handlebar switches – check . . . . .see Chapter	8
Handlebar switches – removal and installation . . . . .see Chapter	8
Handlebars and levers – removal and installation	5
Rear shock absorber – removal, inspection and installation	10
Rear suspension linkage – removal, inspection and installation	11
Sidestand and centrestand – check . . . . .see Chapter	1
Sidestand and centrestand – lubrication . . . . .see Chapter	1
Sidestand and centrestand – removal and installation	4
Sidestand switch – check and renewal . . . . .see Chapter	8
Steering head bearings – freeplay check and adjustment . . . . .see Chapter	1
Steering head bearings – inspection and renewal	9
Steering head bearings – lubrication . . . . .see Chapter	1
Steering stem – removal and installation	8
Suspension – adjustments	12
Suspension – check . . . . .see Chapter	1
Swingarm – inspection and bearing renewal	14
Swingarm – removal and installation	13
Swingarm and suspension linkage bearings – lubrication . . . . .see Chapter	1

Degrees of difficulty

| Easy, suitable for novice with little experience | | Fairly easy, suitable for beginner with some experience | | Fairly difficult, suitable for competent DIY mechanic | | Difficult, suitable for experienced DIY mechanic | | Very difficult, suitable for expert DIY or professional | |

Specifications

Front forks
Fork oil type . . . . 10W fork oil or equivalent
Fork oil capacity
   1994 and 1995 models . . . . 444 cc
   1996 models . . . . 444 cc
   1997-on models . . . . 441 cc
Fork oil level*
   1994 and 1995 models . . . . 133 mm
   1996 models . . . . 113 mm
   1997-on models . . . . 135 mm
Fork spring free length
   1994 and 1995 models
      Standard . . . . 505 mm
      Service limit . . . . 500 mm
   1996-on models
      Standard . . . . 399.5 mm
      Service limit . . . . 395.5 mm
Fork tube runout limit . . . . 0.2 mm

*Oil level is measured from the top of the tube with the fork spring removed and the leg fully compressed.

Final drive
Final drive oil type and capacity . . . . see Chapter 1

5•2 Frame, suspension and final drive

Torque wrench settings

Gearchange lever pivot bolt	30 Nm
Centrestand pivot bolt nuts	56 Nm
Handlebar holder clamp bolts	23 Nm
Fork clamp bolts (top yoke)	30 Nm
Fork clamp bolts (bottom yoke)	38 Nm
Damper rod Allen bolt	30 Nm
Fork top bolt	23 Nm
Steering stem nut	110 Nm
Rear shock absorber upper mounting nut	40 Nm
Rear shock absorber lower mounting nut	48 Nm
Rear suspension linkage arm and linkage rod nuts	48 Nm
Swingarm pivot bolt (left side)	100 Nm
Swingarm pivot adjuster bolt (right side)	7 Nm
Swingarm pivot adjuster bolt locknut	100 Nm
Rear brake torque arm nut	26 Nm
Final drive housing nuts	42 Nm

1 General information

All models use a tubular steel cradle frame with a removable section on the right-hand side.

Front suspension is by a pair of oil-damped telescopic forks which use a conventional-type damper. On 1996-on models the forks are adjustable for spring pre-load.

At the rear, an alloy swingarm acts on a single shock absorber via a three-way linkage. The shock absorber is adjustable for spring pre-load.

The drive to the rear wheel is by shaft, housed inside the left-hand longitudinal section of the swingarm. The final drive housing turns the drive through 90° to the rear wheel.

2 Frame – inspection and repair

1 The frame should not require attention unless accident damage has occurred. In most cases, a new frame is the only satisfactory remedy for such damage. A few frame specialists have the jigs and other equipment necessary for straightening the frame to the required standard of accuracy, but even then there is no simple way of assessing to what extent the frame may have been over stressed.

2 After the machine has accumulated a lot of miles, the frame should be examined closely for signs of cracking or splitting at the welded joints. Loose engine mount bolts can cause ovaling or fracturing of the mounts themselves. Minor damage can often be repaired by welding, depending on the extent and nature of the damage.

3 Remember that a frame which is out of alignment will cause handling problems. If misalignment is suspected as the result of an accident, it will be necessary to strip the machine completely so the frame can be thoroughly checked.

3 Footrest, brake pedal and gearchange lever – removal and installation

Front footrest

Removal

1 Remove the split pin from the bottom of the pivot pin, then withdraw the pivot pin and remove the footrest, noting the fitting of the return spring (see illustration).

2 The footrest rubbers can be renewed by removing the screws on the underside of the footrest (see illustration 3.6).

Installation

3 Installation is the reverse of removal. Use a new split pin to secure the pivot pin.

Rear footrest

Removal

4 On 1994 and 1995 models, remove the split pin from the bottom of the pivot pin, then withdraw the pivot pin and remove the footrest, noting the fitting of the detent plate, ball and spring – take care they do not spring out when removing the footrest.

5 On all other models, unscrew the nut from the bottom of the pivot bolt, then withdraw the bolt and remove the footrest, noting the fitting of the detent plates, ball and spring – take care they do not spring out when removing the footrest (see illustration). Also note the collar for the pivot bolt.

6 The footrest rubbers can be renewed by removing the screws on the underside of the footrest (see illustration).

Installation

7 Installation is the reverse of removal. On 1994 and 1995 models, use a new split pin to secure the pivot pin.

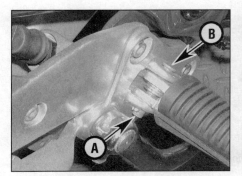

3.1 Remove the split pin (A) and withdraw the pivot pin (B)

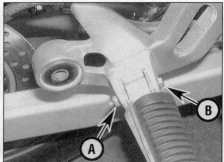

3.5 Unscrew the nut (A) and remove the pivot bolt (B)

3.6 The rubber is held by two screws (arrowed)

Frame, suspension and final drive 5•3

3.8 Brake pedal pinch bolt (arrowed)

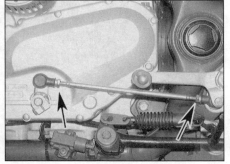

3.10a Slacken the locknuts (arrowed) and thread the rod out of the lever and arm

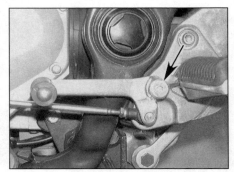

3.10b Unscrew the pivot bolt (arrowed) and remove the lever, noting the washers

Brake pedal

Removal

8 Unscrew the brake pedal pinch bolt and slide the pedal off the shaft, noting any alignment marks **(see illustration)**. If no marks are visible, make your own before removing the pedal so that it can be correctly aligned with the shaft on installation.

Installation

9 Installation is the reverse of removal. Align the pedal as noted on removal and tighten the pinchbolt securely. It is advisable to clean up the shaft splines and apply some grease to prevent difficulty in removing the pedal at a later stage.

Gearchange lever

Removal

10 To remove the lever on its own, slacken the gearchange lever linkage rod locknuts, then unscrew the rod and separate it from the lever and the arm (the rod is reverse-threaded on one end and so will simultaneously unscrew from both lever and arm when turned in the one direction) **(see illustration)**. Note the how far the rod is threaded into the lever and arm as this determines the height of the lever relative to the footrest. Unscrew the lever pivot bolt and remove the lever, noting the washers on the outside and the inside **(see illustration)**.

11 To remove the lever with the linkage rod and arm as an assembly, first unscrew the gearchange lever linkage arm pinchbolt and slide the arm off the shaft, noting any alignment marks **(see illustration)**. If no marks are visible, make your own before removing the arm so that it can be correctly aligned with the shaft on installation. Unscrew the lever pivot bolt and remove the lever, noting the washer on the outside and the inside **(see illustration 3.10b)**.

Installation

12 Installation is the reverse of removal, noting the following:
a) Apply grease to the gear lever pivot.
b) If removed, align the gearchange linkage arm with the shaft as noted on removal **(see illustration 3.11)**.
c) Tighten the lever pivot bolt to the torque setting specified at the beginning of the Chapter.
d) Adjust the gear lever height as required by screwing the rod in or out of the lever and arm. Tighten the locknuts securely **(see illustration 3.10a)**.

4 Sidestand and centrestand – removal and installation

Sidestand

1 Put the motorcycle securely on the centrestand.

2 Unhook the stand springs and remove the link plate, noting how it fits **(see illustration)**. Unscrew the pivot bolt and remove the washer and hook plate, then draw the stand off the pivot.
3 On installation apply grease to the pivot and to the contact surfaces of the stand and bracket. Apply a suitable non-permanent thread locking compound to the bolt threads. Tighten the bolt securely. Fit the link plate and reconnect the sidestand springs. Check that the springs hold the stand securely up when not in use – an accident is almost certain to occur if the stand extends while the machine is in motion.
4 Check the operation of the sidestand switch (see Chapter 1).

Centrestand

5 Support the motorcycle using the sidestand or an auxiliary stand.
6 Unhook the stand spring(s), then counter-hold the pivot bolts and unscrew the nuts **(see illustration)**. Withdraw the pivot bolts and remove the stand.
7 On installation apply grease to the pivot sections of the bolts. Tighten the nuts to the torque setting specified at the beginning of the Chapter. Reconnect the spring(s) and check that the stand is held securely up when not in use – an accident is almost certain to occur if the stand extends while the machine is in motion.

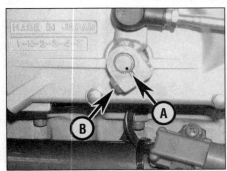

3.11 Note the alignment of the punchmark with the slit (A), then unscrew the pinchbolt (B)

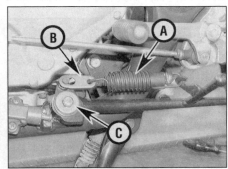

4.2 Sidestand springs (A), link plate (B) and pivot bolt (C)

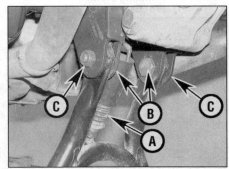

4.6 Centrestand springs (A), pivot bolts (B), nuts (C)

5•4 Frame, suspension and final drive

5.5 Clutch switch wiring connector (A), clutch lever bracket pinch bolt (B)

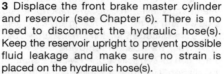

5.7 Handlebar end-weight (arrowed)

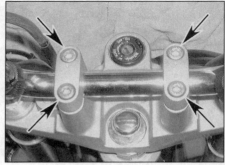

5.8 Unscrew the holder clamp bolts (arrowed) and remove the handlebars

5 Handlebars and levers – removal and installation

Handlebars

Removal

Note: *The handlebars can be displaced from the top yoke for access to the steering stem nut and fork top bolts without having to remove any of the lever or switch assemblies (see Steps 2 and 8).*

1 Remove the fairing and the rear view mirrors (see Chapter 7). **Note:** *The mirrors can remain in place if required, though it is easier if they are removed.*
2 Unscrew the bolt securing the cable guide

5.9a Align the punchmark with the clamp mating surface

to the underside of the top yoke and displace it.
3 Displace the front brake master cylinder and reservoir (see Chapter 6). There is no need to disconnect the hydraulic hose(s). Keep the reservoir upright to prevent possible fluid leakage and make sure no strain is placed on the hydraulic hose(s).
4 Displace the throttle cable housing from the handlebars (see Chapter 3). There is no need to detach the cables from the carburettors.
5 Either remove the clutch lever (see below), or detach the clutch cable from the lever (see Chapter 2). Disconnect the clutch switch wiring connector **(see illustration)**.
6 Displace the handlebar switches (see Chapter 8). There is no need to disconnect the loom wiring connectors.
7 If necessary, remove the handlebar end-weights from the end of the handlebars and remove the grips – the weights themselves thread into the handlebars **(see illustration)**. It may be necessary to slit open the left-hand grip using a sharp blade in order to remove it as they are sometimes stuck in place, though a screwdriver between the grip and the handlebar and some compressed air or spray lubricant directed into the grip will usually work. Depending on your removal method and its success, it may mean using a new grip on assembly. Slacken the clutch lever bracket pinchbolt and slide the bracket off the handlebar **(see illustration 5.5)**.
8 Unscrew the handlebar holder clamp bolts and remove the handlebars **(see illustration)**.

5.9b The arrow on each holder must point to the front

If the handlebars are just being displaced, place some rags over the instrument cluster and surrounding area to act as a cushion and protection.

Installation

9 Installation is the reverse of removal, noting the following.
 a) Align the punchmark on the back of the handlebars with the mating surfaces of the holder **(see illustration)**. Make sure the handlebars are centrally positioned.
 b) Install the holder clamps with the arrows pointing forwards **(see illustration)**, then tighten the front clamp bolt first, followed by the rear bolt, to the torque setting specified at the beginning of the Chapter
 c) Refer to the relevant Chapters as directed for the installation of the handlebar mounted assemblies. Apply some grease between the handlebar and the throttle twistgrip.
 d) Do not forget to reconnect the front brake light switch and clutch switch wiring connectors.
 e) Adjust throttle cable freeplay (see Chapter 1).
 f) Check the operation of all switches and the front brake and clutch before taking the machine on the road.

Front brake lever

Removal

10 Remove the cap from the end of the master cylinder pushrod in the lever, then thread the end nut in to expose the E-clip **(see illustrations)**. Remove the E-clip,

5.10a Remove the cap . . .

5.10b . . . and thread the nut in to expose the E-clip

Frame, suspension and final drive 5•5

5.10c Remove the E-clip . . .

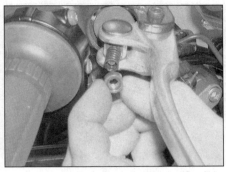

5.10d . . . then thread the nut off . . .

5.10e . . . and remove the spring . . .

5.10f . . . and spring plate

5.11a Unscrew the locknut . . .

then thread the nut off the pushrod and remove the spring and spring plate **(see illustrations)**.

11 Unscrew the lever pivot bolt locknut, then unscrew the pivot bolt and remove the lever **(see illustrations)**. Note the pivot bolt collar in the lever **(see illustration)**.

Installation

12 Installation is the reverse of removal. Apply grease to the pivot bolt shaft and the contact areas between the lever and its bracket.

Clutch lever

Removal

13 Pull the rubber boot off the cable adjuster **(see illustration)**. Slacken the clutch cable adjuster lockring and thread the adjuster fully into the bracket to provide maximum freeplay in the cable **(see illustration)**. Unscrew the lever pivot bolt locknut, then unscrew the pivot bolt and remove the lever, detaching the cable nipple as you do **(see illustration)**.

Installation

14 Installation is the reverse of removal. Apply grease to the pivot bolt shaft and the contact areas between the lever and its bracket, and to the clutch cable nipple. Adjust the clutch cable freeplay (see Chapter 1).

5.11b . . . then the pivot bolt . . .

5.11d . . . noting the collar

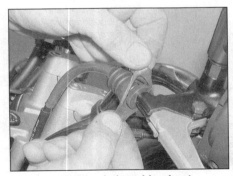

5.13a Pull back the rubber boot . . .

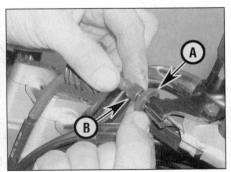

5.13b . . . then slacken the lockring (A) and thread the adjuster (B) in

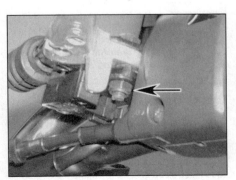

5.13c Unscrew the locknut (arrowed), then unscrew the pivot bolt

5•6 Frame, suspension and final drive

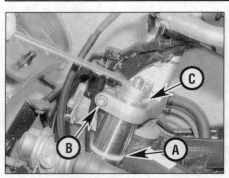

6.6 Release the wiring tie (A), slacken the top yoke clamp bolt (B), and if required slacken the top bolt (C)

6.7a Slacken the clamp bolt (arrowed) in the bottom yoke . . .

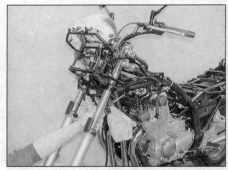

6.7b . . . and draw the fork down out of the yokes

6 Forks – removal and installation

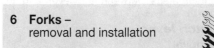

Removal

1 Remove the fairing (see Chapter 7). Displace the handlebars (see Section 5), making sure no strain is placed on the cables, hoses and wiring. Keep the master cylinder reservoir upright.
2 Displace the front brake calipers (see Chapter 6). There is no need to disconnect the hydraulic hoses from the calipers.
3 Remove the front wheel (see Chapter 6).
4 Remove the front mudguard and fork brace (see Chapter 7).
5 Work on each fork individually. Release the cable tie(s) around the top of the fork tube, noting the routing of the wire **(see illustration 6.6)**. Also note the routing of the various cables and hoses around the forks.
6 Slacken the fork clamp bolt in the top yoke **(see illustration)**. If the forks are to be disassembled, or if the fork oil is being changed, it is advisable to slacken the fork top bolt at this stage.
7 Note the alignment or amount of protrusion of the tops of the fork tubes with the top yoke. Slacken but do not remove the fork clamp bolt in the bottom yoke, and remove the fork by twisting it and pulling it downwards **(see illustrations)**.

 If the fork legs are seized in the yokes, spray the area with penetrating oil and allow time for it to soak in before trying again.

Installation

8 Remove all traces of corrosion from the fork tubes and the yokes. Slide the fork up through the bottom yoke and up into the top yoke, making sure the wiring, cables and hoses are the correct side of the fork as noted on removal **(see illustration 6.7b)**. Check that the amount of protrusion of the fork tube above the top yoke is as noted on removal and equal on both sides – Yamaha advise that the tops of the tubes should be flush with the top of the top yoke.
9 Tighten the fork clamp bolt in the bottom yoke to the torque setting specified at the beginning of the Chapter **(see illustration 6.7a)**. If the fork leg has been dismantled or if the fork oil has been changed, the fork top bolt should now be tightened to the specified torque setting **(see illustration 6.6)**. Now tighten the fork clamp bolt in the top yoke to the specified torque settings. Secure the wiring to the fork using the cable tie.

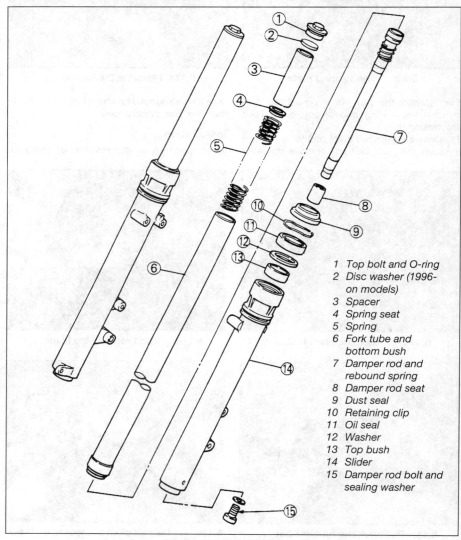

1 Top bolt and O-ring
2 Disc washer (1996-on models)
3 Spacer
4 Spring seat
5 Spring
6 Fork tube and bottom bush
7 Damper rod and rebound spring
8 Damper rod seat
9 Dust seal
10 Retaining clip
11 Oil seal
12 Washer
13 Top bush
14 Slider
15 Damper rod bolt and sealing washer

7.1 Front fork components

Frame, suspension and final drive 5•7

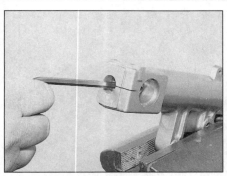

7.2 Slacken the damper rod Allen bolt

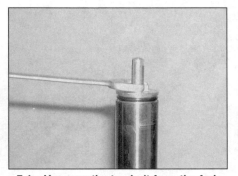

7.4a Unscrew the top bolt from the fork tube

7.4b 1996-on models, remove the disc washer

10 Install the front wheel (see Chapter 6), the front mudguard and fork brace (see Chapter 7), and the brake calipers (see Chapter 6). Make sure the speedometer cable is correctly routed.

11 Install the handlebars (see Section 5) and the fairing (see Chapter 7).

12 Check the operation of the front forks and brakes before taking the machine out on the road.

7 Forks – disassembly, inspection and reassembly

Disassembly

1 Always dismantle the fork legs separately to avoid interchanging parts and thus causing an accelerated rate of wear. Store all components in separate, clearly marked containers **(see illustration opposite)**. On 1996-on models, adjust the spring pre-load to its minimum setting (see Section 12).

2 Before dismantling the fork, it is advised that the damper rod bolt be slackened at this stage. Turn the fork upside down and compress the slider so that the spring exerts maximum pressure on the damper rod head, then have an assistant slacken the damper rod bolt in the base of the fork slider **(see illustration)**. If an assistant is not available, clamp the brake caliper mounting lugs in a soft-jawed vice to support the fork. If the bolt does not slacken, but just turns the damper rod inside the fork, it will have to be done later using a holding tool in the top of the damper (See Step 7).

3 If the fork top bolt was not slackened with the fork in situ, carefully clamp the fork tube in a vice equipped with soft jaws, taking care not to overtighten or score its surface, and slacken the top bolt.

4 Unscrew the fork top bolt from the top of the fork tube **(see illustration)**. On 1996-on models, remove the disc washer **(see illustration)**.

⚠ **Warning: The fork spring is pressing on the fork top bolt (via the spacer) with considerable pressure. Unscrew the bolt very carefully using a ratchet tool and keeping a downward pressure on it, and release it slowly as it is likely to spring clear. It is advisable to wear some form of eye and face protection when carrying out this operation.**

5 Slide the fork tube down into the slider and withdraw the spacer, spring seat and the spring from the tube **(see illustrations)**. Note which way up the spring is fitted.

6 Invert the fork leg over a suitable container and pump the fork vigorously to expel as much fork oil as possible.

7 Remove the previously slackened damper rod bolt and its copper sealing washer from the bottom of the slider **(see illustration 7.2)**. Discard the sealing washer as a new one must be used on reassembly. If the damper rod bolt was not slackened before dismantling the fork, insert either the Yamaha holding tool (Pt. No. 90890-01388 and 01326), or a suitable alternative such as a large nut (that fits snugly into the top of the rod) in a socket on the end of a T-bar extension, into the fork tube and locate it in the top of the damper rod. Alternatively, a length of wood doweling (such as a broom handle) passed down the fork tube and pressed hard into the damper rod head quite often suffices.

8 Invert the fork and withdraw the damper rod from inside the fork tube **(see illustration)**. If required, slide the rebound spring off the damper rod.

9 Carefully prise out the dust seal from the top of the slider to gain access to the oil seal

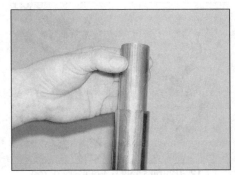

7.5a Withdraw the spacer . . .

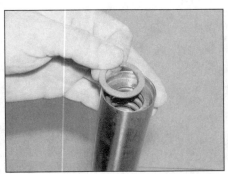

7.5b . . . then remove the spring seat . . .

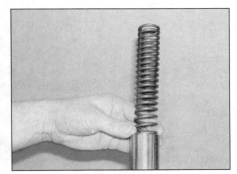

7.5c . . . and withdraw the spring

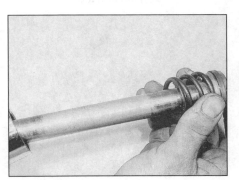

7.8 Withdraw the damper rod with its rebound spring from the tube

5

5•8 Frame, suspension and final drive

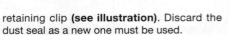

7.9 Prise out the dust seal using a flat-bladed screwdriver

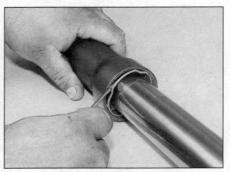

7.10 Prise out the retaining clip using a flat-bladed screwdriver

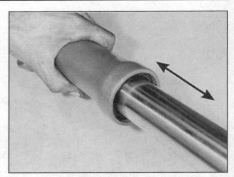

7.11 To separate the inner and outer fork tubes, pull them apart firmly several times – the slide-hammer effect will pull the tubes apart

retaining clip **(see illustration)**. Discard the dust seal as a new one must be used.

10 Carefully remove the retaining clip, taking care not to scratch the surface of the tube **(see illustration)**.

11 To separate the tube from the slider it is necessary to displace the top bush and oil seal. The bottom bush should not pass through the top bush, and this can be used to good effect. Push the tube gently inwards until it stops against the damper rod seat. Take care not to do this forcibly or the seat may be damaged. Then pull the tube sharply outwards until the bottom bush strikes the top bush. Repeat this operation until the top bush and seal are tapped out of the slider **(see illustration)**.

12 With the tube removed, slide off the oil seal, washer and top bush, noting which way up they fit **(see illustration)**. Discard the oil seal as a new one must be used.

Caution: Do not remove the bottom bush from the tube unless it is to be renewed.

13 Tip the damper rod seat out of the slider, noting which way up it fits.

Inspection

14 Clean all parts in solvent and blow them dry with compressed air, if available. Check the fork tube for score marks, scratches, flaking of the chrome finish and excessive or abnormal wear. Look for dents in the tube and replace the tube in both forks with new ones if any are found. Check the fork seal seat for nicks, gouges and scratches. If damage is evident, leaks will occur. Also check the oil seal washer for damage or distortion and replace it with a new one if necessary.

15 Check the fork tube for runout (bending) using V-blocks and a dial gauge, or have it done by a Yamaha dealer or suspension specialists **(see illustration)**. Yamaha do not specify a runout limit, but if the tube is bent beyond the generally accepted limit specified, it should be replaced with a new one.

⚠ *Warning: If the tube is bent, it should not be straightened; replace it with a new one.*

16 Check the spring for cracks and other damage. Measure the spring free length and compare the measurement to the specifications at the beginning of the Chapter. If it is defective or sagged below the service limit, replace the springs in both forks with new ones. Never replace only one spring. Also check the rebound spring.

17 Examine the working surfaces of the two bushes; if worn or scuffed they must be replaced with new ones. To remove the bottom bush from the fork tube, prise it apart at the slit using a flat-bladed screwdriver and slide it off **(see illustration)**. Make sure the new one seats properly.

18 Check the damper rod for damage and wear, and replace it with a new one if necessary.

Reassembly

19 If removed, slide the rebound spring onto the damper rod **(see illustration)**. Insert the damper rod into the fork tube and slide it into

7.12 The oil seal (1), washer (2), top bush (3) and bottom bush (4) will come out with the fork tube

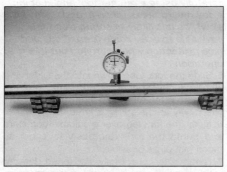

7.15 Check the fork tube for runout using V-blocks and a dial gauge

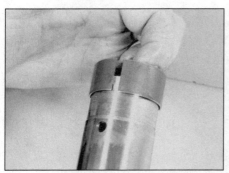

7.17 Prise off the bottom bush using a flat-bladed screwdriver

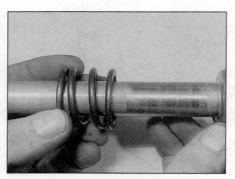

7.19a Slide the rebound spring onto the damper rod . . .

7.19b Fit the seat onto the bottom of the damper rod

Frame, suspension and final drive 5•9

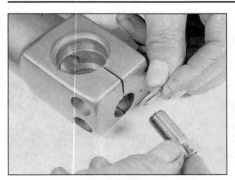

7.20 Apply a thread locking compound to the damper rod bolt and use a new sealing washer

7.21a Install the top bush . . .

7.21b . . . followed by the washer

place so that it projects fully from the bottom of the tube **(see illustration 7.8)**, then fit the seat onto the bottom of the damper rod **(see illustration)**.

20 Oil the fork tube and bottom bush with the specified fork oil and insert the assembly into the slider. Fit a new copper sealing washer to the damper rod bolt and apply a few drops of a suitable non-permanent thread locking compound, then install the bolt into the bottom of the slider **(see illustration)**. Tighten the bolt to the specified torque setting. If the damper rod rotates inside the tube, either use the holding tool used on disassembly (see Step 7), or wait until the fork is fully reassembled before tightening the bolt.

21 Push the fork tube fully into the slider, then oil the top bush and slide it down over the tube **(see illustration)**. Press the bush squarely into its recess in the slider as far as possible, then install the oil seal washer **(see illustration)**. Either use the Yamaha service tool or a suitable piece of tubing to tap the bush fully into place; the tubing must be slightly larger in diameter than the fork tube and slightly smaller in diameter than the bush recess in the slider. Take care not to scratch the fork tube during this operation; it is best to make sure that the fork tube is pushed fully into the slider so that any accidental scratching is confined to the area above the oil seal.

22 When the bush is seated fully and squarely in its recess in the slider (remove the washer to check, wipe the recess clean, then reinstall the washer), install the new oil seal. Smear the seal's lips with lithium-based grease and slide it over the tube so that its markings face upwards and drive the seal into place as described above until the retaining clip groove is visible above the seal **(see illustration)**.

 Place the old oil seal on top of the new one to protect it when driving the seal into place.

23 Once the seal is correctly seated, fit the retaining clip, making sure it is correctly located in its groove **(see illustration)**.

7.22 Make sure the oil seal is the correct way up

24 Lubricate the lips of the new dust seal then slide it down the fork tube and press it into position **(see illustration)**.

25 Slowly pour in the specified quantity of the specified grade of fork oil and pump the fork at least ten times to distribute it evenly **(see illustration)**. Fully compress the fork tube into the slider and measure the fork oil level from the top of the tube **(see illustration)**. Add or subtract fork oil until it is at the level specified at the beginning of the Chapter.

26 Clamp the slider in a soft-jawed vice using the brake caliper mounting lugs, taking care not to overtighten and damage them. Pull the fork tube out of the slider as far as possible then install the spring with its closer wound coils at the top, the spring seat, and the

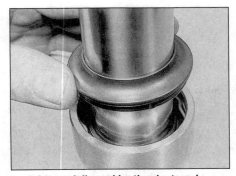

7.24 . . . followed by the dust seal. . .

7.25a Pour the oil into the top of the tube

7.25b Measure the oil level with the fork held vertical

5•10 Frame, suspension and final drive

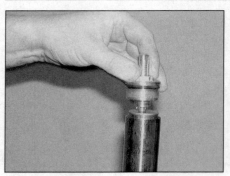
7.27 Thread the top bolt into the fork tube

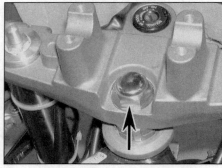
8.5a Unscrew the steering stem nut (arrowed)...

8.5b ... and lift the yoke up off the steering stem

spacer **(see illustrations 7.5c, b and a)**. On 1996-on models, fit the disc washer onto the spacer **(see illustration 7.4b)**.
27 Apply a smear of grease to its new O-ring and thread the bolt into the top of the fork tube **(see illustration)**.

 Warning: It will be necessary to compress the spring by pressing it down using the top bolt to engage the threads of the top bolt with the fork tube. This is a potentially dangerous operation and should be performed with care, using an assistant if necessary. Wipe off any excess oil before starting to prevent the possibility of slipping.

Keep the fork tube fully extended whilst pressing on the spring. Screw the top bolt carefully into the fork tube making sure it is not cross-threaded. **Note:** *The top bolt can be tightened to the specified torque setting at this stage if the tube is held between the padded jaws of a vice, but do not risk distorting the tube by doing so. A better method is to tighten the top bolt when the fork has been installed in the bike and is securely held in the bottom yoke.*

 Use a ratchet-type tool when installing the fork top bolt. This makes it unnecessary to remove the tool from the bolt whilst threading it in making it easier to maintain a downward pressure on the spring.

28 Install the forks (see Section 6). On 1996-on models, adjust the spring pre-load as required (see Section 12).

8 Steering stem – removal and installation

Removal

1 Remove the fuel tank (see Chapter 3). Remove the fairing (see Chapter 7). **Note:** *Although it is not strictly necessary to remove the fairing, doing so will prevent the possibility of damage should a tool slip.*

2 Displace the handlebars from the top yoke (see Chapter 5). Support them so the master cylinder is upright to prevent the possibility of fluid leakage. There is no need to remove assemblies from the handlebars. On 1994 and 1995 models, unscrew the bolt securing the choke knob holder to the top yoke and displace it.
3 Remove the front forks (see Section 6).
4 Disconnect the horn wiring connectors, then unscrew the bolts securing the front brake hose/horn bracket to the bottom yoke. If the top yoke is being removed from the bike rather than just being displaced, trace the wiring from the ignition switch and disconnect it at the connector.
5 Unscrew the steering stem nut and remove it along with its washer, where fitted (1998-on models) **(see illustration)**. Lift the top yoke up off the steering stem and position it clear, using a rag to protect the tank or other components **(see illustration)**.
6 Remove the tabbed lockwasher, noting how it fits, then unscrew and remove the locknut using either a C-spanner, a peg spanner or a drift located in one of the notches **(see illustrations)**. Remove the rubber washer **(see illustration)**.
7 Supporting the bottom yoke, unscrew the adjuster nut using either a C-spanner, a peg-spanner or a drift located in one of the notches, then remove the adjuster nut and the bearing cover from the steering stem **(see illustration)**.

8.6a Remove the lockwasher...

8.6b ... the locknut ...

8.6c ... and the rubber washer

8.7 Unscrew the adjuster nut and remove the bearing cover (arrowed)

Frame, suspension and final drive 5•11

8 Gently lower the bottom yoke and steering stem out of the frame.
9 Remove the inner race and bearing from the top of the steering head **(see illustration)**. Remove the rubber washer, bearing and dust seal from the base of the steering stem. Remove all traces of old grease from the bearings and races and check them for wear or damage as described in Section 9. **Note:** *Do not attempt to remove the races from the steering head or the steering stem unless they are to be replaced with new ones.*

Installation

10 Smear a liberal quantity of lithium-based grease onto the bearing races. Also work some grease well into both the upper and lower bearings. Fit the rubber dust seal over the lower bearing inner race on the steering stem, then fit the bearing and the rubber washer **(see illustration 8.9)**.
11 Carefully lift the steering stem/bottom yoke up through the steering head. Fit the upper bearing and the inner race into the top of the steering head, then install the bearing cover. Thread the adjuster nut onto the steering stem and adjust the bearings as described in Chapter 1.
12 Install the rubber washer and the locknut **(see illustrations 8.6c and b)**. Tighten the locknut finger-tight, then tighten it further until its notches align with those in the adjuster nut. If necessary, counter-hold the adjuster nut and tighten the locknut using a C-spanner or drift until the notches align, but make sure the adjuster nut does not turn as well. Install the tabbed lockwasher so that the tabs fit into the notches in both the locknut and adjuster nut **(see illustration 8.6a)**.
13 Fit the top yoke onto the steering stem **(see illustration 8.5b)**, then install the washer (where fitted) and steering stem nut and tighten it finger-tight. Temporarily install one of the forks to align the top and bottom yokes, and secure it by tightening the bottom yoke clamp bolts only. Now tighten the steering stem nut to the torque setting specified at the beginning of the Chapter.
14 Install the remaining components in a reverse of the removal procedure, referring to the relevant Sections or Chapters, and to the torque settings specified at the beginning of the Chapter.
15 Carry out a check of the steering head bearing freeplay as described in Chapter 1, and if necessary re-adjust.

9 Steering head bearings – inspection and renewal

Inspection

1 Remove the steering stem (see Section 8).
2 Remove all traces of old grease from the bearings and races and check them for wear or damage.
3 The outer races should be polished and free from indentations. Inspect the bearing balls for signs of wear, damage or discoloration, and examine the bearing ball retainer cage for signs of cracks or splits. Spin the bearing balls by hand. They should spin freely and smoothly. If there are any signs of wear on any of the above components both upper and lower bearing assemblies must be renewed as a set. Only remove the outer races in the steering head and the lower bearing inner race on the steering stem if they need to be renewed – do not re-use them once they have been removed.

Renewal

4 The outer races are an interference fit in the steering head and can be tapped from position with a suitable drift **(see illustration)**. Tap firmly and evenly around each race to ensure that it is driven out squarely. It may prove advantageous to curve the end of the drift slightly to improve access.
5 Alternatively, the races can be removed

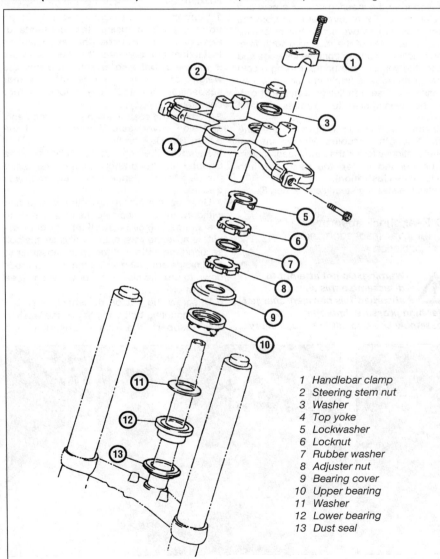

1 Handlebar clamp
2 Steering stem nut
3 Washer
4 Top yoke
5 Lockwasher
6 Locknut
7 Rubber washer
8 Adjuster nut
9 Bearing cover
10 Upper bearing
11 Washer
12 Lower bearing
13 Dust seal

8.9 Steering stem and head bearing assembly

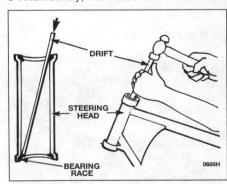

9.4 Drive the bearing races out with a brass drift as shown

5•12 Frame, suspension and final drive

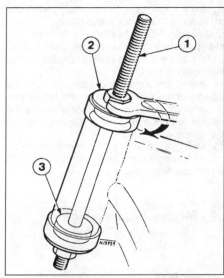

9.6 Drawbolt arrangement for fitting steering stem bearing races

1 Long bolt or threaded bar
2 Thick washer
3 Guide for lower race

using a slide-hammer type bearing extractor; these can often be hired from tool shops.

6 The new outer races can be pressed into the head using a drawbolt arrangement **(see illustration)**, or by using a large diameter tubular drift. Ensure that the drawbolt washer or drift (as applicable) bears only on the outer edge of the race and does not contact the working surface. Alternatively, have the races installed by a Yamaha dealer equipped with the bearing race installing tools.

 Installation of new bearing outer races is made much easier if the races are left overnight in the freezer. This causes them to contract slightly making them a looser fit. Alternatively, use a freeze spray.

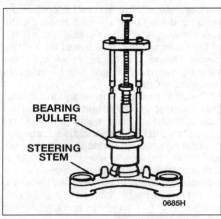

9.7 You may have to use a puller to remove the lower bearing inner race

7 The lower bearing inner race should only be removed from the steering stem if a new one is being fitted. To remove the race from the steering stem, use two screwdrivers placed on opposite sides of the race to work it free, using blocks of wood to improve leverage and protect the yoke, or tap under it using a cold chisel. If the race is firmly in place it will be necessary to use a puller **(see illustration)**. Take the steering stem to a Yamaha dealer if required.

8 Fit the new lower race onto the steering stem. A length of tubing with an internal diameter slightly larger than the steering stem will be needed to tap the new race into position **(see illustration)**.

9 Install the steering stem (see Section 8).

10 Rear shock absorber – removal, inspection and installation

Warning: Do not attempt to disassemble this shock absorber. It is nitrogen-charged under high pressure. Improper disassembly could result in serious injury.

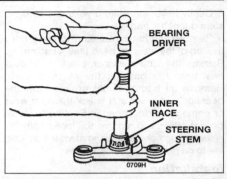

9.8 Drive the new race on using a suitable driver or a length of pipe

Instead, take the shock to a Yamaha dealer or suspension specialist with the proper equipment to do the job.

Removal

1 Support the motorcycle securely in an upright position using the centrestand. Position a support under the rear wheel so that it does not drop when the shock absorber is removed, but also making sure that the weight of the machine is off the rear suspension so that the shock is not compressed.

2 Remove the seat, the right-hand side panel and side cover (see Chapter 7), and the battery (see Chapter 8).

3 Remove the right-hand silencer (see Chapter 3). Though not essential, removing the left-hand silencer as well improves clearance.

4 Unscrew the nut, remove the washer and withdraw the bolt securing the linkage rods to the swingarm **(see illustration)**. Unscrew the nut, remove the washer and withdraw the bolt securing the bottom of the shock absorber to the linkage arm, then swing the arm and rods down to provide clearance for the shock **(see illustration)**.

5 Unscrew the nut on the shock absorber upper mounting bolt and remove the washer, then support the shock absorber and

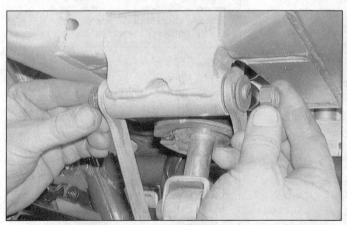

10.4a Unscrew the nut and withdraw the bolt to free the linkage rods

10.4b Unscrew the nut and remove the lower mounting bolt

Frame, suspension and final drive 5•13

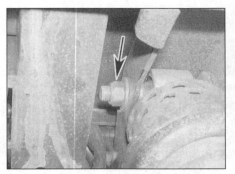

10.5a Unscrew the nut (arrowed) . . .

10.5b . . . and withdraw the upper mounting bolt . . .

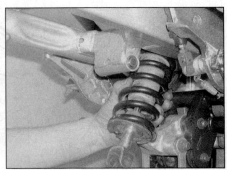

10.5c . . . then lower the shock and remove it

withdraw the bolt via the hole in the battery box **(see illustrations)**. Lift the swingarm and lower the shock out of the frame taking care not to scratch anything **(see illustration)**.
Note: *Earlier models may not have the hole in the battery box, in which case you can either make a hole yourself (if you aren't worried about the damage – the hole can be easily plugged using a rubber blanking grommet), or the alternative is to remove the rear mudguard. To remove the mudguard, remove the left-hand side panel, side cover and fuel tank, then displace the fuel filter, the starter relay and the rear brake master cylinder, release the tail light and turn signal wiring from the bracket and disconnect the wiring connector, then remove the bolts and screws securing the mudguard and draw it back.*

Inspection

6 Inspect the shock absorber for obvious physical damage and the coil spring for looseness, cracks or signs of fatigue.
7 Inspect the damper rod for signs of bending, pitting and oil leakage **(see illustration)**.
8 Inspect the pivot hardware at the top and bottom of the shock for wear or damage.
9 Individual components are not available for the shock absorber. If it is worn or damaged, it must be replaced with a new one.

Installation

10 Installation is the reverse of removal. Apply molybdenum disulphide grease to the shock absorber and linkage rod pivot points. Install the bolts and nuts finger-tight only until all components are in position, then tighten the nuts to the torque settings specified at the beginning of the Chapter. Make sure the top bolt head locates between the raised edges and is held captive **(see illustration)**. Install the shock absorber lower bolt before the linkage rod bolt or the rods will block the hole. Note that unless a special torque wrench is available, it is not possible to tighten the upper nut as access is too restricted, unless the rear mudguard is removed.

11 Rear suspension linkage – removal, inspection and installation

Removal

1 Support the motorcycle securely in an upright position using the centrestand. Position a support under the rear wheel so that it does not drop when the shock absorber lower mounting bolt is removed, but also making sure that the weight of the machine is

10.7 Look for cracks, pitting and oil leakage on the damper rod (arrowed)

off the rear suspension so that the shock is not compressed.
2 Remove the silencers (see Chapter 3).
3 Unscrew the nuts, remove the washers and withdraw the bolts securing the shock absorber and the linkage rods to the linkage arm **(see illustration)**. Note which bolts fit where.
4 Unscrew the nut, remove the washer and withdraw the bolt securing the linkage rods to the swingarm and remove the rods **(see illustration 11.3)**.
5 Unscrew the nut and withdraw bolt securing the linkage arm to the frame and remove the linkage arm, noting which way round it fits **(see illustration 11.3)**.

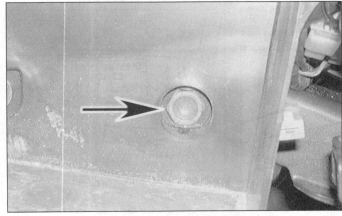

10.10 The top bolt head must locate between the raised edges so it is held captive (arrowed)

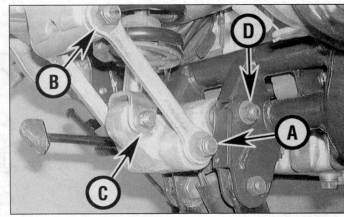

11.3 Linkage rods-to-arm bolt (A), linkage rods-to-swingarm bolt (B), shock lower bolt (C), linkage arm-to-frame bolt (D)

5•14 Frame, suspension and final drive

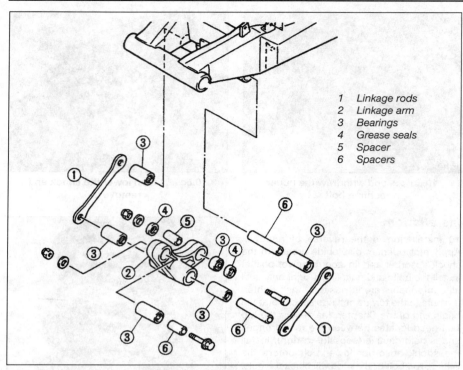

1 Linkage rods
2 Linkage arm
3 Bearings
4 Grease seals
5 Spacer
6 Spacers

11.6 Suspension linkage components

Inspection

6 Withdraw all the spacers from the linkage arm and swingarm, noting their different sizes **(see illustration)**. Lever the grease seals out of the shock absorber mounting on the linkage arm. Thoroughly clean all components, removing all traces of dirt, corrosion and grease.

7 Inspect all components closely, looking for obvious signs of wear such as heavy scoring, or for damage such as cracks or distortion. Slip each spacer back into its bearing and check that there is not an excessive amount of freeplay between the two components. Renew any components as required.

8 Check the condition of the needle roller bearings in the linkage arm and in the bottom of the swingarm. Refer to *Tools and Workshop Tips* (Section 5) in the *Reference* section for more information on bearings. If the linkage rod bearings in the swingarm need to be renewed, remove the swingarm (see Section 13).

9 Worn bearings can be drifted out of their bores, but note that removal will destroy them; new bearings should be obtained before work commences. The new bearings should be pressed or drawn into their bores rather than driven into position. In the absence of a press, a suitable drawbolt tool can be made up as described in *Tools and Workshop Tips* (Section 5) in the *Reference* section.

10 Lubricate the needle roller bearings and the spacers with molybdenum disulphide grease and install the spacers.

11 Check the condition of the grease seals for the shock absorber mounting in the linkage arm and renew them if they are damaged or deteriorated. Press the seals squarely into place.

Installation

12 Installation is the reverse of removal. Apply molybdenum disulphide grease to the pivot points. Install the bolts and nuts finger-tight only until all components are in position, then tighten the nuts to the torque settings specified at the beginning of the Chapter.

12 Suspension – adjustments

Front forks

1 On 1994 and 1995 models, the forks are not adjustable.
2 On all other models the forks are adjustable for spring pre-load, which is adjusted using a suitable spanner on the adjuster flats on the top of the forks. The amount of pre-load is indicated by lines on the adjuster **(see illustration)**. There are seven lines. The standard position is with the 4th line just visible above the top bolt hex. The softest position is with all seven lines visible, and the hardest is with one line visible. Turn the adjuster clockwise to increase pre-load and anti-clockwise to decrease it. Always make sure both adjusters are set equally.

Rear shock absorber

3 The rear shock absorber is adjustable for spring pre-load.
4 Pre-load adjustment is made using a suitable C-spanner (one is provided in the toolkit) to turn the spring seat on the top of the shock absorber **(see illustration)**. There are seven positions. Position 1 is the softest setting and position 7 is the hardest. On 1994 and 1995 models position 4 is the standard setting. On all other models position 3 is the standard setting. Align the setting position required with the adjustment stopper **(see illustration)**.

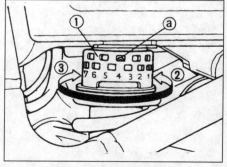

12.4b Rear shock preload adjuster

a Stopper
1 Pre-load adjuster
2 To increase pre-load
3 To decrease pre-load

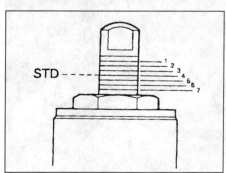

12.2 Fork pre-load adjuster lines

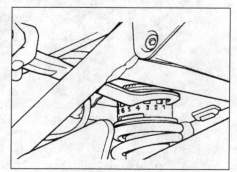

12.4a Use the C-spanner in the bike's toolkit to turn the pre-load adjuster

Frame, suspension and final drive 5•15

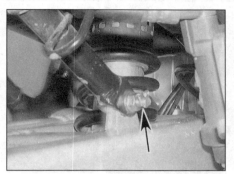

13.3 Remove the split pin (arrowed), then unscrew the nut, withdraw the bolt and detach the torque arm

13.5 Pull the rubber gaiter back off the engine

13.7 Prise the cap off each swingarm pivot

13 Swingarm – removal and installation

Removal

Note: *Before removing the swingarm, it is advisable to perform the rear suspension checks described in Chapter 1 to assess the extent of any wear.*

1 Remove the exhaust silencers (see Chapter 3).
2 Remove the rear wheel (see Chapter 6).
3 Remove the split pin from the bolt securing the torque arm to the swingarm, then unscrew the nut, withdraw the bolt and displace the torque arm **(see illustration)**. Discard the split pin as a new one must be used. Tie the caliper/bracket/torque arm assembly to the frame so that it is out the way, making sure no strain is placed on the hose.
4 Unscrew the nut, remove the washer and withdraw the bolt securing the linkage rods to the swingarm **(see illustration 10.4a)**. Unscrew the nut, remove the washer and withdraw the bolt securing the shock absorber to the linkage arm **(see illustration 10.4b)**. Swing the linkage rods and the linkage arm down.
5 Pull the driveshaft rubber gaiter back off the engine to expose the driveshaft coupling **(see illustration)**.
6 Unless you need to separate the final drive housing and/or the driveshaft from the swingarm (see Section 15), the swingarm can be removed with them installed. Note however that the final drive housing is heavy and will make manoeuvring the swingarm much more difficult. If you do not want to separate them, it is advisable to have an assistant to help you.
7 Prise off the swingarm pivot caps on both sides of the swingarm **(see illustration)**.
8 Slacken the locknut on the pivot bolt on the right-hand side **(see illustration)**.
9 With the aid of an assistant to support the swingarm if necessary, unscrew the pivot bolt on each side and then carefully move the swingarm down and back between the linkage arm and the shock absorber and remove it from the frame **(see illustrations)** – if it wasn't removed, the driveshaft should slip out of the universal joint (UJ) and come away with the swingarm, though if it is tight, it may well disengage from the final drive and remain attached to the UJ.
10 If required and not already removed, withdraw the driveshaft from the front of the swingarm – it is a push-fit into the final drive housing. Note the collars fitted into each side of the swingarm and remove them for safekeeping if required **(see illustration)**. Also remove the rubber gaiter if required.
11 Inspect all components for wear or damage as described in Section 14.

Installation

12 If removed, slide the driveshaft into the swingarm, making sure it locates correctly

13.8 Slacken the pivot bolt locknut (arrowed)

13.9a Unscrew the right-hand pivot bolt . . .

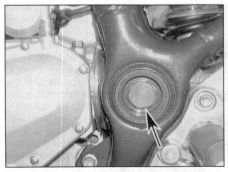

13.9b . . . and the left-hand pivot bolt (arrowed) . . .

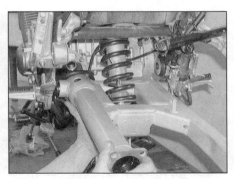

13.9c . . . then manoeuvre the swingarm down and out

13.10 Remove the collar from each side

5•16 Frame, suspension and final drive

13.13a Install the left-hand pivot bolt . . .

13.13b . . . and the right-hand pivot bolt and locknut

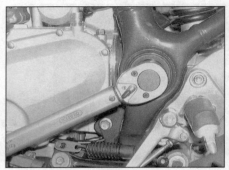

13.14a Tighten the left-hand pivot bolt . . .

13.14b . . . then the right-hand pivot bolt . . .

13.14c . . . then the locknut

into the final drive if it is installed. If removed, fit the rubber gaiter. If removed, fit the collar into each side of the swingarm **(see illustration 13.10)**.

13 Manoeuvre the swingarm into position in the frame, making sure the driveshaft end (if installed) locates into the universal joint **(see illustration 13.9c)**. Fit the pivot bolt into the left-hand side and the pivot bolt and its locknut into the right-hand side **(see illustrations)**.

14 Tighten the left-hand side pivot bolt then the right-hand side pivot bolt to the torque settings specified at the beginning of the Chapter **(see illustrations)**. Now tighten the locknut on the right-hand bolt to the specified torque setting **(see illustration)**. When tightening the locknut, it is essential that the pivot bolt does not move with it. As conventional torque wrenches will not allow the pivot bolt to be counter-held while tightening the locknut, make a reference mark between the bolt and frame to check that it doesn't move. Install the pivot caps.

15 If removed, install the final drive housing (see Section 15). Fit the rubber gaiter back onto the engine **(see illustration 13.5)**.

16 Mount the shock absorber onto the linkage arm and the linkage rods onto the swingarm and tighten the nuts to the specified torque settings **(see illustrations 10.4b and a)**.

17 Fit the brake torque arm onto the swingarm and install the bolt, then tighten the nut to the specified torque setting **(see illustration 13.3)**. Fit a new split pin into the end of the bolt.

18 Install the rear wheel (see Chapter 6).

19 Install the exhaust silencers (see Chapter 3).

20 Check the operation of the rear suspension before taking the machine on the road.

14 Swingarm – inspection and bearing renewal

Inspection

1 Thoroughly clean the swingarm, removing all traces of dirt, corrosion and grease.

2 If not already done, remove the collar from each side of the swingarm **(see illustration 13.10)**.

3 Inspect all components closely, looking for obvious signs of wear such as heavy scoring, and cracks or distortion due to accident damage. Check the bearings for roughness, looseness and any other damage, referring to *Tools and Workshop Tips* (Section 5) in the *Reference* section. Any damaged or worn component must be renewed.

Bearing renewal

4 If not already done, remove the collar from each side of the swingarm **(see illustration 13.10)**. Lever out the grease seals using a flat-bladed screwdriver **(see illustration)**. Discard the seals as new ones should be used. Also remove the collar for the linkage rod bearings **(see illustration)**. Remove the bearings, using a puller or slide-hammer if necessary. Refer to *Tools and Workshop Tips* (Section 5) in the *Reference* section for more information on bearing removal and installation methods.

5 Lubricate the new bearings with molybdenum disulphide grease and fit them into the swingarm. Use the old bearing or a suitable socket or piece of tubing that bears only on the outer race of the bearing and drive them in until fully seated. Press in the grease seals, then install the collars.

14.4a Lever out each grease seal (arrowed)

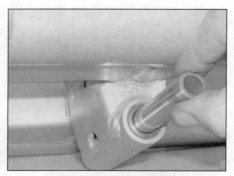

14.4b Withdraw the collar

Frame, suspension and final drive 5•17

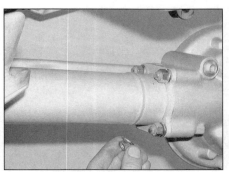

15.3a Unscrew the four nuts . . .

15.3b . . . and draw the housing off the swingarm, bringing the driveshaft with it

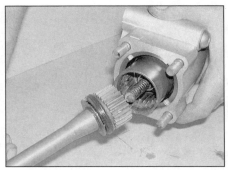

15.3c Pull the driveshaft out of the housing

15 Driveshaft and final drive – removal, inspection and installation

Removal

1 Remove the left-hand side exhaust silencer (see Chapter 3).
2 Remove the rear wheel (see Chapter 6).
3 Support the final drive housing and unscrew the four nuts securing it to the swingarm (see illustration). Remove the housing from the swingarm (see illustration). The driveshaft is a push fit into the final drive housing and a slide fit in the universal joint, and therefore will probably come away with the final drive housing. Separate the driveshaft from the housing (it is a push fit), or withdraw it from the swingarm if it stayed in there (see illustration). Note the spacer in the final drive housing and remove it for safekeeping (see illustration).
4 The universal joint is part of the middle driven gear shaft, which is covered in Chapter 2.

Inspection

5 Inspect the driveshaft splines for wear or damage and the corresponding splines in the universal joint and final drive housing. If wear is evident and there is excessive clearance between the driveshaft and either the final drive housing or the universal joint, the shaft must be replaced with a new one.
6 Check the condition of the seal at the rear of the shaft. If it is worn, deteriorated or damaged, remove the circlip on the front of the shaft and the circlip securing the seal onto the shaft, then slide the washer and seal off the front of the shaft (see illustration). Fit a new seal then slide on the washer and secure them the circlip, making sure it is correctly seated in its groove. Also install the front circlip.
7 Fit the driveshaft into the final drive housing and rotate the shaft. Check that the shaft is able to rotate smoothly and freely and that the power is transmitted correctly through the bevel gear assembly to the output boss. If there are any signs of roughness, stiffness or notchiness, any evidence of wear on the input and output boss splines, or any evidence of oil leakage from the seals, the unit must be disassembled and examined further.
8 If attention to the final drive housing is required, the complete unit should be taken to a Yamaha dealer who will have the necessary special tools and expertise to carry out the rather complicated inspection and overhaul procedure.

Installation

9 Lubricate the splines on both ends of the driveshaft, in the universal joint and in the final drive housing input boss with molybdenum disulphide grease.
10 Check that the spring is still attached to the boss in the final drive housing (see illustration). Fit the driveshaft into the housing and push it in until the seal is felt to locate (see illustration 15.3c).
11 Slide the driveshaft into the swingarm and mount the housing onto the swingarm, making sure the driveshaft locates correctly and fully in the splines of the universal joint (see illustration 15.3b). There is a hole in the front of the swingarm through which the universal joint can be manipulated if required – remove the blanking plug (see illustration). Tighten the housing nuts to the torque setting specified at the beginning of the Chapter (see illustration 15.3a).
12 Fit the spacer into the final drive housing (see illustration 15.3d). Install the rear wheel (see Chapter 6).
13 Install the left-hand side exhaust silencer (see Chapter 3).

15.3d Withdraw the spacer from the housing

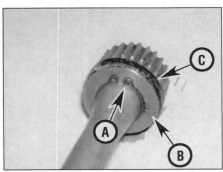

15.6 Remove the circlip (A), the washer (B) and the seal (C)

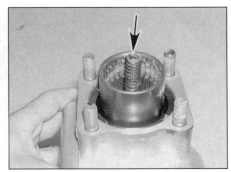

15.10 Make sure the spring (arrowed) is still in place on its boss

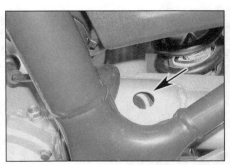

15.11 Remove the blanking plug (arrowed) and manipulate the universal joint to align it if necessary

5•18 Frame, suspension and final drive

Notes

Chapter 6
Brakes, wheels and tyres

Contents

Brake fluid level check . . . . .see *Daily (pre-ride) checks*	
Brake hoses, pipes and unions – inspection and renewal 10	
Brake light switches – check and renewal . . . . .see Chapter 8	
Brake pad wear check . . . . .see Chapter 1	
Brake system – bleeding 11	
Brake system check . . . . .see Chapter 1	
Front brake calipers – removal, overhaul and installation 3	
Front brake discs – inspection, removal and installation 4	
Front brake master cylinder – removal, overhaul and installation . . . 5	
Front brake pads – renewal 2	
Front wheel – removal and installation 14	
General information 1	
Rear brake caliper – removal, overhaul and installation 7	
Rear brake disc – inspection, removal and installation 8	
Rear brake master cylinder – removal, overhaul and installation . . . 9	
Rear brake pads – renewal 6	
Rear wheel – removal and installation 15	
Tyres – general information and fitting 17	
Tyres – pressure, tread depth and condition . . . . .see *Daily (pre-ride) checks*	
Wheel bearings and coupling dampers – removal, inspection and installation 16	
Wheel bearings – check . . . . .see Chapter 1	
Wheels – alignment check 13	
Wheels – general check . . . . .see Chapter 1	
Wheels – inspection and repair 12

Degrees of difficulty

Easy, suitable for novice with little experience	**Fairly easy,** suitable for beginner with some experience	**Fairly difficult,** suitable for competent DIY mechanic	**Difficult,** suitable for experienced DIY mechanic	**Very difficult,** suitable for expert DIY or professional

Specifications

Brakes
Brake fluid type	DOT 4
Front caliper bore ID	
Upper bore	30.20 mm
Lower bore	33.30 mm
Front disc thickness	
Standard	4.0 mm
Service limit	3.5 mm
Front disc maximum runout	0.15 mm
Front master cylinder bore ID	15.87 mm
Rear caliper bore ID	42.85 mm
Rear disc thickness	
Standard	5.0 mm
Service limit	4.5 mm
Rear disc maximum runout	0.15 mm
Rear master cylinder bore ID	14.00 mm

Wheels
Rim size	
Front	17 x MT3.0
Rear	17 x MT4.0
Wheel runout (max)	
Axial (side-to-side)	0.5 mm
Radial (out-of-round)	1.0 mm

Tyres
Tyre pressures	see *Daily (pre-ride) checks*
Tyre sizes*	
Front	120/70-17 58V
Rear	150/70-17 69V

*Refer to the owners handbook, the tyre information label on the swingarm, or your Yamaha dealer for approved tyre brands.

6•2 Brakes, wheels and tyres

Torque wrench settings

Front brake caliper mounting bolts	35 Nm
Front brake caliper slider bolt	22 Nm
Brake hose banjo bolts	30 Nm
Front brake disc bolts	20 Nm
Front brake master cylinder clamp bolts	9 Nm
Rear brake caliper mounting bolts	35 Nm
Rear brake disc bolts	20 Nm
Rear brake master cylinder mounting bolts	30 Nm
Rear brake hose joint piece	30 Nm
Brake caliper bleed valve	6 Nm
Front wheel axle	59 Nm
Front axle clamp bolt	19 Nm
Rear axle nut	105 Nm
Rear axle clamp bolt	16 Nm

1 General information

All models are fitted with cast alloy wheels designed for tubeless tyres only. Both front and rear brakes are hydraulically operated disc brakes.

The front brakes have twin piston sliding calipers, and the rear brake has a single opposed piston caliper.

Caution: Disc brake components rarely require disassembly. Do not disassemble components unless absolutely necessary. If a hydraulic brake line is loosened, the entire system must be disassembled, drained, cleaned and then properly filled and bled upon reassembly. Do not use solvents on internal brake components. Solvents will cause the seals to swell and distort. Use only clean brake fluid or denatured alcohol for cleaning. Use care when working with brake fluid as it can injure your eyes and it will damage painted surfaces and plastic parts.

2 Front brake pads – renewal

⚠️ **Warning: The dust created by the brake system may contain asbestos, which is harmful to your health. Never blow it out with compressed air and don't inhale any of it. An approved filtering mask should be worn when working on the brakes.**

1 Push the brake caliper against the disc so that the pistons are forced back into the caliper – this will provide room for the new pads. Due to the increased friction material thickness of new pads, it may be necessary to remove the master cylinder reservoir cover and diaphragm and siphon out some fluid. If the pistons are difficult to push back, attach a length of clear hose to the bleed valve and place the open end in a suitable container, then open the valve and try again. Take great care not to draw any air into the system. If in doubt, bleed the brakes afterwards (see Section 11).

2 Unscrew the caliper slider bolt **(see illustration)** and pivot the back of the caliper up. Remove the pads, noting how they locate **(see illustration)**.

3 Inspect the surface of each pad for contamination and check that the friction material has not worn beyond its service limit (see Chapter 1, Section 7). If either pad is worn down to or beyond the service limit wear indicator, is fouled with oil or grease, or is heavily scored or damaged by dirt and debris, both sets of pads must be renewed as a set. Note that it is not possible to degrease the friction material; if the pads are contaminated in any way new ones must be fitted.

4 If the pads are in good condition clean them carefully, using a fine wire brush which is completely free of oil and grease to remove all traces of road dirt and corrosion. Using a pointed instrument, clean out the grooves in the friction material and dig out any embedded particles of foreign matter. Any areas of glazing may be removed using emery cloth. Spray with a dedicated brake cleaner to remove any dust.

5 Check the condition of the brake discs (see Section 4).

6 Smear the back of the pads and the leading and trailing edges of the backing material with copper-based grease, making sure that none gets on the friction material. Smear the slider bolt shank with lithium soap based grease.

7 Install the inner pad, making sure it locates correctly against the caliper bracket at both ends **(see illustration)**. Install the outer pad, locating it in the same way. Pivot the caliper down onto the bracket, making sure the pads remain in place **(see illustration)**. Install the

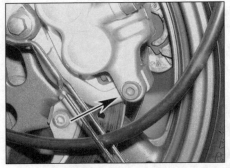

2.2a Unscrew the slider bolt (arrowed) ...

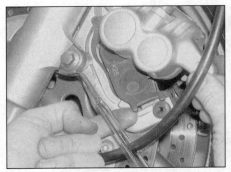

2.2b ... then pivot the rear of the caliper up and remove the pads

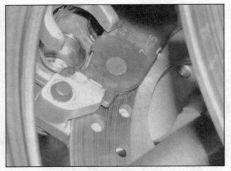

2.7a Make sure the pads locate correctly against the bracket

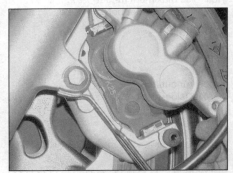

2.7b Pivot the caliper down over the pads and onto the bracket ...

Brakes, wheels and tyres 6•3

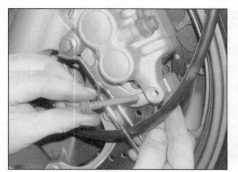

2.7c ... and install the slider bolt

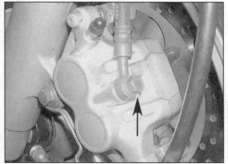

3.1 Remove the brake hose banjo bolt (arrowed) and detach the hose

3.2a Unscrew the brake hose clamp bolt (arrowed) on each side

slider bolt and tighten it to the torque setting specified at the beginning of the Chapter (see illustration).

8 Top up the master cylinder reservoir if necessary (see *Daily (pre-ride) checks*), and install the reservoir diaphragm and cover.

9 Operate the brake lever several times to bring the pads into contact with the disc. Check the operation of the brake before riding the motorcycle.

3 Front brake calipers – removal, overhaul and installation

⚠️ **Warning:** *If a caliper indicates the need for an overhaul (usually due to leaking fluid or sticky operation), all old brake fluid should be flushed from the system. Also, the dust created by the brake system may contain asbestos, which is harmful to your health. Never blow it out with compressed air and don't inhale any of it. An approved filtering mask should be worn when working on the brakes. Do not, under any circumstances, use petroleum-based solvents to clean brake parts. Use the specified clean brake fluid, dedicated brake cleaner or denatured alcohol only, as described.*

Removal

1 If the calipers are just being displaced and not completely removed or overhauled, do not disconnect the brake hose. If the calipers are being completely removed or overhauled, remove the brake hose banjo bolt and detach the hose, noting its alignment with the caliper **(see illustration)**. Plug the hose end or wrap a plastic bag tightly around it to minimise fluid loss and prevent dirt entering the system. Discard the sealing washers as new ones must be used on installation. **Note:** *If you are planning to overhaul the caliper and don't have a source of compressed air to blow out the pistons, just loosen the banjo bolt at this*

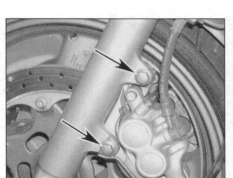

3.2b Unscrew the caliper mounting bolts (arrowed) ...

stage and retighten it lightly. The bike's hydraulic system can then be used to force the pistons out of the body once the pads have been removed. Disconnect the hose once the pistons have been sufficiently displaced.

2 If the brake hose has not been disconnected from the caliper, unscrew the bolt securing the hose to the front fork. On 1997-on models, a pipe links the two calipers, and is joined to the hose by a union – to avoid stressing the pipe, remove the union bolt securing the assembly to the fork on each side and displace each caliper from its disc at the same time **(see illustration)**. Unscrew the caliper mounting bolts and slide

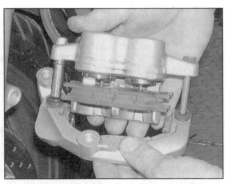

3.3a Slide the caliper off the bracket and remove the pads

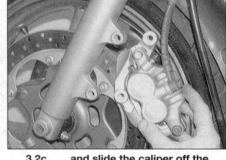

3.2c ... and slide the caliper off the disc

the calipers off their discs, noting the speedometer cable guide secured by the lower bolt on the left-hand caliper **(see illustrations)**.

3 If the calipers are being overhauled, separate each caliper from its bracket by sliding them apart and remove the pads, noting how they locate **(see illustration)**. Remove the pad spring from the caliper **(see illustration 3.15a)**. If required, also remove the guides from the bracket, noting how they fit **(see illustration)**.

Overhaul

4 Clean the exterior of the caliper with

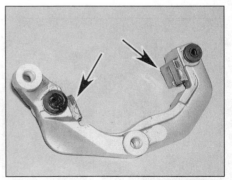

3.3b Remove the pad guides (arrowed) if required

6•4 Brakes, wheels and tyres

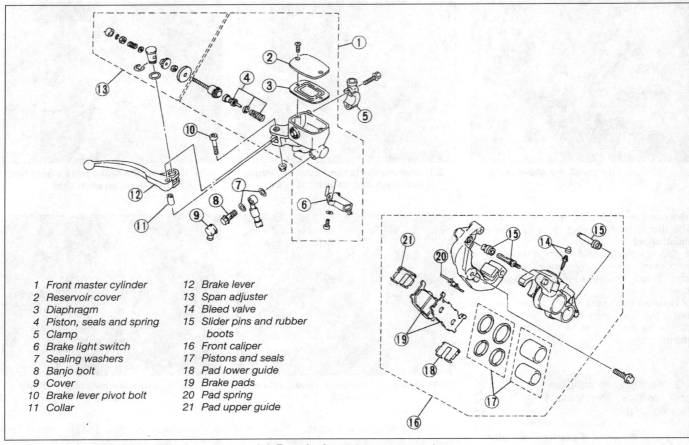

1 Front master cylinder
2 Reservoir cover
3 Diaphragm
4 Piston, seals and spring
5 Clamp
6 Brake light switch
7 Sealing washers
8 Banjo bolt
9 Cover
10 Brake lever pivot bolt
11 Collar
12 Brake lever
13 Span adjuster
14 Bleed valve
15 Slider pins and rubber boots
16 Front caliper
17 Pistons and seals
18 Pad lower guide
19 Brake pads
20 Pad spring
21 Pad upper guide

3.4 Front brake system components

denatured alcohol or brake system cleaner (see illustrations).
5 Displace the pistons as far as possible from the caliper body, either by pumping them out by operating the front brake lever, or by forcing them out using compressed air, then remove them from the caliper. Mark each piston head and caliper body with a felt marker to ensure that the pistons can be matched to their original bores on reassembly. If the compressed air method is used, direct the air into the fluid inlet to force the pistons out of the body. Use only low pressure to ease the pistons out and make sure both pistons are displaced at the same time. If the air pressure is too high and the pistons are forced out, the caliper and/or pistons may be damaged.

⚠ **Warning: Never place your fingers in front of the pistons in an attempt to catch or protect them when applying compressed air, as serious injury could result.**

Caution: Do not try to remove the pistons by levering them out, or by using pliers or any other grips.

6 Using a wooden or plastic tool, remove the dust seals from the caliper bores (see illustration). Discard them as new ones must be used on installation. If a metal tool is being used, take great care not to damage the caliper bores.
7 Remove and discard the piston seals in the same way.
8 Clean the pistons and bores with clean brake fluid of the specified type. If compressed air is available, use it to dry the parts thoroughly (make sure it's filtered and unlubricated).

Caution: Do not, under any circumstances, use a petroleum-based solvent to clean brake parts.

9 Inspect the caliper bores and pistons for signs of corrosion, nicks and burrs and loss of plating. If surface defects are present, the caliper assembly must be renewed. If the necessary measuring equipment is available, compare the dimensions of the caliper bores to those specified at the beginning of the Chapter, and install a new caliper if necessary. If the caliper is in bad shape the master cylinder should also be checked.
10 Lubricate the new piston seals with clean brake fluid and install them in their grooves in the caliper bores. Note that two sizes of bore and piston are used (see Specifications), and care must therefore be taken to ensure that the correct size seals are fitted to the correct bores. The same applies when fitting the new dust seals and pistons.
11 Lubricate the new dust seals with clean brake fluid and install them in their grooves in the caliper bores.
12 Lubricate the pistons with clean brake fluid and install them closed-end first into the caliper bores. Using your thumbs, push the pistons all the way in, making sure they enter the bore squarely.

Installation

13 If the caliper and bracket have been separated, clean the old grease and any

3.6 Use a plastic or wooden tool (such as a pencil) to remove the seals

Brakes, wheels and tyres 6•5

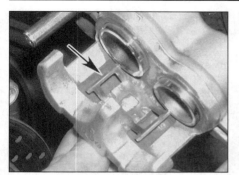

3.15a Install the pad spring (arrowed) . . .

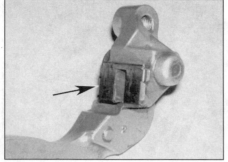

3.15b . . . and each pad guide, making sure they locate correctly

3.15c Position the pads in the caliper and fit the bracket . . .

corrosion off the caliper slider pins and check the rubber boots. If they are damaged or deteriorated, they should be replaced with new ones.

14 Smear the back of the pads and the leading and trailing edges of the backing material with copper-based grease, making sure that none gets on the friction material. Smear the slider pins with lithium soap based grease.

15 If removed, fit the pad spring into the caliper and the guides onto the bracket (see illustrations). Fit the pads into the caliper (see illustration), then slide the caliper and bracket together (see illustration 3.3a), making sure the pads locate correctly around the guides on the bracket (see illustration).

16 Slide the caliper onto the brake disc, making sure the pads sit squarely each side of the disc, on 1997-on models bearing in mind the information in Step 2 (see illustration 3.2c). Install the caliper bolts, not forgetting to secure the speedometer cable guide with the lower bolt on the left-hand caliper, and tighten them to the torque setting specified at the beginning of the Chapter (see illustrations). Attach the brake hose or hose/pipe assembly to the front fork (see illustration).

17 If removed, connect the brake hose to the caliper, using new sealing washers on each side of the fitting. Align the hose as noted on removal (see illustration 3.1). Tighten the banjo bolt to the torque setting specified at

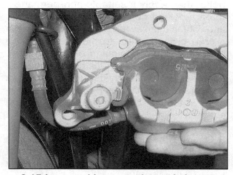

3.15d . . . making sure the pads locate correctly

the beginning of the Chapter. Top up the master cylinder reservoir with DOT 4 brake fluid (see Daily (pre-ride) checks) and bleed the hydraulic system as described in Section 11.

18 Check for leaks and thoroughly test the operation of the brake before riding the motorcycle.

4 Front brake discs – inspection, removal and installation

Inspection

1 Visually inspect the surface of the discs for score marks and other damage. Light

3.16a Install the caliper mounting bolts . . .

scratches are normal after use and won't affect brake operation, but deep grooves and heavy score marks will reduce braking efficiency and accelerate pad wear. If a disc is badly grooved it must be machined or a new one fitted.

2 To check disc runout, position the bike on its centrestand and support it so that the front wheel is raised off the ground. Mount a dial gauge to a fork leg, with the plunger on the gauge touching the surface of the disc about 10 mm (1/2 in) from the outer edge (see illustration). Rotate the wheel and watch the gauge needle, comparing the reading with the limit listed in the Specifications at the beginning of the Chapter. If the runout is greater than the service limit, check the wheel bearings for play (see Chapter 1). If the

3.16b . . . and tighten them to the specified torque

3.16c Fit the hose clamps onto the forks

4.2 Set up a dial gauge with the probe contacting the brake disc, then rotate the wheel to check for runout

6•6 Brakes, wheels and tyres

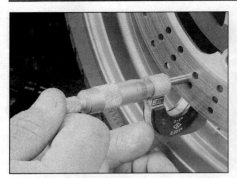

4.3 Using a micrometer to measure disc thickness

4.5 Unscrew the bolts (arrowed) and remove the disc

bearings are worn, install new ones (see Section 16) and repeat this check. If the disc runout is still excessive, a new one will have to be fitted, although machining by an engineer may be possible.

3 The discs must not be machined or allowed to wear down to a thickness less than the service limit as listed in this Chapter's Specifications. The thickness of the disc can be checked with a micrometer or any other measuring tool **(see illustration)**. If the thickness of the disc is less than the service limit, a new one must be fitted.

Removal

4 Remove the wheel (see Section 14).
Caution: Do not lay the wheel down and allow it to rest on either disc – the disc could become warped. Set the wheel on wood blocks so the disc doesn't support the weight of the wheel.
5 Mark the relationship of the disc to the wheel, so it can be installed in the same position. Unscrew the disc retaining bolts, loosening them evenly and a little at a time in a criss-cross pattern to avoid distorting the disc, then remove the disc from the wheel **(see illustration)**.

Installation

6 Mount the disc on the wheel with its marked side facing out, aligning the previously applied matchmarks (if you're reinstalling the original disc).
7 Clean the threads of the disc mounting bolts, then apply a suitable non-permanent thread locking compound. Install the bolts and tighten them evenly and a little at a time in a criss-cross pattern to the torque setting specified at the beginning of the Chapter. Clean off all grease from the brake disc using acetone or brake system cleaner. If a new brake disc has been installed, remove any protective coating from its working surfaces.
8 Install the front wheel (see Section 14).
9 Operate the brake lever several times to bring the pads into contact with the discs. Check the operation of the brakes carefully before riding the bike.

5 Front brake master cylinder – removal, overhaul and installation

1 If the master cylinder is leaking fluid, or if the lever does not produce a firm feel when the brake is applied, and bleeding the brake does not help (see Section 11), and the hydraulic hoses and or pipes and unions are all in good condition, then master cylinder overhaul is recommended.
2 Before disassembling the master cylinder, read through the entire procedure and make sure that you have the correct rebuild kit. Also, you will need some new DOT 4 brake fluid and some clean rags. **Note:** *To prevent damage to the paint from spilled brake fluid,* always cover the fuel tank when working on the master cylinder.
Caution: Disassembly, overhaul and reassembly of the brake master cylinder must be done in a spotlessly clean work area to avoid contamination and possible failure of the brake hydraulic system components.

Removal

Note: *If the master cylinder is being displaced from the handlebar and not being removed completely or overhauled, follow Steps 4 and 7 only.*
3 Loosen, but do not remove, the screws holding the reservoir cover in place.
4 Disconnect the brake light switch wiring connector **(see illustration)**.
5 Remove the front brake lever (see Chapter 5). Remove the rear view mirror (see Chapter 7).
6 Unscrew the brake hose banjo bolt and separate the hose(s) from the master cylinder, noting the alignment **(see illustration 5.4)**. Discard the sealing washers as they must be replaced with new ones. Wrap the end(s) of the hose(s) in a clean rag and suspend in an upright position or bend down carefully and place the open end(s) in a clean container. The objective is to prevent excessive loss of brake fluid, fluid spills and system contamination.
7 Unscrew the master cylinder clamp bolts, then lift the master cylinder away from the handlebar **(see illustration)**.
8 Remove the reservoir cover retaining screws and lift off the cover and the rubber diaphragm. Drain the brake fluid from the reservoir into a suitable container. Wipe any remaining fluid out of the reservoir with a clean rag.
9 Remove the brake light switch (see Chapter 8).
Caution: Do not tip the master cylinder upside down or brake fluid will run out.

Overhaul

10 Thread the adjuster off the pushrod and remove the spring **(see illustrations)**. Counter-hold the pushrod end using the flats,

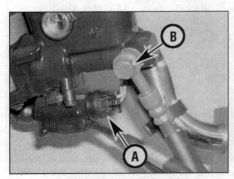

5.4 Brake light switch wiring connector (A), brake hose banjo bolt (B)

5.7 Front brake master cylinder clamp bolts (arrowed)

5.10a Unscrew the adjuster . . .

Brakes, wheels and tyres 6•7

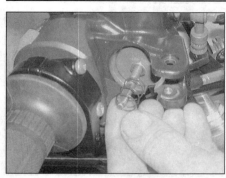

5.10b . . . and remove the spring

5.10c Counter-hold the pushrod and unscrew the nut . . .

5.10d . . . and remove the plate

then unscrew the nut and remove the plate **(see illustrations)**.

11 Remove the rubber boot from the pushrod, noting how it locates in the grooves in the pushrod and master cylinder **(see illustration)**. Depress the pushrod and remove the circlip, then slide out the pushrod, the piston assembly and the spring, noting how they fit **(see illustration)**. Lay the parts out in the proper order to prevent confusion during reassembly **(see illustration 3.4)**.

12 Clean all parts with clean brake fluid. If compressed air is available, use it to dry the parts thoroughly (make sure it's filtered and unlubricated).

Caution: Do not, under any circumstances, use a petroleum-based solvent to clean brake parts.

13 Check the master cylinder bore for corrosion, scratches, nicks and score marks. If the necessary measuring equipment is available, compare the diameter of the bore to that given in the Specifications Section of this Chapter. If damage or wear is evident, the master cylinder must be replaced with a new one. If the master cylinder is in poor condition, then the calipers should be checked as well. Check that the fluid inlet and outlet ports in the master cylinder are clear.

14 The piston assembly and spring are included in the rebuild kit. Use all of the new parts, regardless of the apparent condition of the old ones. If the seals and cup are not already on the piston, fit them according to the layout of the old piston assembly.

15 Install the spring in the master cylinder so that its narrow end faces out.

16 Lubricate the piston, seals and cup with clean brake fluid. Install the assembly into the master cylinder, making sure it is the correct way round **(see illustration 3.4)**. Make sure the lips on the cup do not turn inside out when they are slipped into the bore. Slide in the pushrod and secure it with the circlip **(see illustration 5.11b)**. Fit the rubber boot, making sure it locates in the groove in the master cylinder and on the pushrod **(see illustration 5.11a)**.

17 Slide the plate onto the pushrod and secure it with the nut, counter-holding the pushrod end as you tighten it against the plate **(see illustrations 5.10d and c)**. Fit the spring, then thread the adjuster onto the pushrod **(see illustrations 5.10b and a)**.

18 Inspect the reservoir cover rubber diaphragm and renew it if it is damaged or deteriorated.

Installation

19 Install the brake light switch (see Chapter 8).

20 Attach the master cylinder to the handlebar and, where marked, fit the clamp with its 'UP' mark facing up, aligning the top mating surfaces of the clamp with the punchmark on the handlebar **(see illustration 5.7)**. Tighten first the upper bolt, then the lower bolt to the torque setting specified at the beginning of the Chapter.

21 Connect the brake hose(s) to the master cylinder, using new sealing washers on each side of the union(s), and aligning the hose(s) as noted on removal **(see illustration 5.4)**. Tighten the banjo bolt to the torque setting specified at the beginning of this Chapter.

22 Install the brake lever (see Chapter 5), and the rear view mirror (see Chapter 7).

23 Connect the brake light switch wiring connector **(see illustrations 5.4)**.

24 Fill the fluid reservoir with new DOT 4 brake fluid as described in *Daily (pre-ride) checks*. Refer to Section 11 of this Chapter and bleed the air from the system.

25 Fit the rubber diaphragm, making sure it is correctly seated, and the cover onto the master cylinder reservoir.

26 Check the operation of the front brake before riding the motorcycle.

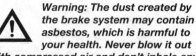

6 Rear brake pads – renewal

⚠ *Warning: The dust created by the brake system may contain asbestos, which is harmful to your health. Never blow it out with compressed air and don't inhale any of it. An approved filtering mask should be worn when working on the brakes.*

1 Press in the edges of the brake pad cover to release its clips and remove it – use a flat-bladed screwdriver if necessary **(see illustration)**. Remove the pad pin retaining clips, then

5.11a Remove the rubber boot . . .

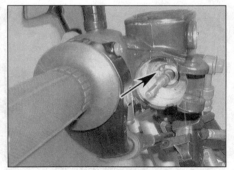

5.11b . . . then depress the pushrod and remove the circlip (arrowed)

6.1a Remove the brake pad cover . . .

6

6•8 Brakes, wheels and tyres

6.1b ... then remove the retaining clips ...

6.1c ... withdraw the pad pins and remove the spring (arrowed) ...

6.1d ... and lift the pads out of the caliper

withdraw the pad pins from the caliper using a suitable pair of pliers and remove the pad spring, noting how it fits (see illustrations). Withdraw the pads from the caliper body (see illustration). If required, remove the anti-chatter shim from the back of each pad, noting how it fits (see illustration 6.7).

2 Inspect the surface of each pad for contamination and check that the friction material has not worn beyond its service limit (see Chapter 1, Section 7). If either pad is worn down to or beyond the service limit wear indicator, is fouled with oil or grease, or is heavily scored or damaged by dirt and debris, both sets of pads must be renewed as a set. Note that it is not possible to degrease the friction material; if the pads are contaminated in any way new ones must be fitted.

3 If the pads are in good condition clean them carefully, using a fine wire brush which is completely free of oil and grease to remove all traces of road dirt and corrosion. Using a pointed instrument, clean out the grooves in the friction material and dig out any embedded particles of foreign matter. Any areas of glazing may be removed using emery cloth. Spray with a dedicated brake cleaner to remove any dust.

4 Check the condition of the brake disc (see Section 8).

5 Remove all traces of corrosion from the pad pins. Check them for signs of damage and renew them if necessary.

6 Push the pistons as far back into the caliper as possible using hand pressure or a piece of wood as leverage. Due to the increased friction material thickness of new pads, it may be necessary to remove the master cylinder reservoir cap and diaphragm and siphon out some fluid. If access to the piston heads is too restricted with the caliper in place, displace it (see Section 7). If the pistons are difficult to push back, attach a length of clear hose to the bleed valve and place the open end in a suitable container, then open the valve and try again. Take great care not to draw any air into the system. If in doubt, bleed the brakes afterwards (see Section 11).

7 Fit the anti-chatter shim onto the back of each pad, making sure the arrow points in the direction of normal disc rotation (see illustration). Smear the backs of the pads and the shank of each pad pin with copper-based grease, making sure that none gets on the front or sides of the pads.

8 Insert the pads into the caliper so that the friction material of each pad is facing the disc (see illustration 6.1d). Insert one of the pad pins, making sure it passes through the hole in each pad, then hook the end of the pad spring under the pin, making sure the longer outer tabs of the spring point in the direction of normal disc rotation (see illustration). Insert the other pad pin, pressing down on the spring end so that the pin fits over it (see illustration). Fit the retaining clips (see illustration). Install the caliper cover (see illustration 6.1a).

9 Top up the master cylinder reservoir if necessary (see Daily (pre-ride) checks).

10 Operate the brake pedal several times to bring the pads into contact with the disc. Check the operation of the brake before riding the motorcycle.

7 Rear brake caliper – removal, overhaul and installation

Warning: *If a caliper indicates the need for an overhaul (usually due to leaking fluid or sticky operation), all old brake fluid should be flushed from the system. Also, the dust created by the brake system may contain asbestos, which is harmful to your*

6.7 Fit the shim with arrow pointing in the direction of disc rotation

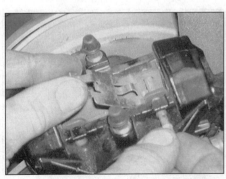

6.8a Insert the front pad pin and hook the spring end under the pin ...

6.8b ... then press the spring onto the pads and insert the other pin

6.8c Secure the pins with the clips

Brakes, wheels and tyres 6•9

health. Never blow it out with compressed air and don't inhale any of it. An approved filtering mask should be worn when working on the brakes. Do not, under any circumstances, use petroleum-based solvents to clean brake parts. Use the specified clean brake fluid, dedicated brake cleaner or denatured alcohol only, as described.

Removal

1 If the calipers are being overhauled, remove the brake pads (see Section 6). If the calipers are just being displaced or removed, the pads can be left in place.

2 If the calipers are just being displaced and not completely removed or overhauled, do not disconnect the brake hose. If the calipers are being overhauled, counter-hold the hose hex then unscrew the locknut and separate the hose from the hose joint in the caliper **(see illustration)**. Plug the hose end or wrap a plastic bag tightly around it to minimise fluid loss and prevent dirt entering the system. Discard the two sealing washers as they must be replaced with new ones. **Note:** *If you are planning to overhaul the caliper and don't have a source of compressed air to blow out the pistons, just loosen the banjo bolt at this stage and retighten it lightly. The bike's hydraulic system can then be used to force the pistons out of the body once the pads have been removed. Disconnect the hose once the pistons have been sufficiently displaced.*

3 Free the brake hose from its clamp on the torque arm **(see illustration)**. Unscrew the caliper mounting bolts, and slide the caliper off the disc **(see illustrations)**.

Overhaul

4 Clean the exterior of the caliper with denatured alcohol or brake system cleaner **(see illustration)**.

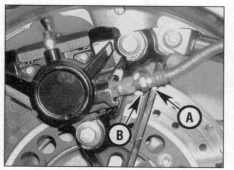

7.2 Counter-hold the hex (A) and unscrew the locknut (B)

7.3a Free the hose from its clamp

7.3b Unscrew the bolts (arrowed) . . .

7.3c . . . and slide the caliper off the disc

5 Using a flat piece of wood, block the piston on one side of the caliper and displace the opposite piston either by pumping it out by operating the rear brake pedal, or by forcing it out using compressed air. Remove the seals (see below) from the bore of the displaced piston, then reinstall the piston and block it using the wood. Now displace the piston from the other side using the same method. Remove the wood and the pistons. Mark each piston head and caliper body with a felt marker to ensure that the pistons can be matched to their original bores on reassembly. If the compressed air method is used, direct the air into the fluid inlet to force the pistons out of the body. Use only low pressure to ease the pistons out. If the air pressure is too high and the pistons are forced out, the caliper and/or pistons may be damaged.

 Warning: *Never place your fingers in front of the pistons in an attempt to catch or protect them when applying compressed air, as serious injury could result.*

Caution: *Do not try to remove the pistons by levering them out, or by using pliers or any other grips.*

6 Using a wooden or plastic tool, remove the dust seals from the caliper bores **(see illustration 3.6)**. Discard them as new ones must be used on installation. If a metal tool is being used, take great care not to damage the caliper bores.

7 Remove and discard the piston seals in the same way.

8 Clean the pistons and bores with clean brake fluid of the specified type. If compressed air is available, use it to dry the parts thoroughly (make sure it's filtered and unlubricated).

Caution: *Do not, under any circumstances, use a petroleum-based solvent to clean brake parts.*

9 Inspect the caliper bores and pistons for signs of corrosion, nicks and burrs and loss of

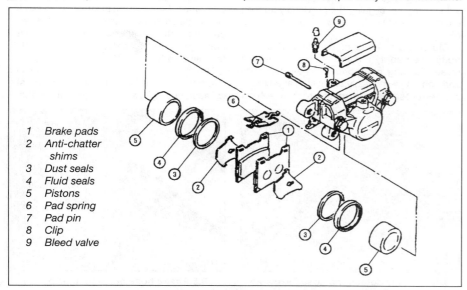

1 Brake pads
2 Anti-chatter shims
3 Dust seals
4 Fluid seals
5 Pistons
6 Pad spring
7 Pad pin
8 Clip
9 Bleed valve

7.4 Rear brake system components

6•10 Brakes, wheels and tyres

7.14 Install the caliper bolts and tighten them to the specified torque

plating. If surface defects are present, the caliper assembly must be renewed. If the necessary measuring equipment is available, compare the dimensions of the caliper bores to those specified at the beginning of the Chapter, and install a new caliper if necessary. If the caliper is in bad shape the master cylinder should also be checked.

10 Lubricate the new piston seals with clean brake fluid and install them in their grooves in the caliper bores.

11 Lubricate the new dust seals with clean brake fluid and install them in their grooves in the caliper bores.

12 Lubricate the pistons with clean brake fluid and install them closed-end first into the caliper bores. Using your thumbs, push the pistons all the way in, making sure they enter the bore squarely.

Installation

13 Slide the caliper onto the brake disc, making sure the pads sit squarely each side of the disc if they weren't removed **(see illustration 7.3c)**.

14 Install the caliper mounting bolts, and tighten them to the torque setting specified at the beginning of the Chapter **(see illustration)**.

15 If detached, fit the brake hose onto the hose joint and tighten the locknut onto the hose, counter-holding the hose hex to prevent the hose twisting **(see illustration 7.2)**. Do not overtighten the locknut. Top up the master cylinder reservoir with DOT 4 brake fluid (see *Daily (pre-ride) checks*) and bleed the hydraulic system as described in Section 11.

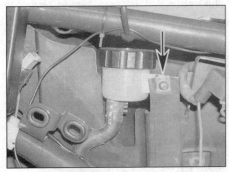

9.4a Remove the screw (arrowed) and drain the reservoir . . .

8.3 Rear brake disc bolts (arrowed)

16 If removed, install the brake pads (see Section 6).

17 Check for leaks and thoroughly test the operation of the brake before riding the motorcycle.

8 Rear brake disc – inspection, removal and installation

Inspection

1 Refer to Section 4 of this Chapter, noting that the dial gauge should be attached to the swingarm.

Removal

2 Remove the rear wheel (see Section 15).

3 Mark the relationship of the disc to the wheel so it can be installed in the same position. Unscrew the disc retaining bolts, loosening them evenly and a little at a time in a criss-cross pattern to avoid distorting the disc, and remove the disc **(see illustration)**.

Installation

4 Install the disc on the wheel with its marked side facing out, aligning the previously applied matchmarks (if you're reinstalling the original disc).

5 Clean the threads of the disc mounting bolts, then apply a suitable non-permanent thread locking compound. Install the bolts and tighten them evenly and a little at a time in a criss-cross pattern to the torque setting

9.4b . . . and detach the hose (arrowed) from the master cylinder

specified at the beginning of the Chapter. Clean off all grease from the brake disc using acetone or brake system cleaner. If a new brake disc has been installed, remove any protective coating from its working surfaces.

6 Install the rear wheel (see Section 15).

7 Operate the brake pedal several times to bring the pads into contact with the disc. Check the operation of the brake carefully before riding the motorcycle.

9 Rear brake master cylinder – removal, overhaul and installation

1 If the master cylinder is leaking fluid, or if the lever does not produce a firm feel when the brake is applied, and bleeding the brake does not help (see Section 11), and the hydraulic hoses are all in good condition, then master cylinder overhaul is recommended.

2 Before disassembling the master cylinder, read through the entire procedure and make sure that you have the correct rebuild kit. Also, you will need some new DOT 4 brake fluid, some clean rags and internal circlip pliers. **Note:** *To prevent damage to the paint from spilled brake fluid, always cover the surrounding components when working on the master cylinder.*

Caution: *Disassembly, overhaul and reassembly of the brake master cylinder must be done in a spotlessly clean work area to avoid contamination and possible failure of the brake hydraulic system components.*

Removal

3 Remove the right-hand side panel (see Chapter 7).

4 Remove the screw securing the master cylinder fluid reservoir to the frame, then unscrew the cap and remove the diaphragm plate and diaphragm and pour the fluid into a container **(see illustration)**. Release the clamp securing the reservoir hose to the union on the master cylinder and detach the hose, being prepared to catch any residual fluid **(see illustration)**.

5 Unscrew the brake hose banjo bolt and separate the brake hose from the master cylinder, noting its alignment **(see illustration)**.

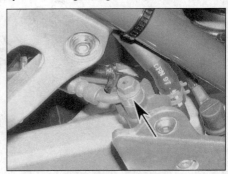

9.5 Brake hose banjo bolt (arrowed)

Brakes, wheels and tyres 6•11

9.6 Remove the split pin (A) and withdraw the clevis pin (B)

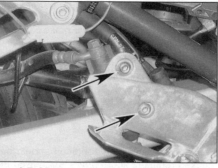

9.7 Master cylinder mounting bolts (arrowed)

9.8 Hold the clevis and slacken the locknut

Discard the two sealing washers as they must be replaced with new ones. Wrap the end of the hose in a clean rag and suspend the hose in an upright position or bend it down carefully and place the open end in a clean container. The objective is to prevent excessive loss of brake fluid, fluid spills and system contamination.

6 Remove the split pin and washer from the clevis pin securing the brake pedal to the master cylinder pushrod (see illustration). Withdraw the clevis pin and separate the pedal from the pushrod. Discard the split pin as a new one must be used.

7 Unscrew the two bolts securing the master cylinder to the bracket and remove the master cylinder (see illustration).

Overhaul

8 If required, mark the position of the clevis locknut on the pushrod, then slacken the locknut and thread the clevis off the pushrod (see illustration). Note the nut fitted inside the clevis and remove it for safekeeping.

9 Dislodge the rubber dust boot from the base of the master cylinder to reveal the pushrod retaining circlip (see illustration).

10 Depress the pushrod and, using circlip pliers, remove the circlip (see illustration). Slide out the piston assembly and spring. If they are difficult to remove, apply low pressure compressed air to the fluid outlet. Lay the parts out in the proper order to prevent confusion during reassembly (see illustration).

11 Clean all of the parts with clean brake fluid.

Caution: Do not, under any circumstances, use a petroleum-based solvent to clean brake parts. If compressed air is available, use it to dry the parts thoroughly (make sure it's filtered and unlubricated).

12 Check the master cylinder bore for corrosion, scratches, nicks and score marks. If the necessary measuring equipment is available, compare the diameter of the bore to that given in the Specifications Section of this Chapter. If damage is evident, the master cylinder must be replaced with a new one. If the master cylinder is in poor condition, then the caliper should be checked as well.

13 Inspect the reservoir hose for cracks or

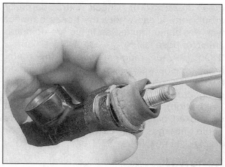

9.9 Remove the dust boot from the bottom of the master cylinder

splits and replace it with a new one if necessary. If required, pull the union from the master cylinder. Discard the bush as a new one must be used.

9.10a Depress the pushrod and remove the circlip

14 The dust boot, circlip, piston assembly and spring are included in the rebuild kit. Use all of the new parts, regardless of the apparent condition of the old ones. Fit them

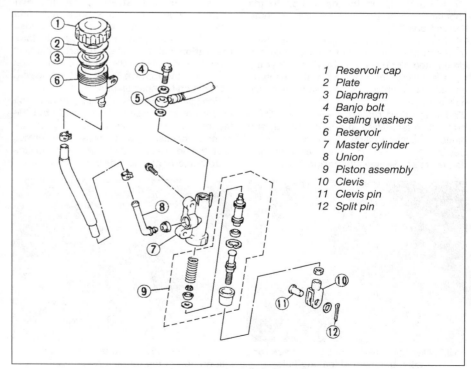

1 Reservoir cap
2 Plate
3 Diaphragm
4 Banjo bolt
5 Sealing washers
6 Reservoir
7 Master cylinder
8 Union
9 Piston assembly
10 Clevis
11 Clevis pin
12 Split pin

9.10b Rear brake master cylinder assembly

according to the layout of the old piston assembly.
15 Fit the spring into the master cylinder.
16 Lubricate the piston assembly with clean brake fluid. Fit the assembly into the master cylinder, making sure it is the correct way round. Make sure the lips on the cup do not turn inside out when they are slipped into the bore.
17 Install and depress the pushrod, then fit a new circlip, making sure it is properly seated in the groove (see illustration 9.10).
18 Install the rubber dust boot, making sure the lip is seated properly in the groove (see illustration 9.9).
19 If removed, fit a new reservoir hose union bush, then push the union into the master cylinder.
20 If removed, thread the clevis locknut and the clevis with its nut onto the master cylinder pushrod end. Position the clevis as noted on removal, then tighten the locknut securely (see illustration 9.8).

Installation
21 Fit the master cylinder onto the footrest bracket and tighten its mounting bolts to the torque setting specified at the beginning of the Chapter (see illustration 9.7).
22 Align the brake pedal with the master cylinder pushrod clevis, then slide in the clevis pin and secure it using a new split pin, not forgetting the washer (see illustration 9.6).
23 Connect the brake hose banjo bolt to the master cylinder, using a new sealing washer on each side of the banjo union. Ensure that the hose is positioned so that it butts against the lug and tighten the banjo bolt to the specified torque setting (see illustrations 9.5).
24 Connect the reservoir hose to the union on the master cylinder and secure it with the clamp (see illustration 9.4b). Check that the hose is secure and clamped at the reservoir end as well. If the clamps have weakened, use new ones.
25 Fill the fluid reservoir with new DOT 4 brake fluid (see Daily (pre-ride) checks) and bleed the system following the procedure in Section 11. Mount the fluid reservoir and tighten its screw (see illustration 9.4a).
26 Install the right-hand side panel (see Chapter 7).
27 Check the operation of the brake carefully before riding the motorcycle.

10 Brake hoses, pipes and unions – inspection and renewal

Inspection
1 Brake hose and pipe condition should be checked regularly and the hoses renewed at the specified interval (see Chapter 1).
2 Twist and flex the rubber hoses while looking for cracks, bulges and seeping fluid (see illustration). Check extra carefully around the areas where the hoses connect with the banjo fittings, as these are common areas for hose failure.
3 On 1997-on models, inspect the metal brake pipe between each front caliper, and on all models check the banjo union fittings connected to the brake hoses (see illustration). If the pipe is damaged or rusted or cracked, a new one must be installed. If the union fittings are rusted, scratched or cracked, fit new hoses.

Renewal
4 The brake hoses have banjo union fittings on each end, with the exception of the rear caliper hose which has a joint piece (see illustration 7.2). Cover the surrounding area with plenty of rags and unscrew the banjo bolt at each end of the hose or pipe, noting its alignment (see illustration). On the rear caliper, counter-hold the hose hex and unscrew the locknut and separate the hose from the joint piece in the caliper (see illustration 7.2). If required, unscrew the joint from the caliper. Free the hose from any clips or guides and remove it. Discard the sealing washers on the hose unions.
5 Position the new hose, making sure it isn't twisted or otherwise strained, and abut the tab on the hose union with the lug on the component casting, where present. Otherwise align the hose as noted on removal. Install the hose banjo bolts using new sealing washers on both sides of the unions. Tighten the banjo bolts to the torque setting specified at the beginning of this Chapter. On the rear caliper, if removed, thread the joint piece into the caliper using a new sealing washer and tighten it to the torque setting specified at the beginning of the Chapter (see illustration 7.2). Fit the hose against the hose joint and tighten the locknut onto the hose, counter-holding the hose hex to prevent the hose twisting. Do not overtighten the locknut. Make sure the hoses are correctly aligned and routed clear of all moving components.
6 Flush the old brake fluid from the system, refill with new DOT 4 brake fluid (see Daily (pre-ride) checks) and bleed the air from the system (see Section 11). Check the operation of the brakes carefully before riding the motorcycle.

11 Brake system – bleeding

1 Bleeding the brakes is simply the process of removing all the air bubbles from the brake fluid reservoirs, the hoses and the brake calipers. Bleeding is necessary whenever a brake system hydraulic connection is loosened, when a component or hose is renewed, or when the master cylinder or caliper is overhauled. Leaks in the system may also allow air to enter, but leaking brake fluid will reveal their presence and warn you of the need for repair.
2 To bleed the brakes, you will need some new DOT 4 brake fluid, a length of clear vinyl or plastic tubing, a small container partially filled with clean brake fluid, some rags and a spanner to fit the brake caliper bleed valves.
3 Cover the fuel tank and other painted components to prevent damage in the event that brake fluid is spilled.
4 When bleeding the rear brake, remove the right-hand side panel (see Chapter 7) for access to the fluid reservoir.
5 Remove the reservoir cap or cover, diaphragm plate (rear reservoir) and diaphragm and slowly pump the brake lever or pedal a few times, until no air bubbles can

10.2 Flex the brake hoses and check for cracks, bulges and leaking fluid

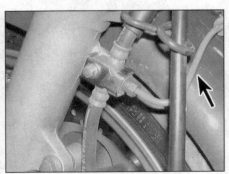

10.3 On 1997-on models, check the condition of the metal pipe on each front caliper (arrowed)

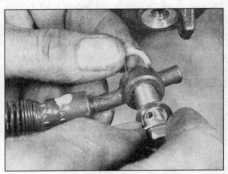

10.4 Remove the banjo bolt and separate the hose from the caliper; there is a sealing washer on each side of the fitting

Brakes, wheels and tyres 6•13

be seen floating up from the holes in the bottom of the reservoir. Doing this bleeds the air from the master cylinder end of the line. Loosely refit the reservoir cap or cover.

6 Pull the dust cap off the bleed valve **(see illustration)**. Attach one end of the clear vinyl or plastic tubing to the bleed valve and submerge the other end in the brake fluid in the container **(see illustration)**.

7 Remove the reservoir cap or cover and check the fluid level. Do not allow the fluid level to drop below the lower mark during the bleeding process.

8 Carefully pump the brake lever or pedal three or four times and hold it in (front) or down (rear) while opening the caliper bleed valve. When the valve is opened, brake fluid will flow out of the caliper into the clear tubing and the lever will move toward the handlebar or the pedal will move down.

9 Retighten the bleed valve, then release the brake lever or pedal gradually. Repeat the process until no air bubbles are visible in the brake fluid leaving the caliper, or if the fluid is being changed until new fluid is coming out, and the lever or pedal is firm when applied. On completion, disconnect the bleeding equipment, then tighten the bleed valve to the torque setting specified at the beginning of the chapter and install the dust cap.

HAYNES HiNT *Old brake fluid is invariably much darker in colour than new fluid, making it easy to see when all old fluid has been expelled from the system.*

10 Install the diaphragm and cap or cover assembly, wipe up any spilled brake fluid and check the entire system for leaks.

HAYNES HiNT *If it's not possible to produce a firm feel to the lever or pedal the fluid my be aerated. Let the brake fluid in the system stabilise for a few hours and then repeat the procedure when the tiny bubbles in the system have settled out.*

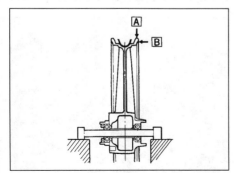
12.2 Check the wheel for radial (out-of-round) runout (A) and axial (side-to-side) runout (B)

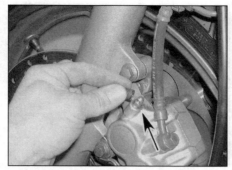
11.6a Brake caliper bleed valve (arrowed)

12 Wheels – inspection and repair

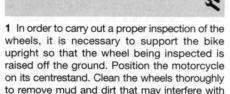

1 In order to carry out a proper inspection of the wheels, it is necessary to support the bike upright so that the wheel being inspected is raised off the ground. Position the motorcycle on its centrestand. Clean the wheels thoroughly to remove mud and dirt that may interfere with the inspection procedure or mask defects. Make a general check of the wheels (see Chapter 1) and tyres (see *Daily (pre-ride) checks*).

2 Attach a dial gauge to the fork slider or the swingarm and position its stem against the side of the rim **(see illustration)**. Spin the wheel slowly and check the axial (side-to-side) runout of the rim. In order to accurately check radial (out of round) runout with the dial gauge, the wheel would have to be removed from the machine, and the tyre from the wheel. With the axle clamped in a vice and the dial gauge positioned on the top of the rim, the wheel can be rotated to check the runout.

3 An easier, though slightly less accurate, method is to attach a stiff wire pointer to the fork slider or the swingarm and position the end a fraction of an inch from the wheel (where the wheel and tyre join). If the wheel is true, the distance from the pointer to the rim will be constant as the wheel is rotated. **Note:** *If wheel runout is excessive, check the wheel or hub bearings very carefully before replacing the wheel.*

4 The wheels should also be visually inspected for cracks, flat spots on the rim and other damage. Look very closely for dents in the area where the tyre bead contacts the rim. Dents in this area may prevent complete sealing of the tyre against the rim, which leads

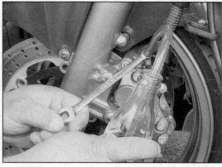
11.6b To bleed the brakes, you need a spanner, a short section of clear tubing, and a clear container half-filled with brake fluid

to deflation of the tyre over a period of time. If damage is evident, or if runout in either direction is excessive, the wheel will have to be replaced with a new one. Never attempt to repair a damaged cast alloy wheel.

13 Wheels – alignment check

1 Misalignment of the wheels, which may be due to a cocked rear wheel or a bent frame or fork yokes, can cause strange and possibly serious handling problems. If the frame or yokes are at fault, repair by a frame specialist or replacement with new parts are the only alternatives.

2 To check the alignment you will need an assistant, a length of string or a perfectly straight piece of wood and a ruler. A plumb bob or other suitable weight will also be required.

3 In order to make a proper check of the wheels it is necessary to support the bike in an upright position, using the centrestand. Measure the width of both tyres at their widest points. Subtract the smaller measurement from the larger measurement, then divide the difference by two. The result is the amount of offset that should exist between the front and rear tyres on both sides.

4 If a string is used, have your assistant hold one end of it about halfway between the floor and the rear axle, touching the rear sidewall of the tyre.

5 Run the other end of the string forward and pull it tight so that it is roughly parallel to the floor **(see illustration)**. Slowly bring the string

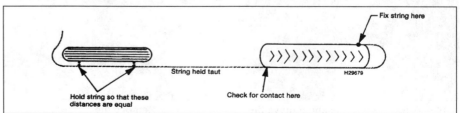
13.5 Wheel alignment check using string

6•14 Brakes, wheels and tyres

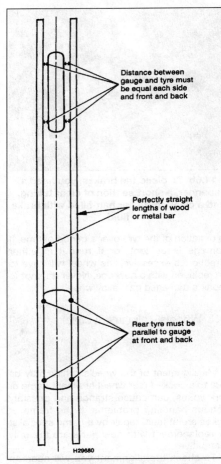

13.7 Wheel alignment check using a straight-edge

14.3 Unscrew the ring (arrowed) and detach the cable

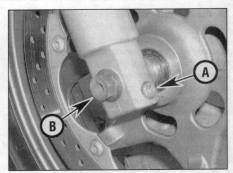

14.4 Slacken the clamp bolt (A) and unscrew the axle (B)

into contact with the front sidewall of the rear tyre, then turn the front wheel until it is parallel with the string. Measure the distance from the front tyre sidewall to the string.

6 Repeat the procedure on the other side of the motorcycle. The distance from the front tyre sidewall to the string should be equal on both sides. If it isn't, check that this is not due to excessive swingarm bearing play (see Chapter 1, Section 17) or to incorrect positioning of wheel spacers if either the front or rear wheel has recently been removed.

7 As previously mentioned, a perfectly straight length of wood or metal bar may be substituted for the string (see illustration). The procedure is the same.

8 If the front-to-back alignment is correct, the wheels still may be out of alignment vertically.

9 Using a plumb bob, or other suitable weight, and a length of string, check the rear wheel to make sure it is vertical. To do this, hold the string against the tyre upper sidewall and allow the weight to settle just off the floor. When the string touches both the upper and lower tyre sidewalls and is perfectly straight, the wheel is vertical. If it is not, place thin spacers under one leg of the stand until it is.

10 Once the rear wheel is vertical, check the front wheel in the same manner. If both wheels are not perfectly vertical, the frame and/or major suspension components are bent.

14 Front wheel – removal and installation

Removal

1 Put the motorcycle on its centrestand and support it under the crankcase so that the front wheel is off the ground. Always make sure the motorcycle is properly supported.

2 Displace the front brake calipers (see Section 3). Support the calipers with a piece of wire or a bungee cord so that no strain is placed on the hydraulic hoses. There is no need to disconnect the hoses from the calipers. **Note:** *Do not operate the front brake lever with the calipers removed.*

3 Unscrew the knurled ring securing the speedometer cable to the drive gear using a pair of pliers and detach the cable **(see illustration)**.

4 Slacken the axle clamp bolt on the bottom of the right-hand fork, then unscrew the axle **(see illustration)**.

5 Support the wheel, then withdraw the axle from the right-hand side **(see illustration)**. Carefully lower the wheel from between the forks, noting how the speedometer drive gear locates against the fork. Use a drift to drive out the axle if required.

6 Remove the spacer from the right-hand side of the wheel and the speedometer drive gear from the left-hand side, noting how they fit **(see illustrations)**.

Caution: Don't lay the wheel down and allow it to rest on either disc – the disc could become warped. Set the wheel on wood blocks so the disc doesn't support the weight of the wheel, or keep it upright.

7 Check the axle for straightness by rolling it on a flat surface such as a piece of plate glass (first wipe off all old grease and remove any corrosion using fine emery cloth). If the equipment is available, place the axle in V-blocks and check for runout using a dial

14.5 Withdraw the axle and remove the wheel

14.6a Remove the spacer . . .

14.6b . . . and the speedometer drive gear housing

Brakes, wheels and tyres 6•15

14.11a Locate the tab (arrowed) on the inside of the fork in the slot in the top of the housing . . .

14.11b . . . and insert the axle

14.11c Tighten the axle to the specified torque, then tighten the clamp bolt

gauge. If the axle is bent, replace it with a new one.
8 Check the condition of the wheel bearings (see Section 16).

Installation

9 Apply lithium based grease to the wheel spacer, the lips of the grease seals, and to the speedometer drive gear. Fit the spacer into the right-hand side of the wheel **(see illustration 14.6a)**. Fit the drive gear into the left-hand side, making sure the drive plate tabs locate in the slots **(see illustration 14.6b)**.
10 Manoeuvre the wheel into position. Apply a thin coat of grease to the axle.
11 Lift the wheel into place between the fork sliders, making sure the spacer and drive gear remain in position, and that the slot in the drive gear locates over the tab on the inside of the fork **(see illustration)**. Slide the axle in from the right-hand side and tighten it to the torque setting specified at the beginning of the Chapter **(see illustrations)**. Now tighten the axle clamp bolt on the bottom of the right-hand fork to the specified torque setting **(see illustration 14.4)**.
12 Install the brake calipers, making sure the pads sit squarely on each side of the discs (see Section 3). Tighten the caliper mounting bolts to the specified torque setting.
13 Fit the speedometer cable into the drive housing and tighten the knurled ring securely **(see illustration)**.
14 Apply the front brake a few times to bring the pads back into contact with the discs. Take the bike off its stand, apply the front brake and pump the front forks a few times to settle all components in position.
15 Check for correct operation of the front brake before riding the motorcycle.

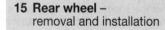

15 Rear wheel –
removal and installation

Removal

1 Position the motorcycle on its centrestand. It is advisable to place a block in front of the front wheel, or to tie the front brake lever back so that the front brake is locked on.

14.13 Insert the cable and tighten the ring securely

2 Displace the rear brake caliper (see Section 7). Support the caliper with a piece of wire or a bungee cord so that no strain is placed on the hydraulic hose. There is no need to disconnect the hose from the caliper. *Note: Do not operate the rear brake pedal with the caliper removed.*
3 Slacken the axle clamp bolt in the rear of the swingarm on the right-hand side **(see illustration)**. Remove the split pin on the bolt securing the torque arm to the swingarm and slacken the nut **(see illustration)**.
4 Unscrew and remove the axle nut and washer **(see illustration)**.
5 Withdraw the axle from the right-hand side, using a screwdriver or metal bar through the hole in the end of the axle as a handle **(see illustration)**. Remove the spacer from

15.3a Slacken the axle clamp bolt (arrowed)

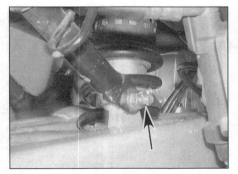

15.3b Remove the split pin (arrowed) and slacken the nut

15.4 Unscrew the axle nut (arrowed) and remove the washer

15.5a Withdraw the axle . . .

6•16 Brakes, wheels and tyres

15.5b ... and remove the swingarm spacer ...

15.5c ... then raise the caliper bracket and torque arm

15.6a Draw the wheel off the final drive housing and manoeuvre it out the back

between the caliper bracket and the swingarm, then raise the caliper bracket and torque arm **(see illustrations)**.

6 Grasp the wheel and draw it to the right until it is clear of the final drive housing, then manoeuvre it clear of the swingarm **(see illustration)**. Remove the wheel spacer from the righthand side of the wheel, noting which way round it fits **(see illustration)**. Note the coupling spacer in the final drive housing and remove it if required **(see illustration 15.10)**.

Caution: *Do not lay the wheel down and allow it to rest on the disc or the final drive coupling shroud – they could become warped or damaged. Set the wheel on wood blocks so that neither component supports the weight of the wheel.*

7 Check the axle for straightness by rolling it on a flat surface such as a piece of plate glass (first wipe off all old grease and remove any corrosion using fine emery cloth). If the axle is bent, renew it.
8 Check the condition of the wheel and coupling bearings (see Section 16).

Installation

9 Apply a thin coat of lithium grease to the wheel spacer and seal lips on the righthand side of the wheel, then install the spacer with its narrower end fitting into the seal **(see illustration 15.6b)**.
10 Apply a thin coat of lithium grease to the axle and the splines of the wheel hub and final drive housing. If removed, fit the coupling spacer into the final drive housing **(see illustration)**.
11 Lift the wheel into position and fit it onto the final drive housing, making sure the splines of the hub and the final drive housing are fully and properly engaged **(see illustration 15.6a)**.
12 Check that the spacer is still in position in the wheel. Lower the caliper bracket so that it aligns with the swingarm and wheel **(see illustration 15.5c)**. Slide the spacer in between the bracket and the swingarm, then install the axle from the righthand side, making sure that it passes through the swingarm spacer, the caliper mounting bracket and the wheel spacer **(see illustration 15.5b)**.

13 Install the washer and axle nut and tighten the nut to the torque setting specified at the beginning of the Chapter **(see illustrations)**.
14 Tighten the axle clamp bolt to the specified torque setting **(see illustration 15.3b)**. Also tighten the torque arm nut to the specified torque and fit a new split pin into the bolt **(see illustration 15.3b)**.
15 Install the brake caliper (see Section 7).
16 Apply the rear brake a few times to bring the pads back into contact with the disc. Move the motorcycle off its stand.
17 Check for correct operation of the rear brake before riding the motorcycle.

16 Wheel bearings and coupling dampers – removal, inspection and installation

Front wheel bearings

Note: *Always renew the wheel bearings in pairs, never individually. Avoid using a high pressure cleaner on the wheel bearing area.*
1 Remove the wheel (see Section 14).
2 Set the wheel on blocks so as not to allow the weight of the wheel to rest on either brake disc.
3 Lever out the grease seal on each side of the wheel using a large flat-bladed screwdriver, taking care not to damage the

15.6b Remove the spacer from the right-hand side of the wheel

15.10 Fit the coupling spacer into the final drive housing

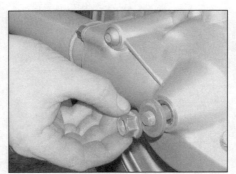
15.13a Fit the washer and nut ...

15.13b ... and tighten the nut to the specified torque

Brakes, wheels and tyres 6•17

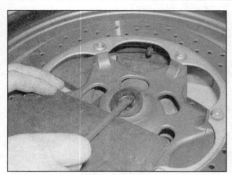

16.3 Lever out the grease seal on each side

16.4a . . . then lever out the retainer plate from the left-hand side . . .

16.4b . . . and remove the drive plate

rim (see illustration). Discard the seals if they are damaged or deteriorated.

 Position a piece of wood against the wheel to prevent the screwdriver shaft damaging it when levering the grease seal out.

4 Remove the retainer plate from the left-hand side of the wheel and remove the speedometer drive plate, noting how it fits (see illustrations).
5 Using a metal rod (preferably a brass drift punch) inserted through the centre of the one bearing, tap evenly around the inner race of the other bearing to drive it from the hub (see illustrations). The bearing spacer will also come out.

6 Lay the wheel on its other side so that the remaining bearing faces down. Drive the bearing out of the wheel using the same technique as above.
7 If the bearings are of the unsealed type or are only sealed on one side, clean them with a high flash-point solvent (one which won't leave any residue) and blow them dry with compressed air (don't let the bearings spin as you dry them). Apply a few drops of oil to the bearing. **Note:** *If the bearing is sealed on both sides don't attempt to clean it.*

 Refer to Tools and Workshop Tips (Section 5) in Reference section for more information about bearings.

8 Hold the outer race of the bearing and rotate the inner race – if the bearing doesn't turn smoothly, has rough spots or is noisy, replace it with a new one.
9 If the bearing is good and can be re-used, wash it in solvent once again and dry it, then pack the bearing with lithium based grease.
10 Thoroughly clean the hub area of the wheel. Install the right-hand bearing into its recess in the hub, with the marked or sealed side facing outwards. Using the old bearing (if new ones are being fitted), a bearing driver or a socket large enough to contact the outer race of the bearing, drive it in until it's completely seated (see illustration).
11 Turn the wheel over and install the bearing spacer. Drive the left-hand bearing into place as described above.
12 Fit the speedometer drive plate into the left-hand side of the wheel, with the drive tabs facing out and aligning the flat tabs with the cutouts in the hub (see illustration 16.4b). Press the retainer plate onto the drive plate (see illustration 16.4a). Apply a smear of lithium based grease to the lips of the seal for that side, then press it into the wheel, using a seal or bearing driver or a suitable socket to drive it into place if necessary (see illustrations). Drive the seal in until it sits against the retainer plate.
13 Apply a smear of lithium based grease to the lips of the other seal, then press it into the right-hand side of the wheel. As this seal sits

16.5a Knock out the bearings using a drift . . .

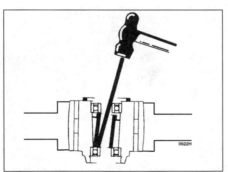

16.5b . . . locating it as shown

16.10 A socket can be used to drive in the bearing

16.12a Fit the grease seal . . .

16.12b . . . and tap it into place

6

6•18 Brakes, wheels and tyres

16.13 Using a piece of wood ensures the seal sits flush with the rim

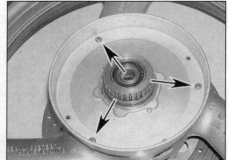

16.15 Undo the screws (arrowed) and remove the shroud

16.16 Lift the final drive coupling out of the wheel

flush with the hub, it is best to knock it into place using a flat piece of wood **(see illustration)**.
14 Clean off all grease from the brake discs using acetone or brake system cleaner then install the wheel (see Section 14).

Rear wheel bearings

Note: *Always renew the wheel bearings in pairs, never individually. Avoid using a high pressure cleaner on the wheel bearing area.*
15 Remove the rear wheel (see Section 15). Remove the screws securing the coupling retaining shroud to the hub and remove the shroud **(see illustration)**.
16 Lift the final drive coupling away from the wheel leaving the rubber dampers in position in the wheel **(see illustration)**.

16.17 Lever out the grease seal

16.21b . . . and the rubber dampers

17 Using a flat-bladed screwdriver, prise out the grease seal from the righthand side of the wheel **(see illustration)**. Discard the seal if it is worn or damaged as a new one should be used.
18 Set the wheel on blocks so as not to allow the weight of the wheel to rest on the brake disc.
19 Remove, inspect and install the bearings as described above in Steps 5 through 11, but note that there are two bearings fitted into the left-hand side of the wheel.
20 Apply a smear of lithium grease to the lips of the grease seal, then press it into the right-hand side of the wheel. As the seal sits flush with the hub, it is best to knock it into place using a flat piece of wood **(see illustration 16.13)**.

16.21a Check the O-ring (arrowed) . . .

16.25a Drive the spacer out of the bearing . . .

21 Inspect the coupling O-ring and the rubber dampers for signs of wear or damage and replace them with new ones if necessary **(see illustrations)**. Apply a smear of grease to the O-ring and fit the coupling onto the wheel, making sure all the damper rubbers are in place **(see illustration 16.16)**.
22 Clean off all grease from the brake disc using acetone or brake system cleaner then install the wheel (see Section 15).

Final drive coupling bearing and dampers

23 Remove the rear wheel (see Section 15). Remove the screws securing the coupling retaining shroud to the hub and remove the shroud **(see illustration 16.15)**.
24 Lift the final drive coupling away from the wheel leaving the rubber dampers in position in the wheel **(see illustration 16.16)**.
25 Support the coupling on blocks of wood and drive the bearing spacer out from the outside using a 14 mm socket **(see illustration)**. Now drive the bearing out from the inside with a bearing driver or 30 mm socket **(see illustration)**.
26 Inspect the bearing as described above in Steps 7 through 9.
27 Thoroughly clean the bearing recess then install the bearing into the recess in the coupling, with the marked or sealed side facing out. Using a bearing driver or a socket large enough to contact the outer race of the

16.25b . . . then drive out the bearing from the inside

Brakes, wheels and tyres 6•19

16.27a A socket can be used to drive in the bearing

16.27b Support the bearing as shown when driving in the spacer

bearing, drive it in until it's completely seated **(see illustration)**. Now drive the spacer into the bearing from the inside, supporting the bearing on a suitable socket to prevent it being driven out **(see illustration)**.

28 Inspect the coupling O-ring and the rubber dampers for signs of wear or damage and replace them with new ones if necessary **(see illustrations 16.21a and b)**. Apply a smear of grease to the O-ring and fit the coupling onto the wheel, making sure all the damper rubbers are in place **(see illustration 16.16)**.

29 Install the coupling shroud and tighten its screws securely **(see illustration 16.15)**.

30 Clean off all grease from the brake disc using acetone or brake system cleaner then install the wheel (see Section 15).

17 Tyres – general information and fitting

General information

1 The wheels fitted on all models are designed to take tubeless tyres only. Tyre sizes are given in the Specifications at the beginning of this chapter.

2 Refer to the Daily (pre-ride) checks listed at the beginning of this manual for tyre maintenance.

Fitting new tyres

3 When selecting new tyres, refer to the tyre information label on the swingarm and the tyre options listed in the owners handbook. Ensure that front and rear tyre types are compatible, the correct size and correct speed rating; if necessary seek advice from a Yamaha dealer or motorcycle tyre fitting specialist **(see illustration)**.

4 It is recommended that tyres are fitted by a motorcycle tyre specialist rather than attempted in the home workshop. This is particularly relevant in the case of tubeless tyres because the force required to break the seal between the wheel rim and tyre bead is substantial, and is usually beyond the capabilities of an individual working with normal tyre levers. Additionally, the specialist will be able to balance the wheels after tyre fitting.

5 Note that punctured tubeless tyres can in some cases be repaired. Refer to a Yamaha dealer or motorcycle tyre fitting specialist for advice.

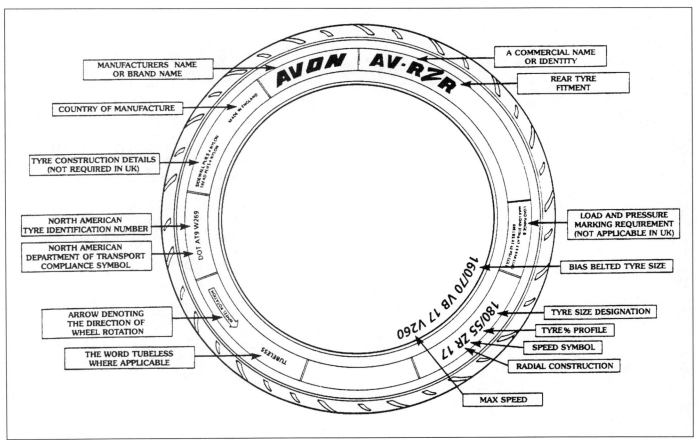

17.3 Common tyre sidewall markings

6•20 Brakes, wheels and tyres

Notes

Chapter 7
Bodywork

Contents

Fairing and body panels – removal and installation 3
Front mudguard – removal and installation 6
General information 1
Rear view mirrors – removal and installation 4
Seat – removal and installation 2
Windshield – removal and installation 5

Degrees of difficulty

Easy, suitable for novice with little experience	Fairly easy, suitable for beginner with some experience	Fairly difficult, suitable for competent DIY mechanic	Difficult, suitable for experienced DIY mechanic	Very difficult, suitable for expert DIY or professional

1 General information

This Chapter covers the procedures necessary to remove and install the body parts. Since many service and repair operations on these motorcycles require the removal of the body parts, the procedures are grouped here and referred to from other Chapters.

In the case of damage to the body parts, it is usually necessary to remove the broken component and replace it with a new (or used) one. The material that the body panels are composed of doesn't lend itself to conventional repair techniques. There are however some shops that specialise in 'plastic welding', so it may be worthwhile seeking the advice of one of these specialists before consigning an expensive component to the bin. Also note that there are a number of kits available for body panel repair.

When attempting to remove any body panel, first study it closely, noting any fasteners and associated fittings, to be sure of returning everything to its correct place on installation. In some cases the aid of an assistant will be required when removing panels, to help avoid the risk of damage to paintwork. Once the evident fasteners have been removed, try to withdraw the panel as described but DO NOT FORCE IT – if it will not release, check that all fasteners have been removed and try again. Where a panel engages another by means of tabs, be careful not to break the tab or its mating slot or to damage the paintwork. Remember that a few moments of patience at this stage will save you a lot of money in replacing broken fairing panels!

When installing a body panel, first study it closely, noting any fasteners and associated fittings removed with it, to be sure of returning everything to its correct place. Check that all fasteners are in good condition, including all trim nuts or clips and damping/rubber mounts; any of these must be renewed if faulty before the panel is reassembled. Check also that all mounting brackets are straight and repair or renew them if necessary before attempting to install the panel. Where assistance was required to remove a panel, make sure your assistant is on hand to install it.

Tighten the fasteners securely, but be careful not to overtighten any of them or the panel may break (not always immediately) due to the uneven stress. Where quick-release fasteners are fitted, turn them 90° anti-clockwise to release them, and 90° clockwise to secure them.

 Note that a small amount of lubricant (liquid soap or similar) applied to the mounting rubber grommets of the seat cowling will assist the lugs to engage without the need for undue pressure.

7•2 Bodywork

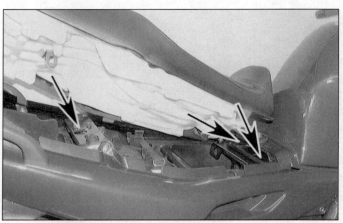

2.2 Locate the tabs at the front under the bracket and the hook into the latch

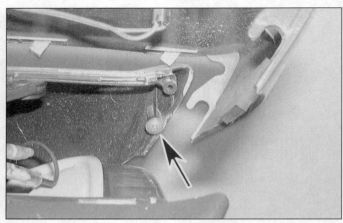

3.1 Note how the hooks on the back of the tail light cover locate over the pegs (arrowed)

2 Seat – removal and installation

Removal

1 Insert the ignition key into the seat lock

3.2 Unscrew the bolts and remove the grabrail

located in the left-hand side cover, and turn it clockwise to unlock the seat. Lift up the back of the seat and draw it rearwards, noting how the tabs at the front locate under the tank bracket.

Installation

2 Installation is the reverse of removal. Locate the tabs at the front of the seat under the tank bracket and the locking hook on the underside of the seat in the latch and press down on the seat to engage it **(see illustration)**.

3 Fairing and body panels – removal and installation

Side panels
Removal

1 Each panel can be removed individually. Remove the seat (see Section 2) Remove the

two screws securing the tail light cover to the side panels and remove the cover, noting how it fits **(see illustration)**.

2 Unscrew the two bolts securing the grab-rail on the side being removed and remove the grab-rail **(see illustration)**. Remove both grab-rails if both panels are being removed.

3 Remove the remaining screws securing the side panel to the frame – there is one at the front and one in the middle **(see illustration)**.

4 Carefully draw the panel away at the front to disengage the lug on the inside of the panel from the grommet, then remove the panel, noting how it fits **(see illustration)**.

Installation

5 Installation is the reverse of removal. Make sure the panel locates correctly.

Side covers
Removal

6 Remove the side panel (see above).

7 Remove the single bolt securing the cover, then carefully draw the cover away to

3.3 Remove the screws (arrowed) . . .

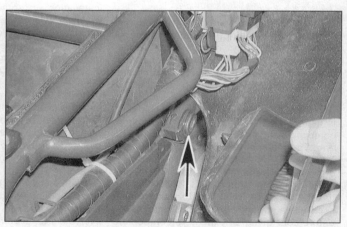

3.4 . . . and draw the panel away to release the peg from the grommet (arrowed)

Bodywork 7•3

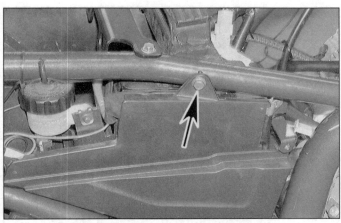

3.7a Unscrew the bolt (arrowed) . . .

3.7b . . . and draw the cover away to release the lug from the grommet (arrowed)

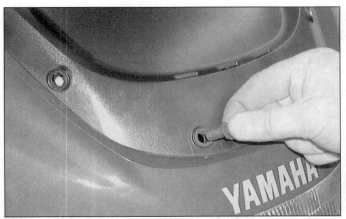

3.9 Pull out the rubber collars

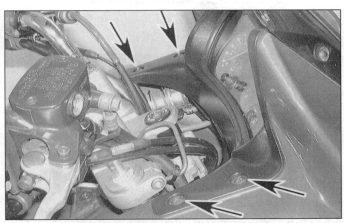

3.10a Undo the screws (arrowed) . . .

release the lug on the inside of the cover at the back from the grommet **(see illustrations)**.

Installation

8 Installation is the reverse of removal. Make sure the panel locates correctly.

Fairing

Removal

9 Remove the windshield (see Section 5). Pull out the rubber collars **(see illustration)**.
10 Remove the four screws securing the cockpit trim panel and remove the panel, noting how it fits **(see illustrations)**.
11 Disconnect the headlight, sidelight and turn signal wiring connectors **(see illustrations)**. If required, remove the turn signals (see Chapter 8).

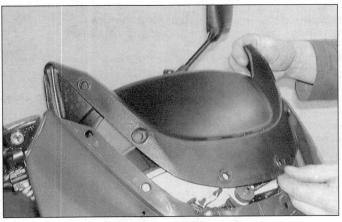

3.10b . . . and remove the trim panel

3.11a Disconnect the headlight wiring connector . . .

7•4 Bodywork

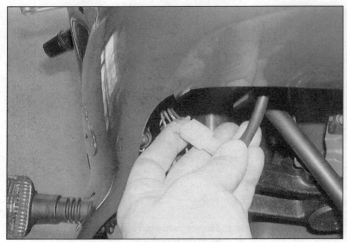
3.11b ... the sidelight wiring connector ...

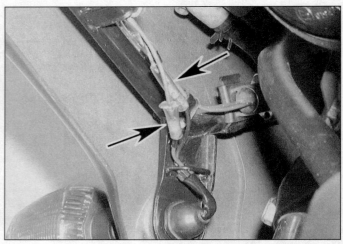
3.11c ... and the turn signal wiring connectors (arrowed) on each side

3.12a Remove the two screws on each side (arrowed) ...

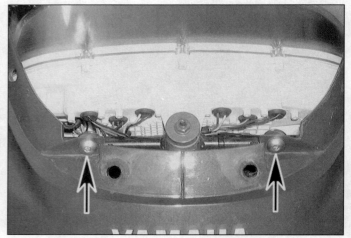
3.12b ... and the two screws at the front (arrowed) ...

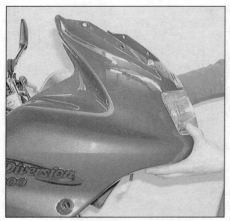
3.13 ... and remove the fairing

12 Remove the six screws securing the fairing to the stay **(see illustrations)**.
13 Carefully draw the fairing assembly forward and remove it – the headlight comes with the fairing **(see illustration)**. Remove the headlight if required (see Chapter 8).

Installation

14 Installation is the reverse of removal. Make sure the wiring connectors are correctly and securely connected. A little grease or other lubricant will help when fitting the rubber collars.

4 **Rear view mirrors –**
   removal and installation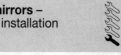

Removal

1 Unscrew the mirror from its mount using the hex on the base of the mirror.

Installation

2 Installation is the reverse of removal. Adjust the mirror as required by slackening the upper nut and moving the stalk round in its base.

Bodywork 7•5

5 Windshield – removal and installation

Removal

1 Remove the screws securing the windshield to the fairing and remove the windshield, noting how it fits **(see illustration)**.

Installation

2 Installation is the reverse of removal. Do not overtighten the screws.

6 Front mudguard – removal and installation

Removal

1 Unscrew the four bolts securing the fork brace, then remove the mudguard. If required, lift off the brace and mounting plates, noting how they fit **(see illustrations)**. If you want to completely remove the left-hand mounting plate, detach the speedometer cable from the wheel by unscrewing the ring and draw the cable out of the plate.

Installation

2 Installation is the reverse of removal.

5.1 Windshield screws (arrowed)

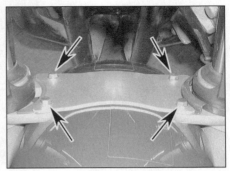

6.1a Unscrew the bolts (arrowed) . . .

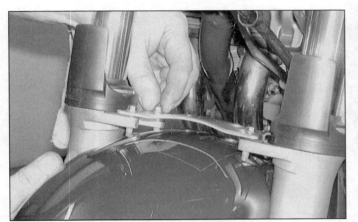

6.1b . . . and draw the mudguard forwards . . .

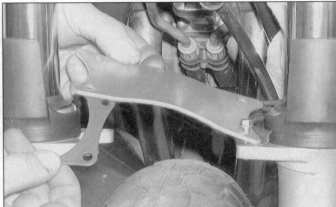

6.1c . . . then remove the brace and mounting plates

7

7•6 Bodywork

Notes

Chapter 8
Electrical system

Contents

Alternator/regulator/rectifier – check, removal and installation 33	Ignition (main) switch – check, removal and installation 18
Battery – charging 4	Ignition system components .... see Chapter 4
Battery – removal, installation, inspection and maintenance 3	Instrument and warning light bulbs – renewal 17
Brake light switches – check and renewal 14	Instrument cluster and speedometer cable –
Brake/tail light bulb – renewal 9	removal and installation 15
Charging system – leakage and output test 32	Instruments – check and renewal 16
Charging system testing – general information and precautions .. 31	Lighting system – check 6
Clutch switch – check and renewal 23	Neutral switch – check, removal and installation 21
Diode (1994 to 1996 models) – check and renewal 25	Oil level sensor – check, removal and installation 27
Electrical system – fault finding 2	Relay assembly – check and renewal 24
Fuses – check and renewal 5	Sidestand switch – check and renewal 22
General information 1	Starter motor – disassembly, inspection and reassembly 30
Handlebar switches – check 19	Starter motor – removal and installation 29
Handlebar switches – removal and installation 20	Starter relay – check and renewal 28
Headlight aim – check and adjustment .... see Chapter 1	Tail light assembly – removal and installation 10
Headlight assembly – removal and installation 8	Turn signal assemblies – removal and installation 13
Headlight bulb and sidelight bulb – renewal 7	Turn signal bulbs – renewal 12
Horn – check and renewal 26	Turn signal circuit – check 11

Degrees of difficulty

| Easy, suitable for novice with little experience | | Fairly easy, suitable for beginner with some experience | | Fairly difficult, suitable for competent DIY mechanic | | Difficult, suitable for experienced DIY mechanic | | Very difficult, suitable for expert DIY or professional | |

Specifications

Battery
Capacity	12V, 12Ah
Type	YTX14-BS
Charge condition	
Fully charged	12.8V
Half-charged	12.3V
Discharged	12V or less
Charging time	until fully charged (12.8V) (see Text)
Current leakage	1 mA (max)
Specific gravity	1.320

Alternator
Nominal output	14V, 33A @ 5000 rpm
Brush length	
Standard	13.7 mm
Service limit (min)	4.7 mm
Stator coil resistance	0.19 to 0.21 ohms @ 20°C
Rotor coil resistance	2.7 to 3.1 ohms @ 20°C

Regulator/rectifier
Regulated output (no load)	14.2 to 14.8V @ 5000 rpm

Starter circuit cut-off relay
Resistance	202 to 248 ohms @ 20°C

8•2 Electrical system

Starter relay
Resistance .... 4.18 to 4.62 ohms @ 20°C

Starter motor
Brush length
  Standard .... 12.0 mm
  Service limit (min) .... 8.5 mm
Commutator diameter
  Standard .... 28 mm
  Service limit (min) .... 27 mm
Mica depth .... 0.6 mm

Fuses
Main 30A
Signals 20A
Headlight 15A
Ignition 10A
Clock 10A
Hazard warning (1997–on models) 10A

Bulbs
Headlight .... 60/55 W halogen
Sidelight .... 4.0 W
Brake/tail light .... 21/5 W
Turn signal lights .... 21 W x 4
Instrument lights .... 3.4 W x 4
Turn signal indicator light .... 3.4 W x 2
Neutral indicator light .... 3.4 W
High beam indicator light .... 3.4 W
Oil level warning light .... 3.4 W
Fuel level warning light .... 3.4 W

Torque wrench settings
Neutral switch .... 20 Nm
Oil level sensor bolts .... 10 Nm
Starter motor mounting bolts .... 12 Nm
Starter motor housing bolts .... 7 Nm
Alternator mounting bolts .... 25 Nm

1 General information

All models have a 12-volt electrical system charged by a three-phase alternator with an integral regulator/rectifier.

The regulator maintains the charging system output within the specified range to prevent overcharging, and the rectifier converts the ac (alternating current) output of the alternator to dc (direct current) to power the lights and other components and to charge the battery. The alternator rotor is mounted in the top of the crankcase and is driven off the crankshaft by a Hy-Vo chain.

The starter motor is mounted on the top of the crankcase. The starting system includes the motor, the battery, the relay and the various wires and switches. If the engine kill switch in the 'RUN' position and the ignition (main) switch is ON, the starter relay allows the starter motor to operate only if the transmission is in neutral (neutral switch on) or, if the transmission is in gear, if the clutch lever is pulled into the handlebar and the sidestand is up.

Note: *Keep in mind that electrical parts, once purchased, cannot be returned. To avoid unnecessary expense, make very sure the faulty component has been positively identified before buying a replacement part.*

2 Electrical system – fault finding

Warning: To prevent the risk of short circuits, the ignition (main) switch must always be OFF and the battery negative (–ve) terminal should be disconnected before any of the bike's other electrical components are disturbed. Don't forget to reconnect the terminal securely once work is finished or if battery power is needed for circuit testing.

1 A typical electrical circuit consists of an electrical component, the switches, relays, etc. related to that component and the wiring and connectors that hook the component to both the battery and the frame. To aid in locating a problem in any electrical circuit, refer to the wiring diagrams at the end of this Chapter.
2 Before tackling any troublesome electrical circuit, first study the wiring diagram (see end of Chapter) thoroughly to get a complete picture of what makes up that individual circuit. Trouble spots, for instance, can often be narrowed down by noting if other components related to that circuit are operating properly or not. If several components or circuits fail at one time, chances are the fault lies in the fuse or earth (ground) connection, as several circuits often are routed through the same fuse and earth (ground) connections.
3 Electrical problems often stem from simple causes, such as loose or corroded connections or a blown fuse. Prior to any electrical fault finding, always visually check the condition of the fuse, wires and connections in the problem circuit. Intermittent failures can be especially frustrating, since you can't always duplicate the failure when it's convenient to test. In such situations, a good practice is to clean all connections in the affected circuit, whether or not they appear to be good. All of the connections and wires should also be wiggled to check for looseness which can cause intermittent failure.
4 If testing instruments are going to be utilised, use the wiring diagram to plan where you will make the necessary connections in order to accurately pinpoint the trouble spot.
5 The basic tools needed for electrical fault finding include a battery and bulb test circuit,

Electrical system 8•3

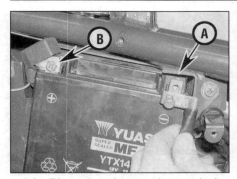

3.2a Disconnect the negative terminal first (A), then the positive (B)

3.2b Slide the battery out of its box

a continuity tester, a test light, and a jumper wire. A multimeter capable of reading volts, ohms and amps is also very useful as an alternative to the above, and is necessary for performing more extensive tests and checks.

 HAYNES HiNT *Refer to Fault Finding Equipment in the Reference section for details of how to use electrical test equipment.*

3 Battery – removal, installation, inspection and maintenance

Caution: Be extremely careful when handling or working around the battery. The electrolyte is very caustic and an explosive gas (hydrogen) is given off when the battery is charging.

Removal and installation

1 Remove the right-hand side panel and cover (see Chapter 7).
2 Unscrew the negative (–ve) terminal bolt first and disconnect the lead from the battery **(see illustration)**. Lift up the insulating cover to access the positive (+ve) terminal, then unscrew the bolt and disconnect the lead. Remove the battery from the bike **(see illustration)**.
3 On installation, clean the battery terminals and lead ends with a wire brush or knife and emery paper. Reconnect the leads, connecting the positive (+ve) terminal first.
4 Install the right-hand side panel and cover (see Chapter 7).

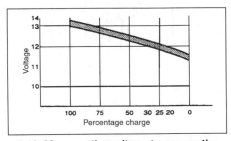

3.10 Measure the voltage to assess the condition of the battery from the chart

HAYNES HiNT *Battery corrosion can be kept to a minimum by applying a layer of petroleum jelly to the terminals after the cables have been connected.*

Inspection and maintenance

5 The battery fitted on all models is of the maintenance free (sealed) type, therefore requiring no specific maintenance. However, the following checks should still be regularly performed.
6 Check the battery terminals and leads for tightness and corrosion. If corrosion is evident, unscrew the terminal screws and disconnect the leads from the battery, disconnecting the negative (–ve) terminal first, and clean the terminals and lead ends with a wire brush or knife and emery paper. Reconnect the leads, connecting the negative (–ve) terminal last, and apply a thin coat of petroleum jelly to the connections to slow further corrosion.
7 The battery case should be kept clean to prevent current leakage, which can discharge the battery over a period of time (especially when it sits unused). Wash the outside of the case with a solution of baking soda and water. Rinse the battery thoroughly, then dry it.
8 Look for cracks in the case and renew the battery if any are found. If acid has been spilled on the frame or battery box, neutralise it with a baking soda and water solution, dry it thoroughly, then touch up any damaged paint.
9 If the motorcycle sits unused for long periods of time, disconnect the cables from

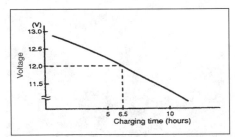

4.1 Measure the voltage to determine the charging time required

the battery terminals, negative (–ve) terminal first. Refer to Section 4 and charge the battery once every month to six weeks.
10 The condition of the battery can be assessed by measuring the voltage present at the battery terminals, and comparing the figure against the chart **(see illustration)**. Disconnect the battery leads (see above), then connect the voltmeter positive (+ve) probe to the battery positive (+ve) terminal, and the negative (–ve) probe to the battery negative (–ve) terminal. When fully charged there should be 12.8 volts (or more) present. If the voltage falls below 12.3 volts the battery must be removed, disconnecting the negative (–ve) terminal first, and recharged as described in Section 4.

4 Battery – charging

Caution: Be extremely careful when handling or working around the battery. The electrolyte is very caustic and an explosive gas (hydrogen) is given off when the battery is charging.

1 Remove the battery (see Section 3). If not already done, refer to Section 3, Step 10, and check the open circuit voltage of the battery. Refer to the chart and read off the charging time required according to the voltage reading taken **(see illustration)**.
2 Connect the charger to the battery, making sure that the positive (+ve) lead on the charger is connected to the positive (+ve) terminal on the battery, and the negative (–ve) lead is connected to the negative (–ve) terminal. The battery should be charged for the specified time, or until the voltage across the terminals reaches 12.8V (allow the battery to stabilise for 30 minutes after charging before taking a voltage reading). Exceeding this can cause the battery to overheat, buckling the plates and rendering it useless. Few owners will have access to an expensive current controlled charger, so if a normal domestic charger is used check that after a possible initial peak, the charge rate falls to a safe level **(see illustration)**. If the battery becomes hot

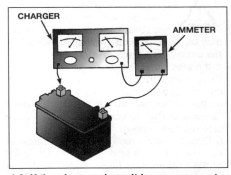

4.2 If the charger doesn't have an ammeter built in, connect one in series as shown. DO NOT connect the ammeter between the battery terminals or it will be ruined

8•4 Electrical system

during charging **stop**. Further charging will cause damage. **Note:** *In emergencies the battery can be charged at a higher rate of around 3.0 amps for a period of 1 hour. However, this is not recommended and the low amp charge is by far the safer method of charging the battery.*

3 If the recharged battery discharges rapidly if left disconnected it is likely that an internal short caused by physical damage or sulphation has occurred. A new battery will be required. A sound item will tend to lose its charge at about 1% per day.

4 Install the battery (see Section 3).

5 If the motorcycle sits unused for long periods of time, charge the battery once every month to six weeks and leave it disconnected.

5 Fuses – check and renew

1 The electrical system is protected by fuses of different ratings. The fuseboxes are located behind the right-hand side panel – the main fuse is housed in its own box, while the circuit fuses are housed together in another fusebox **(see illustrations)**.

2 To access all the fuses, remove the right-hand side panel (see Chapter 7). To access the fuses within the fusebox, unclip the fusebox lid **(see illustration)**. Note that on 1997-on models, the turn signal fuse is housed adjacent to the fusebox lid as the hazard warning system fuse has been installed inside the box.

3 The fuses can be removed and checked visually. If you can't pull the fuse out with your fingertips, use a suitable pair of pliers. A blown fuse is easily identified by a break in the element **(see illustration)**, or can be tested for continuity using an ohmmeter or continuity tester – if there is no continuity, it has blown. Each fuse is clearly marked with its rating and must only be replaced by a fuse of the correct rating. Spare fuses are housed in the fusebox. If a spare fuse is used, always replace it so that a spare of each rating is carried on the bike at all times.

⚠ **Warning:** *Never put in a fuse of a higher rating or bridge the terminals with any other substitute, however temporary it may be. Serious damage may be done to the circuit, or a fire may start.*

4 If a fuse blows, be sure to check the wiring circuit very carefully for evidence of a short-circuit. Look for bare wires and chafed, melted or burned insulation. If the fuse is renewed before the cause is located, the new fuse will blow immediately.

5 Occasionally a fuse will blow or cause an open-circuit for no obvious reason. Corrosion of the fuse ends and fusebox terminals may occur and cause poor fuse contact. If this happens, remove the corrosion with a wire brush or emery paper, then spray the fuse end and terminals with electrical contact cleaner.

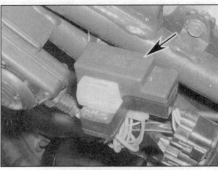

5.1a Fusebox (arrowed)

5.1b Main fuse (arrowed)

6 Lighting system – check
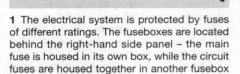

1 The battery provides power for operation of the headlight, tail light, brake light, turn signals and instrument cluster lights. If none of the lights operate, always check battery voltage before proceeding. Low battery voltage indicates either a faulty battery or a defective charging system. Refer to Section 3 for battery checks and Sections 31 and 32 for charging system tests. Also, check the condition of the fuses (see Section 5). When checking for a blown filament in a bulb, it is advisable to back up a visual check with a continuity test of the filament as it is not always apparent that a bulb has blown. When testing for continuity, remember that on tail light and turn signal bulbs it is often the metal body of the bulb which is the ground or earth.

Headlight

2 If the headlight fails to work, check the bulb first (see Section 7), then the fuse (see Section 5), and the wiring connector, then check for battery voltage at the yellow (HI beam) and/or green (LO beam) wire terminal on the supply side of the headlight wiring connector. If voltage is present, check the earth (ground) circuit for an open or poor connection.

3 If no voltage is indicated, check the wiring between the headlight, the lighting switches and the ignition switch, then check the switches themselves.

Tail light

4 If the tail light fails to work, check the bulb and the bulb terminals and wiring connector first (see Section 9), then the fuse, then check for battery voltage at the blue/red wire terminal on the supply side of the tail light wiring connector, with the ignition switch and lighting switch ON. If voltage is present, check for continuity between the wiring connector terminals on the tail light side of the wiring connector and the corresponding terminals in the bulbholder. If voltage and continuity are present, check the earth (ground) circuit for an open or poor connection.

5 If no voltage is indicated, check the wiring between the tail light, the lighting switch and the ignition switch, then check the switches themselves.

Brake light

6 If the brake light fails to work, check the bulb and the bulb terminals and wiring connector first (see Section 9), then the fuse, then check for battery voltage at the yellow wire terminal on the supply side of the tail light wiring connector, with the ignition switch ON and the brake lever or pedal applied. If voltage is present, check the earth (ground) circuit for an open or poor connection.

5.2 Unclip the lid to access the fuses within

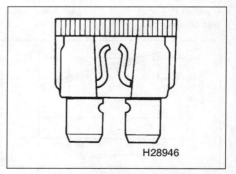

5.3 A blown fuse can be identified by a break in its element

Electrical system 8•5

7.1a Disconnect the wiring connector (arrowed) . . .

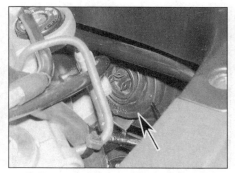
7.1b . . . and remove the dust cover (arrowed)

7.2a Release the clip (arrowed) . . .

7 If no voltage is indicated, check the brake light switches (see Section 14), then the wiring between the tail light and the switches.

Instrument and warning lights

8 See Section 17 for instrument and warning light bulb renewal.

Turn signal lights

9 If one light fails to work, check the bulb and the bulb terminals first, then the wiring connectors. If none of the turn signals work, first check the fuse.
10 If the fuse is good, see Section 11 for turn signal circuit check.

7 Headlight bulb and sidelight bulb – renewal

Note: *The headlight bulb is of the quartz-halogen type. Do not touch the bulb glass as skin acids will shorten the bulb's service life. If the bulb is accidentally touched, it should be wiped carefully when cold with a rag soaked in methylated spirit and dried before fitting.*

 Warning: Allow the bulb time to cool before removing it if the headlight has just been on.

Headlight

Note: *Access to the bulb is quite restricted with the fairing installed, so if difficulty is encountered, remove the fairing (see Chapter 7).*
1 Disconnect the wiring connector from the back of the headlight assembly and remove the rubber dust cover, noting how it fits **(see illustrations)**.
2 Release the bulb retaining clip, noting how it fits, then remove the bulb **(see illustrations)**.
3 Fit the new bulb, bearing in mind the information in the **Note** above. Make sure the tabs on the bulb fit correctly in the slots in the bulb housing, and secure it in position with the retaining clip.
4 Install the dust cover, making sure it is correctly seated and with the 'TOP' mark at the top, and connect the wiring connector **(see illustration 7.1b)**.
5 Check the operation of the headlight.

Sidelight

6 Carefully release the bulbholder from the bottom of the headlight **(see illustration)**. Carefully pull the bulb out of the holder **(see illustration)**. Install the new bulb, then fit the bulbholder into the headlight.
7 Check the operation of the sidelight.

7.2b . . . and remove the bulb

8 Headlight assembly – removal and installation

Removal

1 Remove the fairing (see Chapter 7).
2 Remove the four screws securing the headlight assembly and lift it out of the fairing **(see illustration)**.

Installation

3 Installation is the reverse of removal. Make sure all the wiring is correctly connected and secured. Check the operation of the headlight and sidelight. Check the headlight aim (see Chapter 1).

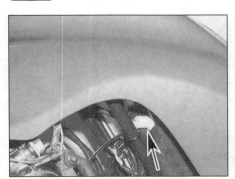
7.6a Release the bulbholder from the headlight (arrowed)

7.6b . . . then remove the bulb from the holder

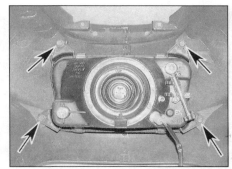
8.2 Remove the screws (arrowed) and lift the headlight out of the fairing

8•6 Electrical system

9.1a Undo the screws (arrowed) . . .

9.1b . . . and remove the lens

9.2 Release the bulb from the taillight

9 Brake/tail light bulb – renewal

1 Remove the screws securing the tail light lens and remove the lens **(see illustrations)**.
2 Push the bulb into the holder and twist it anti-clockwise to remove it **(see illustration)**.
3 Check the socket terminals for corrosion and clean them if necessary. Line up the pins of the new bulb with the slots in the socket, then push the bulb in and turn it clockwise until it locks into place. **Note:** *The pins on the bulb are offset so it can only be installed one way. It is a good idea to use a paper towel or dry cloth when handling the new bulb to prevent injury if the bulb should break and to increase bulb life.*

4 Check the condition of the rubber seal in the groove in the tail light and replace it with a new one if it is damaged or deteriorated **(see illustration)**. Make sure it is located correctly in its groove. Fit the lens, making sure the rubber seal stays in place, and secure it with the screws. Do not overtighten the screws or the lens could be damaged.

10 Tail light assembly – removal and installation

Removal

1 Remove the seat and the left-hand side panel (see Chapter 7). Disconnect the tail light and turn signal wiring connectors and free the wiring from any ties **(see illustrations)**.

2 Unscrew the bolts securing the tail light and draw it out the back, bringing the wiring with it **(see illustration)**.

Installation

3 Installation is the reverse of removal. Check the operation of the tail light and the brake light.

11 Turn signal circuit – check

1 Most turn signal problems are the result of a burned out bulb or corroded socket. This is especially true when the turn signals function properly in one direction, but fail to flash in the other direction. Check the bulbs and the sockets (see Section 12) and the wiring connectors. Also, check the fuse (see Section 5) and the switch (see Section 19).
2 The battery provides power for operation of the turn signal lights, so if they do not operate, also check the battery voltage. Low battery voltage indicates either a faulty battery or a defective charging system. Refer to Section 3 for battery checks and Sections 31 and 32 for charging system tests.
3 If the bulbs, sockets, connectors, fuse, switch and battery are good, check the turn signal relay, which is mounted behind the left-hand side panel **(see illustration)**. Remove the panel for access (see Chapter 7).
4 Check for voltage at the brown wire

9.4 Check the condition of the rubber seal (arrowed), and that it is seated in its groove

10.1a Disconnect the taillight wiring connector . . .

10.1b . . . and the turn signal wiring connectors

10.2 . . . then unscrew the bolts (arrowed) and remove the taillight

11.3 Turn signal relay (arrowed)

Electrical system 8•7

11.5 Hazard warning relay (arrowed) – 1997-on models

12.1 Remove the screw and detach the lens . . .

12.2 . . . and remove the bulb

(brown/red on 1997-on models) in the relay wiring connector with the ignition ON. If no voltage is present, using the appropriate wiring diagram at the end of this Chapter check the wiring between the relay and the ignition (main) switch. If voltage was present, check for voltage at the brown/white wire with the ignition ON, and with the switch turned to either LEFT or RIGHT. If no voltage is present, replace the relay with a new one. If voltage was present, check the wiring between the relay, turn signal switch and turn signal lights for continuity. Turn the ignition OFF when the check is complete.

5 1997-on models incorporate a hazard warning function in the turn signal circuit, whereby all four turn signals flash simultaneously when the hazard warning switch is ON. The switch is housed in the left-hand handlebar switch (see Section 20), and the system has its own relay. To test the hazard relay, remove the left-hand side panel (see Chapter 7) and disconnect the wiring connector **(see illustration)**. Set a multimeter to the ohms x 1 scale and connect the positive (+ve) probe to the blue/red wire terminal on the relay and the negative (–ve) probe to the brown/red wire terminal. There should be continuity. If not, replace the relay with a new one. Now connect the positive (+ve) probe to the brown wire terminal (i.e. the terminal next to the blue/red), and the

negative (–ve) probe to the brown/red terminal. There should be no continuity. Leaving the meter connected, and using a fully-charged 12 volt battery and two insulated jumper wires, connect the battery positive (+ve) lead to the brown wire terminal (i.e. the terminal next to the black), and the negative (–ve) lead to the black wire terminal. There should now be continuity. If the relay doesn't behave as stated, replace it with a new one.

12 Turn signal bulbs – renewal

1 Remove the screw securing the turn signal lens and remove the lens, noting how it fits **(see illustration)**.
2 Push the bulb into the holder and twist it anti-clockwise to remove it **(see illustration)**. Check the socket terminals for corrosion and clean them if necessary. Line up the pins of the new bulb with the slots in the socket, then push the bulb in and turn it clockwise until it locks into place.
3 Fit the lens onto the holder, making sure the tab locates correctly **(see illustration)**. Do not overtighten the screw as the lens could be damaged.

13 Turn signal assemblies – removal and installation

Front
Removal
1 Disconnect the turn signal wiring connectors and draw the wiring out of its guide **(see illustration)**. Pull the cap off the nut on the inside of the fairing, then unscrew the nut and slide it off the wiring **(see illustration)**. Draw the turn signal out of the fairing, taking care not to snag the wiring as you pull it through.

Installation
2 Installation is the reverse of removal. Make sure the wiring is correctly routed and securely connected. Check the operation of the turn signals.

Rear
Removal
3 Remove the seat, then remove the two screws securing the tail light cover and remove the cover, noting how it locates (see Chapter 7).
4 Disconnect the turn signal wiring connectors **(see illustration 10.1b)**.

12.3 Make sure the tab locates correctly when fitting the lens

13.1a Disconnect the wiring connectors (arrowed) and draw the wiring from the guide . . .

13.1b . . . then pull off the cap, unscrew the nut and remove the turn signal

8•8 Electrical system

13.5 The turn signal is secured by a nut (arrowed) on the inside of the mudguard

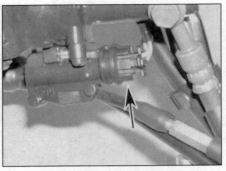

14.2 Front brake switch wiring connector (arrowed)

14.3a Rear brake light switch (arrowed)

5 Unscrew the nut securing the turn signal to the inside of the mudguard (see illustration). Draw the turn signal out of the mudguard, taking care not to snag the wiring as you pull it through.

Installation

6 Installation is the reverse of removal. Make sure the wiring is correctly routed and securely connected. Check the operation of the turn signals.

14 Brake light switches – check and renewal

Circuit check

1 Before checking the switches, and if not already done, check the brake light circuit (see Section 6, Step 6).
2 The front brake light switch is mounted on the underside of the brake master cylinder. Disconnect the wiring connector from the switch (see illustration). Using a continuity tester, connect the probes to the terminals of the switch. With the brake lever at rest, there should be no continuity. With the brake lever applied, there should be continuity. If the switch does not behave as described, replace it with a new one.
3 The rear brake light switch is mounted on the inside of the frame on the right-hand side, above the brake pedal (see illustration).

Remove the right-hand side panel and displace the ignition control unit to access the wiring connector (see Chapters 7 and 4). Trace the wiring from the switch and disconnect it at the connector (see illustration). Using a continuity tester, connect the probes to the terminals on the switch side of the wiring connector. With the brake pedal at rest, there should be no continuity. With the brake pedal applied, there should be continuity. If the switch does not behave as described, replace it with a new one.
4 If the switches are good, check for voltage at the brown wire terminal on the connector with the ignition switch ON – there should be battery voltage. If there's no voltage present, check the wiring between the switch and the ignition switch (see Wiring Diagrams at the end of this Chapter).

Switch renewal

Front brake light switch

5 The switch is mounted on the underside of the brake master cylinder. Disconnect the wiring connector from the switch (see illustration 14.2).
6 Remove the screws and washers securing the switch to the bottom of the master cylinder and remove the switch, noting how the plunger locates against the plate (see illustration).
7 Installation is the reverse of removal. Make

sure the plunger locates correctly against the plate (see illustration). The switch isn't adjustable.

Rear brake light switch

8 The switch is mounted on the inside of the frame on the right-hand side, above the brake pedal (see illustration 14.3a). Remove the right-hand side panel and displace the ignition control unit to access the wiring connector (see Chapters 7 and 4). Trace the wiring from the switch and disconnect it at the connector (see illustration 14.3b). Free the wiring from any clips or ties and feed it through to the switch.
9 Detach the lower end of the switch spring from the brake pedal, then unscrew and remove the switch.
10 Installation is the reverse of removal. Make sure the brake light is activated just before the rear brake pedal takes effect. If adjustment is necessary, hold the switch and turn the adjusting ring on the switch body until the brake light is activated when required.

15 Instrument cluster and speedometer cable – removal and installation

Instrument cluster

Removal

1 Remove the fairing (see Chapter 7).

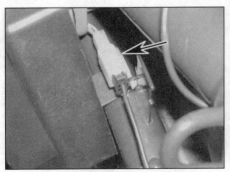

14.3b Rear brake switch wiring connector (arrowed)

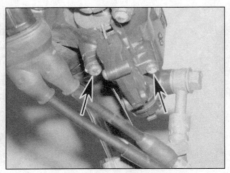

14.6 Undo the screws (arrowed) and remove the switch

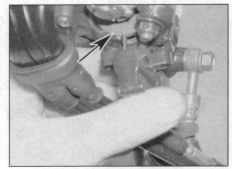

14.7 Make sure the plunger (arrowed) locates correctly against the outside of the plate

Electrical system 8•9

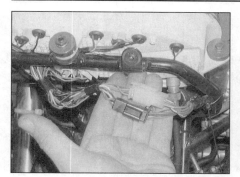

15.2 Disconnect the wiring connectors

15.3 Unscrew the ring and detach the cable

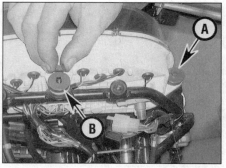

15.4a Unscrew the bolt on each side (A) and the nut (B) and remove the washers . . .

2 Release the instrument cluster wiring from any clips on the fairing stay and disconnect the wiring connectors (see illustration).
3 Unscrew the knurled ring securing the speedometer cable to the back of the speedometer and detach the cable (see illustration).
4 Unscrew the two bolts and one nut securing the instrument cluster to the stay and remove the washers (see illustration). Lift the instrument cluster off and retrieve the collars (see illustration).

Installation

5 Installation is the reverse of removal. Fit the collars into the mounting dampers after locating the instrument cluster (see illustration). Make sure that the speedometer cable and wiring connectors are correctly routed and secured.

Speedometer cable

Removal

6 Remove the fairing (see Chapter 7).
7 Unscrew the knurled ring securing the speedometer cable to the back of the speedometer and detach the cable (see illustration 15.3).
8 Unscrew the knurled ring securing the speedometer cable to the drive gear on the front wheel and detach the cable (see illustration).

9 Remove the cable from the bike, noting its routing through the guides.

Installation

10 Connect the cable upper end to the speedometer and tighten the knurled ring securely (see illustration 15.3).
11 Feed the cable down through its guides and connect it to the drive housing on the front wheel and tighten the knurled ring securely (see illustration 15.8).
12 Install the fairing (see Chapter 7).
13 Check that the cable doesn't restrict steering movement or interfere with any other components.

16 Instruments – check and renewal

Speedometer

Check

1 Special instruments are required to properly check the operation of this meter. If it is believed to be faulty, take the motorcycle to a Yamaha dealer for assessment. Before doing this, make sure that the fault is not due to a faulty cable or drive gear, either at

15.4b . . . then remove the instrument cluster and retrieve the collars

the front wheel or at the instruments (see Step 2).
2 Remove the speedometer cable (see Section 15), and check that it is not seized or broken. Replace it with a new one if necessary. Remove the front wheel (see Chapter 7), and check that the drive gear rotates freely. Clean and re-grease it. Replace it with a new one if necessary. Similarly check the driven gear on the back of the instrument cluster.

Renewal

3 Remove the instrument cluster (see Section 15).
4 Unscrew the odometer trip reset knob (see illustration). Remove the casing screws from

15.5 Install the collars after the instruments

15.8 Unscrew the ring and detach the cable

16.4a Unscrew the trip knob

8•10 Electrical system

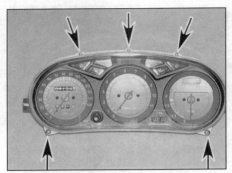

16.4b Undo the screws (arrowed) . . .

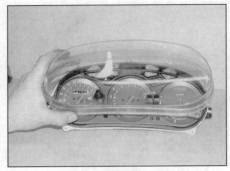

16.4c . . . and remove the front cover . . .

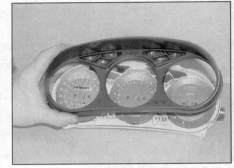

16.4d . . . and the shroud

the front of the cluster and lift off the cover and shroud **(see illustrations)**.

5 Remove the two screws securing the speedometer to the casing **(see illustration)**. Carefully withdraw the speedometer from the front.

6 Installation is the reverse of removal.

Tachometer

Check

7 Special instruments are required to properly check the operation of this meter. If it is believed to be faulty, take the motorcycle to a Yamaha dealer for assessment.

Renewal

8 Remove the instrument cluster (see Section 15).

9 Unscrew the odometer trip reset knob **(see illustration 16.4a)**. Remove the casing screws from the front of the cluster and lift off the cover and shroud **(see illustrations 16.4b, c and d)**.

10 Remove the screws and washers securing the three tachometer wires and detach the wires, noting which fits where **(see illustration)**. Remove the two screws securing the tachometer to the casing. Carefully withdraw the tachometer from the front.

11 Installation is the reverse of removal. Make sure the wiring is correctly connected. As you look at the back of the cluster, the brown wire is for the left-hand terminal, the black for the middle terminal, and the grey for the right-hand terminal **(see illustration 16.10)**.

Fuel gauge

Check

12 See Chapter 3.

Renewal

13 Remove the instrument cluster (see Section 15).

14 Unscrew the odometer trip reset knob **(see illustration 16.4a)**. Remove the casing screws from the front of the cluster and lift off the cover and shroud **(see illustrations 16.4b, c and d)**.

15 Remove the screws securing the three fuel gauge wires and detach the wires, noting which fits where **(see illustration)**. Carefully withdraw the fuel gauge from the front.

16 Installation is the reverse of removal. Make sure the wiring is correctly connected. As you look at the back of the cluster, the green wire is for the right-hand terminal, the black for the middle terminal, and the brown for the left-hand terminal **(see illustration 16.15)**.

Clock

Check

17 If the battery has been disconnected, the clock must be reset by first setting it to read 1-00 AM, and then setting it to read the correct time. The clock is set by using the 'H' and 'M' buttons (hours and minutes respectively) on the front of the instrument cluster.

18 If the clock stops working, first check the fuse (see Section 5), then the battery (see Section 3).

19 If the clock still does not work, remove the fairing (see Chapter 7). Disconnect the instrument cluster wiring connector with the red, green, blue, yellow/black, dark green and dark brown coloured wires **(see illustration 15.2)**.

20 Using a multimeter or voltmeter set to the dc volts x 20 scale, check for battery voltage at the red wire terminal on the loom side of the connector with the ignition switch ON. If no voltage is present, check the wiring between the connector and the ignition switch for loose or damaged connections, broken wiring or shorts to earth.

21 If all the wiring and power to the clock is good, and the clock does not work or cannot be reset as described above, then it is faulty and must be replaced with a new one.

Renewal

22 Remove the instrument cluster (see Section 15).

23 Unscrew the odometer trip reset knob **(see illustration 16.4a)**. Remove the casing screws from the front of the cluster and lift off the cover and shroud **(see illustrations 16.4b, c and d)**.

24 Remove the tachometer (see above).

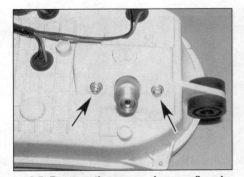

16.5 Remove the screws (arrowed) and draw the speedometer out from the front

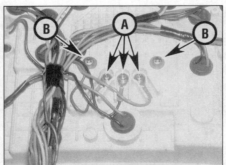

16.10 Remove the screws (A) and detach the wires, then remove the instrument screws (B)

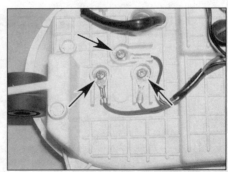

16.15 Remove the screws (arrowed) and detach the wires

Electrical system 8•11

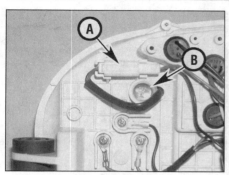

16.25 Disconnect the wiring connector (A) and remove the blanking plug (B)

17.2a Pull out the bulbholder . . .

17.2b . . . and remove the bulb

25 Disconnect the clock wiring connector on the back of the cluster, then remove the blanking plug **(see illustration)**. Remove the screws and washers securing the clock and remove the clock from the front, drawing the wiring connector through the hole in the casing as you do.
26 Installation is the reverse of removal.

17 Instrument and warning light bulbs – renewal

1 Remove the fairing (see Chapter 7).
2 Carefully pull the bulbholder out of the instrument casing, then pull the bulb out of

18.1 Disconnect the ignition switch wiring connectors

the bulbholder **(see illustrations)**. If access to some of the bulbs is too restricted, displace the cluster from its mounts (see Section 15).
3 If the socket contacts are dirty or corroded, scrape them clean and spray with electrical contact cleaner before a new bulb is installed. Carefully push the new bulb into the holder and push the holder into the casing.
4 Install the fairing (see Chapter 7).

18 Ignition (main) switch – check, removal and installation

 Warning: To prevent the risk of short circuits, remove the right-hand side panel and disconnect the battery negative (–ve) lead before making any ignition (main) switch checks.

Check

1 Remove the fuel tank and air filter housing (see Chapter 3). Trace the ignition (main) switch wiring back from the base of the switch and disconnect it at the connectors **(see illustration)**.
2 Using an ohmmeter or a continuity tester, check the continuity of the connector terminal pairs (see Wiring Diagrams at the end of this Chapter). Continuity should exist between the terminals connected by a solid line on the

diagram when the switch is in the indicated position.
3 If the switch fails any of the tests, replace it with a new one.

Removal

4 Remove the fuel tank and air filter housing (see Chapter 3). Trace the ignition (main) switch wiring back from the base of the switch and disconnect it at the connectors **(see illustration 18.1)**. Draw the wiring through to the switch, freeing it from any clips or ties and noting its routing.
5 Remove the fairing (see Chapter 7). **Note:** *Although it is not strictly necessary to remove the fairing, doing so will prevent the possibility of damage should a tool slip.*
6 Displace the handlebars from the top yoke (see Chapter 5). Support them so the master cylinder is upright to prevent the possibility of fluid leakage. There is no need to remove the switch assemblies from the handlebars. On 1994 and 1995 models, unscrew the bolt securing the choke knob holder to the top yoke and displace it.
7 Slacken the fork clamp bolts in the top yoke **(see illustration)**.
8 Unscrew the steering stem nut and remove it along with its washer, where fitted (1998-on models) **(see illustration)**.
9 Gently ease the top yoke upwards off the fork tubes and remove it **(see illustration)**.
10 Two shear-head bolts mount the ignition switch to the underside of the top yoke **(see**

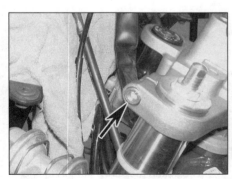

18.7 Slacken the fork clamp bolt (arrowed) on each side . . .

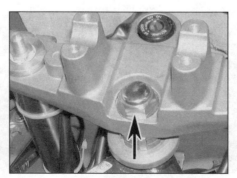

18.8 . . . then unscrew the steering stem nut (arrowed) . . .

18.9 . . . and ease the yoke up off the steering stem and forks

8•12 Electrical system

18.10 Ignition switch bolts (arrowed)

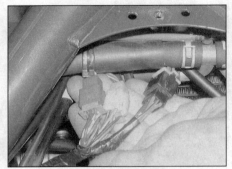

19.3 Handlebar switch wiring connectors

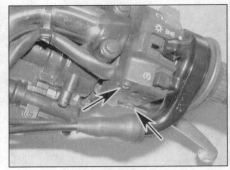

20.3a Right-hand switch housing screws (arrowed)

illustration). The heads of the bolts must be knocked round using a suitable punch or drift, or drilled off, before the switch can be removed. Mount the yoke in a vice equipped with soft jaws and padded out with rags to do this. Remove the bolts and withdraw the switch from the top yoke.

Installation

11 Installation is the reverse of removal. Tighten the new bolts until the heads shear off. Make sure wiring connectors are securely connected and correctly routed. Tighten the steering stem nut first, then the fork clamp bolts, to the torque settings specified at the beginning of Chapter 5.

19 Handlebar switches – check

1 Generally speaking, the switches are reliable and trouble-free. Most troubles, when they do occur, are caused by dirty or corroded contacts, but wear and breakage of internal parts is a possibility that should not be overlooked. If breakage does occur, the entire switch and related wiring harness will have to be replaced with a new one, as individual parts are not available.
2 The switches can be checked for continuity using an ohmmeter or a continuity test light.
3 Remove the fuel tank and air filter housing to access the switch wiring connectors (see Chapter 3). Trace the wiring harness of the switch in question back to its connectors and disconnect them **(see illustration)**.
4 Check for continuity between the terminals of the switch harness with the switch in the various positions (i.e. switch off – no continuity, switch on – continuity) – see *Wiring Diagrams* at the end of this Chapter.
5 If the continuity check indicates a problem exists, refer to Section 20, remove the switch and spray the switch contacts with electrical contact cleaner. If they are accessible, the contacts can be scraped clean with a knife or polished with crocus cloth. If switch components are damaged or broken, it should be obvious when the switch is disassembled.

20 Handlebar switches – removal and installation

Removal

1 If the switch is to be removed from the bike, rather than just displaced from the handlebar, trace the wiring harness of the switch in question back to its connectors and disconnect them **(see illustration 19.3)**. Remove the fuel tank and air filter housing to access the connectors (see Chapter 3). Work back along the harness, freeing it from all the relevant clips and ties, whilst noting its correct routing.
2 Disconnect the wiring connector(s) from the brake light switch (if removing the right-hand switch) or the clutch switch (if removing the left-hand switch) **(see illustration 14.2 or 23.2)**.
3 Remove the handlebar switch screws and free the switch from the handlebar by separating the halves **(see illustrations)**. On 1996-on models, if removing the left-hand switch, remove the choke cable lever, noting how it fits.

Installation

4 Installation is the reverse of removal. On 1996-on models, refer to Chapter 3 for installation of the choke cable, if required. Make sure the locating pin in the switch housing locates in the hole in the handlebar **(see illustration)**. Make sure the wiring connectors are correctly routed and securely connected.

21 Neutral switch – check, removal and installation

Check

1 Before checking the electrical circuit, check the bulb (see Section 17) and fuse (see Section 5).
2 The switch is located in the bottom of the engine on the left-hand side. Make sure the transmission is in neutral. Slacken the screw and disconnect the wiring connector from the switch **(see illustration)**.
3 With the wire disconnected and the ignition switched ON, the neutral light should be out. If

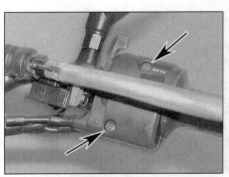

20.3b Left-hand switch housing screws (arrowed)

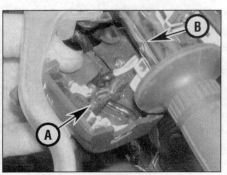

20.4 Locate the pin (A) in the hole (B)

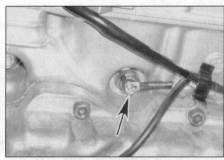

21.2 Slacken the screw (arrowed) and detach the wiring connector from the neutral switch

Electrical system 8•13

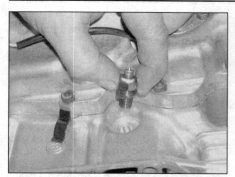

21.7 Unscrew the switch and remove it

22.2 Sidestand switch wiring connector (arrowed)

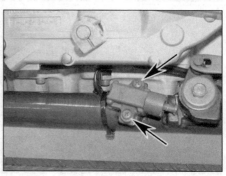

22.7 The sidestand switch is secured by two screws (arrowed)

not, the wire between the connector and instrument cluster must be earthed (grounded) at some point. Now touch the wire to a good earth on the engine. The neutral light should come on. If not, there is a broken wire or connector.
4 Check for continuity between the switch terminal and the crankcase. With the transmission in neutral, there should be continuity. With the transmission in gear, there should be no continuity. If the tests prove otherwise, then the switch is faulty.
5 If the continuity tests prove the switch is good, check for voltage at the brown wire terminal on the wiring loom side of the instrument cluster wiring connector using a test light and with the ignition switch ON – remove the fairing to access the connector **(see illustration 15.2)**. If there's no voltage present, check the wire between the connector and fusebox (see *Wiring Diagrams* at the end of this Chapter). If the voltage is good, check the wiring between the connector and the bulbholder, then check the starter circuit cut-off relay and other components in the starter circuit as described in the relevant sections of this Chapter. If all components are good, check the wiring between the various components (see *Wiring Diagrams* at the end of this book).

Removal

6 The switch is located in the bottom of the engine on the left-hand side. Make sure the transmission is in neutral. Drain the engine oil (see Chapter 1). Slacken the screw and disconnect the wiring connector from the switch **(see illustration 21.2)**.
7 Unscrew the switch and remove it from the engine **(see illustration)**. Check the condition of the sealing washer and discard it if it is damaged or deformed.

Installation

8 Install the switch using a new sealing washer if necessary and tighten it to the torque setting specified at the beginning of the Chapter **(see illustration 21.7)**.
9 Connect the wiring and tighten the screw **(see illustration 21.2)**. Check the operation of the switch. Fill the engine with oil (see Chapter 1).

22 Sidestand switch – check and renewal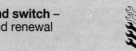

Check

1 The sidestand switch is mounted on the sidestand. The switch is part of the safety circuit which prevents or stops the engine running if the transmission is in gear whilst the sidestand is down, and prevents the engine from starting if the transmission is in gear unless the sidestand is up, and unless the clutch is pulled in. Before checking the electrical circuit, check the fuse (see Section 5).
2 To access the wiring connector, remove the fuel tank (see Chapter 3). Trace the wiring from the switch and disconnect it at the connector **(see illustration)**.
3 Check the operation of the switch using an ohmmeter or continuity test light. Connect the meter probes to the terminals on the switch side of the connector. With the sidestand up there should be continuity (zero resistance) between the terminals, and with the stand down there should be no continuity (infinite resistance).
4 If the switch does not perform as expected, it is defective and must be renewed.
5 If the switch is good, check the starter circuit cut-off relay and other components in the starter circuit as described in the relevant sections of this Chapter. If all components are good, check the wiring between the various components (see *Wiring Diagrams* at the end of this book).

Renewal

6 The sidestand switch is mounted on the sidestand. Remove the fuel tank (see Chapter 3) to access the wiring connector. Trace the wiring from the switch and disconnect it at the connector **(see illustration 22.2)**. Work back along the switch wiring, freeing it from any relevant retaining clips and ties, noting its correct routing.
7 Remove the screws securing the switch and remove the switch, noting how it fits **(see illustration)**.

8 Fit the new switch, making sure the plunger locates correctly, and tighten the screws securely.
9 Make sure the wiring is correctly routed up to the connector and retained by all the necessary clips and ties.
10 Reconnect the wiring connector and check the operation of the sidestand switch.
11 Install the fuel tank (see Chapter 3).

23 Clutch switch – check and renewal

Check

1 The clutch switch is mounted on the underside of the clutch lever bracket. The switch is part of the safety circuit which prevents or stops the engine running if the transmission is in gear whilst the sidestand is down, and prevents the engine from starting if the transmission is in gear unless the sidestand is up and the clutch lever is pulled in. The switch isn't adjustable.
2 To check the switch, disconnect the wiring connector **(see illustration)**. Connect the probes of an ohmmeter or a continuity test light to the two switch terminals. With the clutch lever pulled in, continuity should be indicated. With the clutch lever out, no continuity (infinite resistance) should be indicated.
3 If the switch is good, check the starter circuit cut-off relay and other components in the starter circuit as described in the relevant

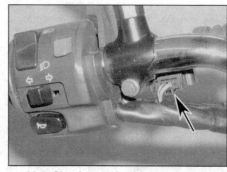

23.2 Clutch switch wiring connector (arrowed)

8•14 Electrical system

24.2 Relay assembly (arrowed)

sections of this Chapter. If all components are good, check the wiring between the various components (see *Wiring Diagrams* at the end of this book).

Renewal

4 The clutch switch is mounted on the underside of the clutch lever bracket.
5 Disconnect the wiring connector **(see illustration 23.2)**, then remove the screw and detach the switch.
6 Installation is the reverse of removal.

24 Relay assembly – check and renewal

Starter circuit cut-off relay

Check

1 The starter circuit cut-off relay is incorporated in the relay assembly. It is part of the safety circuit which prevents or stops the engine running if the transmission is in gear whilst the sidestand is down, and prevents the engine from starting if the transmission is in gear unless the sidestand is up and the clutch lever is pulled in. The relay is quite complicated internally, containing diodes, resistors and switches, and performs many functions. Due to the extensive (though not complicated) nature of the tests for the relay, the best way to determine whether it is faulty is to substitute it with a new or known-to-be-good one, and see whether the fault is cured.
2 If the starter circuit is faulty, first check the fuse (see Section 5). The relay assembly is located behind the left-hand side panel. Remove the panel for access (see Chapter 7). Disconnect the relay wiring connector and remove the relay **(see illustration)**.
3 Set a multimeter to the ohms x 1 scale and connect the positive (+ve) probe to the blue wire terminal, and the negative (–ve) probe to the blue/white terminal. There should be no continuity. Leaving the meter connected, and using a fully-charged 12 volt battery and two insulated jumper wires, connect the battery positive (+ve) lead to the red/black wire terminal, and the negative (–ve) lead to the black/yellow wire terminal. There should now be continuity. If the relay doesn't behave as stated, replace it with a new one.
4 Using an ohmmeter or continuity tester, connect the positive (+ve) probe to the light blue wire terminal, and the negative (–ve) probe to the blue/yellow wire terminal. Now reverse the probes. There should be continuity in one direction and no continuity in the other. If the diode indicates the same condition in both directions it has failed and the relay assembly should be renewed.
5 Using an ohmmeter or continuity tester, connect the positive (+ve) probe to the light blue wire terminal, and the negative (–ve) probe to the black/yellow. Now reverse the probes. There should be continuity in one direction and no continuity in the other. If the diode indicates the same condition in both directions it has failed and the relay assembly should be renewed.
6 Using an ohmmeter or continuity tester, connect the positive (+ve) probe to the blue wire terminal, and the negative (–ve) probe to the red/blue wire terminal. Now reverse the probes. There should be continuity in one direction and no continuity in the other. If the diode indicates the same condition in both directions it has failed and the relay assembly should be renewed.
7 Using an ohmmeter or continuity tester, connect the positive (+ve) probe to the blue wire terminal, and the negative (–ve) probe to the green/red wire terminal. Now reverse the probes. There should be continuity in one direction and no continuity in the other. If the diode indicates the same condition in both directions it has failed and the relay assembly should be renewed.
8 If the relay is good, check the other components in the starter circuit as described in the relevant sections of this Chapter. If all components are good, check the wiring between the various components (see *Wiring Diagrams* at the end of this book).

Renewal

9 The starter cut-off relay is incorporated in the relay assembly located behind the left-hand side panel. Remove the panel for access (see Chapter 7). Disconnect the relay wiring connector and remove the relay **(see illustration 24.2)**.
10 Installation is the reverse of removal.

Oil level sensor resister

11 The sensor resister is housed inside the relay assembly.
12 Using an ohmmeter set to the ohms x 100 scale, connect the positive (+ve) probe to the black/red wire terminal, and the negative (–ve) probe to the red/blue wire terminal. The meter should show between 202.5 and 247.5 ohms resistance. If the relay doesn't behave as stated, replace it with a new one.

Fuel pump relay

13 The fuel pump relay is housed inside the relay assembly. Refer to Chapter 3 for details.

25 Diode (1994 to 1996 models) – check and renewal

Check

1 The diode is a small block that plugs into the main wiring harness, and is part of the safety circuit which prevents or stops the engine running if the transmission is in gear whilst the sidestand is down, and prevents the engine from starting if the transmission is in gear unless the sidestand is up and the clutch lever is pulled in (see *Wiring Diagrams* at the end of the Chapter).
2 Remove the insulating tape, then disconnect the diode from the harness.
3 Using an ohmmeter or continuity tester, connect the positive (+ve) probe to the light blue wire terminal of the diode and the negative (–ve) probe to the light green wire terminal. Now reverse the probes. There should be continuity in one direction and no continuity in the other direction. If the diode doesn't behave as stated, replace it with a new one.
4 If the diode is good, check the starter circuit cut-off relay and other components in the starter circuit as described in the relevant sections of this Chapter. If all components are good, check the wiring between the various components (see *Wiring Diagrams* at the end of this book).

Renewal

5 The diode is a small block that plugs into the main wiring harness.
6 Remove the insulating tape, then disconnect the diode from the harness and connect the new one.

26 Horn – check and renewal

Check

1 If the horn, doesn't work, first check the fuse (see Section 5) and the battery (see Section 3).
2 The horn is mounted on the bottom yoke. Remove the fairing for best access to it (see Chapter 7).
3 Unplug the wiring connectors from the horn **(see illustration)**. Using two jumper wires,

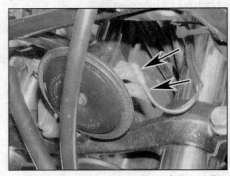

26.3 Horn wiring connectors (arrowed)

Electrical system 8•15

26.6 Horn mounting bolt (arrowed)

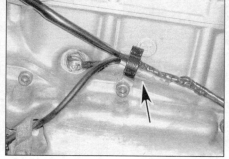

27.5a Oil level sensor wiring connector (arrowed)

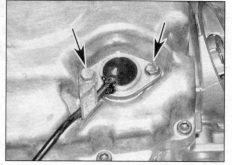

27.5b Unscrew the bolts (arrowed) and remove the sensor

apply battery voltage directly to the terminals on the horn. If the horn sounds, check the switch (see Section 19) and the wiring between the switch and the horn (see *Wiring Diagrams* at the end of this Chapter).
4 If the horn doesn't sound, replace it with a new one.

Renewal

5 The horn is mounted on the bottom yoke. Remove the fairing for best access to it (see Chapter 7).
6 Unplug the wiring connectors from the horn **(see illustration 25.3)**. Unscrew the bolt securing the horn and remove it from the bike **(see illustration)**.
7 Install the horn and securely tighten the bolt. Connect the wiring connectors to the horn. Install the fairing (see Chapter 7).

27 Oil level sensor – check, removal and installation

Check

1 With the ignition switch ON and the kill switch in the 'RUN' position, the oil level warning light should not come on, indicating that the oil level is good. If the light does come on, check the oil level (see *Daily (pre-ride) checks*). If the oil level is good, check the sensor and relay (see Steps 3 and 4).
2 Start the engine. The oil level warning light should come on when the starter button is pressed and extinguish when it is released. If the light does not come on, stop the engine and check the bulb (see Section 17). If the bulb is good, check for continuity in the wire between the sensor bullet connector and the loom side of the instrument cluster wiring connector. Also check for continuity between the cluster side of the connector and the bulb holder. Not that there is a resister fitted inside the relay assembly (see Section 24) to stabilise the signals to the oil level warning light, thus preventing it flickering when cornering or braking hard. Test the resister as described in Section 24.
3 To check the sensor, remove it from the sump (see Steps 4 and 5 below). Connect one

probe of an ohmmeter or continuity tester to the sensor wire and the other probe to its base. With the sensor in its normal installed position (wiring at the bottom), there should be continuity. Turn the sensor upside down. There should be no continuity. If either condition does not occur, replace the sensor with a new one.

Removal

4 Drain the engine oil (see Chapter 1).
5 Trace the wiring back from the sensor and disconnect it at the single bullet connector **(see illustration)**. Free it from its clamp. Unscrew the two bolts securing the sensor to the bottom of the sump and withdraw it from the sump, being prepared to catch any residue oil **(see illustration)**. Discard the O-ring as a new one must be used.

Installation

6 Fit a new O-ring onto the oil level sensor, then fit the sensor into the sump. Tighten its bolts to the torque setting specified at the beginning of the Chapter.
7 Connect the wiring at the connector **(see illustration 27.5a)** and check the operation of the sensor (see Steps 1 to 4 above). Secure the wiring in its clamp.
8 Fill the engine with oil (see Chapter 1).

28 Starter relay – check and renewal

Check

1 If the starter circuit is faulty, first check the fuse (see Section 5).
2 Remove the fuel tank (see Chapter 3). Lift the rubber terminal cover and unscrew the bolt securing the starter motor lead to the front terminal **(see illustration)**; position the lead away from the relay terminal. With the ignition switch ON, the engine kill switch in the RUN position, and the transmission in neutral, press the starter switch. The relay should be heard to click.
3 If the relay doesn't click, switch off the ignition and remove the relay as described below; test it as follows.

4 Set a multimeter to the ohms x 1 scale and connect it across the relay's starter motor and battery lead terminals **(see illustration 28.2)**. Using a fully-charged 12 volt battery and two insulated jumper wires, connect the positive (+ve) terminal of the battery to the red/white wire terminal on the relay, and the negative (–ve) terminal to the blue/white wire terminal on the relay. At this point the relay should be heard to click and the multimeter read 0 ohms (continuity). If this is the case the relay is proved good. If the relay does not click when battery voltage is applied and indicates no continuity (infinite resistance) across its terminals, it is faulty and must be replaced with a new one.
5 The relay can be checked by measuring its resistance across the red/white and blue/white wire terminals. The resistance should be as specified at the beginning of this Chapter.
6 If the relay is good, check for battery voltage at the red/white wire terminal on the loom side of the relay wiring connector when the starter button is pressed. If voltage is present, check the other components in the starter circuit as described in the relevant sections of this Chapter. If no voltage was present, or if all components are good, check the wiring between the various components (see *Wiring Diagrams* at the end of this book).

Renewal

7 Disconnect the battery (see Section 3). Remove the fuel tank (see Chapter 3).

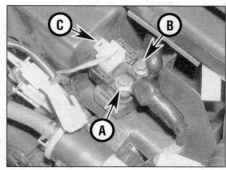

28.2 Starter motor lead (A), battery lead (B), starter relay wiring connector (C)

8•16 Electrical system

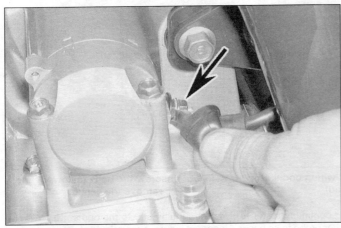

29.2 Pull back the rubber cover and unscrew the terminal nut (arrowed)

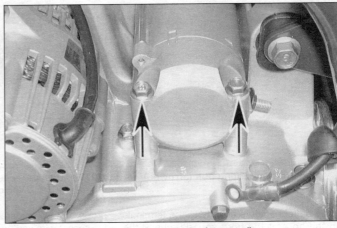

29.3a Unscrew the bolts (arrowed) . . .

8 Unscrew the two bolts securing the starter motor and battery leads to the relay and detach the leads **(see illustration 28.2)**. Displace the relay with its rubber sleeve from its mounting lug on the frame. Disconnect the relay wiring connector and remove the relay.
9 Installation is the reverse of removal. The starter motor lead connects to the front terminal, and the battery lead to the rear terminal **(see illustration 28.2)**. Make sure the terminal nuts are securely tightened. Connect the negative (–ve) lead last when reconnecting the battery.

29 Starter motor – removal and installation

Removal

1 Remove the right-hand side panel (see Chapter 7). Disconnect the battery negative (–ve) lead. The starter motor is mounted on the crankcase.
2 Peel back the rubber terminal cover and unscrew the nut securing the lead to the starter motor **(see illustration)**. Detach the lead.
3 Detach the breather hose from the crankcase cover. Unscrew the two bolts securing the starter motor **(see illustration)**. Draw the starter motor out of the crankcase and remove it from the machine **(see illustration)**.
4 Remove the O-ring on the end of the starter motor and discard it as a new one must be used.

Installation

5 Fit a new O-ring onto the end of the starter motor, making sure it is seated in its groove, and smear it with grease **(see illustration)**.
6 Manoeuvre the motor into position and slide it into the crankcase **(see illustration 29.3b)**. Ensure that the starter motor teeth mesh correctly with those of the starter idle/reduction gear. Apply a suitable non-permanent thread locking compound to the threads of the bolts, then tighten them to the torque setting specified at the beginning of the Chapter **(see illustration)**.
7 Connect the lead to the starter motor and secure it with the nut **(see illustration 29.2)**. Make sure the rubber cover is correctly seated over the terminal.
8 Connect the battery negative (–ve) lead and install the side panel (see Chapter 7).

29.3b . . . and remove the starter motor

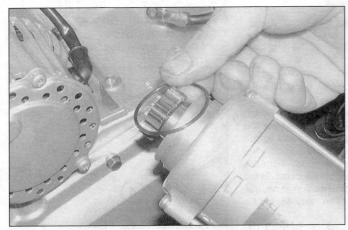

29.5 Fit a new O-ring onto the starter motor

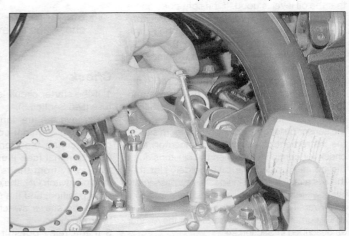

29.6 Apply a threadlock to the bolts and tighten them to the specified torque

Electrical system 8•17

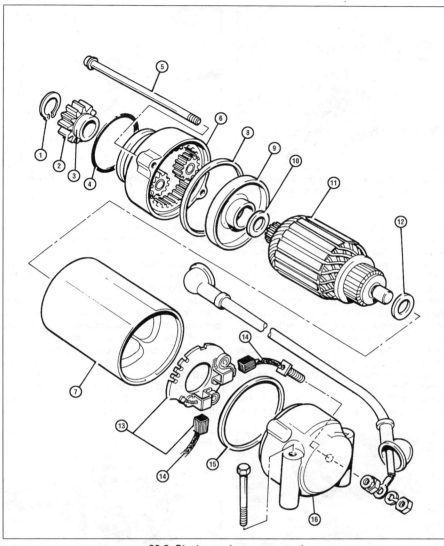

30.2 Starter motor components

1 Circlip
2 Drive gear
3 Ring
4 O-ring
5 Long bolt
6 Reduction gear housing
7 Main housing
8 O-ring
9 End plate
10 Washer
11 Armature
12 Shim(s)
13 Brushplate
14 Brushes
15 O-ring
16 End cover

30 Starter motor – disassembly, inspection and reassembly

Disassembly

1 Remove the starter motor (see Section 29).
2 Make alignment marks between the main housing and both end covers **(see illustration)**.
3 Unscrew and remove the two long housing bolts **(see illustration)**. Remove the reduction gear housing and the O-ring from the front of the motor **(see illustrations)**.
4 Remove the end plate and the washer, then draw the main housing off the armature **(see illustrations)**. Remove the O-ring.

30.3a Unscrew and remove the two long bolts (arrowed) . . .

30.3b . . . then remove the gear housing . . .

30.3c . . . and the O-ring

30.4a Remove the end plate . . .

30.4b . . . and the washer

8•18 Electrical system

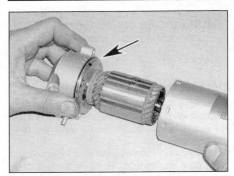

30.4c Draw the main housing off the armature and remove the O-ring (arrowed)

30.5a Draw the armature out of the end cover, noting how it locates against the brushes . . .

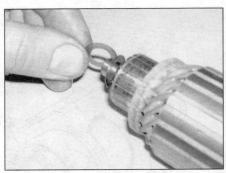

30.5b . . . and remove the shims

5 Withdraw the armature from the brush plate assembly and end cover **(see illustration)**. Remove the shims from the shaft end **(see illustration)**.

6 Draw the terminal bolt brush out of its holder **(see illustration)**. Withdraw the brushplate assembly from the end cover, noting how it fits **(see illustration 30.16)**.

7 If required, unscrew the nut from the terminal bolt, noting which way it fits onto the bolt, and remove the insulating base and O-ring, noting their order **(see illustration)**.

Inspection

8 The parts of the starter motor that are most likely to wear are the brushes. Measure the length of the brushes and compare the results to the service limit in this Chapter's Specifications **(see illustration)**. If the brushes are not worn excessively, nor cracked, chipped, or otherwise damaged, they may be re-used. Otherwise, replace them with new ones.

9 Inspect the commutator for scoring, scratches and discoloration. The commutator can be cleaned and polished with crocus cloth, but do not use sandpaper or emery paper. After cleaning, wipe away any residue with a cloth soaked in electrical system cleaner or denatured alcohol. Measure the diameter of the commutator and compare the reading with the service limit in the Specifications **(see illustration)**. If it has worn below the service limit, replace the armature with a new one. Measure the depth of the insulating Mica below the surface of the commutator bars. If the Mica is less than the depth specified, scrape it away until the specified depth is reached.

10 Using an ohmmeter or a continuity test light, check for continuity between the commutator bars **(see illustration)**. Continuity should exist between each bar and all of the others. Also, check for continuity between the commutator bars and the armature shaft **(see illustration)**. There should be no continuity (infinite resistance) between the commutator and the shaft. If the checks indicate otherwise, the armature is defective.

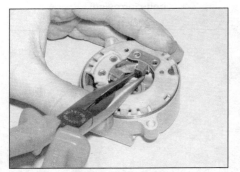

30.6 Draw the terminal brush bolt out of its holder

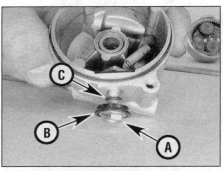

30.7 Unscrew the nut (A) and remove the insulating base (B) and O-ring (C)

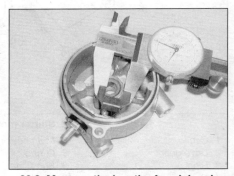

30.8 Measure the length of each brush

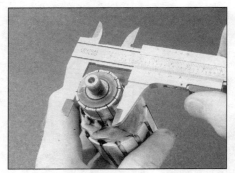

30.9 Measure the diameter of the commutator

30.10a Continuity should exist between the commutator bars

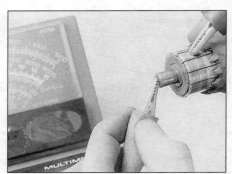

30.10b There should be no continuity between the commutator bars and the armature shaft

Electrical system 8•19

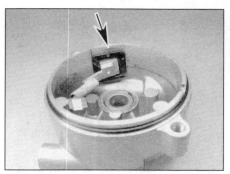

30.15 Make sure the bolt locates correctly (arrowed)

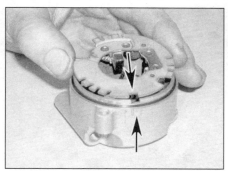

30.16 Make sure the brushplate aligns correctly with the end cover (arrowed)

30.20 Fit the reduction gear housing, locating the pin into the notch

11 Check for continuity between the brush and the brushplate, and between the brush and its terminal bolt. There should be continuity in both cases.

12 Inspect the reduction gear and the drive gear for worn, cracked, chipped and broken teeth. Also inspect the housing for cracks or wear. If the gear or housing is damaged or worn, replace the starter motor with a new one.

13 Inspect the end cover for signs of cracks or wear. Inspect the magnets in the main housing and the housing itself for cracks.

14 Replace the housing O-rings with new ones if they are worn, damaged or deteriorated.

Reassembly

15 Fit the terminal bolt through the rear cover, then install the O-ring and insulating base (see illustration 30.7). Make sure the bolt base locates correctly inside the end cover (see illustration). Install the terminal nut, making sure it is the correct way up, and tighten it securely.

16 Fit the brushplate assembly into the rear cover making sure it is correctly aligned (see illustration). Fit the brushes back into their holders (see illustration 30.6).

17 Fit the shims onto the end of the shaft (see illustration 30.5b). Insert the armature into the rear cover taking care not to damage the brushes (see illustration 30.5a). As it is inserted, locate the brushes on the commutator bars. Check that each brush is securely pressed against the commutator by its spring and is free to move easily in its holder.

18 Fit the O-ring onto the end cover (see illustration 30.4c). Fit the main housing over the armature, aligning the marks made on removal.

19 Fit the washer onto the end of the armature, then install the end plate, aligning the notch with the tab (see illustrations 30.4b and a). Fit the O-ring onto the housing (see illustration 30.3c).

20 Smear some molybdenum disulphide grease over the reduction gears. Install the reduction gear housing, making sure the marks made on removal are correctly aligned

and the pin fits into the notch (see illustration). Apply a suitable non-permanent thread locking compound to the long housing bolts and tighten them to the torque setting specified at the beginning of the Chapter (see illustration 30.3a).

21 Install the starter motor (see Section 29).

31 Charging system testing – general information and precautions

1 If the performance of the charging system is suspect, the system as a whole should be checked first, followed by testing of the individual components. **Note:** *Before beginning the checks, make sure the battery is fully charged and that all system connections are clean and tight.*

2 Checking the output of the charging system and the performance of the various components within the charging system requires the use of a multimeter (with voltage, current and resistance checking facilities).

3 When making the checks, follow the procedures carefully to prevent incorrect connections or short circuits, as irreparable damage to electrical system components may result if short circuits occur.

4 If a multimeter is not available, the job of checking the charging system should be left to a Yamaha dealer.

32 Charging system – leakage and output test

1 If the charging system of the machine is thought to be faulty, remove the right-hand side panel (see Chapter 7) and perform the following checks.

Leakage test

Caution: *Always connect an ammeter in series, never in parallel with the battery, otherwise it will be damaged. Do not turn the ignition ON or operate the starter motor when the ammeter is connected – a sudden surge in current will blow the meter's fuse.*

2 Turn the ignition switch OFF and disconnect the lead from the battery negative (–ve) terminal.

3 Set the multimeter to the Amps function and connect its negative (–ve) probe to the battery negative (–ve) terminal, and positive (+ve) probe to the disconnected negative (–ve) lead (see illustration). Always set the meter to a high amps range initially and then bring it down to the mA (milli Amps) range; if there is a high current flow in the circuit it may blow the meter's fuse.

4 No current flow should be indicated. If current leakage is indicated (generally greater than 0.1 mA), there is a short circuit in the wiring. Using the wiring diagrams at the end of this book, systematically disconnect individual electrical components, checking the meter each time until the source is identified.

5 If no leakage is indicated, disconnect the meter and connect the negative (–ve) lead to the battery, tightening it securely

Output test

6 Start the engine and warm it up to normal operating temperature. Remove the right-hand side panel (see Chapter 7).

7 To check the regulated voltage output, allow the engine to idle and connect a multimeter set to the 0-20 volts DC scale

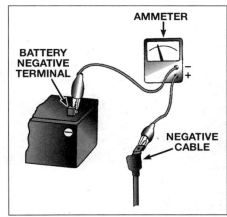

32.3 Checking the charging system leakage rate – connect the meter as shown

8•20 Electrical system

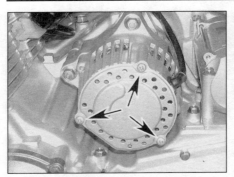

33.1 Undo the screws (arrowed) and remove the cover

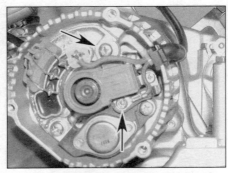

33.2a Undo the screws (arrowed) and remove the brushholder . . .

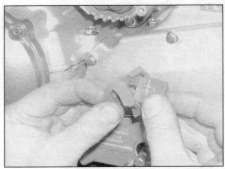

33.2b . . . then remove the cover . . .

(voltmeter) across the terminals of the battery (positive (+ve) lead to battery positive (+ve) terminal, negative (–ve) lead to battery negative (–ve) terminal). Slowly increase the engine speed to 5000 rpm and note the reading obtained. The regulated voltage should be as specified at the beginning of the Chapter. If the voltage is outside these limits, check the alternator/regulator/rectifier (see Section 33).

 Clues to a faulty regulator are constantly blowing bulbs, with brightness varying considerably with engine speed, and battery overheating.

33 Alternator/regulator/rectifier – check, removal and installation

Check

1 Remove the three screws securing the alternator end cover and remove the cover **(see illustration)**.

2 Remove the screws securing the brush holder, noting the lead secured by the bottom screw, and remove the holder, noting how it fits **(see illustration)**. Remove the cover from the holder **(see illustration)**. Inspect the holder for any signs of damage. Measure the length of the brushes and compare the results to the service limit in this Chapter's Specifications **(see illustration)**. If the brushes are not worn excessively, nor cracked, chipped, or otherwise damaged, they may be re-used. Otherwise, replace them with new ones. Clean the slip rings (the rings on the shaft which contact the brushes) with a rag moistened with some solvent.

3 To check the rotor coil resistance, first remove the brushholder (see above), then set a multimeter to the ohms x 1 (ohmmeter) scale and measure the resistance between the slip rings (the rings on the shaft which contact the brushes) and compare the reading to the Specifications. If it is higher than specified, replace the rotor with a new one.

4 To check the stator coil resistance, set a multimeter to the ohms x 1 (ohmmeter) scale and measure the resistance between each of the white wires coming out of the left-hand side of the alternator, taking a total of three readings, then check for continuity between each terminal and ground (earth) **(see illustration)**. If the stator coil windings are in good condition the three readings should be within the range shown in the Specifications at the beginning of the Chapter, and there should be no continuity (infinite resistance) between any of the terminals and ground (earth). If not, the alternator stator coil assembly is faulty and should be replaced with a new one.

5 Check for continuity between the slip rings and the armature housing. There should be no continuity (infinite resistance). If there is continuity, renew the rotor.

6 Yamaha do not provide any test Specifications for the regulator and rectifier. If none of the checks made here or in other Sections of the Chapter reveal any faults, then take the assembly to a Yamaha dealer for further tests. Individual components are available.

Removal

7 Remove the fuel tank (see Chapter 3).
8 Trace the wiring from the alternator/regulator/rectifier and disconnect it

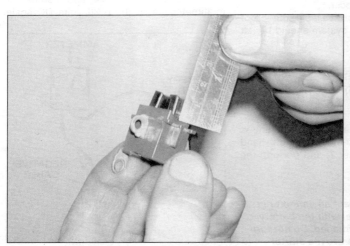

33.2c . . . and inspect the brushes

33.4 Check the stator coil resistance by testing between the three wires (arrowed) as described

Electrical system 8•21

33.8 Alternator wiring connector

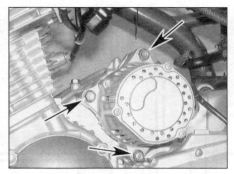

33.9a Unscrew the three bolts (arrowed) . . .

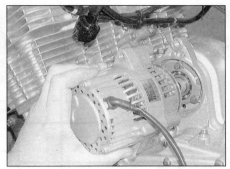

33.9b . . . and remove the alternator

at the connector **(see illustration)**. Feed the wiring back to the alternator assembly.

9 Unscrew the three bolts securing the alternator assembly to the crankcase and withdraw it **(see illustrations)**. Discard the O-ring as a new one must be used.

Installation

10 Installation is the reverse of removal. Use a new O-ring **(see illustration)**. Apply a suitable non-permanent thread locking compound to the alternator bolts and tighten them to the torque setting specified at the beginning of the Chapter **(see illustration)**.

33.10a Use a new O-ring . . .

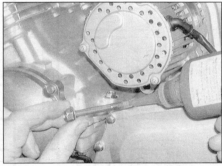

33.10b . . . and apply a threadlock to the bolts

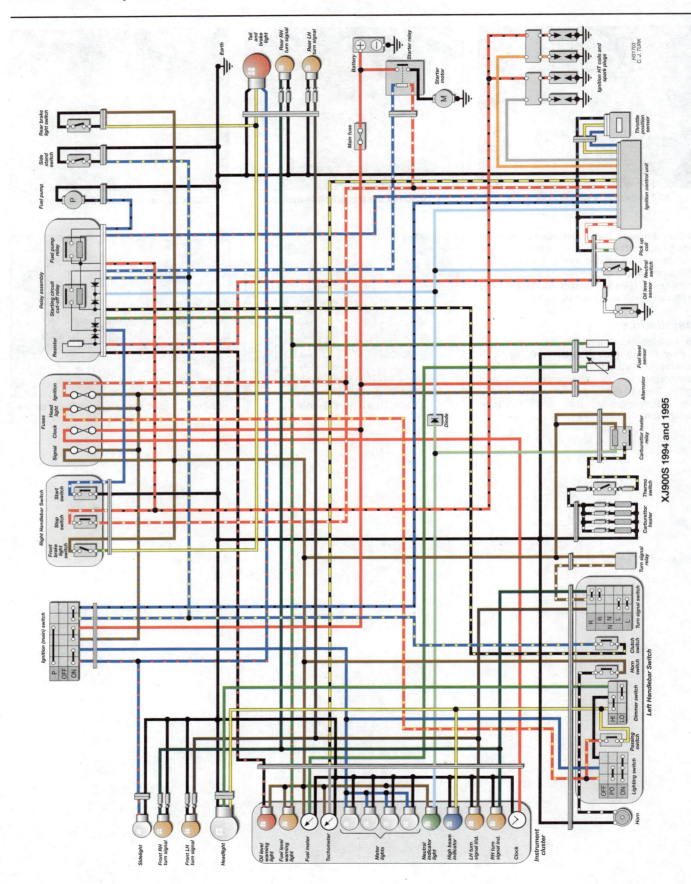

Electrical system 8•23

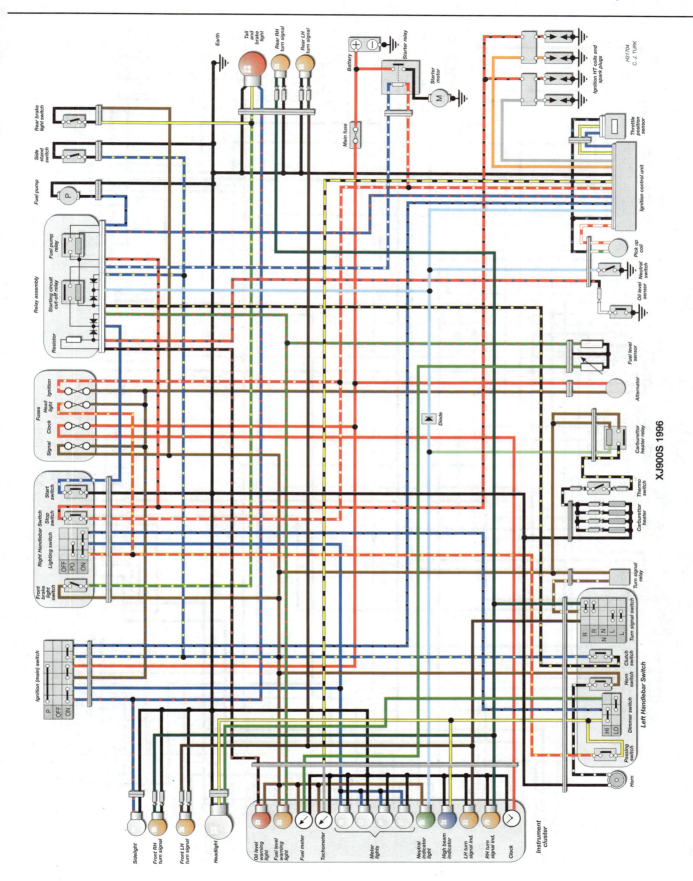

8•24 Electrical system

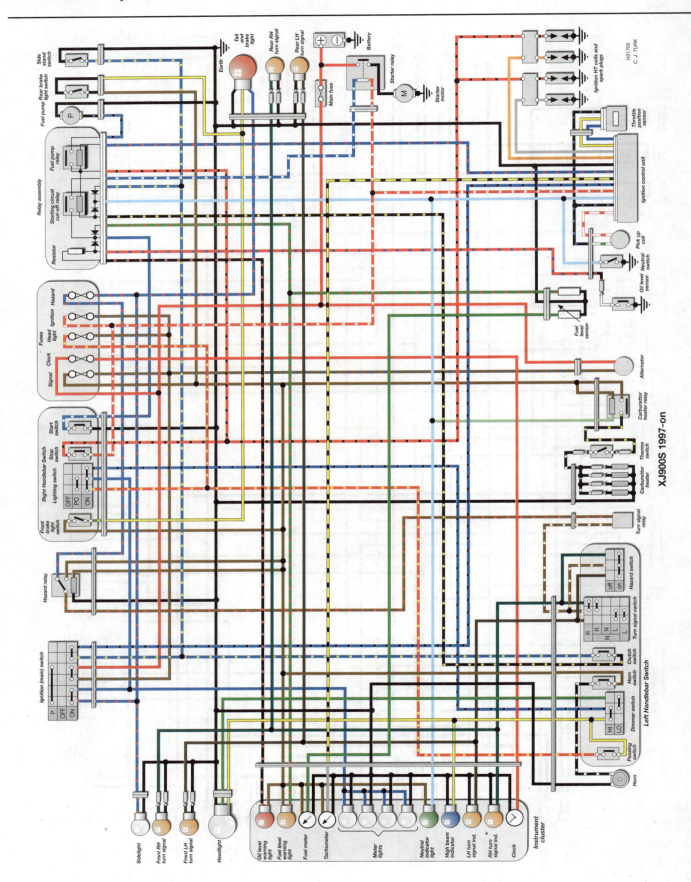

Reference REF•1

Dimensions and Weights	REF•1	Storage	REF•27
Tools and Workshop Tips	REF•2	Fault Finding	REF•30
Conversion Factors	REF•20	Fault Finding Equipment	REF•39
Motorcycle Chemicals and Lubricants	REF•21	Technical Terms Explained	REF•43
MOT Test Checks	REF•22	Index	REF•47

Dimensions and weights

Overall length	2230 mm
Overall width	
1994 and 1995 models	735 mm
1996-on models	750 mm
Overall height	1300 mm
Seat height	795 mm
Wheelbase	1505 mm
Ground clearance	130 mm
Weight (with fuel and oil)	265 kg

REF•2 Tools and Workshop Tips

Buying tools

A toolkit is a fundamental requirement for servicing and repairing a motorcycle. Although there will be an initial expense in building up enough tools for servicing, this will soon be offset by the savings made by doing the job yourself. As experience and confidence grow, additional tools can be added to enable the repair and overhaul of the motorcycle. Many of the specialist tools are expensive and not often used so it may be preferable to hire them, or for a group of friends or motorcycle club to join in the purchase.

As a rule, it is better to buy more expensive, good quality tools. Cheaper tools are likely to wear out faster and need to be renewed more often, nullifying the original saving.

Warning: To avoid the risk of a poor quality tool breaking in use, causing injury or damage to the component being worked on, always aim to purchase tools which meet the relevant national safety standards.

The following lists of tools do not represent the manufacturer's service tools, but serve as a guide to help the owner decide which tools are needed for this level of work. In addition, items such as an electric drill, hacksaw, files, soldering iron and a workbench equipped with a vice, may be needed. Although not classed as tools, a selection of bolts, screws, nuts, washers and pieces of tubing always come in useful.

For more information about tools, refer to the Haynes *Motorcycle Workshop Practice TechBook* (Bk. No. 3470).

Manufacturer's service tools

Inevitably certain tasks require the use of a service tool. Where possible an alternative tool or method of approach is recommended, but sometimes there is no option if personal injury or damage to the component is to be avoided. Where required, service tools are referred to in the relevant procedure.

Service tools can usually only be purchased from a motorcycle dealer and are identified by a part number. Some of the commonly-used tools, such as rotor pullers, are available in aftermarket form from mail-order motorcycle tool and accessory suppliers.

Maintenance and minor repair tools

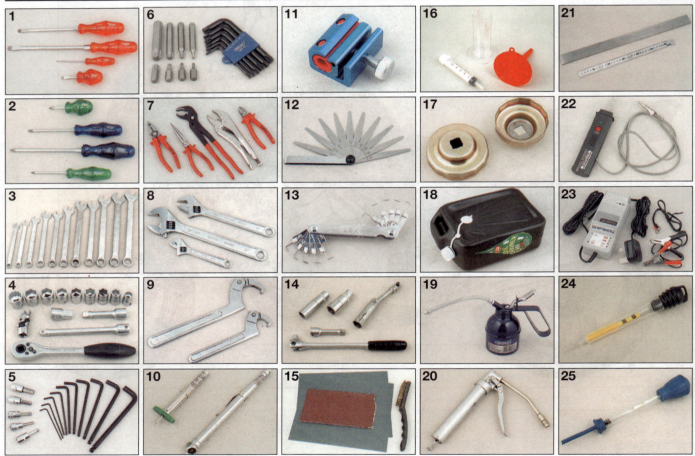

1 Set of flat-bladed screwdrivers
2 Set of Phillips head screwdrivers
3 Combination open-end and ring spanners
4 Socket set (3/8 inch or 1/2 inch drive)
5 Set of Allen keys or bits
6 Set of Torx keys or bits
7 Pliers, cutters and self-locking grips (Mole grips)
8 Adjustable spanners
9 C-spanners
10 Tread depth gauge and tyre pressure gauge
11 Cable oiler clamp
12 Feeler gauges
13 Spark plug gap measuring tool
14 Spark plug spanner or deep plug sockets
15 Wire brush and emery paper
16 Calibrated syringe, measuring vessel and funnel
17 Oil filter adapters
18 Oil drainer can or tray
19 Pump type oil can
20 Grease gun
21 Straight-edge and steel rule
22 Continuity tester
23 Battery charger
24 Hydrometer (for battery specific gravity check)
25 Anti-freeze tester (for liquid-cooled engines)

Tools and Workshop Tips REF•3

Repair and overhaul tools

1 Torque wrench (small and mid-ranges)
2 Conventional, plastic or soft-faced hammers
3 Impact driver set
4 Vernier gauge
5 Circlip pliers (internal and external, or combination)
6 Set of cold chisels and punches
7 Selection of pullers
8 Breaker bars
9 Chain breaking/riveting tool set
10 Wire stripper and crimper tool
11 Multimeter (measures amps, volts and ohms)
12 Stroboscope (for dynamic timing checks)
13 Hose clamp (wingnut type shown)
14 Clutch holding tool
15 One-man brake/clutch bleeder kit

Specialist tools

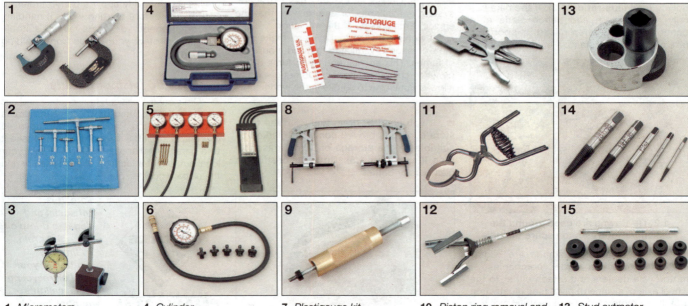

1 Micrometers (external type)
2 Telescoping gauges
3 Dial gauge
4 Cylinder compression gauge
5 Vacuum gauges (left) or manometer (right)
6 Oil pressure gauge
7 Plastigauge kit
8 Valve spring compressor (4-stroke engines)
9 Piston pin drawbolt tool
10 Piston ring removal and installation tool
11 Piston ring clamp
12 Cylinder bore hone (stone type shown)
13 Stud extractor
14 Screw extractor set
15 Bearing driver set

REF•4 Tools and Workshop Tips

1 Workshop equipment and facilities

The workbench

● Work is made much easier by raising the bike up on a ramp - components are much more accessible if raised to waist level. The hydraulic or pneumatic types seen in the dealer's workshop are a sound investment if you undertake a lot of repairs or overhauls **(see illustration 1.1)**.

1.1 Hydraulic motorcycle ramp

● If raised off ground level, the bike must be supported on the ramp to avoid it falling. Most ramps incorporate a front wheel locating clamp which can be adjusted to suit different diameter wheels. When tightening the clamp, take care not to mark the wheel rim or damage the tyre - use wood blocks on each side to prevent this.

● Secure the bike to the ramp using tie-downs **(see illustration 1.2)**. If the bike has only a sidestand, and hence leans at a dangerous angle when raised, support the bike on an auxiliary stand.

1.2 Tie-downs are used around the passenger footrests to secure the bike

● Auxiliary (paddock) stands are widely available from mail order companies or motorcycle dealers and attach either to the wheel axle or swingarm pivot **(see illustration 1.3)**. If the motorcycle has a centrestand, you can support it under the crankcase to prevent it toppling whilst either wheel is removed **(see illustration 1.4)**.

1.3 This auxiliary stand attaches to the swingarm pivot

1.4 Always use a block of wood between the engine and jack head when supporting the engine in this way

Fumes and fire

● Refer to the Safety first! page at the beginning of the manual for full details. Make sure your workshop is equipped with a fire extinguisher suitable for fuel-related fires (Class B fire - flammable liquids) - it is not sufficient to have a water-filled extinguisher.

● Always ensure adequate ventilation is available. Unless an exhaust gas extraction system is available for use, ensure that the engine is run outside of the workshop.

● If working on the fuel system, make sure the workshop is ventilated to avoid a build-up of fumes. This applies equally to fume build-up when charging a battery. Do not smoke or allow anyone else to smoke in the workshop.

Fluids

● If you need to drain fuel from the tank, store it in an approved container marked as suitable for the storage of petrol (gasoline) **(see illustration 1.5)**. Do not store fuel in glass jars or bottles.

1.5 Use an approved can only for storing petrol (gasoline)

● Use proprietary engine degreasers or solvents which have a high flash-point, such as paraffin (kerosene), for cleaning off oil, grease and dirt - never use petrol (gasoline) for cleaning. Wear rubber gloves when handling solvent and engine degreaser. The fumes from certain solvents can be dangerous - always work in a well-ventilated area.

Dust, eye and hand protection

● Protect your lungs from inhalation of dust particles by wearing a filtering mask over the nose and mouth. Many frictional materials still contain asbestos which is dangerous to your health. Protect your eyes from spouts of liquid and sprung components by wearing a pair of protective goggles **(see illustration 1.6)**.

1.6 A fire extinguisher, goggles, mask and protective gloves should be at hand in the workshop

● Protect your hands from contact with solvents, fuel and oils by wearing rubber gloves. Alternatively apply a barrier cream to your hands before starting work. If handling hot components or fluids, wear suitable gloves to protect your hands from scalding and burns.

What to do with old fluids

● Old cleaning solvent, fuel, coolant and oils should not be poured down domestic drains or onto the ground. Package the fluid up in old oil containers, label it accordingly, and take it to a garage or disposal facility. Contact your local authority for location of such sites or ring the oil care hotline.

Note: It is antisocial and illegal to dump oil down the drain. To find the location of your local oil recycling bank, call this number free.

0800 66 33 66

In the USA, note that any oil supplier must accept used oil for recycling.

Tools and Workshop Tips

2 Fasteners -
screws, bolts and nuts

Fastener types and applications

Bolts and screws

● Fastener head types are either of hexagonal, Torx or splined design, with internal and external versions of each type (see illustrations 2.1 and 2.2); splined head fasteners are not in common use on motorcycles. The conventional slotted or Phillips head design is used for certain screws. Bolt or screw length is always measured from the underside of the head to the end of the item (see illustration 2.11).

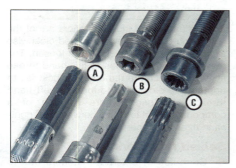

2.1 Internal hexagon/Allen (A), Torx (B) and splined (C) fasteners, with corresponding bits

2.2 External Torx (A), splined (B) and hexagon (C) fasteners, with corresponding sockets

● Certain fasteners on the motorcycle have a tensile marking on their heads, the higher the marking the stronger the fastener. High tensile fasteners generally carry a 10 or higher marking. Never replace a high tensile fastener with one of a lower tensile strength.

Washers (see illustration 2.3)

● Plain washers are used between a fastener head and a component to prevent damage to the component or to spread the load when torque is applied. Plain washers can also be used as spacers or shims in certain assemblies. Copper or aluminium plain washers are often used as sealing washers on drain plugs.

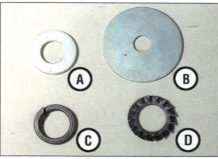

2.3 Plain washer (A), penny washer (B), spring washer (C) and serrated washer (D)

● The split-ring spring washer works by applying axial tension between the fastener head and component. If flattened, it is fatigued and must be renewed. If a plain (flat) washer is used on the fastener, position the spring washer between the fastener and the plain washer.
● Serrated star type washers dig into the fastener and component faces, preventing loosening. They are often used on electrical earth (ground) connections to the frame.
● Cone type washers (sometimes called Belleville) are conical and when tightened apply axial tension between the fastener head and component. They must be installed with the dished side against the component and often carry an OUTSIDE marking on their outer face. If flattened, they are fatigued and must be renewed.
● Tab washers are used to lock plain nuts or bolts on a shaft. A portion of the tab washer is bent up hard against one flat of the nut or bolt to prevent it loosening. Due to the tab washer being deformed in use, a new tab washer should be used every time it is disturbed.
● Wave washers are used to take up endfloat on a shaft. They provide light springing and prevent excessive side-to-side play of a component. Can be found on rocker arm shafts.

Nuts and split pins

● Conventional plain nuts are usually six-sided (see illustration 2.4). They are sized by thread diameter and pitch. High tensile nuts carry a number on one end to denote their tensile strength.

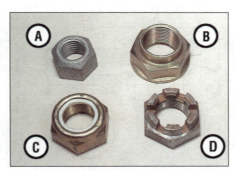

2.4 Plain nut (A), shouldered locknut (B), nylon insert nut (C) and castellated nut (D)

● Self-locking nuts either have a nylon insert, or two spring metal tabs, or a shoulder which is staked into a groove in the shaft - their advantage over conventional plain nuts is a resistance to loosening due to vibration. The nylon insert type can be used a number of times, but must be renewed when the friction of the nylon insert is reduced, ie when the nut spins freely on the shaft. The spring tab type can be reused unless the tabs are damaged. The shouldered type must be renewed every time it is disturbed.
● Split pins (cotter pins) are used to lock a castellated nut to a shaft or to prevent slackening of a plain nut. Common applications are wheel axles and brake torque arms. Because the split pin arms are deformed to lock around the nut a new split pin must always be used on installation - always fit the correct size split pin which will fit snugly in the shaft hole. Make sure the split pin arms are correctly located around the nut (see illustrations 2.5 and 2.6).

2.5 Bend split pin (cotter pin) arms as shown (arrows) to secure a castellated nut

2.6 Bend split pin (cotter pin) arms as shown to secure a plain nut

Caution: *If the castellated nut slots do not align with the shaft hole after tightening to the torque setting, tighten the nut until the next slot aligns with the hole - never slacken the nut to align its slot.*

● R-pins (shaped like the letter R), or slip pins as they are sometimes called, are sprung and can be reused if they are otherwise in good condition. Always install R-pins with their closed end facing forwards (see illustration 2.7).

REF•6 Tools and Workshop Tips

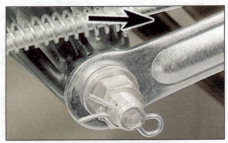

2.7 Correct fitting of R-pin. Arrow indicates forward direction

Circlips (see illustration 2.8)

● Circlips (sometimes called snap-rings) are used to retain components on a shaft or in a housing and have corresponding external or internal ears to permit removal. Parallel-sided (machined) circlips can be installed either way round in their groove, whereas stamped circlips (which have a chamfered edge on one face) must be installed with the chamfer facing away from the direction of thrust load **(see illustration 2.9)**.

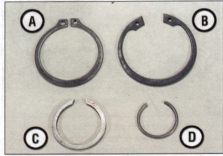

2.8 External stamped circlip (A), internal stamped circlip (B), machined circlip (C) and wire circlip (D)

● Always use circlip pliers to remove and install circlips; expand or compress them just enough to remove them. After installation, rotate the circlip in its groove to ensure it is securely seated. If installing a circlip on a splined shaft, always align its opening with a shaft channel to ensure the circlip ends are well supported and unlikely to catch **(see illustration 2.10)**.

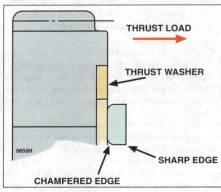

2.9 Correct fitting of a stamped circlip

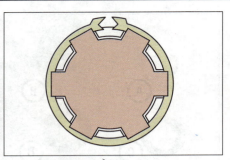

2.10 Align circlip opening with shaft channel

● Circlips can wear due to the thrust of components and become loose in their grooves, with the subsequent danger of becoming dislodged in operation. For this reason, renewal is advised every time a circlip is disturbed.

● Wire circlips are commonly used as piston pin retaining clips. If a removal tang is provided, long-nosed pliers can be used to dislodge them, otherwise careful use of a small flat-bladed screwdriver is necessary. Wire circlips should be renewed every time they are disturbed.

Thread diameter and pitch

● Diameter of a male thread (screw, bolt or stud) is the outside diameter of the threaded portion **(see illustration 2.11)**. Most motorcycle manufacturers use the ISO (International Standards Organisation) metric system expressed in millimetres, eg M6 refers to a 6 mm diameter thread. Sizing is the same for nuts, except that the thread diameter is measured across the valleys of the nut.

● Pitch is the distance between the peaks of the thread **(see illustration 2.11)**. It is expressed in millimetres, thus a common bolt size may be expressed as 6.0 x 1.0 mm (6 mm thread diameter and 1 mm pitch). Generally pitch increases in proportion to thread diameter, although there are always exceptions.

● Thread diameter and pitch are related for conventional fastener applications and the accompanying table can be used as a guide. Additionally, the AF (Across Flats), spanner or socket size dimension of the bolt or nut **(see illustration 2.11)** is linked to thread and pitch specification. Thread pitch can be measured with a thread gauge **(see illustration 2.12)**.

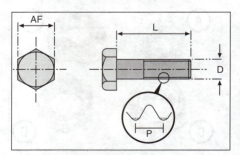

2.11 Fastener length (L), thread diameter (D), thread pitch (P) and head size (AF)

2.12 Using a thread gauge to measure pitch

AF size	Thread diameter x pitch (mm)
8 mm	M5 x 0.8
8 mm	M6 x 1.0
10 mm	M6 x 1.0
12 mm	M8 x 1.25
14 mm	M10 x 1.25
17 mm	M12 x 1.25

● The threads of most fasteners are of the right-hand type, ie they are turned clockwise to tighten and anti-clockwise to loosen. The reverse situation applies to left-hand thread fasteners, which are turned anti-clockwise to tighten and clockwise to loosen. Left-hand threads are used where rotation of a component might loosen a conventional right-hand thread fastener.

Seized fasteners

● Corrosion of external fasteners due to water or reaction between two dissimilar metals can occur over a period of time. It will build up sooner in wet conditions or in countries where salt is used on the roads during the winter. If a fastener is severely corroded it is likely that normal methods of removal will fail and result in its head being ruined. When you attempt removal, the fastener thread should be heard to crack free and unscrew easily - if it doesn't, stop there before damaging something.

● A smart tap on the head of the fastener will often succeed in breaking free corrosion which has occurred in the threads **(see illustration 2.13)**.

● An aerosol penetrating fluid (such as WD-40) applied the night beforehand may work its way down into the thread and ease removal. Depending on the location, you may be able to make up a Plasticine well around the fastener head and fill it with penetrating fluid.

2.13 A sharp tap on the head of a fastener will often break free a corroded thread

Tools and Workshop Tips

- If you are working on an engine internal component, corrosion will most likely not be a problem due to the well lubricated environment. However, components can be very tight and an impact driver is a useful tool in freeing them (see illustration 2.14).

2.14 Using an impact driver to free a fastener

- Where corrosion has occurred between dissimilar metals (eg steel and aluminium alloy), the application of heat to the fastener head will create a disproportionate expansion rate between the two metals and break the seizure caused by the corrosion. Whether heat can be applied depends on the location of the fastener - any surrounding components likely to be damaged must first be removed (see illustration 2.15). Heat can be applied using a paint stripper heat gun or clothes iron, or by immersing the component in boiling water - wear protective gloves to prevent scalding or burns to the hands.

2.15 Using heat to free a seized fastener

- As a last resort, it is possible to use a hammer and cold chisel to work the fastener head unscrewed (see illustration 2.16). This will damage the fastener, but more importantly extreme care must be taken not to damage the surrounding component.

> **Caution:** Remember that the component being secured is generally of more value than the bolt, nut or screw - when the fastener is freed, do not unscrew it with force, instead work the fastener back and forth when resistance is felt to prevent thread damage.

2.16 Using a hammer and chisel to free a seized fastener

Broken fasteners and damaged heads

- If the shank of a broken bolt or screw is accessible you can grip it with self-locking grips. The knurled wheel type stud extractor tool or self-gripping stud puller tool is particularly useful for removing the long studs which screw into the cylinder mouth surface of the crankcase or bolts and screws from which the head has broken off (see illustration 2.17). Studs can also be removed by locking two nuts together on the threaded end of the stud and using a spanner on the lower nut (see illustration 2.18).

2.17 Using a stud extractor tool to remove a broken crankcase stud

2.18 Two nuts can be locked together to unscrew a stud from a component

- A bolt or screw which has broken off below or level with the casing must be extracted using a screw extractor set. Centre punch the fastener to centralise the drill bit, then drill a hole in the fastener (see illustration 2.19). Select a drill bit which is approximately half to three-quarters the

2.19 When using a screw extractor, first drill a hole in the fastener ...

diameter of the fastener and drill to a depth which will accommodate the extractor. Use the largest size extractor possible, but avoid leaving too small a wall thickness otherwise the extractor will merely force the fastener walls outwards wedging it in the casing thread.

- If a spiral type extractor is used, thread it anti-clockwise into the fastener. As it is screwed in, it will grip the fastener and unscrew it from the casing (see illustration 2.20).

2.20 ... then thread the extractor anti-clockwise into the fastener

- If a taper type extractor is used, tap it into the fastener so that it is firmly wedged in place. Unscrew the extractor (anti-clockwise) to draw the fastener out.

>  **Warning: Stud extractors are very hard and may break off in the fastener if care is not taken - ask an engineer about spark erosion if this happens.**

- Alternatively, the broken bolt/screw can be drilled out and the hole retapped for an oversize bolt/screw or a diamond-section thread insert. It is essential that the drilling is carried out squarely and to the correct depth, otherwise the casing may be ruined - if in doubt, entrust the work to an engineer.
- Bolts and nuts with rounded corners cause the correct size spanner or socket to slip when force is applied. Of the types of spanner/socket available always use a six-point type rather than an eight or twelve-point type - better grip

REF•8 Tools and Workshop Tips

2.21 Comparison of surface drive ring spanner (left) with 12-point type (right)

is obtained. Surface drive spanners grip the middle of the hex flats, rather than the corners, and are thus good in cases of damaged heads **(see illustration 2.21).**

● Slotted-head or Phillips-head screws are often damaged by the use of the wrong size screwdriver. Allen-head and Torx-head screws are much less likely to sustain damage. If enough of the screw head is exposed you can use a hacksaw to cut a slot in its head and then use a conventional flat-bladed screwdriver to remove it. Alternatively use a hammer and cold chisel to tap the head of the fastener around to slacken it. Always replace damaged fasteners with new ones, preferably Torx or Allen-head type.

HAYNES HiNT

A dab of valve grinding compound between the screw head and screwdriver tip will often give a good grip.

Thread repair

● Threads (particularly those in aluminium alloy components) can be damaged by overtightening, being assembled with dirt in the threads, or from a component working loose and vibrating. Eventually the thread will fail completely, and it will be impossible to tighten the fastener.

● If a thread is damaged or clogged with old locking compound it can be renovated with a thread repair tool (thread chaser) **(see illustrations 2.22 and 2.23);** special thread

2.22 A thread repair tool being used to correct an internal thread

2.23 A thread repair tool being used to correct an external thread

chasers are available for spark plug hole threads. The tool will not cut a new thread, but clean and true the original thread. Make sure that you use the correct diameter and pitch tool. Similarly, external threads can be cleaned up with a die or a thread restorer file **(see illustration 2.24).**

2.24 Using a thread restorer file

● It is possible to drill out the old thread and retap the component to the next thread size. This will work where there is enough surrounding material and a new bolt or screw can be obtained. Sometimes, however, this is not possible - such as where the bolt/screw passes through another component which must also be suitably modified, also in cases where a spark plug or oil drain plug cannot be obtained in a larger diameter thread size.

● The diamond-section thread insert (often known by its popular trade name of Heli-Coil) is a simple and effective method of renewing the thread and retaining the original size. A kit can be purchased which contains the tap, insert and installing tool **(see illustration 2.25).** Drill out the damaged thread with the size drill specified **(see illustration 2.26).** Carefully retap the thread **(see illustration 2.27).** Install the

2.25 Obtain a thread insert kit to suit the thread diameter and pitch required

2.26 To install a thread insert, first drill out the original thread . . .

2.27 . . . tap a new thread . . .

2.28 . . . fit insert on the installing tool . . .

2.29 . . . and thread into the component . . .

2.30 . . . break off the tang when complete

insert on the installing tool and thread it slowly into place using a light downward pressure **(see illustrations 2.28 and 2.29).** When positioned between a 1/4 and 1/2 turn below the surface withdraw the installing tool and use the break-off tool to press down on the tang, breaking it off **(see illustration 2.30).**

● There are epoxy thread repair kits on the market which can rebuild stripped internal threads, although this repair should not be used on high load-bearing components.

Tools and Workshop Tips   REF•9

Thread locking and sealing compounds

● Locking compounds are used in locations where the fastener is prone to loosening due to vibration or on important safety-related items which might cause loss of control of the motorcycle if they fail. It is also used where important fasteners cannot be secured by other means such as lockwashers or split pins.

● Before applying locking compound, make sure that the threads (internal and external) are clean and dry with all old compound removed. Select a compound to suit the component being secured - a non-permanent general locking and sealing type is suitable for most applications, but a high strength type is needed for permanent fixing of studs in castings. Apply a drop or two of the compound to the first few threads of the fastener, then thread it into place and tighten to the specified torque. Do not apply excessive thread locking compound otherwise the thread may be damaged on subsequent removal.

● Certain fasteners are impregnated with a dry film type coating of locking compound on their threads. Always renew this type of fastener if disturbed.

● Anti-seize compounds, such as copper-based greases, can be applied to protect threads from seizure due to extreme heat and corrosion. A common instance is spark plug threads and exhaust system fasteners.

3 Measuring tools and gauges

Feeler gauges

● Feeler gauges (or blades) are used for measuring small gaps and clearances **(see illustration 3.1)**. They can also be used to measure endfloat (sideplay) of a component on a shaft where access is not possible with a dial gauge.

● Feeler gauge sets should be treated with care and not bent or damaged. They are etched with their size on one face. Keep them clean and very lightly oiled to prevent corrosion build-up.

3.1 Feeler gauges are used for measuring small gaps and clearances - thickness is marked on one face of gauge

● When measuring a clearance, select a gauge which is a light sliding fit between the two components. You may need to use two gauges together to measure the clearance accurately.

Micrometers

● A micrometer is a precision tool capable of measuring to 0.01 or 0.001 of a millimetre. It should always be stored in its case and not in the general toolbox. It must be kept clean and never dropped, otherwise its frame or measuring anvils could be distorted resulting in inaccurate readings.

● External micrometers are used for measuring outside diameters of components and have many more applications than internal micrometers. Micrometers are available in different size ranges, eg 0 to 25 mm, 25 to 50 mm, and upwards in 25 mm steps; some large micrometers have interchangeable anvils to allow a range of measurements to be taken. Generally the largest precision measurement you are likely to take on a motorcycle is the piston diameter.

● Internal micrometers (or bore micrometers) are used for measuring inside diameters, such as valve guides and cylinder bores. Telescoping gauges and small hole gauges are used in conjunction with an external micro-meter, whereas the more expensive internal micrometers have their own measuring device.

External micrometer

Note: *The conventional analogue type instrument is described. Although much easier to read, digital micrometers are considerably more expensive.*

● Always check the calibration of the micrometer before use. With the anvils closed (0 to 25 mm type) or set over a test gauge (for

3.2 Check micrometer calibration before use

the larger types) the scale should read zero **(see illustration 3.2)**; make sure that the anvils (and test piece) are clean first. Any discrepancy can be adjusted by referring to the instructions supplied with the tool. Remember that the micrometer is a precision measuring tool - don't force the anvils closed, use the ratchet (4) on the end of the micrometer to close it. In this way, a measured force is always applied.

● To use, first make sure that the item being measured is clean. Place the anvil of the micrometer (1) against the item and use the thimble (2) to bring the spindle (3) lightly into contact with the other side of the item **(see illustration 3.3)**. Don't tighten the thimble down because this will damage the micrometer - instead use the ratchet (4) on the end of the micrometer. The ratchet mechanism applies a measured force preventing damage to the instrument.

● The micrometer is read by referring to the linear scale on the sleeve and the annular scale on the thimble. Read off the sleeve first to obtain the base measurement, then add the fine measurement from the thimble to obtain the overall reading. The linear scale on the sleeve represents the measuring range of the micrometer (eg 0 to 25 mm). The annular scale

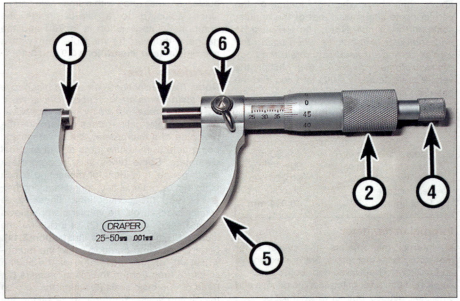

3.3 Micrometer component parts

1	Anvil	3	Spindle	5	Frame
2	Thimble	4	Ratchet	6	Locking lever

REF•10 Tools and Workshop Tips

on the thimble will be in graduations of 0.01 mm (or as marked on the frame) - one full revolution of the thimble will move 0.5 mm on the linear scale. Take the reading where the datum line on the sleeve intersects the thimble's scale. Always position the eye directly above the scale otherwise an inaccurate reading will result.

In the example shown the item measures 2.95 mm **(see illustration 3.4)**:

Linear scale	2.00 mm
Linear scale	0.50 mm
Annular scale	0.45 mm
Total figure	**2.95 mm**

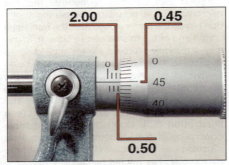

3.4 Micrometer reading of 2.95 mm

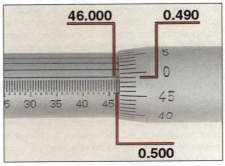

3.5 Micrometer reading of 46.99 mm on linear and annular scales . . .

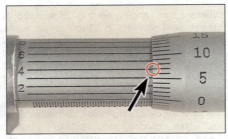

3.6 . . . and 0.004 mm on vernier scale

3.7 Expand the telescoping gauge in the bore, lock its position . . .

3.8 . . . then measure the gauge with a micrometer

3.9 Expand the small hole gauge in the bore, lock its position . . .

3.10 . . . then measure the gauge with a micrometer

Most micrometers have a locking lever (6) on the frame to hold the setting in place, allowing the item to be removed from the micrometer.
● Some micrometers have a vernier scale on their sleeve, providing an even finer measurement to be taken, in 0.001 increments of a millimetre. Take the sleeve and thimble measurement as described above, then check which graduation on the vernier scale aligns with that of the annular scale on the thimble **Note:** *The eye must be perpendicular to the scale when taking the vernier reading - if necessary rotate the body of the micrometer to ensure this.* Multiply the vernier scale figure by 0.001 and add it to the base and fine measurement figures.

In the example shown the item measures 46.994 mm **(see illustrations 3.5 and 3.6)**:

Linear scale (base)	46.000 mm
Linear scale (base)	00.500 mm
Annular scale (fine)	00.490 mm
Vernier scale	00.004 mm
Total figure	**46.994 mm**

Internal micrometer

● Internal micrometers are available for measuring bore diameters, but are expensive and unlikely to be available for home use. It is suggested that a set of telescoping gauges and small hole gauges, both of which must be used with an external micrometer, will suffice for taking internal measurements on a motorcycle.
● Telescoping gauges can be used to measure internal diameters of components. Select a gauge with the correct size range, make sure its ends are clean and insert it into the bore. Expand the gauge, then lock its position and withdraw it from the bore **(see illustration 3.7)**. Measure across the gauge ends with a micrometer **(see illustration 3.8)**.
● Very small diameter bores (such as valve guides) are measured with a small hole gauge. Once adjusted to a slip-fit inside the component, its position is locked and the gauge withdrawn for measurement with a micrometer **(see illustrations 3.9 and 3.10)**.

Vernier caliper

Note: *The conventional linear and dial gauge type instruments are described. Digital types are easier to read, but are far more expensive.*
● The vernier caliper does not provide the precision of a micrometer, but is versatile in being able to measure internal and external diameters. Some types also incorporate a depth gauge. It is ideal for measuring clutch plate friction material and spring free lengths.
● To use the conventional linear scale vernier, slacken off the vernier clamp screws (1) and set its jaws over (2), or inside (3), the item to be measured **(see illustration 3.11)**. Slide the jaw into contact, using the thumbwheel (4) for fine movement of the sliding scale (5) then tighten the clamp screws (1). Read off the main scale (6) where the zero on the sliding scale (5) intersects it, taking the whole number to the left of the zero; this provides the base measurement. View along the sliding scale and select the division which lines up exactly with any of the divisions on the main scale, noting that the divisions usually represents 0.02 of a millimetre. Add this fine measurement to the base measurement to obtain the total reading.

Tools and Workshop Tips   REF•11

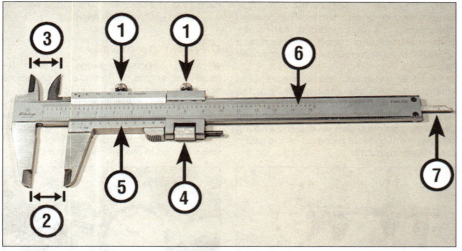

3.11 Vernier component parts (linear gauge)

1 Clamp screws	3 Internal jaws	5 Sliding scale	7 Depth gauge
2 External jaws	4 Thumbwheel	6 Main scale	

In the example shown the item measures 55.92 mm **(see illustration 3.12)**:

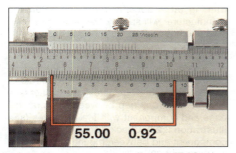

3.12 Vernier gauge reading of 55.92 mm

Base measurement	55.00 mm
Fine measurement	00.92 mm
Total figure	**55.92 mm**

● Some vernier calipers are equipped with a dial gauge for fine measurement. Before use, check that the jaws are clean, then close them fully and check that the dial gauge reads zero. If necessary adjust the gauge ring accordingly. Slacken the vernier clamp screw (1) and set its jaws over (2), or inside (3), the item to be measured **(see illustration 3.13)**. Slide the jaws into contact, using the thumbwheel (4) for fine movement. Read off the main scale (5) where the edge of the sliding scale (6) intersects it, taking the whole number to the left of the zero; this provides the base measurement. Read off the needle position on the dial gauge (7) scale to provide the fine measurement; each division represents 0.05 of a millimetre. Add this fine measurement to the base measurement to obtain the total reading.

In the example shown the item measures 55.95 mm **(see illustration 3.14)**:

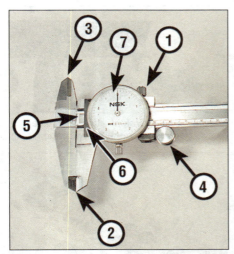

3.13 Vernier component parts (dial gauge)

1 Clamp screw	5 Main scale
2 External jaws	6 Sliding scale
3 Internal jaws	7 Dial gauge
4 Thumbwheel	

Base measurement	55.00 mm
Fine measurement	00.95 mm
Total figure	**55.95 mm**

3.14 Vernier gauge reading of 55.95 mm

Plastigauge

● Plastigauge is a plastic material which can be compressed between two surfaces to measure the oil clearance between them. The width of the compressed Plastigauge is measured against a calibrated scale to determine the clearance.

● Common uses of Plastigauge are for measuring the clearance between crankshaft journal and main bearing inserts, between crankshaft journal and big-end bearing inserts, and between camshaft and bearing surfaces. The following example describes big-end oil clearance measurement.

● Handle the Plastigauge material carefully to prevent distortion. Using a sharp knife, cut a length which corresponds with the width of the bearing being measured and place it carefully across the journal so that it is parallel with the shaft **(see illustration 3.15)**. Carefully install both bearing shells and the connecting rod. Without rotating the rod on the journal tighten its bolts or nuts (as applicable) to the specified torque. The connecting rod and bearings are then disassembled and the crushed Plastigauge examined.

3.15 Plastigauge placed across shaft journal

● Using the scale provided in the Plastigauge kit, measure the width of the material to determine the oil clearance **(see illustration 3.16)**. Always remove all traces of Plastigauge after use using your fingernails.

Caution: Arriving at the correct clearance demands that the assembly is torqued correctly, according to the settings and sequence (where applicable) provided by the motorcycle manufacturer.

3.16 Measuring the width of the crushed Plastigauge

REF•12 Tools and Workshop Tips

Dial gauge or DTI (Dial Test Indicator)

● A dial gauge can be used to accurately measure small amounts of movement. Typical uses are measuring shaft runout or shaft endfloat (sideplay) and setting piston position for ignition timing on two-strokes. A dial gauge set usually comes with a range of different probes and adapters and mounting equipment.

● The gauge needle must point to zero when at rest. Rotate the ring around its periphery to zero the gauge.

● Check that the gauge is capable of reading the extent of movement in the work. Most gauges have a small dial set in the face which records whole millimetres of movement as well as the fine scale around the face periphery which is calibrated in 0.01 mm divisions. Read off the small dial first to obtain the base measurement, then add the measurement from the fine scale to obtain the total reading.

In the example shown the gauge reads 1.48 mm (see illustration 3.17):

Base measurement	1.00 mm
Fine measurement	0.48 mm
Total figure	**1.48 mm**

3.17 Dial gauge reading of 1.48 mm

● If measuring shaft runout, the shaft must be supported in vee-blocks and the gauge mounted on a stand perpendicular to the shaft. Rest the tip of the gauge against the centre of the shaft and rotate the shaft slowly whilst watching the gauge reading (see illustration 3.18). Take several measurements along the length of the shaft and record the maximum gauge reading as the amount of runout in the shaft. **Note:** *The reading obtained will be total runout at that point - some manufacturers specify that the runout figure is halved to compare with their specified runout limit.*

3.18 Using a dial gauge to measure shaft runout

● Endfloat (sideplay) measurement requires that the gauge is mounted securely to the surrounding component with its probe touching the end of the shaft. Using hand pressure, push and pull on the shaft noting the maximum endfloat recorded on the gauge (see illustration 3.19).

3.19 Using a dial gauge to measure shaft endfloat

● A dial gauge with suitable adapters can be used to determine piston position BTDC on two-stroke engines for the purposes of ignition timing. The gauge, adapter and suitable length probe are installed in the place of the spark plug and the gauge zeroed at TDC. If the piston position is specified as 1.14 mm BTDC, rotate the engine back to 2.00 mm BTDC, then slowly forwards to 1.14 mm BTDC.

Cylinder compression gauges

● A compression gauge is used for measuring cylinder compression. Either the rubber-cone type or the threaded adapter type can be used. The latter is preferred to ensure a perfect seal against the cylinder head. A 0 to 300 psi (0 to 20 Bar) type gauge (for petrol/gasoline engines) will be suitable for motorcycles.

● The spark plug is removed and the gauge either held hard against the cylinder head (cone type) or the gauge adapter screwed into the cylinder head (threaded type) (see illustration 3.20). Cylinder compression is measured with the engine turning over, but not running - carry out the compression test as described in *Fault Finding Equipment*. The gauge will hold the reading until manually released.

3.20 Using a rubber-cone type cylinder compression gauge

Oil pressure gauge

● An oil pressure gauge is used for measuring engine oil pressure. Most gauges come with a set of adapters to fit the thread of the take-off point (see illustration 3.21). If the take-off point specified by the motorcycle manufacturer is an external oil pipe union, make sure that the specified replacement union is used to prevent oil starvation.

3.21 Oil pressure gauge and take-off point adapter (arrow)

● Oil pressure is measured with the engine running (at a specific rpm) and often the manufacturer will specify pressure limits for a cold and hot engine.

Straight-edge and surface plate

● If checking the gasket face of a component for warpage, place a steel rule or precision straight-edge across the gasket face and measure any gap between the straight-edge and component with feeler gauges (see illustration 3.22). Check diagonally across the component and between mounting holes (see illustration 3.23).

3.22 Use a straight-edge and feeler gauges to check for warpage

3.23 Check for warpage in these directions

Tools and Workshop Tips　REF•13

- Checking individual components for warpage, such as clutch plain (metal) plates, requires a perfectly flat plate or piece or plate glass and feeler gauges.

4 Torque and leverage

What is torque?

- Torque describes the twisting force about a shaft. The amount of torque applied is determined by the distance from the centre of the shaft to the end of the lever and the amount of force being applied to the end of the lever; distance multiplied by force equals torque.
- The manufacturer applies a measured torque to a bolt or nut to ensure that it will not slacken in use and to hold two components securely together without movement in the joint. The actual torque setting depends on the thread size, bolt or nut material and the composition of the components being held.
- Too little torque may cause the fastener to loosen due to vibration, whereas too much torque will distort the joint faces of the component or cause the fastener to shear off. Always stick to the specified torque setting.

Using a torque wrench

- Check the calibration of the torque wrench and make sure it has a suitable range for the job. Torque wrenches are available in Nm (Newton-metres), kgf m (kilograms-force metre), lbf ft (pounds-feet), lbf in (inch-pounds). Do not confuse lbf ft with lbf in.
- Adjust the tool to the desired torque on the scale (see illustration 4.1). If your torque wrench is not calibrated in the units specified, carefully convert the figure (see *Conversion Factors*). A manufacturer sometimes gives a torque setting as a range (8 to 10 Nm) rather than a single figure - in this case set the tool midway between the two settings. The same torque may be expressed as 9 Nm ± 1 Nm. Some torque wrenches have a method of locking the setting so that it isn't inadvertently altered during use.

- Install the bolts/nuts in their correct location and secure them lightly. Their threads must be clean and free of any old locking compound. Unless specified the threads and flange should be dry - oiled threads are necessary in certain circumstances and the manufacturer will take this into account in the specified torque figure. Similarly, the manufacturer may also specify the application of thread-locking compound.
- Tighten the fasteners in the specified sequence until the torque wrench clicks, indicating that the torque setting has been reached. Apply the torque again to double-check the setting. Where different thread diameter fasteners secure the component, as a rule tighten the larger diameter ones first.
- When the torque wrench has been finished with, release the lock (where applicable) and fully back off its setting to zero - do not leave the torque wrench tensioned. Also, do not use a torque wrench for slackening a fastener.

Angle-tightening

- Manufacturers often specify a figure in degrees for final tightening of a fastener. This usually follows tightening to a specific torque setting.
- A degree disc can be set and attached to the socket (see illustration 4.2) or a protractor can be used to mark the angle of movement on the bolt/nut head and the surrounding casting (see illustration 4.3).

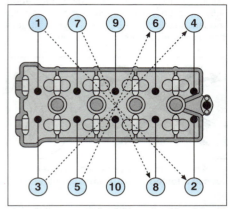

4.2 Angle tightening can be accomplished with a torque-angle gauge . . .

4.1 Set the torque wrench index mark to the setting required, in this case 12 Nm

4.3 . . . or by marking the angle on the surrounding component

Loosening sequences

- Where more than one bolt/nut secures a component, loosen each fastener evenly a little at a time. In this way, not all the stress of the joint is held by one fastener and the components are not likely to distort.
- If a tightening sequence is provided, work in the REVERSE of this, but if not, work from the outside in, in a criss-cross sequence (see illustration 4.4).

4.4 When slackening, work from the outside inwards

Tightening sequences

- If a component is held by more than one fastener it is important that the retaining bolts/nuts are tightened evenly to prevent uneven stress build-up and distortion of sealing faces. This is especially important on high-compression joints such as the cylinder head.
- A sequence is usually provided by the manufacturer, either in a diagram or actually marked in the casting. If not, always start in the centre and work outwards in a criss-cross pattern (see illustration 4.5). Start off by securing all bolts/nuts finger-tight, then set the torque wrench and tighten each fastener by a small amount in sequence until the final torque is reached. By following this practice,

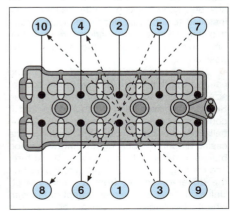

4.5 When tightening, work from the inside outwards

REF•14 Tools and Workshop Tips

the joint will be held evenly and will not be distorted. Important joints, such as the cylinder head and big-end fasteners often have two- or three-stage torque settings.

Applying leverage

● Use tools at the correct angle. Position a socket wrench or spanner on the bolt/nut so that you pull it towards you when loosening. If this can't be done, push the spanner without curling your fingers around it **(see illustration 4.6)** - the spanner may slip or the fastener loosen suddenly, resulting in your fingers being crushed against a component.

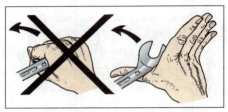

4.6 If you can't pull on the spanner to loosen a fastener, push with your hand open

● Additional leverage is gained by extending the length of the lever. The best way to do this is to use a breaker bar instead of the regular length tool, or to slip a length of tubing over the end of the spanner or socket wrench.
● If additional leverage will not work, the fastener head is either damaged or firmly corroded in place (see *Fasteners*).

5 Bearings

Bearing removal and installation

Drivers and sockets

● Before removing a bearing, always inspect the casing to see which way it must be driven out - some casings will have retaining plates or a cast step. Also check for any identifying markings on the bearing and if installed to a certain depth, measure this at this stage. Some roller bearings are sealed on one side - take note of the original fitted position.
● Bearings can be driven out of a casing using a bearing driver tool (with the correct size head) or a socket of the correct diameter. Select the driver head or socket so that it contacts the outer race of the bearing, not the balls/rollers or inner race. Always support the casing around the bearing housing with wood blocks, otherwise there is a risk of fracture. The bearing is driven out with a few blows on the driver or socket from a heavy mallet. Unless access is severely restricted (as with wheel bearings), a pin-punch is not recommended unless it is moved around the bearing to keep it square in its housing.

● The same equipment can be used to install bearings. Make sure the bearing housing is supported on wood blocks and line up the bearing in its housing. Fit the bearing as noted on removal - generally they are installed with their marked side facing outwards. Tap the bearing squarely into its housing using a driver or socket which bears only on the bearing's outer race - contact with the bearing balls/rollers or inner race will destroy it **(see illustrations 5.1 and 5.2)**.
● Check that the bearing inner race and balls/rollers rotate freely.

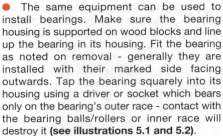

5.1 Using a bearing driver against the bearing's outer race

5.2 Using a large socket against the bearing's outer race

Pullers and slide-hammers

● Where a bearing is pressed on a shaft a puller will be required to extract it **(see illustration 5.3)**. Make sure that the puller clamp or legs fit securely behind the bearing and are unlikely to slip out. If pulling a bearing

5.3 This bearing puller clamps behind the bearing and pressure is applied to the shaft end to draw the bearing off

off a gear shaft for example, you may have to locate the puller behind a gear pinion if there is no access to the race and draw the gear pinion off the shaft as well **(see illustration 5.4)**.

Caution: Ensure that the puller's centre bolt locates securely against the end of the shaft and will not slip when pressure is applied. Also ensure that puller does not damage the shaft end.

5.4 Where no access is available to the rear of the bearing, it is sometimes possible to draw off the adjacent component

● Operate the puller so that its centre bolt exerts pressure on the shaft end and draws the bearing off the shaft.
● When installing the bearing on the shaft, tap only on the bearing's inner race - contact with the balls/rollers or outer race with destroy the bearing. Use a socket or length of tubing as a drift which fits over the shaft end **(see illustration 5.5)**.

5.5 When installing a bearing on a shaft use a piece of tubing which bears only on the bearing's inner race

● Where a bearing locates in a blind hole in a casing, it cannot be driven or pulled out as described above. A slide-hammer with knife-edged bearing puller attachment will be required. The puller attachment passes through the bearing and when tightened expands to fit firmly behind the bearing **(see illustration 5.6)**. By operating the slide-hammer part of the tool the bearing is jarred out of its housing **(see illustration 5.7)**.
● It is possible, if the bearing is of reasonable weight, for it to drop out of its housing if the casing is heated as described opposite. If this

Tools and Workshop Tips   REF•15

5.6 Expand the bearing puller so that it locks behind the bearing . . .

5.7 . . . attach the slide hammer to the bearing puller

method is attempted, first prepare a work surface which will enable the casing to be tapped face down to help dislodge the bearing - a wood surface is ideal since it will not damage the casing's gasket surface. Wearing protective gloves, tap the heated casing several times against the work surface to dislodge the bearing under its own weight **(see illustration 5.8).**

5.8 Tapping a casing face down on wood blocks can often dislodge a bearing

● Bearings can be installed in blind holes using the driver or socket method described above.

Drawbolts

● Where a bearing or bush is set in the eye of a component, such as a suspension linkage arm or connecting rod small-end, removal by drift may damage the component. Furthermore, a rubber bushing in a shock absorber eye cannot successfully be driven out of position. If access is available to a engineering press, the task is straightforward. If not, a drawbolt can be fabricated to extract the bearing or bush.

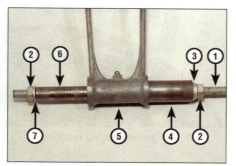

5.9 Drawbolt component parts assembled on a suspension arm

1. Bolt or length of threaded bar
2. Nuts
3. Washer (external diameter greater than tubing internal diameter)
4. Tubing (internal diameter sufficient to accommodate bearing)
5. Suspension arm with bearing
6. Tubing (external diameter slightly smaller than bearing)
7. Washer (external diameter slightly smaller than bearing)

5.10 Drawing the bearing out of the suspension arm

● To extract the bearing/bush you will need a long bolt with nut (or piece of threaded bar with two nuts), a piece of tubing which has an internal diameter larger than the bearing/bush, another piece of tubing which has an external diameter slightly smaller than the bearing/bush, and a selection of washers **(see illustrations 5.9 and 5.10)**. Note that the pieces of tubing must be of the same length, or longer, than the bearing/bush.

● The same kit (without the pieces of tubing) can be used to draw the new bearing/bush back into place **(see illustration 5.11)**.

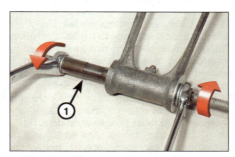

5.11 Installing a new bearing (1) in the suspension arm

Temperature change

● If the bearing's outer race is a tight fit in the casing, the aluminium casing can be heated to release its grip on the bearing. Aluminium will expand at a greater rate than the steel bearing outer race. There are several ways to do this, but avoid any localised extreme heat (such as a blow torch) - aluminium alloy has a low melting point.

● Approved methods of heating a casing are using a domestic oven (heated to 100°C) or immersing the casing in boiling water **(see illustration 5.12)**. Low temperature range localised heat sources such as a paint stripper heat gun or clothes iron can also be used **(see illustration 5.13)**. Alternatively, soak a rag in boiling water, wring it out and wrap it around the bearing housing.

> ⚠ **Warning:** All of these methods require care in use to prevent scalding and burns to the hands. Wear protective gloves when handling hot components.

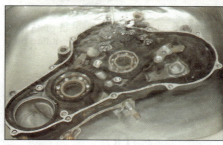

5.12 A casing can be immersed in a sink of boiling water to aid bearing removal

5.13 Using a localised heat source to aid bearing removal

● If heating the whole casing note that plastic components, such as the neutral switch, may suffer - remove them beforehand.

● After heating, remove the bearing as described above. You may find that the expansion is sufficient for the bearing to fall out of the casing under its own weight or with a light tap on the driver or socket.

● If necessary, the casing can be heated to aid bearing installation, and this is sometimes the recommended procedure if the motorcycle manufacturer has designed the housing and bearing fit with this intention.

REF•16 Tools and Workshop Tips

- Installation of bearings can be eased by placing them in a freezer the night before installation. The steel bearing will contract slightly, allowing easy insertion in its housing. This is often useful when installing steering head outer races in the frame.

Bearing types and markings

- Plain shell bearings, ball bearings, needle roller bearings and tapered roller bearings will all be found on motorcycles **(see illustrations 5.14 and 5.15)**. The ball and roller types are usually caged between an inner and outer race, but uncaged variations may be found.

5.14 Shell bearings are either plain or grooved. They are usually identified by colour code (arrow)

5.15 Tapered roller bearing (A), needle roller bearing (B) and ball journal bearing (C)

- Shell bearings (often called inserts) are usually found at the crankshaft main and connecting rod big-end where they are good at coping with high loads. They are made of a phosphor-bronze material and are impregnated with self-lubricating properties.
- Ball bearings and needle roller bearings consist of a steel inner and outer race with the balls or rollers between the races. They require constant lubrication by oil or grease and are good at coping with axial loads. Taper roller bearings consist of rollers set in a tapered cage set on the inner race; the outer race is separate. They are good at coping with axial loads and prevent movement along the shaft - a typical application is in the steering head.
- Bearing manufacturers produce bearings to ISO size standards and stamp one face of the bearing to indicate its internal and external diameter, load capacity and type **(see illustration 5.16)**.
- Metal bushes are usually of phosphor-bronze material. Rubber bushes are used in suspension mounting eyes. Fibre bushes have also been used in suspension pivots.

5.16 Typical bearing marking

Bearing fault finding

- If a bearing outer race has spun in its housing, the housing material will be damaged. You can use a bearing locking compound to bond the outer race in place if damage is not too severe.
- Shell bearings will fail due to damage of their working surface, as a result of lack of lubrication, corrosion or abrasive particles in the oil **(see illustration 5.17)**. Small particles of dirt in the oil may embed in the bearing material whereas larger particles will score the bearing and shaft journal. If a number of short journeys are made, insufficient heat will be generated to drive off condensation which has built up on the bearings.

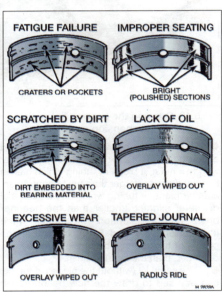

5.17 Typical bearing failures

- Ball and roller bearings will fail due to lack of lubrication or damage to the balls or rollers. Tapered-roller bearings can be damaged by overloading them. Unless the bearing is sealed on both sides, wash it in paraffin (kerosene) to remove all old grease then allow it to dry. Make a visual inspection looking to dented balls or rollers, damaged cages and worn or pitted races **(see illustration 5.18)**.
- A ball bearing can be checked for wear by listening to it when spun. Apply a film of light oil to the bearing and hold it close to the ear - hold the outer race with one hand and spin the inner race with the other hand **(see illustration 5.19)**. The bearing should be almost silent when spun; if it grates or rattles it is worn.

5.18 Example of ball journal bearing with damaged balls and cages

5.19 Hold outer race and listen to inner race when spun

6 Oil seals

Oil seal removal and installation

- Oil seals should be renewed every time a component is dismantled. This is because the seal lips will become set to the sealing surface and will not necessarily reseal.
- Oil seals can be prised out of position using a large flat-bladed screwdriver **(see illustration 6.1)**. In the case of crankcase seals, check first that the seal is not lipped on the inside, preventing its removal with the crankcases joined.

6.1 Prise out oil seals with a large flat-bladed screwdriver

- New seals are usually installed with their marked face (containing the seal reference code) outwards and the spring side towards the fluid being retained. In certain cases, such as a two-stroke engine crankshaft seal, a double lipped seal may be used due to there being fluid or gas on each side of the joint.

Tools and Workshop Tips   REF•17

● Use a bearing driver or socket which bears only on the outer hard edge of the seal to install it in the casing - tapping on the inner edge will damage the sealing lip.

Oil seal types and markings

● Oil seals are usually of the single-lipped type. Double-lipped seals are found where a liquid or gas is on both sides of the joint.
● Oil seals can harden and lose their sealing ability if the motorcycle has been in storage for a long period - renewal is the only solution.
● Oil seal manufacturers also conform to the ISO markings for seal size - these are moulded into the outer face of the seal **(see illustration 6.2)**.

6.2 These oil seal markings indicate inside diameter, outside diameter and seal thickness

7 Gaskets and sealants

Types of gasket and sealant

● Gaskets are used to seal the mating surfaces between components and keep lubricants, fluids, vacuum or pressure contained within the assembly. Aluminium gaskets are sometimes found at the cylinder joints, but most gaskets are paper-based. If the mating surfaces of the components being joined are undamaged the gasket can be installed dry, although a dab of sealant or grease will be useful to hold it in place during assembly.
● RTV (Room Temperature Vulcanising) silicone rubber sealants cure when exposed to moisture in the atmosphere. These sealants are good at filling pits or irregular gasket faces, but will tend to be forced out of the joint under very high torque. They can be used to replace a paper gasket, but first make sure that the width of the paper gasket is not essential to the shimming of internal components. RTV sealants should not be used on components containing petrol (gasoline).
● Non-hardening, semi-hardening and hard setting liquid gasket compounds can be used with a gasket or between a metal-to-metal joint. Select the sealant to suit the application: universal non-hardening sealant can be used on virtually all joints; semi-hardening on joint faces which are rough or damaged; hard setting sealant on joints which require a permanent bond and are subjected to high temperature and pressure. **Note:** *Check first if the paper gasket has a bead of sealant impregnated in its surface before applying additional sealant.*
● When choosing a sealant, make sure it is suitable for the application, particularly if being applied in a high-temperature area or in the vicinity of fuel. Certain manufacturers produce sealants in either clear, silver or black colours to match the finish of the engine. This has a particular application on motorcycles where much of the engine is exposed.
● Do not over-apply sealant. That which is squeezed out on the outside of the joint can be wiped off, whereas an excess of sealant on the inside can break off and clog oilways.

Breaking a sealed joint

● Age, heat, pressure and the use of hard setting sealant can cause two components to stick together so tightly that they are difficult to separate using finger pressure alone. Do not resort to using levers unless there is a pry point provided for this purpose **(see illustration 7.1)** or else the gasket surfaces will be damaged.
● Use a soft-faced hammer **(see illustration 7.2)** or a wood block and conventional hammer to strike the component near the mating surface. Avoid hammering against cast extremities since they may break off. If this method fails, try using a wood wedge between the two components.

> **Caution: If the joint will not separate, double-check that you have removed all the fasteners.**

7.1 If a pry point is provided, apply gently pressure with a flat-bladed screwdriver

7.2 Tap around the joint with a soft-faced mallet if necessary - don't strike cooling fins

Removal of old gasket and sealant

● Paper gaskets will most likely come away complete, leaving only a few traces stuck on

Most components have one or two hollow locating dowels between the two gasket faces. If a dowel cannot be removed, do not resort to gripping it with pliers - it will almost certainly be distorted. Install a close-fitting socket or Phillips screwdriver into the dowel and then grip the outer edge of the dowel to free it.

the sealing faces of the components. It is imperative that all traces are removed to ensure correct sealing of the new gasket.
● Very carefully scrape all traces of gasket away making sure that the sealing surfaces are not gouged or scored by the scraper **(see illustrations 7.3, 7.4 and 7.5)**. Stubborn deposits can be removed by spraying with an aerosol gasket remover. Final preparation of

7.3 Paper gaskets can be scraped off with a gasket scraper tool . . .

7.4 . . . a knife blade . . .

7.5 . . . or a household scraper

REF•18 Tools and Workshop Tips

7.6 Fine abrasive paper is wrapped around a flat file to clean up the gasket face

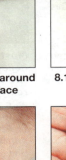

7.7 A kitchen scourer can be used on stubborn deposits

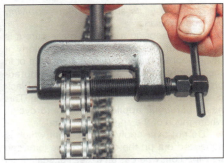

8.1 Tighten the chain breaker to push the pin out of the link . . .

8.2 . . . withdraw the pin, remove the tool . . .

8.3 . . . and separate the chain link

8.4 Insert the new soft link, with O-rings, through the chain ends . . .

8.5 . . . install the O-rings over the pin ends . . .

8.6 . . . followed by the sideplate

8.7 Push the sideplate into position using a clamp

the gasket surface can be made with very fine abrasive paper or a plastic kitchen scourer **(see illustrations 7.6 and 7.7)**.

● Old sealant can be scraped or peeled off components, depending on the type originally used. Note that gasket removal compounds are available to avoid scraping the components clean; make sure the gasket remover suits the type of sealant used.

8 Chains

Breaking and joining final drive chains

● Drive chains for all but small bikes are continuous and do not have a clip-type connecting link. The chain must be broken using a chain breaker tool and the new chain securely riveted together using a new soft rivet-type link. Never use a clip-type connecting link instead of a rivet-type link, except in an emergency. Various chain breaking and riveting tools are available, either as separate tools or combined as illustrated in the accompanying photographs - read the instructions supplied with the tool carefully.

> ⚠ **Warning: The need to rivet the new link pins correctly cannot be overstressed - loss of control of the motorcycle is very likely to result if the chain breaks in use.**

● Rotate the chain and look for the soft link. The soft link pins look like they have been deeply centre-punched instead of peened over like all the other pins **(see illustration 8.9)** and its sideplate may be a different colour. Position the soft link midway between the sprockets and assemble the chain breaker tool over one of the soft link pins **(see illustration 8.1)**. Operate the tool to push the pin out through the chain **(see illustration 8.2)**. On an O-ring chain, remove the O-rings **(see illustration 8.3)**. Carry out the same procedure on the other soft link pin.

> **Caution: Certain soft link pins (particularly on the larger chains) may require their ends to be filed or ground off before they can be pressed out using the tool.**

● Check that you have the correct size and strength (standard or heavy duty) new soft link - do not reuse the old link. Look for the size marking on the chain sideplates **(see illustration 8.10)**.

● Position the chain ends so that they are engaged over the rear sprocket. On an O-ring chain, install a new O-ring over each pin of the link and insert the link through the two chain ends **(see illustration 8.4)**. Install a new O-ring over the end of each pin, followed by the sideplate (with the chain manufacturer's marking facing outwards) **(see illustrations 8.5 and 8.6)**. On an unsealed chain, insert the link through the two chain ends, then install the sideplate with the chain manufacturer's marking facing outwards.

● Note that it may not be possible to install the sideplate using finger pressure alone. If using a joining tool, assemble it so that the plates of the tool clamp the link and press the sideplate over the pins **(see illustration 8.7)**. Otherwise, use two small sockets placed over

Tools and Workshop Tips   REF•19

8.8 Assemble the chain riveting tool over one pin at a time and tighten it fully

8.9 Pin end correctly riveted (A), pin end unriveted (B)

the rivet ends and two pieces of the wood between a G-clamp. Operate the clamp to press the sideplate over the pins.
● Assemble the joining tool over one pin (following the maker's instructions) and tighten the tool down to spread the pin end securely **(see illustrations 8.8 and 8.9)**. Do the same on the other pin.

> **Warning: Check that the pin ends are secure and that there is no danger of the sideplate coming loose. If the pin ends are cracked the soft link must be renewed.**

Final drive chain sizing

● Chains are sized using a three digit number, followed by a suffix to denote the chain type **(see illustration 8.10)**. Chain type is either standard or heavy duty (thicker sideplates), and also unsealed or O-ring/X-ring type.
● The first digit of the number relates to the pitch of the chain, ie the distance from the centre of one pin to the centre of the next pin **(see illustration 8.11)**. Pitch is expressed in eighths of an inch, as follows:

8.10 Typical chain size and type marking

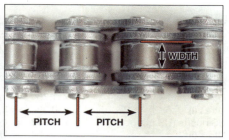

8.11 Chain dimensions

Sizes commencing with a 4 (eg 428) have a pitch of 1/2 inch (12.7 mm)

Sizes commencing with a 5 (eg 520) have a pitch of 5/8 inch (15.9 mm)

Sizes commencing with a 6 (eg 630) have a pitch of 3/4 inch (19.1 mm)

● The second and third digits of the chain size relate to the width of the rollers, again in imperial units, eg the 525 shown has 5/16 inch (7.94 mm) rollers **(see illustration 8.11)**.

9 Hoses

Clamping to prevent flow

● Small-bore flexible hoses can be clamped to prevent fluid flow whilst a component is worked on. Whichever method is used, ensure that the hose material is not permanently distorted or damaged by the clamp.
a) A brake hose clamp available from auto accessory shops **(see illustration 9.1)**.
b) A wingnut type hose clamp **(see illustration 9.2)**.

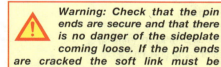

9.1 Hoses can be clamped with an automotive brake hose clamp . . .

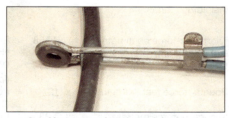

9.2 . . . a wingnut type hose clamp . . .

c) Two sockets placed each side of the hose and held with straight-jawed self-locking grips **(see illustration 9.3)**.
d) Thick card each side of the hose held between straight-jawed self-locking grips **(see illustration 9.4)**.

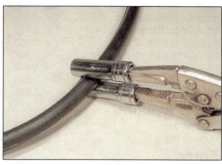

9.3 . . . two sockets and a pair of self-locking grips . . .

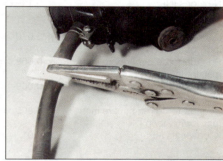

9.4 . . . or thick card and self-locking grips

Freeing and fitting hoses

● Always make sure the hose clamp is moved well clear of the hose end. Grip the hose with your hand and rotate it whilst pulling it off the union. If the hose has hardened due to age and will not move, slit it with a sharp knife and peel its ends off the union **(see illustration 9.5)**.
● Resist the temptation to use grease or soap on the unions to aid installation; although it helps the hose slip over the union it will equally aid the escape of fluid from the joint. It is preferable to soften the hose ends in hot water and wet the inside surface of the hose with water or a fluid which will evaporate.

9.5 Cutting a coolant hose free with a sharp knife

REF•20 Conversion Factors

Length (distance)
Inches (in)	x 25.4	= Millimetres (mm)	x 0.0394	= Inches (in)
Feet (ft)	x 0.305	= Metres (m)	x 3.281	= Feet (ft)
Miles	x 1.609	= Kilometres (km)	x 0.621	= Miles

Volume (capacity)
Cubic inches (cu in; in³)	x 16.387	= Cubic centimetres (cc; cm³)	x 0.061	= Cubic inches (cu in; in³)
Imperial pints (Imp pt)	x 0.568	= Litres (l)	x 1.76	= Imperial pints (Imp pt)
Imperial quarts (Imp qt)	x 1.137	= Litres (l)	x 0.88	= Imperial quarts (Imp qt)
Imperial quarts (Imp qt)	x 1.201	= US quarts (US qt)	x 0.833	= Imperial quarts (Imp qt)
US quarts (US qt)	x 0.946	= Litres (l)	x 1.057	= US quarts (US qt)
Imperial gallons (Imp gal)	x 4.546	= Litres (l)	x 0.22	= Imperial gallons (Imp gal)
Imperial gallons (Imp gal)	x 1.201	= US gallons (US gal)	x 0.833	= Imperial gallons (Imp gal)
US gallons (US gal)	x 3.785	= Litres (l)	x 0.264	= US gallons (US gal)

Mass (weight)
Ounces (oz)	x 28.35	= Grams (g)	x 0.035	= Ounces (oz)
Pounds (lb)	x 0.454	= Kilograms (kg)	x 2.205	= Pounds (lb)

Force
Ounces-force (ozf; oz)	x 0.278	= Newtons (N)	x 3.6	= Ounces-force (ozf; oz)
Pounds-force (lbf; lb)	x 4.448	= Newtons (N)	x 0.225	= Pounds-force (lbf; lb)
Newtons (N)	x 0.1	= Kilograms-force (kgf; kg)	x 9.81	= Newtons (N)

Pressure
Pounds-force per square inch (psi; lbf/in²; lb/in²)	x 0.070	= Kilograms-force per square centimetre (kgf/cm²; kg/cm²)	x 14.223	= Pounds-force per square inch (psi; lbf/in²; lb/in²)
Pounds-force per square inch (psi; lbf/in²; lb/in²)	x 0.068	= Atmospheres (atm)	x 14.696	= Pounds-force per square inch (psi; lbf/in²; lb/in²)
Pounds-force per square inch (psi; lbf/in²; lb/in²)	x 0.069	= Bars	x 14.5	= Pounds-force per square inch (psi; lbf/in²; lb/in²)
Pounds-force per square inch (psi; lbf/in²; lb/in²)	x 6.895	= Kilopascals (kPa)	x 0.145	= Pounds-force per square inch (psi; lbf/in²; lb/in²)
Kilopascals (kPa)	x 0.01	= Kilograms-force per square centimetre (kgf/cm²; kg/cm²)	x 98.1	= Kilopascals (kPa)
Millibar (mbar)	x 100	= Pascals (Pa)	x 0.01	= Millibar (mbar)
Millibar (mbar)	x 0.0145	= Pounds-force per square inch (psi; lbf/in²; lb/in²)	x 68.947	= Millibar (mbar)
Millibar (mbar)	x 0.75	= Millimetres of mercury (mmHg)	x 1.333	= Millibar (mbar)
Millibar (mbar)	x 0.401	= Inches of water (inH₂O)	x 2.491	= Millibar (mbar)
Millimetres of mercury (mmHg)	x 0.535	= Inches of water (inH₂O)	x 1.868	= Millimetres of mercury (mmHg)
Inches of water (inH₂O)	x 0.036	= Pounds-force per square inch (psi; lbf/in²; lb/in²)	x 27.68	= Inches of water (inH₂O)

Torque (moment of force)
Pounds-force inches (lbf in; lb in)	x 1.152	= Kilograms-force centimetre (kgf cm; kg cm)	x 0.868	= Pounds-force inches (lbf in; lb in)
Pounds-force inches (lbf in; lb in)	x 0.113	= Newton metres (Nm)	x 8.85	= Pounds-force inches (lbf in; lb in)
Pounds-force inches (lbf in; lb in)	x 0.083	= Pounds-force feet (lbf ft; lb ft)	x 12	= Pounds-force inches (lbf in; lb in)
Pounds-force feet (lbf ft; lb ft)	x 0.138	= Kilograms-force metres (kgf m; kg m)	x 7.233	= Pounds-force feet (lbf ft; lb ft)
Pounds-force feet (lbf ft; lb ft)	x 1.356	= Newton metres (Nm)	x 0.738	= Pounds-force feet (lbf ft; lb ft)
Newton metres (Nm)	x 0.102	= Kilograms-force metres (kgf m; kg m)	x 9.804	= Newton metres (Nm)

Power
Horsepower (hp)	x 745.7	= Watts (W)	x 0.0013	= Horsepower (hp)

Velocity (speed)
Miles per hour (miles/hr; mph)	x 1.609	= Kilometres per hour (km/hr; kph)	x 0.621	= Miles per hour (miles/hr; mph)

Fuel consumption*
Miles per gallon (mpg)	x 0.354	= Kilometres per litre (km/l)	x 2.825	= Miles per gallon (mpg)

Temperature

Degrees Fahrenheit = (°C x 1.8) + 32   Degrees Celsius (Degrees Centigrade; °C) = (°F - 32) x 0.56

* It is common practice to convert from miles per gallon (mpg) to litres/100 kilometres (l/100km), where mpg x l/100 km = 282

Motorcycle Chemicals and Lubricants REF•21

A number of chemicals and lubricants are available for use in motorcycle maintenance and repair. They include a wide variety of products ranging from cleaning solvents and degreasers to lubricants and protective sprays for rubber, plastic and vinyl.

● **Contact point/spark plug cleaner** is a solvent used to clean oily film and dirt from points, grime from electrical connectors and oil deposits from spark plugs. It is oil free and leaves no residue. It can also be used to remove gum and varnish from carburettor jets and other orifices.

● **Carburettor cleaner** is similar to contact point/spark plug cleaner but it usually has a stronger solvent and may leave a slight oily reside. It is not recommended for cleaning electrical components or connections.

● **Brake system cleaner** is used to remove grease or brake fluid from brake system components (where clean surfaces are absolutely necessary and petroleum-based solvents cannot be used); it also leaves no residue.

● **Silicone-based lubricants** are used to protect rubber parts such as hoses and grommets, and are used as lubricants for hinges and locks.

● **Multi-purpose grease** is an all purpose lubricant used wherever grease is more practical than a liquid lubricant such as oil. Some multi-purpose grease is coloured white and specially formulated to be more resistant to water than ordinary grease.

● **Gear oil** (sometimes called gear lube) is a specially designed oil used in transmissions and final drive units, as well as other areas where high friction, high temperature lubrication is required. It is available in a number of viscosities (weights) for various applications.

● **Motor oil**, of course, is the lubricant specially formulated for use in the engine. It normally contains a wide variety of additives to prevent corrosion and reduce foaming and wear. Motor oil comes in various weights (viscosity ratings) of from 5 to 80. The recommended weight of the oil depends on the seasonal temperature and the demands on the engine. Light oil is used in cold climates and under light load conditions; heavy oil is used in hot climates and where high loads are encountered. Multi-viscosity oils are designed to have characteristics of both light and heavy oils and are available in a number of weights from 5W-20 to 20W-50.

● **Petrol additives** perform several functions, depending on their chemical makeup. They usually contain solvents that help dissolve gum and varnish that build up on carburettor and inlet parts. They also serve to break down carbon deposits that form on the inside surfaces of the combustion chambers. Some additives contain upper cylinder lubricants for valves and piston rings.

● **Brake and clutch fluid** is a specially formulated hydraulic fluid that can withstand the heat and pressure encountered in brake/clutch systems. Care must be taken that this fluid does not come in contact with painted surfaces or plastics. An opened container should always be resealed to prevent contamination by water or dirt.

● **Chain lubricants** are formulated especially for use on motorcycle final drive chains. A good chain lube should adhere well and have good penetrating qualities to be effective as a lubricant inside the chain and on the side plates, pins and rollers. Most chain lubes are either the foaming type or quick drying type and are usually marketed as sprays. Take care to use a lubricant marked as being suitable for O-ring chains.

● **Degreasers** are heavy duty solvents used to remove grease and grime that may accumulate on engine and frame components. They can be sprayed or brushed on and, depending on the type, are rinsed with either water or solvent.

● **Solvents** are used alone or in combination with degreasers to clean parts and assemblies during repair and overhaul. The home mechanic should use only solvents that are non-flammable and that do not produce irritating fumes.

● **Gasket sealing compounds** may be used in conjunction with gaskets, to improve their sealing capabilities, or alone, to seal metal-to-metal joints. Many gasket sealers can withstand extreme heat, some are impervious to petrol and lubricants, while others are capable of filling and sealing large cavities. Depending on the intended use, gasket sealers either dry hard or stay relatively soft and pliable. They are usually applied by hand, with a brush, or are sprayed on the gasket sealing surfaces.

● **Thread locking compound** is an adhesive locking compound that prevents threaded fasteners from loosening because of vibration. It is available in a variety of types for different applications.

● **Moisture dispersants** are usually sprays that can be used to dry out electrical components such as the fuse block and wiring connectors. Some types can also be used as treatment for rubber and as a lubricant for hinges, cables and locks.

● **Waxes and polishes** are used to help protect painted and plated surfaces from the weather. Different types of paint may require the use of different types of wax polish. Some polishes utilise a chemical or abrasive cleaner to help remove the top layer of oxidised (dull) paint on older vehicles. In recent years, many non-wax polishes (that contain a wide variety of chemicals such as polymers and silicones) have been introduced. These non-wax polishes are usually easier to apply and last longer than conventional waxes and polishes.

REF•22 MOT Test Checks

About the MOT Test

In the UK, all vehicles more than three years old are subject to an annual test to ensure that they meet minimum safety requirements. A current test certificate must be issued before a machine can be used on public roads, and is required before a road fund licence can be issued. Riding without a current test certificate will also invalidate your insurance.

For most owners, the MOT test is an annual cause for anxiety, and this is largely due to owners not being sure what needs to be checked prior to submitting the motorcycle for testing. The simple answer is that a fully roadworthy motorcycle will have no difficulty in passing the test.

This is a guide to getting your motorcycle through the MOT test. Obviously it will not be possible to examine the motorcycle to the same standard as the professional MOT tester, particularly in view of the equipment required for some of the checks. However, working through the following procedures will enable you to identify any problem areas before submitting the motorcycle for the test.

It has only been possible to summarise the test requirements here, based on the regulations in force at the time of printing. Test standards are becoming increasingly stringent, although there are some exemptions for older vehicles. More information about the MOT test can be obtained from the TSO publications, *How Safe is your Motorcycle* and *The MOT Inspection Manual for Motorcycle Testing*.

Many of the checks require that one of the wheels is raised off the ground. If the motorcycle doesn't have a centre stand, note that an auxiliary stand will be required. Additionally, the help of an assistant may prove useful.

Certain exceptions apply to machines under 50 cc, machines without a lighting system, and Classic bikes - if in doubt about any of the requirements listed below seek confirmation from an MOT tester prior to submitting the motorcycle for the test.

Check that the frame number is clearly visible.

> **HAYNES HiNT** *If a component is in borderline condition, the tester has discretion in deciding whether to pass or fail it. If the motorcycle presented is clean and evidently well cared for, the tester may be more inclined to pass a borderline component than if the motorcycle is scruffy and apparently neglected.*

Electrical System

Lights, turn signals, horn and reflector

✔ With the ignition on, check the operation of the following electrical components. **Note:** *The electrical components on certain small-capacity machines are powered by the generator, requiring that the engine is run for this check.*

a) Headlight and tail light. Check that both illuminate in the low and high beam switch positions.
b) Position lights. Check that the front position (or sidelight) and tail light illuminate in this switch position.
c) Turn signals. Check that all flash at the correct rate, and that the warning light(s) function correctly. Check that the turn signal switch works correctly.
d) Hazard warning system (where fitted). Check that all four turn signals flash in this switch position.
e) Brake stop light. Check that the light comes on when the front and rear brakes are independently applied. Models first used on or after 1st April 1986 must have a brake light switch on each brake.
f) Horn. Check that the sound is continuous and of reasonable volume.

✔ Check that there is a red reflector on the rear of the machine, either mounted separately or as part of the tail light lens.
✔ Check the condition of the headlight, tail light and turn signal lenses.

Headlight beam height

✔ The MOT tester will perform a headlight beam height check using specialised beam setting equipment **(see illustration 1)**. This equipment will not be available to the home mechanic, but if you suspect that the headlight is incorrectly set or may have been maladjusted in the past, you can perform a rough test as follows.

✔ Position the bike in a straight line facing a brick wall. The bike must be off its stand, upright and with a rider seated. Measure the height from the ground to the centre of the headlight and mark a horizontal line on the wall at this height. Position the motorcycle 3.8 metres from the wall and draw a vertical line up the wall central to the centreline of the motorcycle. Switch to dipped beam and check that the beam pattern falls slightly lower than the horizontal line and to the left of the vertical line **(see illustration 2)**.

Headlight beam height checking equipment

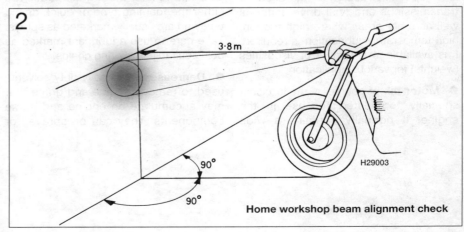

Home workshop beam alignment check

MOT Test Checks REF•23

Exhaust System and Final Drive

Exhaust

✔ Check that the exhaust mountings are secure and that the system does not foul any of the rear suspension components.
✔ Start the motorcycle. When the revs are increased, check that the exhaust is neither holed nor leaking from any of its joints. On a linked system, check that the collector box is not leaking due to corrosion.
✔ Note that the exhaust decibel level ("loudness" of the exhaust) is assessed at the discretion of the tester. If the motorcycle was first used on or after 1st January 1985 the silencer must carry the BSAU 193 stamp, or a marking relating to its make and model, or be of OE (original equipment) manufacture. If the silencer is marked NOT FOR ROAD USE, RACING USE ONLY or similar, it will fail the MOT.

Final drive

✔ On chain or belt drive machines, check that the chain/belt is in good condition and does not have excessive slack. Also check that the sprocket is securely mounted on the rear wheel hub. Check that the chain/belt guard is in place.
✔ On shaft drive bikes, check for oil leaking from the drive unit and fouling the rear tyre.

Steering and Suspension

Steering

✔ With the front wheel raised off the ground, rotate the steering from lock to lock. The handlebar or switches must not contact the fuel tank or be close enough to trap the rider's hand. Problems can be caused by damaged lock stops on the lower yoke and frame, or by the fitting of non-standard handlebars.
✔ When performing the lock to lock check, also ensure that the steering moves freely without drag or notchiness. Steering movement can be impaired by poorly routed cables, or by overtight head bearings or worn bearings. The tester will perform a check of the steering head bearing lower race by mounting the front wheel on a surface plate, then performing a lock to lock check with the weight of the machine on the lower bearing (see illustration 3).
✔ Grasp the fork sliders (lower legs) and attempt to push and pull on the forks (see

Front wheel mounted on a surface plate for steering head bearing lower race check

illustration 4). Any play in the steering head bearings will be felt. Note that in extreme cases, wear of the front fork bushes can be misinterpreted for head bearing play.
✔ Check that the handlebars are securely mounted.
✔ Check that the handlebar grip rubbers are secure. They should by bonded to the bar left end and to the throttle cable pulley on the right end.

Front suspension

✔ With the motorcycle off the stand, hold the front brake on and pump the front forks up and down (see illustration 5). Check that they are adequately damped.

Checking the steering head bearings for freeplay

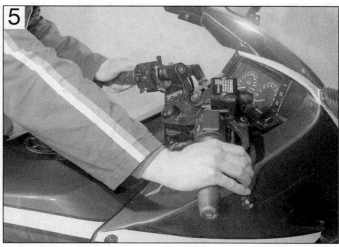

Hold the front brake on and pump the front forks up and down to check operation

REF•24 MOT Test Checks

Inspect the area around the fork dust seal for oil leakage (arrow)

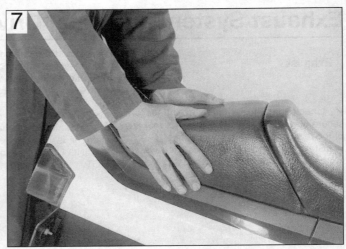

Bounce the rear of the motorcycle to check rear suspension operation

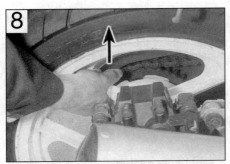

Checking for rear suspension linkage play

✔ Inspect the area above and around the front fork oil seals **(see illustration 6)**. There should be no sign of oil on the fork tube (stanchion) nor leaking down the slider (lower leg). On models so equipped, check that there is no oil leaking from the anti-dive units.

✔ On models with swingarm front suspension, check that there is no freeplay in the linkage when moved from side to side.

Rear suspension

✔ With the motorcycle off the stand and an assistant supporting the motorcycle by its handlebars, bounce the rear suspension **(see illustration 7)**. Check that the suspension components do not foul on any of the cycle parts and check that the shock absorber(s) provide adequate damping.

✔ Visually inspect the shock absorber(s) and check that there is no sign of oil leakage from its damper. This is somewhat restricted on certain single shock models due to the location of the shock absorber.

✔ With the rear wheel raised off the ground, grasp the wheel at the highest point and attempt to pull it up **(see illustration 8)**. Any play in the swingarm pivot or suspension linkage bearings will be felt as movement.

Note: *Do not confuse play with actual suspension movement.* Failure to lubricate suspension linkage bearings can lead to bearing failure **(see illustration 9)**.

✔ With the rear wheel raised off the ground, grasp the swingarm ends and attempt to move the swingarm from side to side and forwards and backwards - any play indicates wear of the swingarm pivot bearings **(see illustration 10)**.

Worn suspension linkage pivots (arrows) are usually the cause of play in the rear suspension

Grasp the swingarm at the ends to check for play in its pivot bearings

MOT Test Checks REF•25

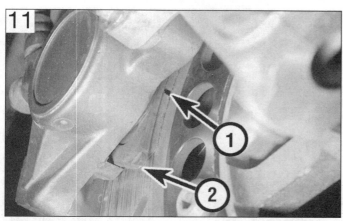

Brake pad wear can usually be viewed without removing the caliper. Most pads have wear indicator grooves (1) and some also have indicator tangs (2)

On drum brakes, check the angle of the operating lever with the brake fully applied. Most drum brakes have a wear indicator pointer and scale.

Brakes, Wheels and Tyres

Brakes

✔ With the wheel raised off the ground, apply the brake then free it off, and check that the wheel is about to revolve freely without brake drag.

✔ On disc brakes, examine the disc itself. Check that it is securely mounted and not cracked.

✔ On disc brakes, view the pad material through the caliper mouth and check that the pads are not worn down beyond the limit (see illustration 11).

✔ On drum brakes, check that when the brake is applied the angle between the operating lever and cable or rod is not too great (see illustration 12). Check also that the operating lever doesn't foul any other components.

✔ On disc brakes, examine the flexible hoses from top to bottom. Have an assistant hold the brake on so that the fluid in the hose is under pressure, and check that there is no sign of fluid leakage, bulges or cracking. If there are any metal brake pipes or unions, check that these are free from corrosion and damage. Where a brake-linked anti-dive system is fitted, check the hoses to the anti-dive in a similar manner.

✔ Check that the rear brake torque arm is secure and that its fasteners are secured by self-locking nuts or castellated nuts with split-pins or R-pins (see illustration 13).

✔ On models with ABS, check that the self-check warning light in the instrument panel works.

✔ The MOT tester will perform a test of the motorcycle's braking efficiency based on a calculation of rider and motorcycle weight. Although this cannot be carried out at home, you can at least ensure that the braking systems are properly maintained. For hydraulic disc brakes, check the fluid level, lever/pedal feel (bleed of air if its spongy) and pad material. For drum brakes, check adjustment, cable or rod operation and shoe lining thickness.

Wheels and tyres

✔ Check the wheel condition. Cast wheels should be free from cracks and if of the built-up design, all fasteners should be secure. Spoked wheels should be checked for broken, corroded, loose or bent spokes.

✔ With the wheel raised off the ground, spin the wheel and visually check that the tyre and wheel run true. Check that the tyre does not foul the suspension or mudguards.

✔ With the wheel raised off the ground, grasp the wheel and attempt to move it about the axle (spindle) (see illustration 14). Any play felt here indicates wheel bearing failure.

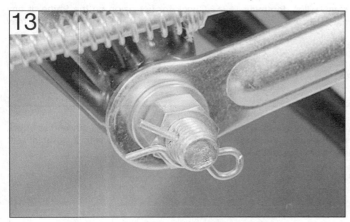

Brake torque arm must be properly secured at both ends

Check for wheel bearing play by trying to move the wheel about the axle (spindle)

REF•26 MOT Test Checks

Checking the tyre tread depth

Tyre direction of rotation arrow can be found on tyre sidewall

Castellated type wheel axle (spindle) nut must be secured by a split pin or R-pin

Two straightedges are used to check wheel alignment

✔ Check the tyre tread depth, tread condition and sidewall condition **(see illustration 15)**.
✔ Check the tyre type. Front and rear tyre types must be compatible and be suitable for road use. Tyres marked NOT FOR ROAD USE, COMPETITION USE ONLY or similar, will fail the MOT.

✔ If the tyre sidewall carries a direction of rotation arrow, this must be pointing in the direction of normal wheel rotation **(see illustration 16)**.
✔ Check that the wheel axle (spindle) nuts (where applicable) are properly secured. A self-locking nut or castellated nut with a split-pin or R-pin can be used **(see illustration 17)**.
✔ Wheel alignment is checked with the motorcycle off the stand and a rider seated. With the front wheel pointing straight ahead, two perfectly straight lengths of metal or wood and placed against the sidewalls of both tyres **(see illustration 18)**. The gap each side of the front tyre must be equidistant on both sides. Incorrect wheel alignment may be due to a cocked rear wheel (often as the result of poor chain adjustment) or in extreme cases, a bent frame.

General checks and condition

✔ Check the security of all major fasteners, bodypanels, seat, fairings (where fitted) and mudguards.

✔ Check that the rider and pillion footrests, handlebar levers and brake pedal are securely mounted.

✔ Check for corrosion on the frame or any load-bearing components. If severe, this may affect the structure, particularly under stress.

Sidecars

A motorcycle fitted with a sidecar requires additional checks relating to the stability of the machine and security of attachment and swivel joints, plus specific wheel alignment (toe-in) requirements. Additionally, tyre and lighting requirements differ from conventional motorcycle use. Owners are advised to check MOT test requirements with an official test centre.

Storage REF•27

Preparing for storage

Before you start

If repairs or an overhaul is needed, see that this is carried out now rather than left until you want to ride the bike again.

Give the bike a good wash and scrub all dirt from its underside. Make sure the bike dries completely before preparing for storage.

Engine

● Remove the spark plug(s) and lubricate the cylinder bores with approximately a teaspoon of motor oil using a spout-type oil can **(see illustration 1)**. Reinstall the spark plug(s). Crank the engine over a couple of times to coat the piston rings and bores with oil. If the bike has a kickstart, use this to turn the engine over. If not, flick the kill switch to the OFF position and crank the engine over on the starter **(see illustration 2)**. If the nature on the ignition system prevents the starter operating with the kill switch in the OFF position, remove the spark plugs and fit them back in their caps; ensure that the plugs are earthed (grounded) against the cylinder head when the starter is operated **(see illustration 3)**.

 Warning: It is important that the plugs are earthed (grounded) away from the spark plug holes otherwise there is a risk of atomised fuel from the cylinders igniting.

> **HAYNES HiNT** On a single cylinder four-stroke engine, you can seal the combustion chamber completely by positioning the piston at TDC on the compression stroke.

● Drain the carburettor(s) otherwise there is a risk of jets becoming blocked by gum deposits from the fuel **(see illustration 4)**.

● If the bike is going into long-term storage, consider adding a fuel stabiliser to the fuel in the tank. If the tank is drained completely, corrosion of its internal surfaces may occur if left unprotected for a long period. The tank can be treated with a rust preventative especially for this purpose. Alternatively, remove the tank and pour half a litre of motor oil into it, install the filler cap and shake the tank to coat its internals with oil before draining off the excess. The same effect can also be achieved by spraying WD40 or a similar water-dispersant around the inside of the tank via its flexible nozzle.

● Make sure the cooling system contains the correct mix of antifreeze. Antifreeze also contains important corrosion inhibitors.

● The air intakes and exhaust can be sealed off by covering or plugging the openings. Ensure that you do not seal in any condensation; run the engine until it is hot,

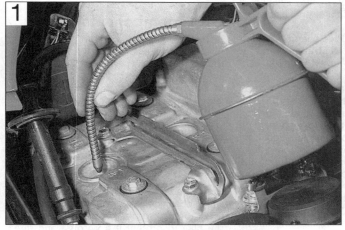

Squirt a drop of motor oil into each cylinder

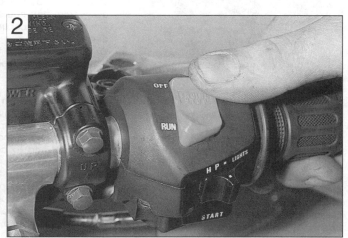

Flick the kill switch to OFF . . .

. . . and ensure that the metal bodies of the plugs (arrows) are earthed against the cylinder head

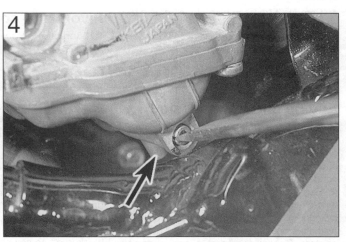

Connect a hose to the carburettor float chamber drain stub (arrow) and unscrew the drain screw

REF•28 Storage

Exhausts can be sealed off with a plastic bag

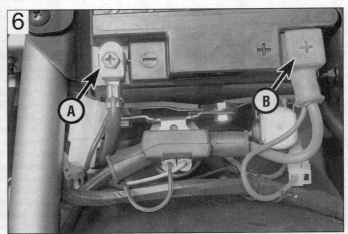
Disconnect the negative lead (A) first, followed by the positive lead (B)

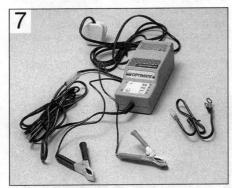
Use a suitable battery charger - this kit also assess battery condition

then switch off and allow to cool. Tape a piece of thick plastic over the silencer end(s) **(see illustration 5)**. Note that some advocate pouring a tablespoon of motor oil into the silencer(s) before sealing them off.

Battery
● Remove it from the bike - in extreme cases of cold the battery may freeze and crack its case **(see illustration 6)**.

● Check the electrolyte level and top up if necessary (conventional refillable batteries). Clean the terminals.
● Store the battery off the motorcycle and away from any sources of fire. Position a wooden block under the battery if it is to sit on the ground.
● Give the battery a trickle charge for a few hours every month **(see illustration 7)**.

Tyres
● Place the bike on its centrestand or an auxiliary stand which will support the motorcycle in an upright position. Position wood blocks under the tyres to keep them off the ground and to provide insulation from damp. If the bike is being put into long-term storage, ideally both tyres should be off the ground; not only will this protect the tyres, but will also ensure that no load is placed on the steering head or wheel bearings.
● Deflate each tyre by 5 to 10 psi, no more or the beads may unseat from the rim, making subsequent inflation difficult on tubeless tyres.

Pivots and controls
● Lubricate all lever, pedal, stand and footrest pivot points. If grease nipples are fitted to the rear suspension components, apply lubricant to the pivots.
● Lubricate all control cables.

Cycle components
● Apply a wax protectant to all painted and plastic components. Wipe off any excess, but don't polish to a shine. Where fitted, clean the screen with soap and water.
● Coat metal parts with Vaseline (petroleum jelly). When applying this to the fork tubes, do not compress the forks otherwise the seals will rot from contact with the Vaseline.
● Apply a vinyl cleaner to the seat.

Storage conditions
● Aim to store the bike in a shed or garage which does not leak and is free from damp.
● Drape an old blanket or bedspread over the bike to protect it from dust and direct contact with sunlight (which will fade paint). This also hides the bike from prying eyes. Beware of tight-fitting plastic covers which may allow condensation to form and settle on the bike.

Getting back on the road

Engine and transmission
● Change the oil and replace the oil filter. If this was done prior to storage, check that the oil hasn't emulsified - a thick whitish substance which occurs through condensation.
● Remove the spark plugs. Using a spout-type oil can, squirt a few drops of oil into the cylinder(s). This will provide initial lubrication as the piston rings and bores comes back into contact. Service the spark plugs, or fit new ones, and install them in the engine.

● Check that the clutch isn't stuck on. The plates can stick together if left standing for some time, preventing clutch operation. Engage a gear and try rocking the bike back and forth with the clutch lever held against the handlebar. If this doesn't work on cable-operated clutches, hold the clutch lever back against the handlebar with a strong elastic band or cable tie for a couple of hours **(see illustration 8)**.
● If the air intakes or silencer end(s) were blocked off, remove the bung or cover used.
● If the fuel tank was coated with a rust

Hold clutch lever back against the handlebar with elastic bands or a cable tie

Storage REF•29

preventative, oil or a stabiliser added to the fuel, drain and flush the tank and dispose of the fuel sensibly. If no action was taken with the fuel tank prior to storage, it is advised that the old fuel is disposed of since it will go off over a period of time. Refill the fuel tank with fresh fuel.

Frame and running gear

● Oil all pivot points and cables.
● Check the tyre pressures. They will definitely need inflating if pressures were reduced for storage.
● Lubricate the final drive chain (where applicable).
● Remove any protective coating applied to the fork tubes (stanchions) since this may well destroy the fork seals. If the fork tubes weren't protected and have picked up rust spots, remove them with very fine abrasive paper and refinish with metal polish.
● Check that both brakes operate correctly. Apply each brake hard and check that it's not possible to move the motorcycle forwards, then check that the brake frees off again once released. Brake caliper pistons can stick due to corrosion around the piston head, or on the sliding caliper types, due to corrosion of the slider pins. If the brake doesn't free after repeated operation, take the caliper off for examination. Similarly drum brakes can stick

due to a seized operating cam, cable or rod linkage.
● If the motorcycle has been in long-term storage, renew the brake fluid and clutch fluid (where applicable).
● Depending on where the bike has been stored, the wiring, cables and hoses may have been nibbled by rodents. Make a visual check and investigate disturbed wiring loom tape.

Battery

● If the battery has been previously removal and given top up charges it can simply be reconnected. Remember to connect the positive cable first and the negative cable last.
● On conventional refillable batteries, if the battery has not received any attention, remove it from the motorcycle and check its electrolyte level. Top up if necessary then charge the battery. If the battery fails to hold a charge and a visual checks show heavy white sulphation of the plates, the battery is probably defective and must be renewed. This is particularly likely if the battery is old. Confirm battery condition with a specific gravity check.
● On sealed (MF) batteries, if the battery has not received any attention, remove it from the motorcycle and charge it according to the information on the battery case - if the battery fails to hold a charge it must be renewed.

Starting procedure

● If a kickstart is fitted, turn the engine over a couple of times with the ignition OFF to distribute oil around the engine. If no kickstart is fitted, flick the engine kill switch OFF and the ignition ON and crank the engine over a couple of times to work oil around the upper cylinder components. If the nature of the ignition system is such that the starter won't work with the kill switch OFF, remove the spark plugs, fit them back into their caps and earth (ground) their bodies on the cylinder head. Reinstall the spark plugs afterwards.
● Switch the kill switch to RUN, operate the choke and start the engine. If the engine won't start don't continue cranking the engine - not only will this flatten the battery, but the starter motor will overheat. Switch the ignition off and try again later. If the engine refuses to start, go through the fault finding procedures in this manual. **Note:** *If the bike has been in storage for a long time, old fuel or a carburettor blockage may be the problem. Gum deposits in carburettors can block jets - if a carburettor cleaner doesn't prove successful the carburettors must be dismantled for cleaning.*

● Once the engine has started, check that the lights, turn signals and horn work properly.

● Treat the bike gently for the first ride and check all fluid levels on completion. Settle the bike back into the maintenance schedule.

REF•30 Fault Finding

This Section provides an easy reference-guide to the more common faults that are likely to afflict your machine. Obviously, the opportunities are almost limitless for faults to occur as a result of obscure failures, and to try and cover all eventualities would require a book. Indeed, a number have been written on the subject.

Successful troubleshooting is not a mysterious 'black art' but the application of a bit of knowledge combined with a systematic and logical approach to the problem. Approach any troubleshooting by first accurately identifying the symptom and then checking through the list of possible causes, starting with the simplest or most obvious and progressing in stages to the most complex.

Take nothing for granted, but above all apply liberal quantities of common sense.

The main symptom of a fault is given in the text as a major heading below which are listed the various systems or areas which may contain the fault. Details of each possible cause for a fault and the remedial action to be taken are given, in brief, in the paragraphs below each heading. Further information should be sought in the relevant Chapter.

1 Engine doesn't start or is difficult to start

- [ ] Starter motor doesn't rotate
- [ ] Starter motor rotates but engine does not turn over
- [ ] Starter works but engine won't turn over (seized)
- [ ] No fuel flow
- [ ] Engine flooded
- [ ] No spark or weak spark
- [ ] Compression low
- [ ] Stalls after starting
- [ ] Rough idle

2 Poor running at low speed

- [ ] Spark weak
- [ ] Fuel/air mixture incorrect
- [ ] Compression low
- [ ] Poor acceleration

3 Poor running or no power at high speed

- [ ] Firing incorrect
- [ ] Fuel/air mixture incorrect
- [ ] Compression low
- [ ] Knocking or pinking
- [ ] Miscellaneous causes

4 Overheating

- [ ] Engine overheats
- [ ] Firing incorrect
- [ ] Fuel/air mixture incorrect
- [ ] Compression too high
- [ ] Engine load excessive
- [ ] Lubrication inadequate
- [ ] Miscellaneous causes

5 Clutch problems

- [ ] Clutch slipping
- [ ] Clutch not disengaging completely

6 Gearchanging problems

- [ ] Doesn't go into gear, or lever doesn't return
- [ ] Jumps out of gear
- [ ] Overselects

7 Abnormal engine noise

- [ ] Knocking or pinking
- [ ] Piston slap or rattling
- [ ] Valve noise
- [ ] Other noise

8 Abnormal driveline noise

- [ ] Clutch noise
- [ ] Transmission noise
- [ ] Final drive noise

9 Abnormal frame and suspension noise

- [ ] Front end noise
- [ ] Shock absorber noise
- [ ] Brake noise

10 Oil level indicator light comes on

- [ ] Engine lubrication system
- [ ] Electrical system

11 Excessive exhaust smoke

- [ ] White smoke
- [ ] Black smoke
- [ ] Brown smoke

12 Poor handling or stability

- [ ] Handlebar hard to turn
- [ ] Handlebar shakes or vibrates excessively
- [ ] Handlebar pulls to one side
- [ ] Poor shock absorbing qualities

13 Braking problems

- [ ] Brakes are spongy, don't hold
- [ ] Brake lever or pedal pulsates
- [ ] Brakes drag

14 Electrical problems

- [ ] Battery dead or weak
- [ ] Battery overcharged

Fault Finding REF•31

1 Engine doesn't start or is difficult to start

Starter motor doesn't rotate

- [ ] Engine kill switch OFF.
- [ ] Fuse blown. Check main fuse and ignition circuit fuse (Chapter 8).
- [ ] Battery voltage low. Check and recharge battery (Chapter 8).
- [ ] Starter motor defective. Make sure the wiring to the starter is secure. Make sure the starter relay clicks when the start button is pushed. If the relay clicks, then the fault is in the wiring or motor.
- [ ] Starter relay faulty. Check it according to the procedure in Chapter 8.
- [ ] Starter switch not contacting. The contacts could be wet, corroded or dirty. Disassemble and clean the switch (Chapter 8).
- [ ] Wiring open or shorted. Check all wiring connections and harnesses to make sure that they are dry, tight and not corroded. Also check for broken or frayed wires that can cause a short to ground (earth) (see wiring diagram, Chapter 8).
- [ ] Ignition (main) switch defective. Check the switch according to the procedure in Chapter 8. Replace the switch with a new one if it is defective.
- [ ] Engine kill switch defective. Check for wet, dirty or corroded contacts. Clean or renew the switch as necessary (Chapter 8).
- [ ] Faulty neutral, side stand or clutch switch. Check the wiring to each switch and the switch itself according to the procedures in Chapter 8.
- [ ] Faulty starter circuit cut-off relay or diode. Check according to the procedure in Chapter 8.

Starter motor rotates but engine does not turn over

- [ ] Starter clutch defective. Inspect and repair or renew (Chapter 2).
- [ ] Damaged idler or starter gears. Inspect and renew the damaged parts (Chapter 2).
- [ ] Worn or broken Hy-vo chain and/or sprockets. Inspect and renew the damaged parts (Chapter 2).

Starter works but engine won't turn over (seized)

- [ ] Seized engine caused by one or more internally damaged components. Failure due to wear, abuse or lack of lubrication. Damage can include seized valves, followers, camshafts, pistons, crankshaft, connecting rod bearings, or transmission gears or bearings. Refer to Chapter 2 for engine disassembly.

No fuel flow

- [ ] No fuel in tank.
- [ ] Fuel tap filter clogged. Remove the tap and clean it and the filter (Chapter 3).
- [ ] Fuel line clogged. Pull the fuel line loose and carefully blow through it.
- [ ] Float needle valve clogged. For all of the valves to be clogged, either a very bad batch of fuel with an unusual additive has been used, or some other foreign material has entered the tank. Many times after a machine has been stored for many months without running, the fuel turns to a varnish-like liquid and forms deposits on the inlet needle valves and jets. The carburettors should be removed and overhauled if draining the float chambers doesn't solve the problem (Chapter 3).
- [ ] Fuel pump or its relay faulty. Check as described in Chapter 3.

Engine flooded

- [ ] Fuel level too high. Check and adjust as necessary (Chapter 3).
- [ ] Float needle valve worn or stuck open. A piece of dirt, rust or other debris can cause the valve to seat improperly, causing excess fuel to be admitted to the float chamber. In this case, the float chamber should be cleaned and the needle valve and seat inspected. If the needle and seat are worn, then the leaking will persist and the parts should be replaced with new ones (Chapter 3).
- [ ] Starting technique incorrect. Under normal circumstances (i.e., if all the carburettor functions are sound) the machine should start with little or no throttle. When the engine is cold, the choke should be operated and the engine started without opening the throttle. When the engine is at operating temperature, only a very slight amount of throttle should be necessary. If the engine is flooded hold the throttle fully open while cranking the engine. This will allow additional air to reach the cylinders.

No spark or weak spark

- [ ] Ignition switch OFF.
- [ ] Engine kill switch turned to the OFF position.
- [ ] Battery voltage low. Check and recharge the battery as necessary (Chapter 8).
- [ ] Spark plugs dirty, defective or worn out. Locate the reason for the fouled plugs using the spark plug condition chart at the end of this manual and follow the plug maintenance procedures in Chapter 1.
- [ ] Spark plug caps or secondary (HT) wiring faulty. Check condition. Renew either or both components if cracks or deterioration are evident (Chapter 4).
- [ ] Spark plug caps not making good contact. Make sure that the plug caps fit snugly over the plug ends.
- [ ] Ignition control unit defective. Check the unit, referring to Chapter 4 for details.
- [ ] Pick-up coil defective. Check the coil, referring to Chapter 4 for details.
- [ ] Ignition HT coils defective. Check the coils, referring to Chapter 4.
- [ ] Ignition or kill switch shorted. This is usually caused by water, corrosion, damage or excessive wear. The switches can be disassembled and cleaned with electrical contact cleaner. If cleaning does not help, renew the switches (Chapter 8).
- [ ] Wiring shorted or broken between:
  - a) *Ignition (main) switch and engine kill switch (or blown fuse)*
  - b) *Ignition control unit and engine kill switch*
  - c) *Ignition control unit and ignition HT coils*
  - d) *Ignition HT coils and spark plugs*
  - e) *Ignition control unit and pick-up coil*
- [ ] Make sure that all wiring connections are clean, dry and tight. Look for chafed and broken wires (Chapters 4 and 8).

Compression low

- [ ] Spark plugs loose. Remove the plugs and inspect their threads. Reinstall and tighten to the specified torque (Chapter 1).
- [ ] Cylinder head not sufficiently tightened down. If the cylinder head is suspected of being loose, then there's a chance that the gasket or head is damaged if the problem has persisted for any length of time. The head nuts should be tightened to the proper torque in the correct sequence (Chapter 2).
- [ ] Improper valve clearance. This means that the valve is not closing completely and compression pressure is leaking past the valve. Check and adjust the valve clearances (Chapter 1).
- [ ] Cylinder and/or piston worn. Excessive wear will cause compression pressure to leak past the rings. This is usually accompanied by worn rings as well. A top-end overhaul is necessary (Chapter 2).
- [ ] Piston rings worn, weak, broken, or sticking. Broken or sticking piston rings usually indicate a lubrication or carburation problem that causes excess carbon deposits or seizures to form on the pistons and rings. Top-end overhaul is necessary (Chapter 2).
- [ ] Piston ring-to-groove clearance excessive. This is caused by excessive wear of the piston ring lands. Piston renewal is necessary (Chapter 2).
- [ ] Cylinder head gasket damaged. If the head is allowed to become loose, or if excessive carbon build-up on the piston crown and combustion chamber causes extremely high compression, the head gasket may leak. Retorquing the head is not always sufficient to restore the seal, so gasket renewal is necessary (Chapter 2).

REF•32 Fault Finding

1 Engine doesn't start or is difficult to start (continued)

Compression low (continued)
- [ ] Cylinder head warped. This is caused by overheating or improperly tightened head nuts. Machine shop resurfacing or head renewal is necessary (Chapter 2).
- [ ] Valve spring broken or weak. Caused by component failure or wear; the springs must be renewed (Chapter 2).
- [ ] Valve not seating properly. This is caused by a bent valve (from over-revving or improper valve adjustment), burned valve or seat (improper carburation) or an accumulation of carbon deposits on the seat (from carburation or lubrication problems). The valves must be cleaned and/or renewed and the seats serviced if possible (Chapter 2).

Stalls after starting
- [ ] Improper choke action. Make sure the choke linkage shaft is getting a full stroke and staying in the out position (Chapter 3).
- [ ] Ignition malfunction (Chapter 4).
- [ ] Carburettor malfunction (Chapter 3).
- [ ] Fuel contaminated. The fuel can be contaminated with either dirt or water, or can change chemically if the machine is allowed to sit for

several months or more. Drain the tank and float chambers (Chapter 3).
- [ ] Intake air leak. Check for loose carburettor-to-intake manifold connections, loose or missing vacuum gauge adapter screws or hoses, or loose carburettor tops (Chapter 3).
- [ ] Engine idle speed incorrect. Turn idle adjusting screw until the engine idles at the specified rpm (Chapter 1).

Rough idle
- [ ] Ignition malfunction (Chapter 4).
- [ ] Idle speed incorrect (Chapter 1).
- [ ] Carburettors not synchronised. Adjust carburettors with vacuum gauge or manometer set (Chapter 1).
- [ ] Carburettor malfunction (Chapter 3).
- [ ] Fuel contaminated. The fuel can be contaminated with either dirt or water, or can change chemically if the machine is allowed to sit for several months or more. Drain the tank and float chambers (Chapter 3).
- [ ] Intake air leak. Check for loose carburettor-to-intake manifold connections, loose or missing vacuum gauge adapter screws or hoses, or loose carburettor tops (Chapter 3).
- [ ] Air filter clogged. Renew the air filter element (Chapter 1).

2 Poor running at low speed

Spark weak
- [ ] Battery voltage low. Check and recharge battery (Chapter 8).
- [ ] Spark plugs fouled, defective or worn out (Chapter 1)
- [ ] Spark plug cap or HT wiring defective (Chapters 1 and 4).
- [ ] Spark plug caps not making contact. Make sure they are properly connected.
- [ ] Incorrect spark plugs. Wrong type, heat range or cap configuration. Check and install correct plugs (Chapter 1).
- [ ] Ignition control unit defective (Chapter 4).
- [ ] Pick-up coil defective (Chapter 4).
- [ ] Ignition HT coils defective (Chapter 4).

Fuel/air mixture incorrect
- [ ] Pilot screws out of adjustment (Chapter 3).
- [ ] Pilot jet or air passage clogged. Remove and overhaul the carburettors (Chapter 3).
- [ ] Air bleed holes clogged. Remove carburettor and blow out all passages (Chapter 3).
- [ ] Air filter clogged, poorly sealed or missing (Chapter 1).
- [ ] Air filter housing poorly sealed. Look for cracks, holes or loose clamps and renew or repair defective parts (Chapter 3).
- [ ] Fuel level too high or too low. Check the level (Chapter 3).
- [ ] Carburettor intake manifolds loose. Check for cracks, breaks, tears or loose clamps. Replace the rubber intake manifold joints if split or perished (Chapter 3).

Compression low
- [ ] Spark plugs loose. Remove the plugs and inspect their threads. Reinstall and tighten to the specified torque (Chapter 1).
- [ ] Cylinder head not sufficiently tightened down. If the cylinder head is suspected of being loose, then there's a chance that the gasket or head is damaged if the problem has persisted for any length of time. The head nuts should be tightened to the proper torque in the correct sequence (Chapter 2).
- [ ] Improper valve clearance. This means that the valve is not closing completely and compression pressure is leaking past the valve. Check and adjust the valve clearances (Chapter 1).
- [ ] Cylinder and/or piston worn. Excessive wear will cause compression pressure to leak past the rings. This is usually

accompanied by worn rings as well. A top-end overhaul is necessary (Chapter 2).
- [ ] Piston rings worn, weak, broken, or sticking. Broken or sticking piston rings usually indicate a lubrication or carburation problem that causes excess carbon deposits or seizures to form on the pistons and rings. Top-end overhaul is necessary (Chapter 2).
- [ ] Piston ring-to-groove clearance excessive. This is caused by excessive wear of the piston ring lands. Piston renewal is necessary (Chapter 2).
- [ ] Cylinder head gasket damaged. If the head is allowed to become loose, or if excessive carbon build-up on the piston crown and combustion chamber causes extremely high compression, the head gasket may leak. Retorquing the head is not always sufficient to restore the seal, so gasket renewal is necessary (Chapter 2).
- [ ] Cylinder head warped. This is caused by overheating or improperly tightened head nuts. Machine shop resurfacing or head renewal is necessary (Chapter 2).
- [ ] Valve spring broken or weak. Caused by component failure or wear; the springs must be renewed (Chapter 2).
- [ ] Valve not seating properly. This is caused by a bent valve (from over-revving or improper valve adjustment), burned valve or seat (improper carburation) or an accumulation of carbon deposits on the seat (from carburation or lubrication problems). The valves must be cleaned and/or renewed and the seats serviced if possible (Chapter 2).

Poor acceleration
- [ ] Carburettors leaking or dirty. Overhaul the carburettors (Chapter 3).
- [ ] Timing not advancing. Faulty pick-up coil or Ignition control unit (Chapter 4).
- [ ] Carburettors not synchronised. Adjust them with a vacuum gauge set or manometer (Chapter 1).
- [ ] Engine oil viscosity too high. Using a heavier oil than that recommended in Chapter 1 can damage the oil pump or lubrication system and cause drag on the engine.
- [ ] Brakes dragging. Usually caused by debris which has entered the brake piston seals, or from a warped disc or bent axle. Repair as necessary (Chapter 6).

Fault Finding REF•33

3 Poor running or no power at high speed

Firing incorrect

- [ ] Air filter restricted. Clean or renew filter (Chapter 1).
- [ ] Spark plugs fouled, defective or worn out (Chapter 1).
- [ ] Spark plug cap or HT wiring defective (Chapters 1 and 4).
- [ ] Spark plug caps not making contact. Make sure they are properly connected.
- [ ] Incorrect spark plugs. Wrong type, heat range or cap configuration. Check and install correct plugs (Chapter 1).
- [ ] Ignition control unit defective (Chapter 4).
- [ ] Pick-up coil defective (Chapter 4).
- [ ] Ignition HT coils defective (Chapter 4).

Fuel/air mixture incorrect

- [ ] Air bleed holes clogged. Remove carburettor and blow out all passages (Chapter 3).
- [ ] Air filter clogged, poorly sealed or missing (Chapter 1).
- [ ] Air filter housing poorly sealed. Look for cracks, holes or loose clamps and renew or repair defective parts (Chapter 3).
- [ ] Fuel level too high or too low. Check the float height (Chapter 3).
- [ ] Carburettor intake manifolds loose. Check for cracks, breaks, tears or loose clamps. Renew the rubber intake manifold joints if split or perished (Chapter 3).
- [ ] Jet needle incorrectly positioned or worn Check and adjust or renew (Chapter 3).
- [ ] Main jet clogged. Dirt, water or other contaminants can clog the main jets. Clean the fuel tap filter, the in-line filter, the float chamber area, and the jets and carburettor orifices (Chapter 3).
- [ ] Main jet wrong size. The standard jetting is for sea level atmospheric pressure and oxygen content. Check jet size (Chapter 3).
- [ ] Throttle shaft-to-carburettor body clearance excessive. Overhaul carburettors, renewing worn parts or complete carburettor assembly if necessary (Chapter 3).

Compression low

- [ ] Spark plugs loose. Remove the plugs and inspect their threads. Reinstall and tighten to the specified torque (Chapter 1).
- [ ] Cylinder head not sufficiently tightened down. If the cylinder head is suspected of being loose, then there's a chance that the gasket or head is damaged if the problem has persisted for any length of time. The head nuts should be tightened to the proper torque in the correct sequence (Chapter 2).
- [ ] Improper valve clearance. This means that the valve is not closing completely and compression pressure is leaking past the valve. Check and adjust the valve clearances (Chapter 1).
- [ ] Cylinder and/or piston worn. Excessive wear will cause compression pressure to leak past the rings. This is usually accompanied by worn rings as well. A top-end overhaul is necessary (Chapter 2).
- [ ] Piston rings worn, weak, broken, or sticking. Broken or sticking piston rings usually indicate a lubrication or carburation problem that causes excess carbon deposits or seizures to form on the pistons and rings. Top-end overhaul is necessary (Chapter 2).
- [ ] Piston ring-to-groove clearance excessive. This is caused by excessive wear of the piston ring lands. Piston renewal is necessary (Chapter 2).
- [ ] Cylinder head gasket damaged. If the head is allowed to become loose, or if excessive carbon build-up on the piston crown and combustion chamber causes extremely high compression, the head gasket may leak. Retorquing the head is not always sufficient to restore the seal, so gasket renewal is necessary (Chapter 2).
- [ ] Cylinder head warped. This is caused by overheating or improperly tightened head nuts. Machine shop resurfacing or head renewal is necessary (Chapter 2).
- [ ] Valve spring broken or weak. Caused by component failure or wear; the springs must be renewed (Chapter 2).
- [ ] Valve not seating properly. This is caused by a bent valve (from over-revving or improper valve adjustment), burned valve or seat (improper carburation) or an accumulation of carbon deposits on the seat (from carburation or lubrication problems). The valves must be cleaned and/or renewed and the seats serviced if possible (Chapter 2).

Knocking or pinking

- [ ] Carbon build-up in combustion chamber. Use of a fuel additive that will dissolve the adhesive bonding the carbon particles to the crown and chamber is the easiest way to remove the build-up. Otherwise, the cylinder head will have to be removed and decarbonised (Chapter 2).
- [ ] Incorrect or poor quality fuel. Old or improper grades of fuel can cause detonation. This causes the piston to rattle, thus the knocking or pinking sound. Drain old fuel and always use the recommended fuel grade (Chapter 3).
- [ ] Spark plug heat range incorrect. Uncontrolled detonation indicates the plug heat range is too hot. The plug in effect becomes a glow plug, raising cylinder temperatures. Install the proper heat range plug (Chapter 1).
- [ ] Improper air/fuel mixture. This will cause the cylinder to run hot, which leads to detonation. Clogged jets or an air leak can cause this imbalance (Chapter 3).

Miscellaneous causes

- [ ] Throttle valve doesn't open fully. Adjust the throttle grip freeplay (Chapter 1).
- [ ] Clutch slipping. May be caused by loose or worn clutch components. Overhaul clutch (Chapter 2).
- [ ] Timing not advancing. Ignition control unit faulty (Chapter 4).
- [ ] Engine oil viscosity too high. Using a heavier oil than the one recommended in Chapter 1 can damage the oil pump or lubrication system and cause drag on the engine.
- [ ] Brakes dragging. Usually caused by debris which has entered the brake piston seals, or from a warped disc or bent axle. Repair as necessary.

REF•34 Fault Finding

4 Overheating

Firing incorrect

- [ ] Spark plugs fouled, defective or worn out (Chapter 1).
- [ ] Incorrect spark plugs (Chapter 1).
- [ ] Faulty ignition HT coils (Chapter 4).

Fuel/air mixture incorrect

- [ ] Main jet clogged. Dirt, water and other contaminants can clog the main jets. Clean the fuel tap filter, the fuel pump in-line filter, the float chamber area and the jets and carburettor orifices (Chapter 3).
- [ ] Main jet wrong size. The standard jetting is for sea level atmospheric pressure and oxygen content. Check jet size (Chapter 3).
- [ ] Air filter clogged, poorly sealed or missing (Chapter 1).
- [ ] Air filter housing poorly sealed. Look for cracks, holes or loose clamps and renew or repair (Chapter 3).
- [ ] Fuel level too low. Check the level (Chapter 3).
- [ ] Carburettor intake manifolds loose. Check for cracks, breaks, tears or loose clamps. Renew the rubber intake manifold joints if split or perished (Chapter 3).

Compression too high

- [ ] Carbon build-up in combustion chamber. Use of a fuel additive that will dissolve the adhesive bonding the carbon particles to the piston crown and chamber is the easiest way to remove the build-up. Otherwise, the cylinder head will have to be removed and decarbonised (Chapter 2).
- [ ] Improperly machined head surface or installation of incorrect gasket during engine assembly (Chapter 2).

Engine load excessive

- [ ] Clutch slipping. Can be caused by damaged, loose or worn clutch components. Overhaul clutch (Chapter 2).

- [ ] Engine oil level too high. The addition of too much oil will cause pressurisation of the crankcase and inefficient engine operation. Check Specifications and drain to proper level (Chapter 1).
- [ ] Engine oil viscosity too high. Using a heavier oil than the one recommended in Chapter 1 can damage the oil pump or lubrication system as well as cause drag on the engine.
- [ ] Brakes dragging. Usually caused by debris which has entered the brake piston seals, or from a warped disc or bent axle. Repair as necessary.
- [ ] Excessive friction in moving engine parts due to inadequate lubrication, worn bearings or incorrect assembly. Overhaul engine (Chapter 2).

Lubrication inadequate

- [ ] Engine oil level too low. Friction caused by intermittent lack of lubrication or from oil that is overworked can cause overheating. The oil provides a definite cooling function in the engine. Check the oil level (Chapter 1).
- [ ] Poor quality engine oil or incorrect viscosity or type. Oil is rated not only according to viscosity but also according to type. Some oils are not rated high enough for use in this engine. Check the Specifications section and change to the correct oil (Chapter 1).
- [ ] Worn oil pump or clogged oil passages. Check oil pump and clean passages (Chapter 2).

Miscellaneous causes

- [ ] Engine cooling fins clogged with debris.
- [ ] Modification to exhaust system. Most aftermarket exhaust systems cause the engine to run leaner, which make them run hotter. When installing an accessory exhaust system, always rejet the carburettors.

5 Clutch problems

Clutch slipping

- [ ] Cable freeplay insufficient. Check and adjust cable (Chapter 1).
- [ ] Friction plates worn or warped. Overhaul the clutch assembly (Chapter 2).
- [ ] Plain plates warped (Chapter 2).
- [ ] Clutch springs broken or weak. Old or heat-damaged (from slipping clutch) springs should be replaced with new ones (Chapter 2).
- [ ] Clutch release mechanism defective. Replace any defective parts (Chapter 2).
- [ ] Clutch centre or housing unevenly worn. This causes improper engagement of the plates. Renew the damaged or worn parts (Chapter 2).

Clutch not disengaging completely

- [ ] Cable freeplay excessive. Check and adjust cable (Chapter 1).
- [ ] Clutch plates warped or damaged. This will cause clutch drag, which in turn will cause the machine to creep. Overhaul the clutch assembly (Chapter 2).

- [ ] Clutch spring tension uneven. Usually caused by a sagged or broken spring. Check and renew the springs as a set (Chapter 2).
- [ ] Engine oil deteriorated. Old, thin, worn out oil will not provide proper lubrication for the plates, causing the clutch to drag. Renew the oil and filter (Chapter 1).
- [ ] Engine oil viscosity too high. Using a heavier oil than recommended in Chapter 1 can cause the plates to stick together, putting a drag on the engine. Change to the correct weight oil (Chapter 1).
- [ ] Clutch housing seized on input shaft. Lack of lubrication, severe wear or damage can cause the guide to seize on the shaft. Overhaul of the clutch, and perhaps transmission, may be necessary to repair the damage (Chapter 2).
- [ ] Clutch release mechanism defective. Overhaul the clutch cover components (Chapter 2).
- [ ] Loose clutch centre nut. Causes drum and centre misalignment putting a drag on the engine. Engagement adjustment continually varies. Overhaul the clutch assembly (Chapter 2).

Fault Finding REF•35

6 Gearchanging problems

Doesn't go into gear or lever doesn't return

☐ Clutch not disengaging. See above.
☐ Selector fork(s) bent or seized. Often caused by dropping the machine or from lack of lubrication. Overhaul the transmission (Chapter 2).
☐ Gear(s) stuck on shaft. Most often caused by a lack of lubrication or excessive wear in transmission bearings and bushes. Overhaul the transmission (Chapter 2).
☐ Gear selector drum binding. Caused by lubrication or bearing failure or excessive wear. Renew the drum and bearing (Chapter 2).
☐ Gearchange lever return spring weak or broken (Chapter 2).
☐ Gearchange lever broken. Splines stripped out of lever or shaft, caused by allowing the lever to get loose or from dropping the machine. Renew necessary parts (Chapter 2).
☐ Gearchange mechanism stopper arm broken or worn. Full engagement and rotary movement of selector drum results. Renew the arm (Chapter 2).
☐ Stopper arm spring broken. Allows arm to float, causing sporadic shift operation. Renew the spring (Chapter 2).

Jumps out of gear

☐ Selector fork(s) worn. Overhaul the transmission (Chapter 2).
☐ Gear groove(s) worn. Overhaul the transmission (Chapter 2).
☐ Gear dogs or dog slots worn or damaged. The gears should be inspected and renewed. No attempt should be made to service the worn parts (Chapter 2).

Overselects

☐ Stopper arm spring weak or broken (Chapter 2).
☐ Gearchange shaft return spring post broken or distorted (Chapter 2).

7 Abnormal engine noise

Knocking or pinking

☐ Carbon build-up in combustion chamber. Use of a fuel additive that will dissolve the adhesive bonding the carbon particles to the piston crown and chamber is the easiest way to remove the build-up. Otherwise, the cylinder head will have to be removed and decarbonised (Chapter 2).
☐ Incorrect or poor quality fuel. Old or improper fuel can cause detonation. This causes the pistons to rattle, thus the knocking or pinking sound. Drain the old fuel and always use the recommended grade fuel (Chapter 3).
☐ Spark plug heat range incorrect. Uncontrolled detonation indicates that the plug heat range is too hot. The plug in effect becomes a glow plug, raising cylinder temperatures. Install the proper heat range plug (Chapter 1).
☐ Improper air/fuel mixture. This will cause the cylinders to run hot and lead to detonation. Clogged jets or an air leak can cause this imbalance (Chapter 3).

Piston slap or rattling

☐ Cylinder-to-piston clearance excessive. Caused by improper assembly. Inspect and overhaul top-end parts (Chapter 2).
☐ Connecting rod bent. Caused by over-revving, trying to start a badly flooded engine or from ingesting a foreign object into the combustion chamber. Renew the damaged parts (Chapter 2).
☐ Piston pin or piston pin bore worn or seized from wear or lack of lubrication. Renew damaged parts (Chapter 2).
☐ Piston ring(s) worn, broken or sticking. Overhaul the top-end (Chapter 2).
☐ Piston seizure damage. Usually from lack of lubrication or overheating. Renew the pistons and bore the cylinders, as necessary (Chapter 2).

☐ Connecting rod upper or lower end clearance excessive. Caused by excessive wear or lack of lubrication. Renew worn parts (Chapter 2).

Valve noise

☐ Incorrect valve clearances. Adjust the clearances (Chapter 1).
☐ Valve spring broken or weak. Check and renew weak valve springs (Chapter 2).
☐ Camshaft or cylinder head worn or damaged. Lack of lubrication at high rpm is usually the cause of damage. Insufficient oil or failure to change the oil at the recommended intervals are the chief causes. Since there are no replaceable bearings in the head, the head itself will have to be renewed if there is excessive wear or damage (Chapter 2).

Other noise

☐ Cylinder head gasket leaking (Chapter 1).
☐ Exhaust pipe leaking at cylinder head connection. Caused by improper fit of pipe(s) or loose exhaust flange. All exhaust fasteners should be tightened evenly and carefully. Failure to do this will lead to a leak (Chapter 3).
☐ Crankshaft runout excessive. Caused by a bent crankshaft (from over-revving) or damage from an upper cylinder component failure. Can also be attributed to dropping the machine on either of the crankshaft ends (Chapter 2).
☐ Engine mounting bolts loose. Tighten all engine mount bolts (Chapter 2).
☐ Crankshaft bearings worn (Chapter 2).
☐ Cam chain tensioner defective. Renew the tensioner (Chapter 2).
☐ Cam chain, sprockets or guides worn (Chapter 2).

REF•36 Fault Finding

8 Abnormal driveline noise

Clutch noise
- [ ] Clutch housing/friction plate clearance excessive (Chapter 2).
- [ ] Loose or damaged clutch pressure plate and/or bolts (Chapter 2).

Transmission noise
- [ ] Bearings worn. Also includes the possibility that the shafts are worn. Overhaul the transmission (Chapter 2).
- [ ] Gears worn or chipped (Chapter 2).
- [ ] Metal chips jammed in gear teeth. Probably pieces from a broken clutch, gear or selector mechanism that were picked up by the gears. This will cause early bearing failure (Chapter 2).

- [ ] Engine oil level too low. Causes a howl from transmission. Also affects engine power and clutch operation (Chapter 1).

Final drive noise
- [ ] Final drive oil level low (Chapter 1).
- [ ] Final drive gear lash incorrect (Chapter 5).
- [ ] Final drive gears worn or damaged (Chapter 5).
- [ ] Final drive bearings worn (Chapter 5).
- [ ] Driveshaft splines worn and slipping (Chapter 5).
- [ ] Wheel coupling damper worn. Renew the damper (Chapter 5).

9 Abnormal frame and suspension noise

Front end noise
- [ ] Low fluid level or improper viscosity oil in forks. This can sound like spurting and is usually accompanied by irregular fork action (Chapter 5).
- [ ] Spring weak or broken. Makes a clicking or scraping sound. Fork oil, when drained, will have a lot of metal particles in it (Chapter 5).
- [ ] Steering head bearings loose or damaged. Clicks when braking. Check and adjust or renew as necessary (Chapters 1 and 5).
- [ ] Fork yokes loose. Make sure all clamp pinch bolts are tight (Chapter 5).
- [ ] Fork tube bent. Good possibility if machine has been dropped. Replace tube with a new one (Chapter 5).
- [ ] Front axle or axle clamp bolt loose. Tighten them to the specified torque (Chapter 6).

Rear end noise
- [ ] Shock absorber fluid level incorrect. Indicates a leak caused by defective seal. Shock will be covered with oil. Renew shock or seek advice on repair from a Yamaha dealer or suspension specialist (Chapter 5).
- [ ] Defective shock absorber with internal damage. This is in the body of the shock and can't be remedied. The shock must be replaced with a new one (Chapter 5).
- [ ] Bent or damaged shock body. Replace the shock with a new one (Chapter 5).

- [ ] Loose or worn shock absorber or suspension linkage mountings. Check and tighten or renew as required (see Chapter 5).
- [ ] Suspension linkage components or bearings damaged. Check and renew as required (Chapter 5).
- [ ] Swingarm pivots loose or bearings worn or damaged. Check and tighten or renew as required (Chapter 5).

Brake noise
- [ ] Squeal caused by pad shim not installed or positioned correctly (Chapter 6).
- [ ] Squeal caused by dust on brake pads. Usually found in combination with glazed pads. Clean using brake cleaning solvent (Chapter 6).
- [ ] Contamination of brake pads. Oil, brake fluid or dirt causing brake to chatter or squeal. Clean or renew pads (Chapter 6).
- [ ] Pads glazed. Caused by excessive heat from prolonged use or from contamination. Do not use sandpaper, emery cloth, carborundum cloth or any other abrasive to roughen the pad surfaces as abrasives will stay in the pad material and damage the disc. A very fine flat file can be used, but pad renewal is suggested as a cure (Chapter 6).
- [ ] Disc warped. Can cause a chattering, clicking or intermittent squeal. Usually accompanied by a pulsating lever and uneven braking. Renew the disc (Chapter 6).
- [ ] Loose or worn wheel bearings. Check and renew as needed (Chapter 6).

10 Oil level indicator light comes on

Engine lubrication system
- [ ] Engine oil level low. Inspect for leak or other problem causing low oil level and add recommended oil (Chapter 1).

Electrical system
- [ ] Oil level sensor defective. Check the sensor and renew it if it is defective (Chapter 8).
- [ ] Oil level indicator light circuit defective. Check for pinched, shorted, disconnected or damaged wiring (Chapter 8).

Fault Finding   REF•37

11 Excessive exhaust smoke

White smoke

- ☐ Piston oil ring worn. The ring may be broken or damaged, causing oil from the crankcase to be pulled past the piston into the combustion chamber. Replace the rings with new ones (Chapter 2).
- ☐ Cylinders worn, cracked, or scored. Caused by overheating or oil starvation. The cylinders will have to be rebored and new pistons installed (Chapter 2).
- ☐ Valve oil seal damaged or worn. Replace oil seals with new ones (Chapter 2).
- ☐ Valve guide worn. Perform a complete valve job (Chapter 2).
- ☐ Engine oil level too high, which causes the oil to be forced past the rings. Drain oil to the proper level (Chapter 1).
- ☐ Head gasket broken between oil return and cylinder. Causes oil to be pulled into the combustion chamber. Renew the head gasket and check the head for warpage (Chapter 2).
- ☐ Abnormal crankcase pressurisation, which forces oil past the rings. Clogged ventilation system or breather hose (Chapter 2).

Black smoke

- ☐ Air filter clogged. Clean or renew the element (Chapter 1).
- ☐ Main jet too large or loose. Compare the jet size to the Specifications (Chapter 3).

- ☐ Choke cable or linkage shaft stuck, causing fuel to be pulled through choke circuit (Chapter 3).
- ☐ Fuel level too high. Check and adjust the float height(s) as necessary (Chapter 3).
- ☐ Float needle valve held off needle seat. Clean the float chambers and fuel line and renew the needles and seats if necessary (Chapter 3).

Brown smoke

- ☐ Main jet too small or clogged. Lean condition caused by wrong size main jet or by a restricted orifice. Clean float chambers and jets and compare jet size to Specifications (Chapter 3).
- ☐ Fuel flow insufficient. Float needle valve stuck closed due to chemical reaction with old fuel. Float height incorrect. Restricted fuel line. Clean line and float chamber and adjust floats if necessary (Chapter 3).
- ☐ Fuel level too low. Check and adjust the float height(s) as necessary (Chapter 3).
- ☐ Carburettor intake manifold clamps loose (Chapter 3).
- ☐ Air filter poorly sealed or not installed (Chapter 1).

12 Poor handling or stability

Handlebar hard to turn

- ☐ Steering head bearing adjuster nut too tight. Check adjustment (Chapter 1).
- ☐ Bearings damaged. Roughness can be felt as the bars are turned from side-to-side. Renew bearings and races (Chapter 5).
- ☐ Races dented or worn. Denting results from wear in only one position (e.g., straight ahead), from a collision or hitting a pothole or from dropping the machine. Renew races and bearings (Chapter 5).
- ☐ Steering stem lubrication inadequate. Causes are grease getting hard from age or being washed out by high pressure car washes. Disassemble steering head and repack bearings (Chapter 5).
- ☐ Steering stem bent. Caused by a collision, hitting a pothole or by dropping the machine. Renew damaged part. Don't try to straighten the steering stem (Chapter 5).
- ☐ Front tyre air pressure too low (Daily (pre-ride) checks).

Handlebar shakes or vibrates excessively

- ☐ Tyres worn or wheels out of balance (Chapter 6).
- ☐ Swingarm bearings worn. Renew worn bearings (Chapter 5).
- ☐ Rim(s) warped or damaged. Inspect wheels for runout (Chapter 6).
- ☐ Wheel bearings worn. Worn front or rear wheel bearings can cause poor tracking. Worn front bearings will cause wobble (Chapter 6).
- ☐ Handlebar clamp bolts loose (Chapter 5).
- ☐ Fork yoke bolts loose. Tighten them to the specified torque (Chapter 5).
- ☐ Engine mounting bolts loose. Will cause excessive vibration with increased engine rpm (Chapter 2).

Handlebar pulls to one side

- ☐ Frame bent. Definitely suspect this if the machine has been dropped. May or may not be accompanied by cracking near the bend. Renew the frame (Chapter 5).
- ☐ Wheels out of alignment. Caused by improper location of axle spacers or from bent steering stem or frame (Chapter 5).
- ☐ Swingarm bent or twisted. Caused by age (metal fatigue) or impact damage. Renew the swingarm (Chapter 5).
- ☐ Steering stem bent. Caused by impact damage or by dropping the motorcycle. Renew the steering stem (Chapter 5).
- ☐ Fork tube bent. Disassemble the forks and renew the damaged parts (Chapter 5).
- ☐ Fork oil level uneven. Check and add or drain as necessary (Chapter 5).

Poor shock absorbing qualities

- ☐ Too hard:
  - a) Fork oil level excessive (Chapter 5).
  - b) Fork oil viscosity too high. Use a lighter oil (see the Specifications in Chapter 5).
  - c) Fork tube bent. Causes a harsh, sticking feeling (Chapter 5).
  - d) Shock shaft or body bent or damaged (Chapter 5).
  - e) Fork internal damage (Chapter 5).
  - f) Shock internal damage.
  - g) Tyre pressure too high (Daily (pre-ride) checks).
- ☐ Too soft:
  - a) Fork or shock oil insufficient and/or leaking (Chapter 5).
  - b) Fork oil level too low (Chapter 5).
  - c) Fork oil viscosity too light (Chapter 5).
  - d) Fork springs weak or broken (Chapter 5).
  - e) Shock internal damage or leakage (Chapter 5).

REF•38 Fault Finding

13 Braking problems

Brakes are spongy, don't hold

- [ ] Air in brake line. Caused by inattention to master cylinder fluid level or by leakage. Locate problem and bleed brakes (Chapter 6).
- [ ] Pad or disc worn (Chapters 1 and 6).
- [ ] Brake fluid leak. Causes air in brake line. Locate problem and bleed brakes (Chapter 6).
- [ ] Contaminated pads. Caused by contamination with oil, grease, brake fluid, etc. Clean or renew pads. Clean disc thoroughly with brake cleaner (Chapter 6).
- [ ] Brake fluid deteriorated. Fluid is old or contaminated. Drain system, replenish with new fluid and bleed the system (Chapter 6).
- [ ] Master cylinder internal parts worn or damaged causing fluid to bypass (Chapter 6).
- [ ] Master cylinder bore scratched by foreign material or broken spring. Repair or renew master cylinder (Chapter 6).
- [ ] Disc warped. Renew disc (Chapter 6).

Brake lever or pedal pulsates

- [ ] Disc warped. Renew disc (Chapter 6).
- [ ] Axle bent. Renew axle (Chapter 6).
- [ ] Brake caliper bolts loose (Chapter 6).
- [ ] Brake caliper sliders damaged or sticking (front caliper), causing caliper to bind. Lubricate the sliders or renew them if they are corroded or bent (Chapter 6).
- [ ] Wheel warped or otherwise damaged (Chapter 6).
- [ ] Wheel bearings damaged or worn (Chapter 6).

Brakes drag

- [ ] Master cylinder piston seized. Caused by wear or damage to piston or cylinder bore (Chapter 6).
- [ ] Lever balky or stuck. Check pivot and lubricate (Chapter 6).
- [ ] Brake caliper binds. Caused by inadequate lubrication or damage to caliper sliders (front caliper) (Chapter 6).
- [ ] Brake caliper piston seized in bore. Caused by wear, corrosion or ingestion of dirt past deteriorated seal (Chapter 6).
- [ ] Brake pad damaged. Pad material separated from backing plate. Usually caused by faulty manufacturing process or from contact with chemicals. Renew pads (Chapter 6).
- [ ] Pads improperly installed (Chapter 6).
- [ ] Pads sticking on retaining pins or in caliper and not returning with pistons. Probably due to dirt and corrosion. Remove the brake pads and clean all corrosion off the retaining pins and caliper, then grease as described (Chapter 5). Check pad retaining pins aren't bent (Chapter 6).

14 Electrical problems

Battery dead or weak

- [ ] Battery faulty. Caused by sulphated plates which are shorted through sedimentation. Also, broken battery terminal making only occasional contact (Chapter 8).
- [ ] Battery cables making poor contact (Chapter 1).
- [ ] Load excessive. Caused by addition of high wattage lights or other electrical accessories.
- [ ] Ignition (main) switch defective. Switch either earths (grounds) internally or fails to shut off system. Renew the switch (Chapter 8).
- [ ] Regulator/rectifier defective (Chapter 8).

- [ ] Alternator stator coil open or shorted (Chapter 8).
- [ ] Wiring faulty. Wiring earthed (grounded) or connections loose in ignition, charging or lighting circuits (Chapter 8).

Battery overcharged

- [ ] Regulator/rectifier defective. Overcharging is noticed when battery gets excessively warm (Chapter 8).
- [ ] Battery defective. Replace battery with a new one (Chapter 8).
- [ ] Battery amperage too low, wrong type or size. Install manufacturer's specified amp-hour battery to handle charging load (Chapter 8).

Fault Finding Equipment   REF•39

Checking engine compression

● Low compression will result in exhaust smoke, heavy oil consumption, poor starting and poor performance. A compression test will provide useful information about an engine's condition and if performed regularly, can give warning of trouble before any other symptoms become apparent.

● A compression gauge will be required, along with an adapter to suit the spark plug hole thread size. Note that the screw-in type gauge/adapter set up is preferable to the rubber cone type.

● Before carrying out the test, first check the valve clearances as described in Chapter 1.

1 Run the engine until it reaches normal operating temperature, then stop it and remove the spark plug(s), taking care not to scald your hands on the hot components.

2 Install the gauge adapter and compression gauge in No. 1 cylinder spark plug hole (see illustration 1).

Screw the compression gauge adapter into the spark plug hole, then screw the gauge into the adapter

3 On kickstart-equipped motorcycles, make sure the ignition switch is OFF, then open the throttle fully and kick the engine over a couple of times until the gauge reading stabilises.

4 On motorcycles with electric start only, the procedure will differ depending on the nature of the ignition system. Flick the engine kill switch (engine stop switch) to OFF and turn the ignition switch ON; open the throttle fully and crank the engine over on the starter motor for a couple of revolutions until the gauge reading stabilises. If the starter will not operate with the kill switch OFF, turn the ignition switch OFF and refer to the next paragraph.

5 Install the spark plugs back into their suppressor caps and arrange the plug electrodes so that their metal bodies are earthed (grounded) against the cylinder head; this is essential to prevent damage to the ignition system as the engine is spun over (see illustration 2). Position the plugs well

All spark plugs must be earthed (grounded) against the cylinder head

away from the plug holes otherwise there is a risk of atomised fuel escaping from the combustion chambers and igniting. As a safety precaution, cover the top of the valve cover with rag. Now turn the ignition switch ON and kill switch ON, open the throttle fully and crank the engine over on the starter motor for a couple of revolutions until the gauge reading stabilises.

6 After one or two revolutions the pressure should build up to a maximum figure and then stabilise. Take a note of this reading and on multi-cylinder engines repeat the test on the remaining cylinders.

7 The correct pressures are given in Chapter 2 Specifications. If the results fall within the specified range and on multi-cylinder engines all are relatively equal, the engine is in good condition. If there is a marked difference between the readings, or if the readings are lower than specified, inspection of the top-end components will be required.

8 Low compression pressure may be due to worn cylinder bores, pistons or rings, failure of the cylinder head gasket, worn valve seals, or poor valve seating.

9 To distinguish between cylinder/piston wear and valve leakage, pour a small quantity of oil into the bore to temporarily seal the piston rings, then repeat the compression tests (see illustration 3). If the readings show

Bores can be temporarily sealed with a squirt of motor oil

a noticeable increase in pressure this confirms that the cylinder bore, piston, or rings are worn. If, however, no change is indicated, the cylinder head gasket or valves should be examined.

10 High compression pressure indicates excessive carbon build-up in the combustion chamber and on the piston crown. If this is the case the cylinder head should be removed and the deposits removed. Note that excessive carbon build-up is less likely with the used on modern fuels.

Checking battery open-circuit voltage

 Warning: The gases produced by the battery are explosive - never smoke or create any sparks in the vicinity of the battery. Never allow the electrolyte to contact your skin or clothing - if it does, wash it off and seek immediate medical attention.

REF•40 Fault Finding Equipment

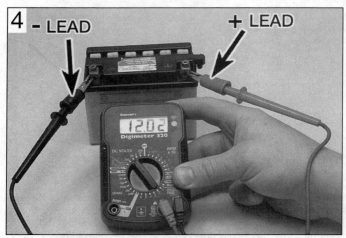

Measuring open-circuit battery voltage

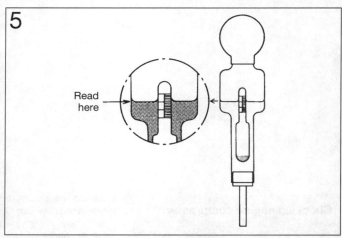

Float-type hydrometer for measuring battery specific gravity

- Before any electrical fault is investigated the battery should be checked.
- You'll need a dc voltmeter or multimeter to check battery voltage. Check that the leads are inserted in the correct terminals on the meter, red lead to positive (+ve), black lead to negative (-ve). Incorrect connections can damage the meter.
- A sound fully-charged 12 volt battery should produce between 12.3 and 12.6 volts across its terminals (12.8 volts for a maintenance-free battery). On machines with a 6 volt battery, voltage should be between 6.1 and 6.3 volts.

1 Set a multimeter to the 0 to 20 volts dc range and connect its probes across the battery terminals. Connect the meter's positive (+ve) probe, usually red, to the battery positive (+ve) terminal, followed by the meter's negative (-ve) probe, usually black, to the battery negative terminal (-ve) **(see illustration 4)**.

2 If battery voltage is low (below 10 volts on a 12 volt battery or below 4 volts on a six volt battery), charge the battery and test the voltage again. If the battery repeatedly goes flat, investigate the motorcycle's charging system.

Checking battery specific gravity (SG)

 Warning: The gases produced by the battery are explosive - never smoke or create any sparks in the vicinity of the battery. Never allow the electrolyte to contact your skin or clothing - if it does, wash it off and seek immediate medical attention.

- The specific gravity check gives an indication of a battery's state of charge.
- A hydrometer is used for measuring specific gravity. Make sure you purchase one which has a small enough hose to insert in the aperture of a motorcycle battery.
- Specific gravity is simply a measure of the electrolyte's density compared with that of water. Water has an SG of 1.000 and fully-charged battery electrolyte is about 26% heavier, at 1.260.
- Specific gravity checks are not possible on maintenance-free batteries. Testing the open-circuit voltage is the only means of determining their state of charge.

1 To measure SG, remove the battery from the motorcycle and remove the first cell cap. Draw

Digital multimeter can be used for all electrical tests

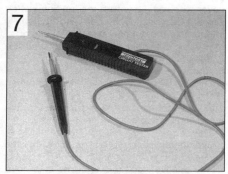

Battery-powered continuity tester

some electrolyte into the hydrometer and note the reading **(see illustration 5)**. Return the electrolyte to the cell and install the cap.

2 The reading should be in the region of 1.260 to 1.280. If SG is below 1.200 the battery needs charging. Note that SG will vary with temperature; it should be measured at 20°C (68°F). Add 0.007 to the reading for every 10°C above 20°C, and subtract 0.007 from the reading for every 10°C below 20°C. Add 0.004 to the reading for every 10°F above 68°F, and subtract 0.004 from the reading for every 10°F below 68°F.

3 When the check is complete, rinse the hydrometer thoroughly with clean water.

Checking for continuity

- The term continuity describes the uninterrupted flow of electricity through an electrical circuit. A continuity check will determine whether an **open-circuit** situation exists.
- Continuity can be checked with an ohmmeter, multimeter, continuity tester or battery and bulb test circuit **(see illustrations 6, 7 and 8)**.

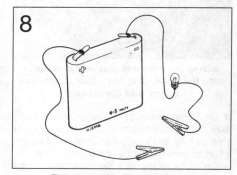

Battery and bulb test circuit

Fault Finding Equipment REF•41

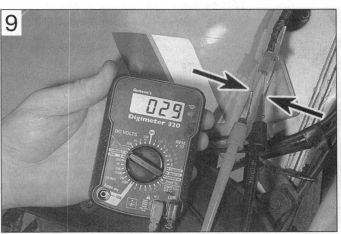

Continuity check of front brake light switch using a meter - note split pins used to access connector terminals

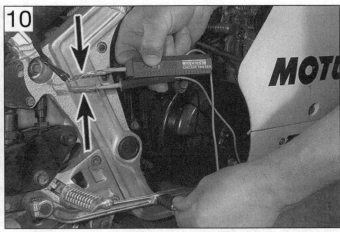

Continuity check of rear brake light switch using a continuity tester

- All of these instruments are self-powered by a battery, therefore the checks are made with the ignition OFF.
- As a safety precaution, always disconnect the battery negative (-ve) lead before making checks, particularly if ignition switch checks are being made.
- If using a meter, select the appropriate ohms scale and check that the meter reads infinity (∞). Touch the meter probes together and check that meter reads zero; where necessary adjust the meter so that it reads zero.
- After using a meter, always switch it OFF to conserve its battery.

Switch checks

1 If a switch is at fault, trace its wiring up to the wiring connectors. Separate the wire connectors and inspect them for security and condition. A build-up of dirt or corrosion here will most likely be the cause of the problem - clean up and apply a water dispersant such as WD40.

2 If using a test meter, set the meter to the ohms x 10 scale and connect its probes across the wires from the switch (see illustration 9). Simple ON/OFF type switches, such as brake light switches, only have two wires whereas combination switches, like the ignition switch, have many internal links. Study the wiring diagram to ensure that you are connecting across the correct pair of wires. Continuity (low or no measurable resistance - 0 ohms) should be indicated with the switch ON and no continuity (high resistance) with it OFF.

3 Note that the polarity of the test probes doesn't matter for continuity checks, although care should be taken to follow specific test procedures if a diode or solid-state component is being checked.

4 A continuity tester or battery and bulb circuit can be used in the same way. Connect its probes as described above (see illustration 10). The light should come on to indicate continuity in the ON switch position, but should extinguish in the OFF position.

Wiring checks

- Many electrical faults are caused by damaged wiring, often due to incorrect routing or chaffing on frame components.
- Loose, wet or corroded wire connectors can also be the cause of electrical problems, especially in exposed locations.

1 A continuity check can be made on a single length of wire by disconnecting it at each end and connecting a meter or continuity tester across both ends of the wire (see illustration 11).

2 Continuity (low or no resistance - 0 ohms) should be indicated if the wire is good. If no continuity (high resistance) is shown, suspect a broken wire.

Checking for voltage

- A voltage check can determine whether current is reaching a component.
- Voltage can be checked with a dc voltmeter, multimeter set on the dc volts scale, test light or buzzer (see illustrations 12 and 13). A meter has the advantage of being able to measure actual voltage.
- When using a meter, check that its leads are inserted in the correct terminals on the meter, red to positive (+ve), black to negative (-ve). Incorrect connections can damage the meter.
- A voltmeter (or multimeter set to the dc volts scale) should always be connected in parallel (across the load). Connecting it in series will destroy the meter.
- Voltage checks are made with the ignition ON.

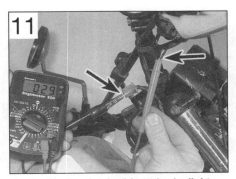

Continuity check of front brake light switch sub-harness

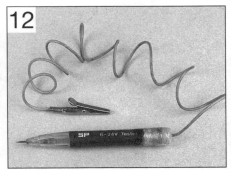

A simple test light can be used for voltage checks

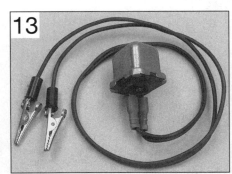

A buzzer is useful for voltage checks

REF•42 Fault Finding Equipment

Checking for voltage at the rear brake light power supply wire using a meter . . .

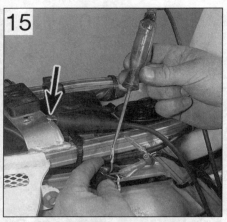

. . . or a test light - note the earth connection to the frame (arrow)

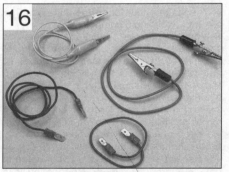

A selection of jumper wires for making earth (ground) checks

1 First identify the relevant wiring circuit by referring to the wiring diagram at the end of this manual. If other electrical components share the same power supply (ie are fed from the same fuse), take note whether they are working correctly - this is useful information in deciding where to start checking the circuit.
2 If using a meter, check first that the meter leads are plugged into the correct terminals on the meter (see above). Set the meter to the dc volts function, at a range suitable for the battery voltage. Connect the meter red probe (+ve) to the power supply wire and the black probe to a good metal earth (ground) on the motorcycle's frame or directly to the battery negative (-ve) terminal **(see illustration 14)**. Battery voltage should be shown on the meter with the ignition switched ON.
3 If using a test light or buzzer, connect its positive (+ve) probe to the power supply terminal and its negative (-ve) probe to a good earth (ground) on the motorcycle's frame or directly to the battery negative (-ve) terminal **(see illustration 15)**. With the ignition ON, the test light should illuminate or the buzzer sound.
4 If no voltage is indicated, work back towards the fuse continuing to check for voltage. When you reach a point where there is voltage, you know the problem lies between that point and your last check point.

Checking the earth (ground)

● Earth connections are made either directly to the engine or frame (such as sensors, neutral switch etc. which only have a positive feed) or by a separate wire into the earth circuit of the wiring harness. Alternatively a short earth wire is sometimes run directly from the component to the motorcycle's frame.
● Corrosion is often the cause of a poor earth connection.
● If total failure is experienced, check the security of the main earth lead from the negative (-ve) terminal of the battery and also the main earth (ground) point on the wiring harness. If corroded, dismantle the connection and clean all surfaces back to bare metal.
1 To check the earth on a component, use an insulated jumper wire to temporarily bypass its earth connection **(see illustration 16)**. Connect one end of the jumper wire between the earth terminal or metal body of the component and the other end to the motorcycle's frame.
2 If the circuit works with the jumper wire installed, the original earth circuit is faulty. Check the wiring for open-circuits or poor connections. Clean up direct earth connections, removing all traces of corrosion and remake the joint. Apply petroleum jelly to the joint to prevent future corrosion.

Tracing a short-circuit

● A short-circuit occurs where current shorts to earth (ground) bypassing the circuit components. This usually results in a blown fuse.

● A short-circuit is most likely to occur where the insulation has worn through due to wiring chafing on a component, allowing a direct path to earth (ground) on the frame.

1 Remove any bodypanels necessary to access the circuit wiring.
2 Check that all electrical switches in the circuit are OFF, then remove the circuit fuse and connect a test light, buzzer or voltmeter (set to the dc scale) across the fuse terminals. No voltage should be shown.
3 Move the wiring from side to side whilst observing the test light or meter. When the test light comes on, buzzer sounds or meter shows voltage, you have found the cause of the short. It will usually shown up as damaged or burned insulation.
4 Note that the same test can be performed on each component in the circuit, even the switch.

Technical Terms Explained REF•43

A

ABS (Anti-lock braking system) A system, usually electronically controlled, that senses incipient wheel lockup during braking and relieves hydraulic pressure at wheel which is about to skid.

Aftermarket Components suitable for the motorcycle, but not produced by the motorcycle manufacturer.

Allen key A hexagonal wrench which fits into a recessed hexagonal hole.

Alternating current (ac) Current produced by an alternator. Requires converting to direct current by a rectifier for charging purposes.

Alternator Converts mechanical energy from the engine into electrical energy to charge the battery and power the electrical system.

Ampere (amp) A unit of measurement for the flow of electrical current. Current = Volts ÷ Ohms.

Ampere-hour (Ah) Measure of battery capacity.

Angle-tightening A torque expressed in degrees. Often follows a conventional tightening torque for cylinder head or main bearing fasteners **(see illustration)**.

Angle-tightening cylinder head bolts

Antifreeze A substance (usually ethylene glycol) mixed with water, and added to the cooling system, to prevent freezing of the coolant in winter. Antifreeze also contains chemicals to inhibit corrosion and the formation of rust and other deposits that would tend to clog the radiator and coolant passages and reduce cooling efficiency.

Anti-dive System attached to the fork lower leg (slider) to prevent fork dive when braking hard.

Anti-seize compound A coating that reduces the risk of seizing on fasteners that are subjected to high temperatures, such as exhaust clamp bolts and nuts.

API American Petroleum Institute. A quality standard for 4-stroke motor oils.

Asbestos A natural fibrous mineral with great heat resistance, commonly used in the composition of brake friction materials. Asbestos is a health hazard and the dust created by brake systems should never be inhaled or ingested.

ATF Automatic Transmission Fluid. Often used in front forks.

ATU Automatic Timing Unit. Mechanical device for advancing the ignition timing on early engines.

ATV All Terrain Vehicle. Often called a Quad.

Axial play Side-to-side movement.

Axle A shaft on which a wheel revolves. Also known as a spindle.

B

Backlash The amount of movement between meshed components when one component is held still. Usually applies to gear teeth.

Ball bearing A bearing consisting of a hardened inner and outer race with hardened steel balls between the two races.

Bearings Used between two working surfaces to prevent wear of the components and a build-up of heat. Four types of bearing are commonly used on motorcycles: plain shell bearings, ball bearings, tapered roller bearings and needle roller bearings.

Bevel gears Used to turn the drive through 90°. Typical applications are shaft final drive and camshaft drive **(see illustration)**.

Bevel gears are used to turn the drive through 90°

BHP Brake Horsepower. The British measurement for engine power output. Power output is now usually expressed in kilowatts (kW).

Bias-belted tyre Similar construction to radial tyre, but with outer belt running at an angle to the wheel rim.

Big-end bearing The bearing in the end of the connecting rod that's attached to the crankshaft.

Bleeding The process of removing air from an hydraulic system via a bleed nipple or bleed screw.

Bottom-end A description of an engine's crankcase components and all components contained there-in.

BTDC Before Top Dead Centre in terms of piston position. Ignition timing is often expressed in terms of degrees or millimetres BTDC.

Bush A cylindrical metal or rubber component used between two moving parts.

Burr Rough edge left on a component after machining or as a result of excessive wear.

C

Cam chain The chain which takes drive from the crankshaft to the camshaft(s).

Canister The main component in an evaporative emission control system (California market only); contains activated charcoal granules to trap vapours from the fuel system rather than allowing them to vent to the atmosphere.

Castellated Resembling the parapets along the top of a castle wall. For example, a castellated wheel axle or spindle nut.

Catalytic converter A device in the exhaust system of some machines which converts certain pollutants in the exhaust gases into less harmful substances.

Charging system Description of the components which charge the battery, ie the alternator, rectifier and regulator.

Circlip A ring-shaped clip used to prevent endwise movement of cylindrical parts and shafts. An internal circlip is installed in a groove in a housing; an external circlip fits into a groove on the outside of a cylindrical piece such as a shaft. Also known as a snap-ring.

Clearance The amount of space between two parts. For example, between a piston and a cylinder, between a bearing and a journal, etc.

Coil spring A spiral of elastic steel found in various sizes throughout a vehicle, for example as a springing medium in the suspension and in the valve train.

Compression Reduction in volume, and increase in pressure and temperature, of a gas, caused by squeezing it into a smaller space.

Compression damping Controls the speed the suspension compresses when hitting a bump.

Compression ratio The relationship between cylinder volume when the piston is at top dead centre and cylinder volume when the piston is at bottom dead centre.

Continuity The uninterrupted path in the flow of electricity. Little or no measurable resistance.

Continuity tester Self-powered bleeper or test light which indicates continuity.

Cp Candlepower. Bulb rating commonly found on US motorcycles.

Crossply tyre Tyre plies arranged in a criss-cross pattern. Usually four or six plies used, hence 4PR or 6PR in tyre size codes.

Cush drive Rubber damper segments fitted between the rear wheel and final drive sprocket to absorb transmission shocks **(see illustration)**.

Cush drive rubbers dampen out transmission shocks

D

Degree disc Calibrated disc for measuring piston position. Expressed in degrees.

Dial gauge Clock-type gauge with adapters for measuring runout and piston position. Expressed in mm or inches.

Diaphragm The rubber membrane in a master cylinder or carburettor which seals the upper chamber.

Diaphragm spring A single sprung plate often used in clutches.

Direct current (dc) Current produced by a dc generator.

Technical Terms Explained

Decarbonisation The process of removing carbon deposits - typically from the combustion chamber, valves and exhaust port/system.
Detonation Destructive and damaging explosion of fuel/air mixture in combustion chamber instead of controlled burning.
Diode An electrical valve which only allows current to flow in one direction. Commonly used in rectifiers and starter interlock systems.
Disc valve (or rotary valve) A induction system used on some two-stroke engines.
Double-overhead camshaft (DOHC) An engine that uses two overhead camshafts, one for the intake valves and one for the exhaust valves.
Drivebelt A toothed belt used to transmit drive to the rear wheel on some motorcycles. A drivebelt has also been used to drive the camshafts. Drivebelts are usually made of Kevlar.
Driveshaft Any shaft used to transmit motion. Commonly used when referring to the final driveshaft on shaft drive motorcycles.

E

Earth return The return path of an electrical circuit, utilising the motorcycle's frame.
ECU (Electronic Control Unit) A computer which controls (for instance) an ignition system, or an anti-lock braking system.
EGO Exhaust Gas Oxygen sensor. Sometimes called a Lambda sensor.
Electrolyte The fluid in a lead-acid battery.
EMS (Engine Management System) A computer controlled system which manages the fuel injection and the ignition systems in an integrated fashion.
Endfloat The amount of lengthways movement between two parts. As applied to a crankshaft, the distance that the crankshaft can move side-to-side in the crankcase.
Endless chain A chain having no joining link. Common use for cam chains and final drive chains.
EP (Extreme Pressure) Oil type used in locations where high loads are applied, such as between gear teeth.
Evaporative emission control system Describes a charcoal filled canister which stores fuel vapours from the tank rather than allowing them to vent to the atmosphere. Usually only fitted to California models and referred to as an EVAP system.
Expansion chamber Section of two-stroke engine exhaust system so designed to improve engine efficiency and boost power.

F

Feeler blade or gauge A thin strip or blade of hardened steel, ground to an exact thickness, used to check or measure clearances between parts.
Final drive Description of the drive from the transmission to the rear wheel. Usually by chain or shaft, but sometimes by belt.
Firing order The order in which the engine cylinders fire, or deliver their power strokes, beginning with the number one cylinder.
Flooding Term used to describe a high fuel level in the carburettor float chambers, leading to fuel overflow. Also refers to excess fuel in the combustion chamber due to incorrect starting technique.
Free length The no-load state of a component when measured. Clutch, valve and fork spring lengths are measured at rest, without any preload.
Freeplay The amount of travel before any action takes place. The looseness in a linkage, or an assembly of parts, between the initial application of force and actual movement. For example, the distance the rear brake pedal moves before the rear brake is actuated.
Fuel injection The fuel/air mixture is metered electronically and directed into the engine intake ports (indirect injection) or into the cylinders (direct injection). Sensors supply information on engine speed and conditions.
Fuel/air mixture The charge of fuel and air going into the engine. See **Stoichiometric ratio**.
Fuse An electrical device which protects a circuit against accidental overload. The typical fuse contains a soft piece of metal which is calibrated to melt at a predetermined current flow (expressed as amps) and break the circuit.

G

Gap The distance the spark must travel in jumping from the centre electrode to the side electrode in a spark plug. Also refers to the distance between the ignition rotor and the pickup coil in an electronic ignition system.
Gasket Any thin, soft material - usually cork, cardboard, asbestos or soft metal - installed between two metal surfaces to ensure a good seal. For instance, the cylinder head gasket seals the joint between the block and the cylinder head.
Gauge An instrument panel display used to monitor engine conditions. A gauge with a movable pointer on a dial or a fixed scale is an analogue gauge. A gauge with a numerical readout is called a digital gauge.
Gear ratios The drive ratio of a pair of gears in a gearbox, calculated on their number of teeth.
Glaze-busting see **Honing**
Grinding Process for renovating the valve face and valve seat contact area in the cylinder head.
Gudgeon pin The shaft which connects the connecting rod small-end with the piston. Often called a piston pin or wrist pin.

H

Helical gears Gear teeth are slightly curved and produce less gear noise that straight-cut gears. Often used for primary drives.

Installing a Helicoil thread insert in a cylinder head

Helicoil A thread insert repair system. Commonly used as a repair for stripped spark plug threads (see illustration).
Honing A process used to break down the glaze on a cylinder bore (also called glaze-busting). Can also be carried out to roughen a rebored cylinder to aid ring bedding-in.
HT (High Tension) Description of the electrical circuit from the secondary winding of the ignition coil to the spark plug.
Hydraulic A liquid filled system used to transmit pressure from one component to another. Common uses on motorcycles are brakes and clutches.
Hydrometer An instrument for measuring the specific gravity of a lead-acid battery.
Hygroscopic Water absorbing. In motorcycle applications, braking efficiency will be reduced if DOT 3 or 4 hydraulic fluid absorbs water from the air - care must be taken to keep new brake fluid in tightly sealed containers.

I

lbf ft Pounds-force feet. An imperial unit of torque. Sometimes written as ft-lbs.
lbf in Pound-force inch. An imperial unit of torque, applied to components where a very low torque is required. Sometimes written as in-lbs.
IC Abbreviation for Integrated Circuit.
Ignition advance Means of increasing the timing of the spark at higher engine speeds. Done by mechanical means (ATU) on early engines or electronically by the ignition control unit on later engines.
Ignition timing The moment at which the spark plug fires, expressed in the number of crankshaft degrees before the piston reaches the top of its stroke, or in the number of millimetres before the piston reaches the top of its stroke.
Infinity (∞) Description of an open-circuit electrical state, where no continuity exists.
Inverted forks (upside down forks) The sliders or lower legs are held in the yokes and the fork tubes or stanchions are connected to the wheel axle (spindle). Less unsprung weight and stiffer construction than conventional forks.

J

JASO Quality standard for 2-stroke oils.
Joule The unit of electrical energy.
Journal The bearing surface of a shaft.

K

Kickstart Mechanical means of turning the engine over for starting purposes. Only usually fitted to mopeds, small capacity motorcycles and off-road motorcycles.
Kill switch Handebar-mounted switch for emergency ignition cut-out. Cuts the ignition circuit on all models, and additionally prevent starter motor operation on others.
km Symbol for kilometre.
kmh Abbreviation for kilometres per hour.

L

Lambda (λ) sensor A sensor fitted in the exhaust system to measure the exhaust gas oxygen content (excess air factor).

Technical Terms Explained

Lapping see **Grinding**.
LCD Abbreviation for Liquid Crystal Display.
LED Abbreviation for Light Emitting Diode.
Liner A steel cylinder liner inserted in a aluminium alloy cylinder block.
Locknut A nut used to lock an adjustment nut, or other threaded component, in place.
Lockstops The lugs on the lower triple clamp (yoke) which abut those on the frame, preventing handlebar-to-fuel tank contact.
Lockwasher A form of washer designed to prevent an attaching nut from working loose.
LT Low Tension Description of the electrical circuit from the power supply to the primary winding of the ignition coil.

M

Main bearings The bearings between the crankshaft and crankcase.
Maintenance-free (MF) battery A sealed battery which cannot be topped up.
Manometer Mercury-filled calibrated tubes used to measure intake tract vacuum. Used to synchronise carburettors on multi-cylinder engines.
Micrometer A precision measuring instrument that measures component outside diameters (see illustration).

Tappet shims are measured with a micrometer

MON (Motor Octane Number) A measure of a fuel's resistance to knock.
Monograde oil An oil with a single viscosity, eg SAE80W.
Monoshock A single suspension unit linking the swingarm or suspension linkage to the frame.
mph Abbreviation for miles per hour.
Multigrade oil Having a wide viscosity range (eg 10W40). The W stands for Winter, thus the viscosity ranges from SAE10 when cold to SAE40 when hot.
Multimeter An electrical test instrument with the capability to measure voltage, current and resistance. Some meters also incorporate a continuity tester and buzzer.

N

Needle roller bearing Inner race of caged needle rollers and hardened outer race. Examples of uncaged needle rollers can be found on some engines. Commonly used in rear suspension applications and in two-stroke engines.
Nm Newton metres.
NOx Oxides of Nitrogen. A common toxic pollutant emitted by petrol engines at higher temperatures.

O

Octane The measure of a fuel's resistance to knock.
OE (Original Equipment) Relates to components fitted to a motorcycle as standard or replacement parts supplied by the motorcycle manufacturer.
Ohm The unit of electrical resistance. Ohms = Volts ÷ Current.
Ohmmeter An instrument for measuring electrical resistance.
Oil cooler System for diverting engine oil outside of the engine to a radiator for cooling purposes.
Oil injection A system of two-stroke engine lubrication where oil is pump-fed to the engine in accordance with throttle position.
Open-circuit An electrical condition where there is a break in the flow of electricity - no continuity (high resistance).
O-ring A type of sealing ring made of a special rubber-like material; in use, the O-ring is compressed into a groove to provide the sealing action.
Oversize (OS) Term used for piston and ring size options fitted to a rebored cylinder.
Overhead cam (sohc) engine An engine with single camshaft located on top of the cylinder head.
Overhead valve (ohv) engine An engine with the valves located in the cylinder head, but with the camshaft located in the engine block or crankcase.
Oxygen sensor A device installed in the exhaust system which senses the oxygen content in the exhaust and converts this information into an electric current. Also called a Lambda sensor.

P

Plastigauge A thin strip of plastic thread, available in different sizes, used for measuring clearances. For example, a strip of Plastigauge is laid across a bearing journal. The parts are assembled and dismantled; the width of the crushed strip indicates the clearance between journal and bearing.
Polarity Either negative or positive earth (ground), determined by which battery lead is connected to the frame (earth return). Modern motorcycles are usually negative earth.
Pre-ignition A situation where the fuel/air mixture ignites before the spark plug fires. Often due to a hot spot in the combustion chamber caused by carbon build-up. Engine has a tendency to 'run-on'.
Pre-load (suspension) The amount a spring is compressed when in the unloaded state. Preload can be applied by gas, spacer or mechanical adjuster.
Premix The method of engine lubrication on older two-stroke engines. Engine oil is mixed with the petrol in the fuel tank in a specific ratio. The fuel/oil mix is sometimes referred to as "petroil".
Primary drive Description of the drive from the crankshaft to the clutch. Usually by gear or chain.
PS Pfedestärke - a German interpretation of BHP.
PSI Pounds-force per square inch. Imperial measurement of tyre pressure and cylinder pressure measurement.
PTFE Polytetrafluroethylene. A low friction substance.
Pulse secondary air injection system A process of promoting the burning of excess fuel present in the exhaust gases by routing fresh air into the exhaust ports.

Q

Quartz halogen bulb Tungsten filament surrounded by a halogen gas. Typically used for the headlight (see illustration).

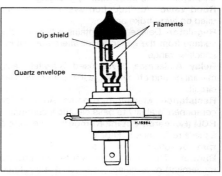

Quartz halogen headlight bulb construction

R

Rack-and-pinion A pinion gear on the end of a shaft that mates with a rack (think of a geared wheel opened up and laid flat). Sometimes used in clutch operating systems.
Radial play Up and down movement about a shaft.
Radial ply tyres Tyre plies run across the tyre (from bead to bead) and around the circumference of the tyre. Less resistant to tread distortion than other tyre types.
Radiator A liquid-to-air heat transfer device designed to reduce the temperature of the coolant in a liquid cooled engine.
Rake A feature of steering geometry - the angle of the steering head in relation to the vertical (see illustration).

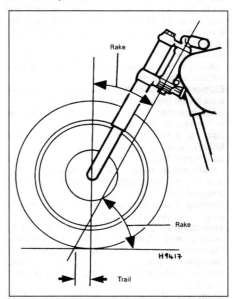

Steering geometry

Technical Terms Explained

Rebore Providing a new working surface to the cylinder bore by boring out the old surface. Necessitates the use of oversize piston and rings.
Rebound damping A means of controlling the oscillation of a suspension unit spring after it has been compressed. Resists the spring's natural tendency to bounce back after being compressed.
Rectifier Device for converting the ac output of an alternator into dc for battery charging.
Reed valve An induction system commonly used on two-stroke engines.
Regulator Device for maintaining the charging voltage from the generator or alternator within a specified range.
Relay A electrical device used to switch heavy current on and off by using a low current auxiliary circuit.
Resistance Measured in ohms. An electrical component's ability to pass electrical current.
RON (Research Octane Number) A measure of a fuel's resistance to knock.
rpm revolutions per minute.
Runout The amount of wobble (in-and-out movement) of a wheel or shaft as it's rotated. The amount a shaft rotates 'out-of-true'. The out-of-round condition of a rotating part.

S

SAE (Society of Automotive Engineers) A standard for the viscosity of a fluid.
Sealant A liquid or paste used to prevent leakage at a joint. Sometimes used in conjunction with a gasket.
Service limit Term for the point where a component is no longer useable and must be renewed.
Shaft drive A method of transmitting drive from the transmission to the rear wheel.
Shell bearings Plain bearings consisting of two shell halves. Most often used as big-end and main bearings in a four-stroke engine. Often called bearing inserts.
Shim Thin spacer, commonly used to adjust the clearance or relative positions between two parts. For example, shims inserted into or under tappets or followers to control valve clearances. Clearance is adjusted by changing the thickness of the shim.
Short-circuit An electrical condition where current shorts to earth (ground) bypassing the circuit components.
Skimming Process to correct warpage or repair a damaged surface, eg on brake discs or drums.
Slide-hammer A special puller that screws into or hooks onto a component such as a shaft or bearing; a heavy sliding handle on the shaft bottoms against the end of the shaft to knock the component free.
Small-end bearing The bearing in the upper end of the connecting rod at its joint with the gudgeon pin.
Spalling Damage to camshaft lobes or bearing journals shown as pitting of the working surface.
Specific gravity (SG) The state of charge of the electrolyte in a lead-acid battery. A measure of the electrolyte's density compared with water.
Straight-cut gears Common type gear used on gearbox shafts and for oil pump and water pump drives.
Stanchion The inner sliding part of the front forks, held by the yokes. Often called a fork tube.
Stoichiometric ratio The optimum chemical air/fuel ratio for a petrol engine, said to be 14.7 parts of air to 1 part of fuel.
Sulphuric acid The liquid (electrolyte) used in a lead-acid battery. Poisonous and extremely corrosive.
Surface grinding (lapping) Process to correct a warped gasket face, commonly used on cylinder heads.

T

Tapered-roller bearing Tapered inner race of caged needle rollers and separate tapered outer race. Examples of taper roller bearings can be found on steering heads.
Tappet A cylindrical component which transmits motion from the cam to the valve stem, either directly or via a pushrod and rocker arm. Also called a cam follower.
TCS Traction Control System. An electronically-controlled system which senses wheel spin and reduces engine speed accordingly.
TDC Top Dead Centre denotes that the piston is at its highest point in the cylinder.
Thread-locking compound Solution applied to fastener threads to prevent slackening. Select type to suit application.
Thrust washer A washer positioned between two moving components on a shaft. For example, between gear pinions on gearshaft.
Timing chain See **Cam Chain**.
Timing light Stroboscopic lamp for carrying out ignition timing checks with the engine running.
Top-end A description of an engine's cylinder block, head and valve gear components.
Torque Turning or twisting force about a shaft.
Torque setting A prescribed tightness specified by the motorcycle manufacturer to ensure that the bolt or nut is secured correctly. Undertightening can result in the bolt or nut coming loose or a surface not being sealed. Overtightening can result in stripped threads, distortion or damage to the component being retained.
Torx key A six-point wrench.
Tracer A stripe of a second colour applied to a wire insulator to distinguish that wire from another one with the same colour insulator. For example, Br/W is often used to denote a brown insulator with a white tracer.
Trail A feature of steering geometry. Distance from the steering head axis to the tyre's central contact point.
Triple clamps The cast components which extend from the steering head and support the fork stanchions or tubes. Often called fork yokes.
Turbocharger A centrifugal device, driven by exhaust gases, that pressurises the intake air. Normally used to increase the power output from a given engine displacement.
TWI Abbreviation for Tyre Wear Indicator. Indicates the location of the tread depth indicator bars on tyres.

U

Universal joint or U-joint (UJ) A double-pivoted connection for transmitting power from a driving to a driven shaft through an angle. Typically found in shaft drive assemblies.
Unsprung weight Anything not supported by the bike's suspension (ie the wheel, tyres, brakes, final drive and bottom (moving) part of the suspension).

V

Vacuum gauges Clock-type gauges for measuring intake tract vacuum. Used for carburettor synchronisation on multi-cylinder engines.
Valve A device through which the flow of liquid, gas or vacuum may be stopped, started or regulated by a moveable part that opens, shuts or partially obstructs one or more ports or passageways. The intake and exhaust valves in the cylinder head are of the poppet type.
Valve clearance The clearance between the valve tip (the end of the valve stem) and the rocker arm or tappet/follower. The valve clearance is measured when the valve is closed. The correct clearance is important - if too small the valve won't close fully and will burn out, whereas if too large noisy operation will result.
Valve lift The amount a valve is lifted off its seat by the camshaft lobe.
Valve timing The exact setting for the opening and closing of the valves in relation to piston position.
Vernier caliper A precision measuring instrument that measures inside and outside dimensions. Not quite as accurate as a micrometer, but more convenient.
VIN Vehicle Identification Number. Term for the bike's engine and frame numbers.
Viscosity The thickness of a liquid or its resistance to flow.
Volt A unit for expressing electrical "pressure" in a circuit. Volts = current x ohms.

W

Water pump A mechanically-driven device for moving coolant around the engine.
Watt A unit for expressing electrical power. Watts = volts x current.
Wear limit see **Service limit**
Wet liner A liquid-cooled engine design where the pistons run in liners which are directly surrounded by coolant **(see illustration)**.

Wet liner arrangement

Wheelbase Distance from the centre of the front wheel to the centre of the rear wheel.
Wiring harness or loom Describes the electrical wires running the length of the motorcycle and enclosed in tape or plastic sheathing. Wiring coming off the main harness is usually referred to as a sub harness.
Woodruff key A key of semi-circular or square section used to locate a gear to a shaft. Often used to locate the alternator rotor on the crankshaft.
Wrist pin Another name for gudgeon or piston pin.

Index REF•47

Note: *References throughout this index are in the form – "Chapter number"•"Page number"*

A

About this manual – 0•9
Air filter
  cleaning and renewal – 1•8
  housing removal and installation – 3•3
Air induction system (AIS)
  check – 1•9
  function, disassembly and reassembly – 3•18
Air/fuel mixture adjustment – 3•4
Alternator
  brushes – 1•22
  drive shaft and starter clutch assembly – 2•40
  regulator/rectifier – 8•20
Asbestos – 0•10

B

Battery
  charging – 8•3
  check – 1•12
  removal, installation, inspection and maintenance – 8•3
  safety – 0•10
  specifications – 8•1
Bearings
  fault finding – REF•14
  removal and installation – REF•14
  steering head – 1•15, 1•18
  suspension linkage – 1•18
  swingarm – 1•18
  types and markings – REF•14
  wheel – 1•12
Bleeding the brake system – 6•12
Bodywork – 7•1 *et seq*
  body panels – 7•2
  fairing – 7•2
  mudguard – 7•5
  rear view mirrors – 7•4
  seat – 7•2
  windshield – 7•5
Brake fluid
  change – 1•20
  level checks – 0•13
Brake light
  bulb – 8•6
  switches – 8•8
Brake pedal removal and installation – 5•2
Brake system check – 1•11
Brakes, wheels and tyres – 6•1 *et seq*
  brake system bleeding – 6•12
  calipers – 1•20, 6•3, 6•8
  discs – 6•5, 6•10
  hoses, pipes and unions – 1•21, 6•12
  master cylinder – 1•20, 6•6, 6•10
  MOT Test checks – REF•25
  pads – 1•10, 6•2, 6•7
  tyres – 6•19
  wheel bearings – 6•16
  wheels – 6•13, 6•14, 6•15
Braking problems – REF•38
Bulbs specifications – 8•2

REF•48 Index

C

Cable(s)
  choke – 1•13, 3•14
  clutch – 2•30
  lubrication – 1•14
  speedometer – 8•8
  throttle – 1•13, 3•12
Calipers
  removal, overhaul and installation
    front – 6•3
    rear – 6•8
Cam chain and tensioner blade removal, inspection and installation – 2•40
Cam chain tensioner and guides removal, inspection and installation – 2•10
Camshafts and followers removal, inspection and installation – 2•11
Carburettors
  disassembly, cleaning and inspection – 3•6
  heating system check – 3•15
  overhaul – 3•4
  reassembly and fuel level check – 3•10
  removal and installation – 3•5
  separation and joining – 3•8
  synchronisation – 1•7
Centrestand
  check – 1•12
  removal and installation – 5•3
Chains – REF•18
Charging system
  leakage and output test – 8•19
  testing (general information and precautions) – 8•19
Chemicals explained – REF•21
Choke cable
  check – 1•13
  removal and installation – 3•14
Clutch
  cable – 2•30
  check and adjustment – 1•12
  fault finding – REF•34
  removal, inspection and installation – 2•25
  switch – 8•13
Component locations – 1•4
Connecting rods removal, inspection and installation – 2•45
Conversion Factors – REF•20
Crankcase
  halves – 2•39
  separation and reassembly – 2•37
Crankshaft and main bearings removal, inspection and installation – 2•43
Cylinder block removal, inspection and installation – 2•20
Cylinder compression check – 1•21
Cylinder head
  disassembly, inspection and reassembly – 2•16
  removal and installation – 2•15

D

Daily (pre-ride) checks – 0•12
Dimensions and Weights – REF•1
Diode (1994 to 1996 models) check and renewal – 8•14
Discs
  inspection, removal and installation
    front – 6•5
    rear – 6•10
Driveshaft removal, inspection and installation – 5•17
Dust, eye and hand protection – REF•4

E

Electrical system – 8•1 *et seq*
  alternator – 8•20
  battery – 8•3
  brake light switches – 8•8
  brake/tail light bulb – 8•6
  charging system testing – 8•19
  clutch switch – 8•13
  diode (1994 to 1996 models) – 8•14
  fault finding – 8•2
  fuses – 8•4
  handlebar switches – 8•12
  headlight assembly – 8•5
  headlight bulb – 8•5
  horn – 8•14
  ignition (main) switch – 8•11
  instrument bulbs – 8•11
  instrument cluster – 8•8
  instruments – 8•9
  lighting system – 8•4
  MOT Test checks – REF•22
  neutral switch – 8•12
  oil level sensor – 8•15
  problems – REF•38
  rectifier – 8•20
  regulator – 8•20
  safety – 0•10
  sidelight bulb – 8•5
  sidestand switch – 8•13
  speedometer cable – 8•8
  starter motor – 8•16, 8•17
  starter relay – 8•15
  tail light assembly – 8•6
  turn signal assemblies – 8•6, 8•7
  warning light bulbs – 8•11
Engine/transmission oil
  change – 1•9, 1•17
  level check – 0•12
  pressure check – 1•21
Engine, clutch and transmission – 2•1 *et seq*
  abnormal engine noise – REF•35
  alternator drive shaft and starter clutch assembly – 2•40
  cam chain and tensioner blade – 2•40
  cam chain tensioner and guides – 2•10
  camshafts and followers – 2•11
  clutch – 2•25
  clutch cable – 2•30
  connecting rods – 2•45
  crankcase – 2•37
  crankcase halves – 2•39
  crankshaft and main bearings – 2•43
  cylinder block – 2•20
  cylinder head – 2•15, 2•16
  disassembly and reassembly – 2•7
  engine numbers – 0•11
  gearchange mechanism – 2•30
  main and connecting rod bearings – 2•42
  major engine repair – 2•5
  middle gear shifts – 2•32
  oil cooler – 2•8
  oil filter housing – 2•8
  oil pump and pressure relief valve – 2•35
  oil sump – 2•34
  operations possible with the engine in the frame – 2•4
  operations requiring engine removal – 2•5
  piston rings – 2•23

Index REF•49

pistons – 2•21
removal and installation – 2•5
running-in procedure – 2•53
selector drum and forks – 2•52
start-up after overhaul – 2•53
transmission shafts – 2•47, 2•48
valve cover – 2•10
valves, valve seats and valve guides – 2•16
Engine fault finding – REF•32
Exhaust system
excessive smoke – REF•37
MOT Test checks – REF•23
removal and installation – 3•15

F

Fairing and body panels removal and installation – 7•2
Fastener types and applications – REF•5
Fault Finding – REF•30
Fault Finding Equipment – REF•39
Filter
air – 1•8
fuel – 1•9
oil – 1•17
Final drive
checks – 0•14, REF•23
oil change – 1•20
oil level check – 1•17
removal, inspection and installation – 5•17
Fire – 0•10, REF•4
Fluids
brake – 0•13, 1•20
recommended – 1•2
storage, removal and disposal – REF•4
Footrest removal and installation – 5•2
Forks
disassembly, inspection and reassembly – 5•7
oil change – 1•22
removal and installation – 5•6
Frame inspection and repair – 5•2
Frame, suspension and final drive – 5•1 *et seq*
abnormal noise – REF•36
brake pedal – 5•2
centrestand – 5•3
driveshaft – 5•17
final drive – 5•17
footrest – 5•2
forks – 5•6, 5•7
frame – 0•11, 5•2
gearchange lever – 5•2
handlebars – 5•4
levers – 5•4
shock absorber – 5•12
sidestand – 5•3
steering head bearings – 5•11
steering stem – 5•10
suspension – 5•14
suspension linkage – 5•13
swingarm – 5•15, 5•16
Fuel and exhaust systems – 3•1 *et seq*
air filter housing – 3•3
air induction system (AIS) – 1•9, 3•18
air/fuel mixture adjustment – 3•4
carburettors – 3•4, 3•5, 3•6, 3•8, 3•10, 3•15
choke cable – 3•14

exhaust system – 3•15
fuel gauge, warning light and sensor – 3•17
fuel pump and relay – 3•17
fuel tank – 3•2, 3•3
fuel tank and fuel tap – 3•2
general information and precautions – 3•2
throttle cables – 3•12
Fuel checks – 0•15
Fuel filter – 1•9
Fuel hoses renewal – 1•22
Fuel system check – 1•9
Fumes – 0•10, REF•4
Fuses
check and renew – 8•4
ratings – 8•2

G

Gaskets – REF•17
Gauges – REF•9
Gearchange
fault finding – REF•35
lever removal and installation – 5•2
mechanism removal, inspection and installation – 2•30

H

Handlebars
removal and installation – 5•4
switches – 8•12
Handling problems – REF•37
Headlight
aim check and adjustment – 1•21
assembly removal and installation – 8•5
bulb renewal – 8•5
Horn check and renewal – 8•14
Hoses
brakes – 1•21, 6•12
clamping, freeing and fitting – REF•19
fuel – 1•22
HT coils check, removal and installation – 4•3

I

Identification numbers – 0•11
Idle speed
check and adjustment – 1•7
specifications – 1•2
Ignition (main) switch check, removal and installation – 8•11
Ignition system – 4•1 *et seq*
control unit – 4•4
HT coils – 4•3
pick-up coil – 4•3
system check – 4•2
throttle position sensor – 4•5
timing – 4•4
Instrument(s)
bulbs renewal – 8•11
cluster removal and installation – 8•8
check and renewal – 8•9
Introduction – 0•4

REF•50 Index

L

Legal checks – 0•15
Lever pivots lubrication – 1•14
Levers (handlebar) removal and installation – 5•4
Lighting system check – 8•4
Lubricants
   explained – REF•21
   recommended – 1•2

M

Main and connecting rod bearings general information – 2•42
Maintenance schedule – 1•3
Major engine repair general information – 2•5
Master cylinder
   removal, overhaul and installation
     front – 6•6
     rear – 6•10
Measuring tools and gauges – REF•9
Micrometers – REF•9
Middle gear shifts removal, inspection and installation – 2•32
Mirrors – 7•4
MOT Test checks – REF•22
Mudguard removal and installation – 7•5

N

Neutral switch check, removal and installation – 8•12
Nuts and bolts tightness check – 1•13

O

Oil cooler removal, inspection and installation – 2•8
Oil filter – 1•17
Oil level indicator light comes on – REF•36
Oil level sensor check, removal and installation – 8•15
Oil pump and pressure relief valve removal, inspection and installation – 2•35
Oil seals – REF•16
Oil sump removal and installation – 2•34
Oil
   correct type and viscosity – 0•12
   disposal facilities – REF•4
   engine – 1•9, 1•17, 1•21
   final drive – 1•17, 1•20
   forks – 1•22

P

Pads
   renewal
     front – 6•2
     rear – 6•7
   wear check – 1•10
Pick-up coil check and renewal – 4•3
Pipes (brake) inspection and renewal – 6•12
Piston rings inspection and installation – 2•23
Pistons removal, inspection and installation – 2•21
Plastigauge – REF•11

R

Rear view mirrors removal and installation – 7•4
Reference – REF•1
Relay assembly check and renewal – 8•14
Routine maintenance and Servicing – 1•1 *et seq*
   air filter – 1•8
   alternator brushes – 1•22
   battery – 1•12
   brake hoses – 1•21
   brake master cylinder and caliper seals – 1•20
   brake pads – 1•10
   brake system – 1•11
   brakes – 1•20
   carburettors – 1•7
   choke cable – 1•13
   clutch – 1•12
   component locations – 1•4
   cylinder compression – 1•21
   engine/transmission oil and filter – 1•9, 1•17, 1•21
   final drive oil – 1•17, 1•20
   front forks – 1•22
   fuel hoses – 1•22
   fuel system and air induction system (AIS) – 1•9
   headlight aim – 1•21
   idle speed – 1•7
   maintenance schedule – 1•3
   nuts and bolts – 1•13
   recommended lubricants and fluids – 1•2
   sidestand/centrestand – 1•12
   spark plugs – 1•6
   stands, lever pivots and cables lubrication – 1•14
   steering head bearings – 1•15, 1•18
   suspension – 1•14
   swingarm bearings – 1•18
   throttle cable – 1•13
   tyres – 1•12
   valve clearances – 1•18
   wheel bearings – 1•12
   wheels – 1•12
Running-in procedure – 2•53

S

Safety checks – 0•15
Safety First! – 0•10
Sealants – REF•17
Seat removal and installation – 7•2
Selector drum and forks removal, inspection and installation – 2•52
Shock absorber removal, inspection and installation – 5•12
Sidecar MOT Test checks – REF•26
Sidelight bulb renewal – 8•5
Sidestand
   check – 1•12
   removal and installation – 5•3
   switch – 8•13
Spare parts – 0•11
Spark plug
   gaps, check and adjustment – 1•6
   types and gap sizes – 1•2
Speedometer cable removal and installation – 8•8
Stands, lever pivots and cables lubrication – 1•14
Starter motor
   disassembly, inspection and reassembly – 8•17
   removal and installation – 8•16

Index REF•51

Starter relay check and renewal – 8•15
Start-up after overhaul – 2•53
Steering checks – 0•14, REF•23
Steering head bearings
    freeplay check and adjustment – 1•15
    inspection and renewal – 5•11
    re-greasing – 1•18
Steering stem removal and installation – 5•10
Storage – REF•27
Suspension
    adjustments – 5•14
    checks – 0•14, 1•14, REF•23
    linkage removal, inspection and installation – 5•13
Swingarm
    bearings re-greasing – 1•18
    inspection and bearing renewal – 5•16
    removal and installation – 5•15

T

Tail light
    assembly, removal and installation – 8•6
    bulb renewal – 8•6
Technical Terms Explained – REF•43
Throttle cable(s)
    check – 1•13
    removal and installation – 3•12
Throttle position sensor check, adjustment and renewal – 4•5
Tools and Workshop Tips – REF•2
Torque and leverage – REF•13
Transmission shafts
    disassembly, inspection and reassembly – 2•48
    removal and installation – 2•47

Turn signal
    assemblies removal and installation – 8•7
    bulbs renewal – 8•7
    circuit check – 8•6
Tyre
    checks – 0•15, 1•12, REF•25
    general information and fitting – 6•19
    pressures – 0•15
    tread depth – 0•15

V

Valve clearances check and adjustment – 1•18
Valve cover removal and installation – 2•10
Valves, valve seats, valve guides servicing – 2•16

W

Warning light bulbs renewal – 8•11
Wheel bearings
    check – 1•12
    removal, inspection and installation – 6•16
Wheels
    alignment check – 6•13
    general check – 1•12
    inspection and repair – 6•13
    MOT Test checks – REF•25
    removal and installation – 6•14, 6•15
Windshield removal and installation – 7•5
Workbenches – REF•4

REF•52 Notes

Haynes Motorcycle Manuals – The Complete List

Title	Book No.
BMW	
BMW 2-valve Twins (70 - 96)	0249
BMW K100 & 75 2-valve Models (83 - 96)	1373
BMW R850 & R1100 4-valve Twins (93 - 97)	3466
BSA	
BSA Bantam (48 - 71)	0117
BSA Unit Singles (58 - 72)	0127
BSA Pre-unit Singles (54 - 61)	0326
BSA A7 & A10 Twins (47 - 62)	0121
BSA A50 & A65 Twins (62 - 73)	0155
DUCATI	
Ducati 600, 750 & 900 2-valve V-Twins (91 - 96)	3290
HARLEY-DAVIDSON	
Harley-Davidson Sportsters (70 - 99)	0702
Harley-Davidson Big Twins (70 - 99)	0703
HONDA	
Honda NB, ND, NP & NS50 Melody (81 - 85) ◊	0622
Honda NE/NB50 Vision & SA50 Vision Met-in (85 - 95) ◊	1278
Honda MB, MBX, MT & MTX50 (80 - 93)	0731
Honda C50, C70 & C90 (67 - 99)	0324
Honda CR80R & CR125R (86 - 97)	2220
Honda XR80R & XR100R (85 - 96)	2218
Honda XL/XR 80, 100, 125, 185 & 200 2-valve Models (78 - 87)	0566
Honda CB100N & CB125N (78 - 86) ◊	0569
Honda H100 & H100S Singles (80 - 92) ◊	0734
Honda CB/CD125T & CM125C Twins (77 - 88) ◊	0571
Honda CG125 (76 - 99) ◊	0433
Honda NS125 (86 - 93) ◊	3056
Honda MBX/MTX125 & MTX200 (83 - 93) ◊	1132
Honda CD/CM185 200T & CM250C 2-valve Twins (77 - 85)	0572
Honda XL/XR 250 & 500 (78 - 84)	0567
Honda XR250L, XR250R & XR400R (86 - 97)	2219
Honda CB250 & CB400N Super Dreams (78 - 84) ◊	0540
Honda CR250R & CR500R (86 - 97)	2222
Honda Elsinore 250 (73 - 75)	0217
Honda CBR400RR Fours (88 - 99)	3552
Honda VFR400 (NC30) & RVF400 (NC35) V-Fours (89 - 98)	3496
Honda CB400 & CB550 Fours (73 - 77)	0262
Honda CX/GL500 & 650 V-Twins (78 - 86)	0442
Honda CBX550 Four (82 - 86) ◊	0940
Honda XL600R & XR600R (83 - 96)	2183
Honda CBR600F1 & 1000F Fours (87 - 96)	1730
Honda CBR600F2 & F3 Fours (91 - 98)	2070
Honda CB650 sohc Fours (78 - 84)	0665
Honda NTV600 & 650 V-Twins (88 - 96)	3243
Honda Shadow VT600 & 750 (USA) (88 - 99)	2312
Honda CB750 sohc Four (69 - 79)	0131
Honda V45/65 Sabre & Magna (82 - 88)	0820
Honda VFR750 & 700 V-Fours (86 - 97)	2101
Honda VFR800 V-Fours (97 - 00)	3703
Honda CB750 & CB900 dohc Fours (78 - 84)	0535
Honda CBR900RR FireBlade (92 - 99)	2161
Honda ST1100 Pan European V-Fours (90 - 97)	3384
Honda Shadow VT1100 (USA) (85 - 98)	2313
Honda GL1000 Gold Wing (75 - 79)	0309
Honda GL1100 Gold Wing (79 - 81)	0669
Honda Gold Wing 1200 (USA) (84 - 87)	2199
Honda Gold Wing 1500 (USA) (88 - 98)	2225
KAWASAKI	
Kawasaki AE/AR 50 & 80 (81 - 95)	1007
Kawasaki KC, KE & KH100 (75 - 99)	1371
Kawasaki KMX125 & 200 (86 - 96) ◊	3046
Kawasaki 250, 350 & 400 Triples (72 - 79)	0134
Kawasaki 400 & 440 Twins (74 - 81)	0281
Kawasaki 400, 500 & 550 Fours (79 - 91)	0910
Kawasaki EN450 & 500 Twins (Ltd/Vulcan) (85 - 93)	2053
Kawasaki EX & ER500 (GPZ500S & ER-5) Twins (87 - 99)	2052
Kawasaki ZX600 (Ninja ZX-6, ZZ-R600) Fours (90 - 97)	2146
Kawasaki ZX-6R Ninja Fours (95 - 98)	3541
Kawasaki ZX600 (GPZ600R, GPX600R, Ninja 600R & RX) & ZX750 (GPX750R, Ninja 750R) Fours (85 - 97)	1780
Kawasaki 650 Four (76 - 78)	0373
Kawasaki 750 Air-cooled Fours (80 - 91)	0574
Kawasaki ZR550 & 750 Zephyr Fours (90 - 97)	3382
Kawasaki ZX750 (Ninja ZX-7 & ZXR750) Fours (89 - 96)	2054
Kawasaki 900 & 1000 Fours (73 - 77)	0222
Kawasaki ZX900, 1000 & 1100 Liquid-cooled Fours (83 - 97)	1681
MOTO GUZZI	
Moto Guzzi 750, 850 & 1000 V-Twins (74 - 78)	0339
MZ	
MZ ETZ Models (81 - 95) ◊	1680
NORTON	
Norton 500, 600, 650 & 750 Twins (57 - 70)	0187
Norton Commando (68 - 77)	0125
PIAGGIO	
Piaggio (Vespa) Scooters (91 - 98)	3492
SUZUKI	
Suzuki GT, ZR & TS50 (77 - 90) ◊	0799
Suzuki TS50X (83 - 99) ◊	1599
Suzuki 100, 125, 185 & 250 Air-cooled Trail bikes (79 - 89)	0797
Suzuki GP100 & 125 Singles (78 - 93) ◊	0576
Suzuki GS, GN, GZ & DR125 Singles (82 - 99) ◊	0888
Suzuki 250 & 350 Twins (68 - 78)	0120
Suzuki GT250X7, GT200X5 & SB200 Twins (78 - 83) ◊	0469
Suzuki GS/GSX250, 400 & 450 Twins (79 - 85)	0736
Suzuki GS500E Twin (89 - 97)	3238
Suzuki GS550 (77 - 82) & GS750 Fours (76 - 79)	0363
Suzuki GS/GSX550 4-valve Fours (83 - 88)	1133
Suzuki GSX-R600 & 750 (96 - 99)	3553
Suzuki GSF600 & 1200 Bandit Fours (95 - 97)	3367
Suzuki GS850 Fours (78 - 88)	0536
Suzuki GS1000 Four (77 - 79)	0484
Suzuki GSX-R750, GSX-R1100 (85 - 92), GSX600F, GSX750F, GSX1100F (Katana) Fours (88 - 96)	2055
Suzuki GS/GSX1000, 1100 & 1150 4-valve Fours (79 - 88)	0737
TRIUMPH	
Triumph Tiger Cub & Terrier (52 - 68)	0414
Triumph 350 & 500 Unit Twins (58 - 73)	0137
Triumph Pre-Unit Twins (47 - 62)	0251
Triumph 650 & 750 2-valve Unit Twins (63 - 83)	0122
Triumph Trident & BSA Rocket 3 (69 - 75)	0136
Triumph Triples & Fours (carburettor engines) (91 - 99)	2162
VESPA	
Vespa P/PX125, 150 & 200 Scooters (78 - 95)	0707
Vespa Scooters (59 - 78)	0126
YAMAHA	
Yamaha DT50 & 80 Trail Bikes (78 - 95) ◊	0800
Yamaha T50 & 80 Townmate (83 - 95) ◊	1247
Yamaha YB100 Singles (73 - 91) ◊	0474
Yamaha RS/RXS100 & 125 Singles (74 - 95)	0331
Yamaha RD & DT125LC (82 - 87) ◊	0887
Yamaha TZR125 (87 - 93) & DT125R (88 - 95) ◊	1655
Yamaha TY50, 80, 125 & 175 (74 - 84) ◊	0464
Yamaha XT & SR125 (82 - 96)	1021
Yamaha 250 & 350 Twins (70 - 79)	0040
Yamaha XS250, 360 & 400 sohc Twins (75 - 84)	0378
Yamaha RD250 & 350LC Twins (80 - 82)	0803
Yamaha RD350 YPVS Twins (83 - 95)	1158
Yamaha RD400 Twin (75 - 79)	0333
Yamaha XT, TT & SR500 Singles (75 - 83)	0342
Yamaha XZ550 Vision V-Twins (82 - 85)	0821
Yamaha FJ, FZ, XJ & YX600 Radian (84 - 92)	2100
Yamaha XJ600S (Diversion, Seca II) & XJ600N Fours (92 - 99)	2145
Yamaha YZF600R Thundercat & FZS600 Fazer (96 - 99)	3702
Yamaha 650 Twins (70 - 83)	0341
Yamaha XJ650 & 750 Fours (80 - 84)	0738
Yamaha XS750 & 850 Triples (76 - 85)	0340
Yamaha TDM850, TRX850 & XTZ750 (89 - 99)	3540
Yamaha FZR600, 750 & 1000 Fours (87 - 96)	2056
Yamaha XV V-Twins (81 - 96)	0802
Yamaha XJ900F Fours (83 - 94)	3239
Yamaha FJ1100 & 1200 Fours (84 - 96)	2057
ATVS	
Honda ATC70, 90, 110, 185 & 200 (71 - 85)	0565
Honda TRX300 Shaft Drive ATVs (88 - 95)	2125
Honda TRX300EX & TRX400EX ATVs (93 - 99)	2318
Polaris ATVs (85 to 97)	2302
Yamaha YT, YFM, YTM & YTZ ATVs (80 - 85)	1154
Yamaha YFS200 Blaster ATV (88 - 98)	2317
Yamaha YFB250 Timberwolf ATV (92 - 96)	2217
Yamaha YFM350 Big Bear and ER ATVs (87 - 95)	2126
Yamaha Warrior and Banshee ATVs (87 - 99)	2314
ATV Basics	10450
TECHNICAL TITLES	
Motorcycle Basics Manual	1083
MOTORCYCLE TECHBOOKS	
Motorcycle Electrical TechBook (3rd Edition)	3471
Motorcycle Fuel Systems TechBook	3514
Motorcycle Workshop Practice TechBook (2nd Edition)	3470

◊ = not available in the USA   **Bold type** = Superbike

The manuals on this page are available through good motorcycle dealers and accessory shops.
In case of difficulty, contact: **Haynes Publishing**
(UK) +44 1963 440635   (USA) +1 805 4986703
(FR) +33 1 47 78 50 50   (SV) +46 18 124016
(Australia/New Zealand) +61 3 9763 8100

MCL08.09/99

Preserving Our Motoring Heritage

> The Model J Duesenberg Derham Tourster. Only eight of these magnificent cars were ever built – this is the only example to be found outside the United States of America

Almost every car you've ever loved, loathed or desired is gathered under one roof at the Haynes Motor Museum. Over 300 immaculately presented cars and motorbikes represent every aspect of our motoring heritage, from elegant reminders of bygone days, such as the superb Model J Duesenberg to curiosities like the bug-eyed BMW Isetta. There are also many old friends and flames. Perhaps you remember the 1959 Ford Popular that you did your courting in? The magnificent 'Red Collection' is a spectacle of classic sports cars including AC, Alfa Romeo, Austin Healey, Ferrari, Lamborghini, Maserati, MG, Riley, Porsche and Triumph.

A Perfect Day Out

Each and every vehicle at the Haynes Motor Museum has played its part in the history and culture of Motoring. Today, they make a wonderful spectacle and a great day out for all the family. Bring the kids, bring Mum and Dad, but above all bring your camera to capture those golden memories for ever. You will also find an impressive array of motoring memorabilia, a comfortable 70 seat video cinema and one of the most extensive transport book shops in Britain. The Pit Stop Cafe serves everything from a cup of tea to wholesome, home-made meals or, if you prefer, you can enjoy the large picnic area nestled in the beautiful rural surroundings of Somerset.

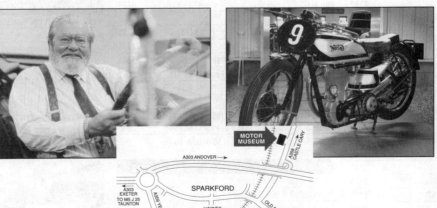

> John Haynes O.B.E., Founder and Chairman of the museum at the wheel of a Haynes Light 12.

> The 1936 490cc sohc-engined International Norton – well known for its racing success

The Museum is situated on the A359 Yeovil to Frome road at Sparkford, just off the A303 in Somerset. It is about 40 miles south of Bristol, and 25 minutes drive from the M5 intersection at Taunton.
Open 9.30am - 5.30pm (10.00am - 4.00pm Winter) 7 days a week, *except Christmas Day, Boxing Day and New Years Day*
Special rates available for schools, coach parties and outings Charitable Trust No. 292048